Robust Design Optimization of Electrical Machines and Devices

Robust Design Optimization of Electrical Machines and Devices

Editors

Tamás Orosz
David Pánek
Anton Rassõlkin
Miklos Kuczmann

MDPI • Basel • Beijing • Wuhan • Barcelona • Belgrade • Manchester • Tokyo • Cluj • Tianjin

Editors
Tamás Orosz
Széchenyi István University
Hungary

David Pánek
University of West Bohemia
Czech Republic

Anton Rassõlkin
Tallinn University of
Technology
Estonia

Miklos Kuczmann
Széchenyi István University
Hungary

Editorial Office
MDPI
St. Alban-Anlage 66
4052 Basel, Switzerland

This is a reprint of articles from the Special Issue published online in the open access journal *Electronics* (ISSN 2079-9292) (available at: https://www.mdpi.com/journal/electronics/special_issues/Optimization_EMD).

For citation purposes, cite each article independently as indicated on the article page online and as indicated below:

LastName, A.A.; LastName, B.B.; LastName, C.C. Article Title. *Journal Name* **Year**, *Volume Number*, Page Range.

ISBN 978-3-0365-6376-3 (Hbk)
ISBN 978-3-0365-6377-0 (PDF)

© 2023 by the authors. Articles in this book are Open Access and distributed under the Creative Commons Attribution (CC BY) license, which allows users to download, copy and build upon published articles, as long as the author and publisher are properly credited, which ensures maximum dissemination and a wider impact of our publications.

The book as a whole is distributed by MDPI under the terms and conditions of the Creative Commons license CC BY-NC-ND.

Contents

Tamás Orosz, David Pánek, Anton Rassõlkin and Miklós Kuczmann
Robust Design Optimization of Electrical Machines and Devices
Reprinted from: *Electronics* 2022, 11, 1427, doi:10.3390/electronics11091427 1

Krisztián Gadó and Tamás Orosz
Robust and Multi-Objective Pareto Design of a Solenoid
Reprinted from: *Electronics* 2021, 10, 2139, doi:10.3390/electronics10172139 5

Mohammad Soltani, Stefano Nuzzo, Davide Barater and Giovanni Franceschini
A Multi-Objective Design Optimization for a Permanent Magnet Synchronous Machine with Hairpin Winding Intended for Transport Applications
Reprinted from: *Electronics* 2021, 10, 3162, doi:10.3390/electronics10243162 21

Hoon-Ki Lee, Tae-Kyoung Bang, Jeong-In Lee, Jong-Hyeon Woo, Hyo-Seob Shin, Ick-Jae Yoon and Jang-Young Choi
Analytical Study and Comparison of Electromagnetic Characteristics of 8-Pole 9-Slot and 8-Pole 12-Slot Permanent Magnet Synchronous Machines Considering Rotor Eccentricity
Reprinted from: *Electronics* 2021, 10, 2036, doi:10.3390/electronics10162036 35

Hamidreza Ghorbani, Mohammadreza Moradian and Mohamed Benbouzid
On the Optimal Selection of Flux Barrier Reconfiguration for a Five-Phase Permanent Magnet Assisted Synchronous Reluctance Machine for Low-Torque Ripple Application
Reprinted from: *Electronics* 2021, 11, 41, doi:10.3390/electronics11010041 45

David A. Elvira-Ortiz, Juan J. Saucedo-Dorantes, Roque A. Osornio-Rios, Daniel Morinigo-Sotelo and Jose A. Antonino-Daviu
Power Quality Monitoring Strategy Based on an Optimized Multi-Domain Feature Selection for the Detection and Classification of Disturbances in Wind Generators
Reprinted from: *Electronics* 2022, 11, 287, doi:10.3390/electronics11020287 61

Sergei V. Zubkov, Ivan A. Parinov and Yulia A. Kuprina
The Structural and Dielectric Properties of $Bi_{3-x}Nd_xTi_{1.5}W_{0.5}O_9$ (x = 0.25, 0.5, 0.75, 1.0)
Reprinted from: *Electronics* 2022, 11, 277, doi:10.3390/electronics11020277 87

Suhaib Ahmad Khan, Mohd Tariq, Asfar Ali Khan, Basem Alamri and Lucian Mihet-Popa
Assessment of Thermophysical Performance of Ester-Based Nanofluids for Enhanced Insulation Cooling in Transformers
Reprinted from: *Electronics* 2022, 11, 376, doi:10.3390/electronics11030376 99

Ramy S. A. Afia, Ehtasham Mustafa and Zoltán Ádám Tamus
Comparison of Mechanical and Low-Frequency Dielectric Properties of Thermally and Thermo-Mechanically Aged Low Voltage CSPE/XLPE Nuclear Power Plant Cables
Reprinted from: *Electronics* 2021, 10, 2728, doi:10.3390/electronics10222728 113

Ekaterina Andriushchenko, Ants Kallaste, Anouar Belahcen, Toomas Vaimann, Anton Rassõlkin, Hamidreza Heidari and Hans Tiismus
Optimization of a 3D-Printed Permanent Magnet Coupling Using Genetic Algorithm and Taguchi Method
Reprinted from: *Electronics* 2021, 10, 494, doi:10.3390/electronics10040494 129

Wagner Benjamim, Imed Jlassi and Antonio J. Marques Cardoso
A Computationally Efficient Model Predictive Current Control of Synchronous Reluctance Motors Based on Hysteresis Comparators
Reprinted from: *Electronics* **2022**, *11*, 379, doi:10.3390/electronics11030379 . . . . **145**

Hamidreza Heidari, Anton Rassõlkin, Arash Razzaghi, Toomas Vaimann, Ants Kallaste, Ekaterina Andriushchenko, Anouar Belahcen, et al.
A Modified Dynamic Model of Single-Sided Linear Induction Motors Considering Longitudinal and Transversal Effects
Reprinted from: *Electronics* **2021**, *10*, 933, doi:10.3390/electronics10080933 . . . . **159**

Qian Zhang, Huijuan Liu, Tengfei Song and Zhenyang Zhang
A Novel, Improved Equivalent Circuit Model for Double-Sided Linear Induction Motor
Reprinted from: *Electronics* **2021**, *10*, 1644, doi:10.3390/electronics10141644 . . . . **173**

David Pánek, Tamás Orosz and Pavel Karban
Performance Comparison of Quantized Control Synthesis Methods of Antenna Arrays
Reprinted from: *Electronics* **2022**, *11*, 994, doi:10.3390/electronics11070994 . . . . **189**

Can Jiang, Jun Yang and Mingwu Fan
Application of Particle Swarm Optimization in the Design of an ICT High-Voltage Power Supply with Dummy Primary Winding
Reprinted from: *Electronics* **2021**, *10*, 1866, doi:10.3390/electronics10151866 . . . . **207**

Editorial

Robust Design Optimization of Electrical Machines and Devices

Tamás Orosz [1,*], David Pánek [2], Anton Rassõlkin [3] and Miklós Kuczmann [1]

[1] Department of Automation, Széchenyi István University, Egyetem ter 1., 9026 Győr, Hungary; kuczmann@sze.hu
[2] Deparment of Theory of Electrical Engineering, University of West Bohemia, Univerzitni 26, 306 14 Plzen, Czech Republic; panek50@kte.zcu.cz
[3] Department of Electrical Power Engineering and Mechatronics, Tallinn University of Technology, Ehitajate Tee 5, 19086 Tallinn, Estonia; anton.rassolkin@taltech.ee
* Correspondence: orosz.tamas@sze.hu

This article introduces a Special Issue (SI) that contains fourteen chosen articles from robust design optimization of electrical machines and devices. Optimization is essential for the research and design of electromechanical devices, especially electrical machines. Finding the optimal solutions may lead to cheaper, more economical products, faster and more efficient production, or more sustainable solutions. However, optimizing such a complex system as an electrical machine is a computationally expensive optimization problem, where many physical domains should be considered together. However, a good, practical design needs to consider the electrical device's design parameters; it should be insensitive to parameter changes or manufacturing tolerances. This Special Issue focused on papers showing how modern artificial intelligence (AI) tools can be used for robust design optimization of electric machines and electrical devices, how these tools can be benchmarked, or the correctness of the result validated.

The articles which are published in this special issue present the latest results of current research fields. Hopefully, the presented models and various application fields will provide useful information for researchers and professionals interested in these techniques themselves or who have other problems from different fields.

Testing and benchmarking the numerical tools for electromagnetic analysis is an important task. The Compumag Society provides openly accessible, challenging benchmark problems (TEAM problems) for testing novel numerical solvers. In [1], the authors deal with a solution of a robust design of a solenoid, and the test problem aims to search for the optimal shape of a coil, which ensures a uniform field distribution in the control region, while the sensitivity and the mass/DC loss of the coil are also considered in the context of robust design. The paper points out that if we are looking for designs with acceptable tolerances, not only symmetrical designs can be favoured. The paper points out the fact that the cheapest solutions are symmetrical setups. They perform worse than the cheapest asymmetric ones in these uniformity and sensitivity criteria. Therefore, some asymmetric solutions that were previously neglected from the solution space can be competitive and interesting for practical design.

A variety of electromechanical systems requires special techniques for optimization; each optimization is unique and focused on specific parameters aimed at performance improvement. In [2], a fast and accurate optimization tool is presented for optimal exploitation of permanent magnet synchronous machine with hairpin winding intended for transport applications. The focus of the optimization is maximizing power density and efficiency. As a benchmark case study, a surface-mounted permanent magnet synchronous motor designed for a student racing competition vehicle was considered. Several optimization steps are presented in the paper, and as a result, the main indexes, such as efficiency, volume power density, and power losses, were improved by 0.15%, 10.55%, and 3.4%, respectively.

Citation: Orosz, T.; Pánek, D.; Rassõlkin, A.; Kuczmann, M. Robust Design Optimization of Electrical Machines and Devices. *Electronics* 2022, 11, 1427. https://doi.org/10.3390/electronics11091427

Received: 20 April 2022
Accepted: 25 April 2022
Published: 29 April 2022

Publisher's Note: MDPI stays neutral with regard to jurisdictional claims in published maps and institutional affiliations.

Copyright: © 2022 by the authors. Licensee MDPI, Basel, Switzerland. This article is an open access article distributed under the terms and conditions of the Creative Commons Attribution (CC BY) license (https://creativecommons.org/licenses/by/4.0/).

Another study on permanent magnet synchronous machines [3] is focused on 8-pole 9-slot and 8-pole 12-slot machines and considers rotor eccentricity. Authors have performed a magnetic field analysis using an analytical method and the torque characteristics for benchmark machines. The optimization is based on perturbation and electromagnetic theories. In both cases, two models (slotted and simplified without slots) were analyzed using the FEM. The research work confirms that the slotted model can obtain similar results, even if the magnetic flux density is predicted without slots and the back-EMF is derived using it. The results obtained using the analytical method are compared with the FEM and experimental results.

The next paper in SI [4] aims to investigate the reconfigurations of rotor flux barriers for a five-phase permanent magnet assisted synchronous reluctance machines. That type of electrical machine is relatively new on the market. However, they are gaining popularity in industrial applications due to their electromagnetic characteristics (robustness, torque/power density, performance, etc.). In this research work, a Lumped Parameter Model conducted to a 2D FEM was applied to the proposed permanent magnet assisted synchronous reluctance motor models under the steady-state condition. Based on the FEM results, the maximum torque, minimum cogging torque, and minimum torque ripples were achieved. As a result, the optimal model of the electrical machine operates at high-performance values with desirable values of line-to-line back-EMF and air-gap flux density.

Wind generators are integrated with electrical machines that require a reliable operation. However, the increasing use of non-linear loads introduces undesired disturbances that may compromise the integrity of the electrical machines inside the wind generator. Ref. [5] proposed a five-step methodology for power quality disturbance detection in grids with the injection of wind farm energy. The proposed method is validated using a set of synthetic signals and is then tested using two different sets of real signals from an IEEE workgroup and from a wind park located in Spain.

In [6], the dielectric properties of a $Bi_3-xNdxTi_{1.5}W_{0.5}O_9$ material is investigated. Many recent studies showed that replacements of atoms in A and also in B-positions of an AP's crystal lattice led to a change in the structure, the dielectric properties and significantly influenced the polarization processes in this compounds. The dependences of the relative permittivity ϵ/ϵ_0 and the tangent of loss $tan\delta$ at different frequencies on temperature were examined in this paper, together with the piezoelectric properties of the material.

Nanotechnology provides an effective way to upgrade the thermophysical characteristics of dielectric oils and creates optimal transformer design. The properties of insulation materials have a significant effect on the optimal transformer design. Ester-based nanofluids (NF) are introduced as an energy-efficient alternative to conventional mineral oils, prepared by dispersing nanoparticles in the base oil. Ref. [7] presents the effect of graphene oxide and TiO_2 nanoparticles on the thermophysical properties of pure natural ester and synthetic ester oils with temperature varied from ambient temperature up to 80 °C. A range of concentrations of graphene oxide (GO) and TiO_2 nanoparticles were used in the study to upgrade the thermophysical properties of ester-based oils. The experimental results show that nanoparticles have a positive effect on the thermal conductivity and viscosity of oils which reduces with an increase in temperature

Low voltage cables are widely used in nuclear power plants and photovoltaic generators. In the case of nuclear power plants the low voltage cables link the system components with the controlling and monitoring instrumentation and control equipment and supplying power to the devices. During the service period these cables are exposed to a wide range of stresses: high-temperature, radiation, mechanical stresses, etc. Since the proper function of the low voltage cables is essential for these power plants' continuous and reliable operation. In [8], the authors examine the effect of mechanical stresses during the aging procedure of these cables, it shows that the Shore D hardness was also higher on the thermo-mechanically aged samples. These findings show the combined aging has a higher impact on the insulation properties. Hence, involving the mechanical stress in the aging procedure of cable qualification enables the design of more robust cables in a harsh environment.

New materials and manufacturing technologies have influence also on design optimization process of electromechanical devices. In [9], the authors present an optimization of a additively manufactured permanent magnet coupling. Two approches are introduced - time-consuming Genetic Algorithm method and faster Taguchi method. The research work analyze the abilities of compared methods within the optimization of studied coupling with minimization of volume and maximization of transmitted torque as objectives. Taking into account that resulting optimal geometry (the clutch volume is reduced by 17%) and characteristics (magnetic torque density is enhanced by more than 20%) achieved by compared methods are nearly identical, the Taguchi method is found to be more time-efficient and effective within the considered optimization problem. The permanent magnet coupling was manufactured and simulation results were validated using an experimental setup.

Model predictive current control has recently become a powerful advanced control technology in industrial drives. In [10], the authors proposed a computationally efficient calcualtion of the current prediction control for synchronous reluctance motors. The porposed methodology can reduce the computational cost by a merging the predictive current control model with a simple hysteresis current control. Therefore, only four voltage vectors should used to predict the current and evaluate the cost function. The proposed methodology can reduce the computation cost of a classical predictve current model by about 20%.

Linear motors are a special type of electrical machine that requires special attention due to nonlinearities caused by side effects. The authors of the paper [11] propose a modified dynamic equivalent circuit model for a linear induction motor. A proposed model considering both longitudinal (speed-dependent) end effect based on conventional Duncan's approach and transverse edge effect investigated by using additional correction factors. In addition, the field-analysis method is used to include the typical linear motors iron saturation effect, the skin effect, and the air-gap leakage effect. Model simulation results show a good agreement between field analysis and FEM estimation of the electrical parameters. Moreover, to validate the proposed paper method, 3-D FEM was employed. Thrust-velocity characteristic of studied linear induction machines shows that the proposed method provides more precision as compared to Duncan's model.

An investigation of linear induction motors in SI continues with work by Zhang et al. in [12]. An improved equivalent circuit model of double-sided linear induction motors that takes into account the linear motor skin effect and the nonzero leakage reluctance of the secondary, longitudinal, and transverse end effects into consideration is proposed. The proposed equivalent circuit is presented described in detail and highlights the modification in comparison with the traditional equivalent circuit with longitudinal and transverse end effects. 3D FEM is used to verify the proposed equivalent circuit model under varying air gap width and frequency. The results show that the equivalent circuit model that takes into account only the longitudinal end effect considered, and the model considered with both longitudinal and transverse end effect have more than 11% errors with the FEM simulation results in the slip range, while the errors between the value of proposed equivalent circuit and simulation are less than 5%.

There is a great potential in small satellite technology for testing new sensors, processes, and technologies for space applications. The design of their receiving antennas for their ground stations needs a careful design to establish stable communication. Paper [13] shows an interesting solution to the antenna design problem with the antenna array technology. This novel approach can have many advantages over parabolic antennas. From a mechanical point of view, it does not require the design and maintenance of the drive system, which sets the azimuth and the elevation angles. Such systems have a simpler feeding network that cannot be disconnected during the connection time. These tools are insensitive to the moisture and weather conditions during the mission. Moreover, with a pattern reconfigurability algorithm, they can support multi-task missions. This work is motivated by the design of an antenna array for a future rotatorless base station for the VZLUSAT group of Czech nano-satellites.

The advancement of a device like an insulated core transformer involves the optimization of several parameters. Special attention must be paid to parameters that affect the uniformity of disk output voltage. In the paper, Ref. [14], the accuracy of the FEM model was verified by comparing test data of the insulated core transformer prototype with the simulation results. Particle Swarm Optimization algorithm was implemented for the design parameters (including the number of secondary winding turns and the compensation capacitance) optimization of dummy primary winding. The optimization results presented in the research work show that the maximum non-uniformity of the disk output voltage is reduced from 11.1% to 4.4% from no-load to a full load for a 200 kV/20 mA for an insulated core transformer prototype. The proposed method improves the performance of the insulated core transformer high voltage power supply and cuts down the design time.

Funding: The research work by Anton Rassõlkin has been supported by the Estonian Research Council under grant PSG453 "Digital twin for propulsion drive of autonomous electric vehicle".

Acknowledgments: For this valuable collection of research works focuses on optimization of electrical machines and devices, the Guest Editors are thankful for all authors who submitted their manuscripts for this SI and congratulate them on publishing their research works with MDPI Electronics. This SI edition would not be possible without the the Academic Editors and all reviewers, our gratitude for their important work. Last but not least, we would like to thank the MDPI team for their support of this SI.

Conflicts of Interest: The authors declare no conflict of interest.

References

1. Gadó, K.; Orosz, T. Robust and Multi-Objective Pareto Design of a Solenoid. *Electronics* **2021**, *10*, 2139. [CrossRef]
2. Soltani, M.; Nuzzo, S.; Barater, D.; Franceschini, G. A Multi-Objective Design Optimization for a Permanent Magnet Synchronous Machine with Hairpin Winding Intended for Transport Applications. *Electronics* **2021**, *10*, 3162. [CrossRef]
3. Lee, H.K.; Bang, T.K.; Lee, J.I.; Woo, J.H.; Shin, H.S.; Yoon, I.J.; Choi, J.Y. Analytical Study and Comparison of Electromagnetic Characteristics of 8-Pole 9-Slot and 8-Pole 12-Slot Permanent Magnet Synchronous Machines Considering Rotor Eccentricity. *Electronics* **2021**, *10*, 2036. [CrossRef]
4. Ghorbani, H.; Moradian, M.; Benbouzid, M. On the Optimal Selection of Flux Barrier Reconfiguration for a Five-Phase Permanent Magnet Assisted Synchronous Reluctance Machine for Low-Torque Ripple Application. *Electronics* **2022**, *11*, 41. [CrossRef]
5. Elvira-Ortiz, D.A.; Saucedo-Dorantes, J.J.; Osornio-Rios, R.A.; Morinigo-Sotelo, D.; Antonino-Daviu, J.A. Power Quality Monitoring Strategy Based on an Optimized Multi-Domain Feature Selection for the Detection and Classification of Disturbances in Wind Generators. *Electronics* **2022**, *11*, 287. [CrossRef]
6. Zubkov, S.V.; Parinov, I.A.; Kuprina, Y.A. The Structural and Dielectric Properties of $Bi_{3-x}Nd_xTi_{1.5}W_{0.5}O_9$ (x = 0.25, 0.5, 0.75, 1.0). *Electronics* **2022**, *11*, 277. [CrossRef]
7. Khan, S.A.; Tariq, M.; Khan, A.A.; Alamri, B.; Mihet-Popa, L. Assessment of Thermophysical Performance of Ester-Based Nanofluids for Enhanced Insulation Cooling in Transformers. *Electronics* **2022**, *11*, 376. [CrossRef]
8. Afia, R.S.A.; Mustafa, E.; Tamus, Z.A. Comparison of Mechanical and Low-Frequency Dielectric Properties of Thermally and Thermo-Mechanically Aged Low Voltage CSPE/XLPE Nuclear Power Plant Cables. *Electronics* **2021**, *10*, 2728. [CrossRef]
9. Andriushchenko, E.; Kallaste, A.; Belahcen, A.; Vaimann, T.; Rassõlkin, A.; Heidari, H.; Tiismus, H. Optimization of a 3D-Printed Permanent Magnet Coupling Using Genetic Algorithm and Taguchi Method. *Electronics* **2021**, *10*, 494. [CrossRef]
10. Benjamim, W.; Jlassi, I.; Cardoso, A.J.M. A Computationally Efficient Model Predictive Current Control of Synchronous Reluctance Motors Based on Hysteresis Comparators. *Electronics* **2022**, *11*, 379. [CrossRef]
11. Heidari, H.; Rassõlkin, A.; Razzaghi, A.; Vaimann, T.; Kallaste, A.; Andriushchenko, E.; Belahcen, A.; Lukichev, D.V. A Modified Dynamic Model of Single-Sided Linear Induction Motors Considering Longitudinal and Transversal Effects. *Electronics* **2021**, *10*, 933. [CrossRef]
12. Zhang, Q.; Liu, H.; Song, T.; Zhang, Z. A Novel, Improved Equivalent Circuit Model for Double-Sided Linear Induction Motor. *Electronics* **2021**, *10*, 1644. [CrossRef]
13. Pánek, D.; Orosz, T.; Karban, P.; Gnawa, D.C.D.; Neghab, H.K. Performance Comparison of Quantized Control Synthesis Methods of Antenna Arrays. *Electronics* **2022**, *11*, 994. [CrossRef]
14. Jiang, C.; Yang, J.; Fan, M. Application of Particle Swarm Optimization in the Design of an ICT High-Voltage Power Supply with Dummy Primary Winding. *Electronics* **2021**, *10*, 1866. [CrossRef]

Article

Robust and Multi-Objective Pareto Design of a Solenoid

Krisztián Gadó and Tamás Orosz *

Montana Knowledge Management Ltd., 1111 Budapest, Hungary; gado.krisztian@montana.hu
* Correspondence: orosz.tamas@montana.hu

Abstract: The optimization of the design of a practical electromagnetic device involves many challenging tasks for new algorithms, especially those involving numerical modeling codes in which objective function calls must be minimized for practical design processes. The Compumag Society provides openly accessible, challenging benchmark problems (TEAM problems) for testing novel numerical solvers. This paper deals with a novel solution for the multi-objective TEAM benchmark problem. This solenoid design test problem aims to search for the optimal shape of a coil, which ensures a uniform field distribution in the control region, while the sensitivity and the mass/DC loss of the coil are also considered in the context of robust design. The main differences from the previously published solutions are that the proposed methodology optimizes all three objectives together, not only as two independent two-dimensional sub-problems. We considered the asymmetrical cases in the solution and found that the symmetrical solutions always produced better uniformity and sensitivity measures. However, the difference between the symmetrical and asymmetrical solutions is insignificant for these objectives. Despite the fact that the cheapest solutions are symmetrical setups, they perform worse than the cheapest asymmetric ones in these uniformity and sensitivity criteria. Therefore, some asymmetric solutions that were previously neglected from the solution space can be competitive and interesting for practical design.

Keywords: optimization; electrical machines; design optimization; finite element method

Citation: Gadó, K.; Orosz, T. Robust and Multi-Objective Pareto Design of a Solenoid. *Electronics* **2021**, *10*, 2139.
https://doi.org/10.3390/ electronics10172139

Academic Editor: Davide Astolfi

Received: 2 August 2021
Accepted: 31 August 2021
Published: 2 September 2021

Publisher's Note: MDPI stays neutral with regard to jurisdictional claims in published maps and institutional affiliations.

Copyright: © 2021 by the authors. Licensee MDPI, Basel, Switzerland. This article is an open access article distributed under the terms and conditions of the Creative Commons Attribution (CC BY) license (https:// creativecommons.org/licenses/by/ 4.0/).

1. Introduction

The practical design of an electrical device usually leads to a multi-objective optimization task. These problems must involve the resolution of many computationally expensive finite-element-methodology-based numerical field calculations. The goal of the approaches that are applied is to reduce the number of function evaluations or to reduce a numerical model's computational cost without a significant loss of accuracy [1,2]. During industrial design processes, not only the physical parameters of a machine, but also the manufacturing tolerances and the different uncertainties should be considered right from the beginning of the design process [3–6].

The goal of a design optimization task differs when it is assessed from a mathematical or industrial perspective. Mathematically, the goal of a design optimization task is to find not only a better solution, but also the global optimum of the task, if it exists [7]. However, models that can be used for optimization are usually simplified ones that do not consider many factors, which is important for the easy and robust manufacturability of the product. Moreover, the design of an electrical device usually leads to a general nonlinear optimization problem. The result of these optimization problems is a Pareto-front, i.e., a set of non-dominated solutions [2,8,9]. From the industrial point of view, solutions that are better than the previous ones are usually considered as optimal ones because many factors are neglected during industrial optimization processes.

The TEAM (Testing Electromagnetic Analysis Methods) (https://www.compumag.org/wp/team/, (accessed on 1 June 2021)) benchmark problems offer a wide variety of test problems for benchmarking the accuracy of numerical solvers, and they are openly available from the website of the International Compumag Society [10]. The subject of our analysis is a multi-objective Pareto optimization of a solenoid, which is cataloged as the 35th benchmark problem in the list [11,12]. The goal of this benchmark is to design a coil that generates a uniform magnetic field in a given control region (Figure 1). The sensitivity to positioning errors of the turns and the power loss or mass of the given design are also considered. This seemingly simple test problem is inspired by a bio-electromagnetic application for Magnetic Fluid Hyperthermia (MFH), where a uniform magnetic field is used to compare the magnetic properties of different nanofluids [5,13–15]. A similar design task should be solved during the design and optimization of induction heating or induction brazing processes [16–22]. The solution of this test problem requires the resolution of a three-objective optimization problem in which the objective functions depend on finite-element-method-based calculations, and one of the objective functions considers the robustness of the solution during the optimization process.

Many solutions were proposed to resolve this problem in the literature [23]. The first paper proposed the DC problem and computed this optimization task through a gradient-based evolutionary algorithm (EA) search [12]. The following paper resolved the same problem with different EAs [24]. This comparison has great importance because several EAs were used to determine inverse electromagnetic tasks. Due to Wolpert's "No-free-lunch" theorem [2,25,26], these metaheuristics must be benchmarked with each other for every kind of optimization task in order to select the most appropriate one. Seo et al. [27] solved this problem with a design sensitivity analysis, which provided almost the same optimization result as the gradient-search-based evolutionary algorithms in a much shorter time. These authors used FEM solvers to calculate the magnetic field. Karban et al. [5] proposed a semi-analytical formula and validated its precision with an hp-adaptive FEM solver [28]. The goal of this semi-analytical formula was to accelerate the solution speed of the magnetostatic problem. This problem was solved by other authors with different evolutionary and genetic algorithms, such as Non-Dominated Sorted Genetic Algorithm (NSGA-II) [29], Wind-Driven Optimization [30], the Micro-Biogeography Inspired Multi-Objective Optimization (μ-BiMo) [31], and the Migration Non-Dominated Sorted Genetic Algorithm (MNSGA-III) [32]. Another paper modified the excitation and solved this problem with the time-harmonic regime as a 2D or a 3D problem, considering the proximity effect of the windings [23]. However, these previously published solutions did not consider the measurement limits and other confounding factors, such as the Earth's magnetic field, which can be greater than the contributions of these effects or the difference between two designs.

This paper proposes an approach for the original DC problem that is different from those of the papers that were mentioned earlier [12,24,27,28], in which the original three-objective problem was resolved as two separate bi-objective problems. The proposed task is handled as a three-objective optimization task because this form of the problem fits better for real-life design tasks. The previous papers excluded asymmetrical solutions from the optimization. However, due to the non-linearity of the optimization problem, some asymmetrical solutions can be competitive with some symmetrical solutions. This 3D solution space is analyzed in this paper, and the analysis makes two other modifications to the parameter space of the problem. Firstly, the boundaries of the radii are changed. Secondly, the number of turns is varied, and the results of these three separate analyses are compared in the paper. The project files of the proposed analysis can be downloaded from the Artap project's homepage (https://github.com/artap-framework/artap/tree/master/examples, (accessed on 1 June 2021)).

2. Formulation of the Problem

The goal of this optimization is to create a uniform field distribution in the control zone with a solenoid [12,23,24]. The solenoid is composed of 20 series of connected, singular turns, with a radial position varying from 5 to 50 mm. These turns have exactly the same size. The width of each turn is $w = 1.5$ mm, the height is $h = 1.0$ mm, and the prescribed DC current density is $j_\phi = 2 \frac{A}{mm^2}$. The flux density should be $B(r,z) = (0, B_0)$ with $B_0 = 2$ mT in the controlled region. The model of the optimized coil is shown in Figure 1, where the green rectangles show the controlled region, and the yellow ones represent the different turns. The main difference from the original description of the TEAM 35 benchmark problem is that the full coil is modeled for asymmetrical calculations, not just the upper half of the solenoid (the description of the examined TEAM benchmark problem can be found at https://www.compumag.org/wp/wp-content/uploads/2021/07/problem-35.pdf, (accessed on 1 September 2021)). The quality of the uniform magnetic field is assessed by using the point values of the magnetic field, which are evenly spaced among 100 points of the controlled region.

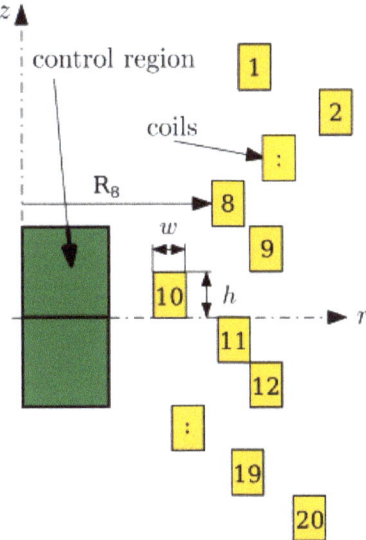

Figure 1. The examined geometry in an axisymmetric arrangement. The green area shows the controlled region in which the magnetic field is considered. Every single turn of the coil is denoted by yellow rectangles; their radii are optimized turn by turn.

Three different objective functions were used to measure the quality of the different solutions. The first one describes the uniformity of the magnetic field in the examined region; the z-component of the flux density is sampled in a 10 × 10 grid. The function takes the maximal difference from the intended flux density ($B_{0z} = 2$ mT) into consideration:

$$F_1 = \max |B_{0z} - B_{iz}|, i = 0, \ldots, 99. \qquad (1)$$

The second function considers the robustness of a given solution. Let $\mathbf{B}(\mathbf{R})$ be the flux density values (2 rows, 100 columns) at a given input $\mathbf{R}$. After that, the $\mathbf{B}^+(\mathbf{X} + \Delta\xi)$ and $\mathbf{B}^-(\mathbf{X} - \Delta\xi)$ vectors need to be computed, where $\Delta\xi = \pm 0.5$ mm and $\mathbf{B}^-(\mathbf{X} - \Delta\xi)$ represents the magnetic flux density change in the case of a 0.5 mm positioning error in a turn. F_2 can be defined in the following way:

$$F_2 = \max\{\|\mathbf{B}_i^+ - \mathbf{B}_i\| + \|\mathbf{B}_i - \mathbf{B}_i^-\|, 0 \leq i \leq 99\}, \qquad (2)$$

where $\|.\|$ means the Euclidean norm and i represents the measurement point in the control region.

The third function represents the mass or the DC loss of the coils. These quantities are proportional to the input. The summation of $\mathbf{R}$ is given by F_3:

$$F_3 = \sum R_j. \qquad (3)$$

where R_j represents the radii of the separate turns. There are 20 different turns in the assembled coils, and their distance from the z-axis can be defined separately (Figure 1).

2.1. Modeling and Optimization Frameworks

The coil model described above was modeled with two different FEM tools: Agros2D, an hp-adaptive FEM solver, and a widely used tool, FEMM, which was used to solve this magnetostatic problem [33,34]. The model was defined by the Adze-modeler (Figure 2), which allowed us to switch between the applied solvers with one command and connect the realized model with Ārtap (Ārtap is available for download from: http://www.agros2 d.org/artap/ (accessed on 1 June 2021) [35]). The workflow for the Adze-modeler can be seen in Figure 2. Different pieces of the geometry can be imported from different file types and can be exported to various FEM solvers by using the same description of the physical model. These parametric FEM models are generated by a function call from Ārtap, which is an optimization framework for robust design optimization. It was developed within the Department of Theoretical Electrical Engineering at the University of West Bohemia in conjunction with a fully hp-adaptive FEM-solver: Agros Suite or Agros2D [28,36,37]. It provides a simple, general interface for facilitating the solution of real-life engineering design problems. The code contains evolutionary and genetic algorithms, wrappers for derivative-free methods, machine learning methods, and an integrated FEM solver. The goal of the realized multi-layered architecture is to separate the problem's definition from those of optimization algorithms and other artificial-intelligence-based methods and to provide automatic parallelization and database connection for the applied algorithms [5,35].

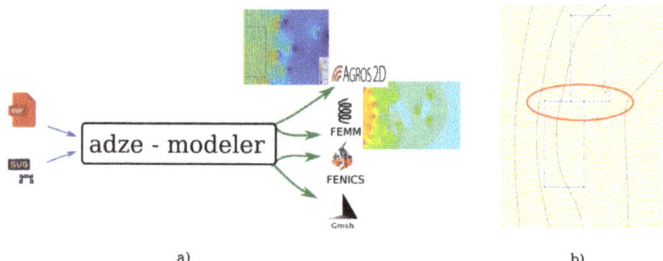

Figure 2. The image (**a**) shows the functionalities used and the workflow that was realized via the Adze-modeler. (**b**) The usage of the collision detection function, which automatically replaces the overlapping edges due to the optimization process.

2.2. Model Validation

The solenoid was simulated in two different ways in this paper. Firstly, the assumptions of symmetry were used, and only the upper half of the model was calculated with the FEM solvers. This model contains the first ten turns, and a Neuman boundary condition is applied at the $z = 0$ axis. This model is exactly the same as that used in the reference calculations [12]. However, the second model contains all 20 turns without using any assumptions of symmetry. The goal of this analysis is to let the optimizer select anti-symmetric solutions. These models were prescribed in Adze-modeler, which could export them for the FEMM or Agros2D models. The following test case was selected from Table 1 [12] to validate the correctness of our FEM models and the calculation of the objectives. Only the results of the symmetrical 10-turn model are presented in this paper, as we found the same results with the asymmetrical 20-turn solenoid model.

The following vector contains all of the design variables for the selected test case (Table 1, [12]):

$$X_1 = [6, 7, 8, 9, 10, 11, 12, 13, 14, 15]. \tag{4}$$

The simulations were performed with Agros2d and FEMM. In the case of Agros2d, an hp-adaptive mesh was set with 0.001% tolerance, while the mesh size was set to 0.5 mm in FEMM. The results and the settings used are summarized in Table 1. It can be seen that the resulting values are in a relatively good agreement with the reference calculations. The absolute value of the differences is a scale of magnitude smaller than the Earth's magnetic field, which can be a possible measurement limit in practice. The results of the F_3 objective calculations are not shown in Table 1 because the value of this function does not depend on the finite element models; it is simply calculated from the sum of the input vectors.

Table 1. The results of the validation run for the X_1 input compared to the reference values of F_1 and F_2.

	F_1 [T]	F_2 [T]	ΔF_1 [T]	ΔF_1 [%]	ΔF_2 [T]	ΔF_2 [%]
Reference	8.18×10^{-4}	3.01×10^{-4}	-	-	-	-
FEMM	8.40×10^{-4}	2.91×10^{-4}	-2.20×10^{-5}	2.69%	1.00×10^{-5}	2.20%
Agros2D	8.36×10^{-4}	2.93×10^{-4}	-1.80×10^{-5}	2.20%	8.00×10^{-6}	-2.66%

2.3. Sensitivity Analysis of the FEM Models

Another comparative analysis was made for calibration purposes. The analysis aimed to minimize the solution time and the computational demand of the optimization task by selecting the smallest mesh that was large enough to solve the task with the required accuracy. The required accuracy was 1% in the F_1 and F_2 metrics because it meant 20 µT in our problem, which is comparable with the Earth's magnetic field. Therefore, it is smaller than the precision of the measurement or the other neglected modeling details.

During the analysis, the Adze-modeler was used to convert and solve a randomly selected geometry for the different FEM tools. This model was solved with different mesh and solver settings (Table 2.) in FEMM [33] and Agros2D [28,36]. The sensitivities of the F_1 and F_2 objective functions with the different mesh settings were compared in a selected geometry (Figure 3).

Table 2. The settings applied for the FEMM- and Agros2d-based calculations.

Parameter	FEMM	Agros2D
Problem type	Magnetostatic	
Analysis type	Steady-state	
Coordinate system	axisymmetric	
Polynomial order	1	2
Mesh settings	Smartmesh = Off	hp-adaptivity
Mesh size	0.1–3	tolerance = 5–0.005%

In Agros2D, the polynomial order (p-adaptivity) was set to 2 for all cases. The mesh refinement (h-adaptivity) was considered with different error indicator settings from 5% to 0.005% (Table 2). FEMM can only use first-order polynomials and does not have any adaptivity. It has a "Smart Mesh" feature that is turned on by default. It generates a dense-enough mesh with Triangle [38] to ensure accurate calculations, but it cannot be parameterized. We set up the same mesh size in all regions by turning off this feature, and this mesh size changed during the comparison process. The settings applied are summarized in Table 2.

The F_1 and F_2 functions were calculated from the point values of the magnetic flux density of the control zone; hence, these functions can be sensitive to the numerical errors of the point values of the magnetic flux density calculations. It can be seen from Figure 3c,d that the B_r and B_z components are sensitive to the mesh applied at the top right corner of the control region (r = 5.0 mm, z = 5.0 mm). There is a huge difference in the convergence speed of the two different FEM solvers applied. The smallest FEMM mesh contains about 5×10^5 nodes, whereas the Agros2D converges to the result in both B_r and B_z. The difference in the case of the radial component is not significant. However, in the case of the axial component, the difference is significant (about 40%).

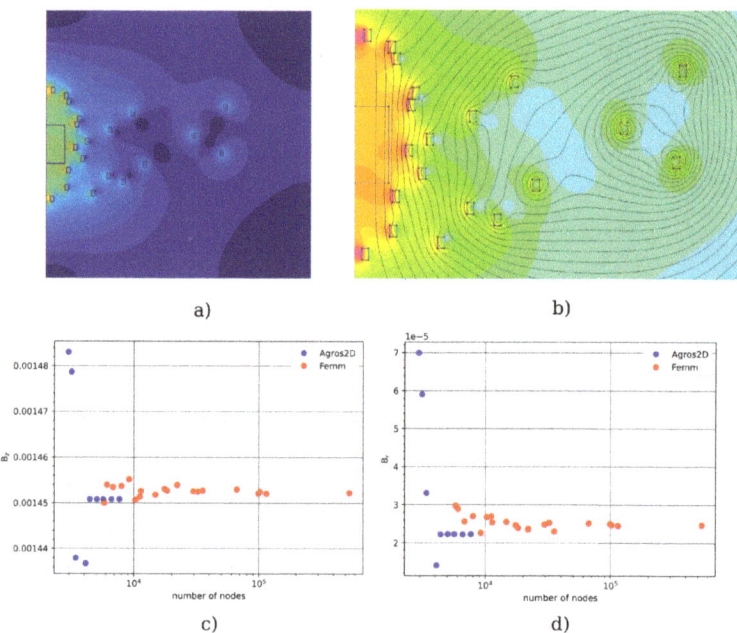

Figure 3. The pictures (**a**,**b**) show the geometry examined and the resulting flux distribution with the Agros2D (**a**) and FEMM software (**b**). The pictures (**c**,**d**) show the convergence of the radial and the axial component of the flux density in the selected (r = 5 mm, z = 5 mm) point.

The same solution is plotted in Figure 4 to visualize the differences in the solutions with the following settings: the error indicator was set to 1% in Agros2d and the smartmesh function was used in FEMM (Figure 4). There is a significant difference in the point values of the magnetic flux density on the right side of the examined region ($r = 5$ mm).

Figure 5 shows that these calculation errors have an effect on the objectives. F_1 considers the maximal difference from the expected value at a single point. These points can cause significant errors during the optimization. The sensitivity of the F_1 and F_2 functions to the mesh selection was examined. It is plotted in Figure 5, where the picture (a) justifies the above-mentioned assumption that the mesh selection has a significant (50%) effect on the values of F_1.

The F_3 function is independent of the mesh selection, and it has a local minimum when all of the radii have the minimum value because it simply depends on the geometry of the coil. Agros2D was used for further calculations with the following settings (Table 3) because it clearly outperformed FEMM during the analyses. The error indicator was set to 1%. Using a more precise calculation seemed pointless because 1% of our target value ($B_0 = 2$ mT) was only 20 µT, which is smaller than the Earth's own magnetic flux density, which would affect the calculation results. If the final application needs more precise results, this effect should also be considered with magnetic and other geometrical simplifications.

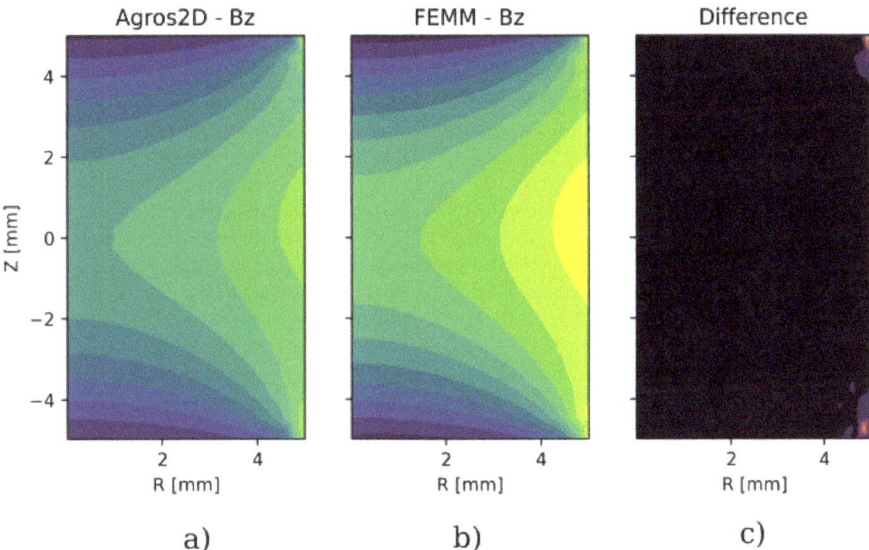

Figure 4. The pictures (**a**,**b**) show the calculated flux density values in the upper half of the examined region with the two types of software compared: Agros2d (**a**) and FEMM (**b**). The third picture (**c**) shows the dependence of the B_z values on the meshing properties.

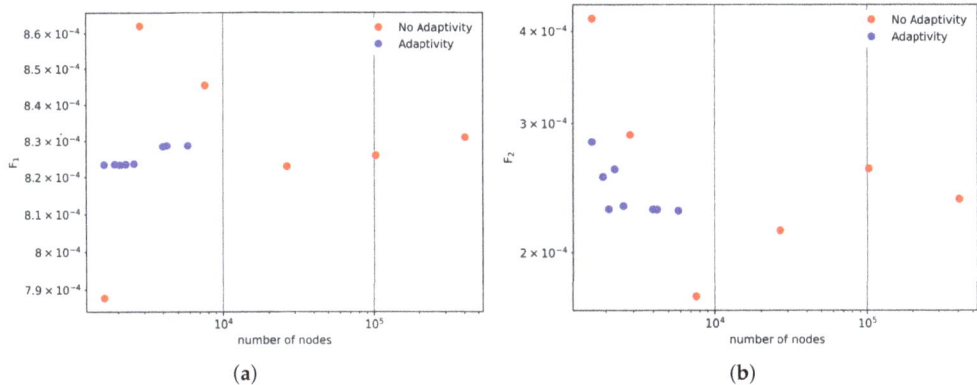

Figure 5. The convergence of the objective functions (F_1 and F_2) in terms of the number of nodes with and without hp-adaptivity. (**a**) The image plots the dependence of F_1, while (**b**) plots the dependence of the F_2 function on the number of nodes.

Table 3. The settings used for Agros2D during the optimization.

Parameter	Agros2D
Problem type	Magnetostatic
Analysis type	Steady-state
Coordinate system	axisymmetric
Polynomial order	2
Mesh settings	hp-adaptivity
Mesh size (tolerance)	1%

3. Results and Discussion

3.1. Optimization of the Three-Objective Problem

The 35th TEAM benchmark problem was optimized as a three-objective optimization task. This approach is the first difference from the previously proposed solutions, where the whole problem was divided into two multi-objective optimization tasks [12,23]. The 2D segments of the three dimensional Pareto surface are plotted and examined in the following subsections and figures. All three objectives were considered during the optimization process because during the design of a product, all of these aspects should considered together. The symmetrical and asymmetrical solutions were optimized separately. The "symmetrical" model refers to the 10-turn geometry, where only the upper half of the solenoid is calculated during the optimization, while the asymmetrical 20-turn model makes it possible to optimize all of the turns separately. Both the "symmetrical" and "asymmetrical" models were calculated with Agros2D with the setup discussed above (Table 3).

The optimization was performed with Artap while using the NSGAII algorithm [29]. In all of the cases, the maximum number of generations was 250 with 100 individuals. In the symmetrical cases, the optimization contained 10 independent variables, while in the asymmetrical cases, the problem contained 20 independent variables.

The following analyses were made for the three cases with the three different settings:

(a) The radii of the first four and the last four turns varied from 1 to 50 mm, while the radii could be changed from 5.5 to 50 mm in the case of the other turns.
(b) The radii of all of the turns could be changed from 5.5 to 50 mm.
(c) The number of turns was reduced to 12, and all of the radii could be changed from 5.5 to 50 mm.

The results of these different optimization tasks are discussed in the following subsections.

3.2. Optimization of Case (a)

First of all, the three-dimensional Pareto surface after the optimization is plotted in Figure 6. It can be seen that the shape of this function is very spiky, and it is hard to localize one distinct optimum. There are many local optima that are close to each other, but most of them are very sensitive to the parameter changes. Optimizing the given solenoid for only one of the selected goal functions can easily lead to a non-robust solution.

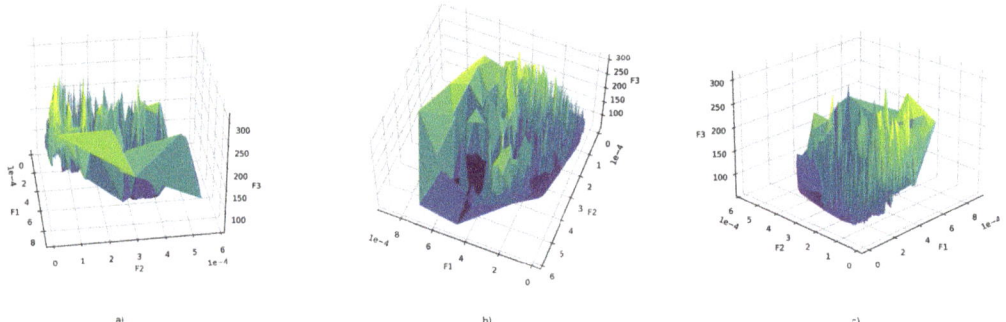

Figure 6. The plots (**a**–**c**) depict the shape of the optimized F_1, F_2, and F_3 objectives, (**a**–**c**) images plots the 3D surface of the objective function from different views.

After the optimization was performed, the results were sorted based on the values of the different objective functions, as can be seen in Figures 7–9. The different sortings indicate different priorities, but the optimization was performed with all three functions considered. For example, the F_1 sorting means that the last generation of solutions was sorted based on the F_1 value, and then the first 100 were selected. This sorting aims to show that the asymmetric solutions can be used just as well as the symmetric ones, and for some criteria, they even outperform the symmetric solutions.

Initially, the solutions from the three-dimensional Pareto plot that had the best values for F_1 were examined (Table 4). This means that these solutions have the best performance for the uniformity objective. As shown in Figure 7a, the F_1 values are in the range of 10–40 µT, which is within the measurement's error. This means that they can be considered equal. This holds on the F_2 axis as well. In terms of price, both variant groupings are in the same price range, but the symmetric setups have a slight advantage. Therefore, the best solutions are symmetrical ones, but there is no significant difference between the best symmetrical and asymmetrical solutions if we consider the uniformity of the solutions.

Table 4. Solutions based on the F_1 sorting in case (a).

	F_1	F_2	F_3	R_1	R_2	R_3	R_4	R_5	R_6	R_7	R_8
Symmetric	1.02×10^{-5}	5.60×10^{-5}	1.18×10^2	3.55	6.09	1.29	5.16	5.76	7.22	7.00	7.50
Asymmetric	2.07×10^{-5}	6.16×10^{-5}	1.00×10^2	1.29	1.47	2.43	5.02	6.42	5.43	6.54	6.80
	R_9	R_{10}	R_{11}	R_{12}	R_{13}	R_{14}	R_{15}	R_{16}	R_{17}	R_{18}	R_{19}	R_{20}
Symmetric	7.50	7.90	7.90	7.50	7.50	7.00	7.22	5.76	5.16	1.29	6.09	3.55
Asymmetric	6.99	7.14	7.18	6.92	6.69	6.67	5.82	5.55	4.47	1.47	4.61	1.06

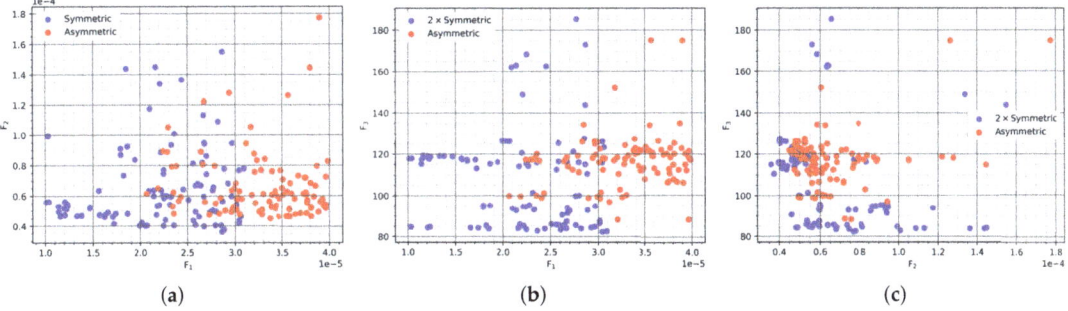

Figure 7. The image shows the first 100 individuals when they are sorted based on uniformity (F_1) in case (a). The blue dots show the symmetric setups, while the asymmetric solutions are depicted in red. (a) The distribution of individuals on the F_1–F_2 axis. (b) The distribution on the F_1–F_3 axis. (c) The distribution on the F_2–F_3 axis.

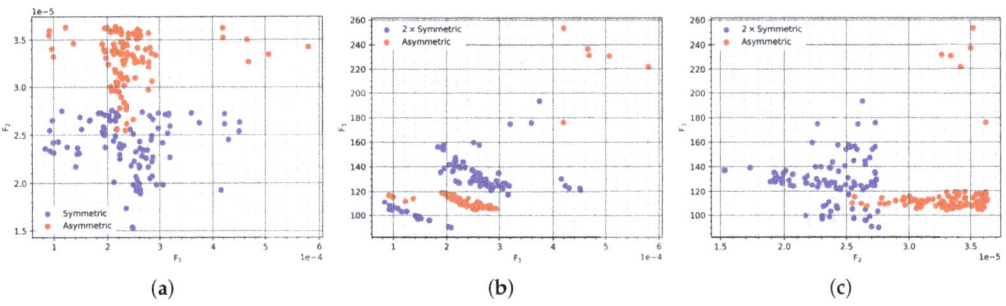

Figure 8. The first 100 individuals from the three-dimensional Pareto front were sorted based on their robustness (F_2) in case (a). The blue dots show the symmetric setups, while the asymmetric solutions are depicted in red. (a) The distribution of individuals on the F_1–F_2 axis. (b) The distribution on the F_1–F_3 axis. (c) The distribution on the F_2–F_3 axis.

Secondly, the most robust solution was sought, and it was a result of an F_2 sorting (Table 5). As shown in Figure 8a, the symmetric setups have an advantage, but they are in the region of the measurement error again, so they can be considered equally robust. In terms of uniformity, the difference is negligible. Regarding the price criteria, the symmetric setups can be slightly cheaper.

Table 5. Solutions based on the F_2 sorting in case (a).

	F_1	F_2	F_3	R_1	R_2	R_3	R_4	R_5	R_6	R_7	R_8
Symmetric	2.49×10^{-4}	1.53×10^{-5}	1.37×10^2	6.82	6.42	3.55	1.97	5.33	7.07	8.99	8.69
Asymmetric	2.34×10^{-4}	2.55×10^{-5}	1.10×10^2	2.51	3.33	2.86	4.44	4.98	6.44	6.92	8.97
	R_9	R_{10}	R_{11}	R_{12}	R_{13}	R_{14}	R_{15}	R_{16}	R_{17}	R_{18}	R_{19}	R_{20}
Symmetric	9.76	9.99	9.99	9.76	8.69	8.99	7.07	5.33	1.97	3.55	6.42	6.82
Asymmetric	7.42	10.82	8.03	8.18	8.39	7.11	6.00	5.01	3.75	1.50	2.57	1.09

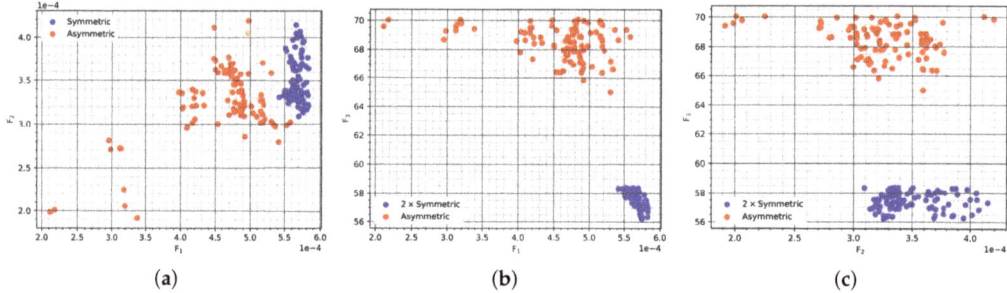

(a) (b) (c)

Figure 9. The image shows the distribution of the 100 cheapest individuals (F_3) in case (**a**). The blue dots show the symmetric setups, while the asymmetric solutions are depicted in red. (**a**) The distribution of individuals on the F_1–F_2 axis. (**b**) The distribution on the F_1–F_3 axis. (**c**) The distribution on the F_2–F_3 axis.

The goal of the third examination was to sort the results by their price (F_3) (Table 6). It can be seen in Figure 9 that the symmetric setups are cheaper by 12–20%, but choosing one of them would be a sub-optimal solution, since the asymmetric setups perform significantly better in terms of accuracy and robustness. The radii of the Pareto-optimal results are plotted in Figure 10a. This violin plot shows the approximate shape of the symmetrical and asymmetrical solutions. The optimizer can set tiny values of the radii for the coils that are placed above or below the homogenized region in these solutions. Most of the Pareto-optimal solutions have at least one turn that has a radius ≤5.5. There is no big difference between the distributions of the radii for the symmetrical and asymmetrical cases. We can conclude that some asymmetrical results that can be competitive with the symmetrical ones exist.

Table 6. Solutions based on the F_3 sorting in case (a).

	F_1	F_2	F_3	R_1	R_2	R_3	R_4	R_5	R_6	R_7	R_8
Symmetric	5.75×10^{-4}	3.26×10^{-4}	5.62×10^1	1.01	1.01	1.00	1.01	1.00	1.02	5.51	5.50
Asymmetric	5.31×10^{-4}	3.59×10^{-4}	6.50×10^1	1.14	1.12	1.01	1.29	1.03	5.48	5.65	5.75
	R_9	R_{10}	R_{11}	R_{12}	R_{13}	R_{14}	R_{15}	R_{16}	R_{17}	R_{18}	R_{19}	R_{20}
Symmetric	5.55	5.51	5.51	5.55	5.50	5.51	1.02	1.00	1.01	1.00	1.01	1.01
Asymmetric	6.03	6.62	5.69	5.67	5.73	5.54	1.31	1.37	1.17	1.07	1.08	1.26

If all of the objective functions are considered, then the symmetrical and asymmetrical variants perform similarly (Table 7) because the difference between them lies in the region of tolerance. The fact that these solutions vary in the values of their radii implies that more than one solution exists for this problem. In Figure 10a, one can see the distribution of the values of the radii for the last 100 individuals with different setups. In Figure 11a, the symmetric and asymmetric setups are compared. In this optimization, all coils are free to move within their logical boundaries. Both setups converge roughly to the same range. The first and last four coils have tiny values of their radii, which makes them hard to manufacture.

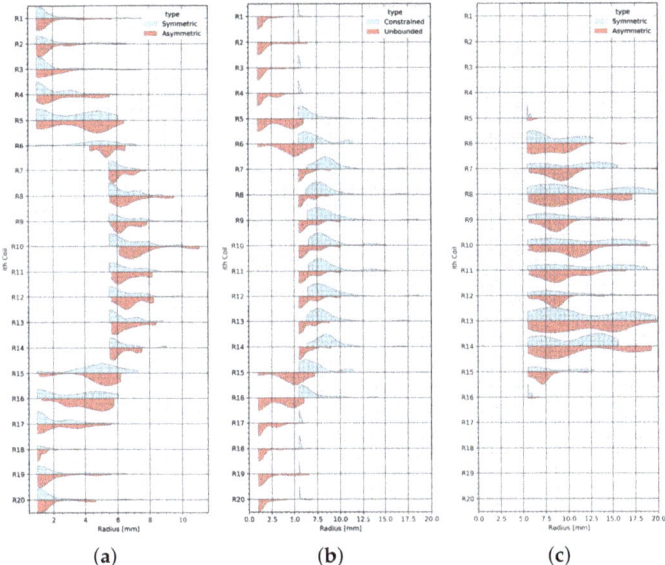

Figure 10. The distribution of the radii of the last 100 unsorted individuals. (**a**) Symmetric and asymmetric setups. All coils are allowed to move freely within the logical boundaries. (**b**) Only the symmetric setups where the coils are first allowed to move freely are shown (red); then, they are constrained in the 5.5–20 mm region (blue). (**c**) The distributions of the radii for the symmetric and asymmetric setups using only 12 coils. All coils were constrained to move within the 5.5–20 mm region.

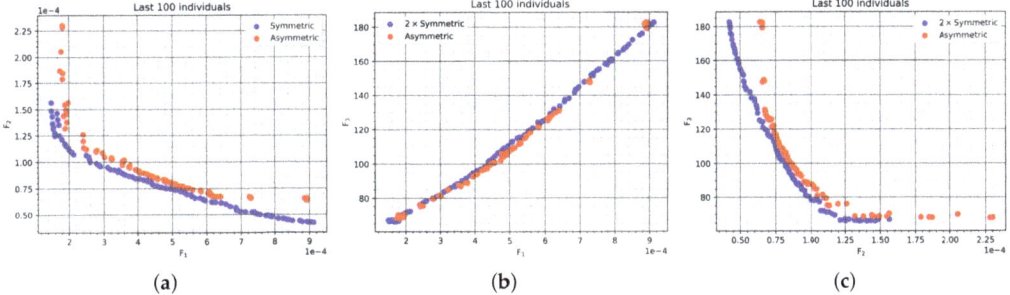

Figure 11. The last 100 individuals if the last generation is not sorted based on any of the conditions. These solutions are lying on the Pareto front. The blue dots show the symmetric setups, while the asymmetric solutions are depicted in red. (**a**) The distribution of individuals on the F_1–F_2 axis. (**b**) The distribution on the F_1–F_3 axis. (**c**) The distribution on the F_2–F_3 axis.

3.3. Optimization with the Parameter Settings of Cases (b) and (c)

The two other optimization runs were carried out on the symmetric variant to examine the impact on the Pareto surface if we neglected the last 3–3 turn from the optimization (case (c)) or did not allow radii smaller than 5.5 mm to be selected (case (b)).

First, in case (b), the optimization was performed with the constraint $5.5 \leq radii \leq 50$ for all coils, as given in the original benchmark problem. This solution excludes the best candidates in the solution space, which have small radii. In the second experiment, we examined if the turns mentioned above were cut out, as described in case (c). The main question during this experiment is that of if we can resolve the task with only a twelve-turn coil instead of the original twenty-turn one.

The results of the optimization in case (b), where the minimum radii of the turns had to be greater than 5.5 mm, are plotted in Figures 10b and 12. Figure 10b shows the distribution of the optimal radii in the two examined cases. The red plot shows the distribution of the radii in the previous symmetric case, while the blue plot shows the new constrained solution. As can be seen from the picture, all of the radii are greater in this case. Therefore, the small turns at the two ends of the coil can significantly improve the uniformity of the magnetic field in the homogenized region. In Figure 12, we can see that the goal function values are significantly worse than in the previous case.

In case (c), we solved both the symmetric and the asymmetric problems with 12 coils instead of 20, as shown in Figure 12. The results can be seen in Figures 12 and 13. If the 100 cheapest solutions are considered, then the reduced number of coils produces better results, especially with an asymmetric setup. In terms of cost, contrary to what one would intuitively expect, the reduced setups cost more than their counterparts by 12–20%. The reason for this small difference is that the twelve-turn variant contains turns with generally bigger radii. This difference is not significant if we compare the price of the coil with the solution of the original problem (constrained, Figure 10b). Regarding the best F_1 and F_2 solutions, the reduced setups perform worse in every way than the 20-coil setups.

Table 7. Last individual in case (a).

	F_1	F_2	F_3	R_1	R_2	R_3	R_4	R_5	R_6	R_7	R_8
Symmetric	5.83×10^{-4}	3.22×10^{-4}	5.67×10^{1}	1.01	1.00	1.01	1.01	1.04	1.15	5.61	5.50
Asymmetric	5.41×10^{-4}	2.79×10^{-4}	6.86×10^{1}	1.16	1.12	1.01	1.67	1.15	4.35	5.84	6.07
	R_9	R_{10}	R_{11}	R_{12}	R_{13}	R_{14}	R_{15}	R_{16}	R_{17}	R_{18}	R_{19}	R_{20}
Symmetric	5.50	5.54	5.54	5.50	5.50	5.61	1.15	1.04	1.01	1.01	1.00	1.01
Asymmetric	5.96	6.71	6.08	6.49	6.38	5.94	1.30	3.15	1.17	1.08	1.03	1.00

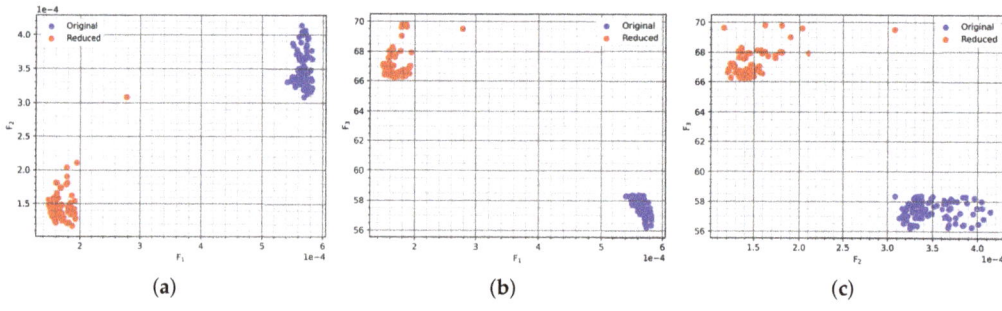

Figure 12. The comparison of the 100 cheapest symmetric solutions. With the blue color, all 20 coils are free to move, and with the red, only 12 coils are used, and they are constrained to move within the 5.5–20 mm region.

After analyzing the solution plot, the search range of the optimized turn radii can be reduced from 5.5–50 to 5.5–20 because the greater radii are not represented in the solution of the three objective problems.

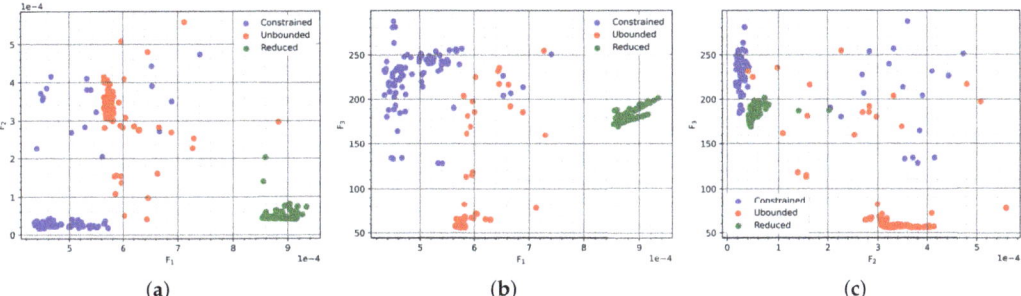

Figure 13. The image shows the last 100 symmetric solutions with various setups. The case where all 20 coils were free to move is in red. The blue color shows when all 20 coils are constrained in the 5.5–20 mm region, and finally, the green color depicts the case where only 12 coils are used, and they are constrained to the 5.5–20 mm region. (**a**) The distribution of the various setups on the F_1–F_2 axis, (**b**) on the F_1–F_3 axis, and (**c**) on the F_2–F_3 axis.

The proposed results and the working version of the realized optimization problem can be downloaded from the Ārtap project's homepage (the proposed solutions are available for download from: http://www.agros2d.org/artap/, accessed on 1 June 2021) together with a semi-analytical solution, and this can be used to validate the performance of FEM-based multi-objective optimization tools.

4. Conclusions

A novel three-variable analysis of the multi-objective TEAM benchmark problem is proposed in this paper. The original benchmark problem contains two similar two-variable Pareto optimizations. Firstly, the proposed coil is optimized to produce a uniform magnetic field in the examined region, and the sensitivity of the coil should also be minimized [12]. Secondly, the uniformity of the magnetic field and the mass of the coil are optimized. In practice, these two problems should be handled together. In this paper, the three objectives mentioned above—the uniformity (F_1), sensitivity (F_2), and price (F_3)—are considered simultaneously. Before optimizing the coil, an FEM simulation was made using two different tools with different mesh settings to find the right FEM setup. It was found that F_1 and F_2 are sensitive to the mesh settings, especially on the right side of the examined region. The FEMM-based calculation of the default (smart mesh function) mesh can produce 100% error in calculating F_1. It was found that the hp-adaptive solver was significantly faster and gave more accurate results. This solver was used to optimize with 1% in the error indicator, which produced an uncertainty of less than 20 µT in the results. This tolerance is acceptable because it is smaller than the measurement error or the Earth's magnetic field, which perturbs the results. This paper shows that this optimization problem is highly nonlinear, and nothing guarantees that only one optimal solution exists. We considered the asymmetrical cases in the solution and found that the symmetrical solutions always produced better solutions for F_1 and F_2. However, the difference between those solutions is insignificant for F_1 and F_2, as it is smaller than 20 µT.

Another interesting discovery is that the cheapest solutions are symmetrical setups, but they perform worse than the cheapest asymmetric ones for F_1 and F_2. We reduced the number of turns from 20 to 12, and we found that the price of the coil was reduced by only about 12–20%, which was below the expectations. Further studies should be carried out to validate the proposed results by performing measurements on at least a single layout, and these measurement results can be used to benchmark the proposed results.

Author Contributions: Conceptualization, T.O.; methodology, T.O., K.G.; software, K.G., T.O.; validation, K.G., T.O.; writing—original draft preparation, T.O., K.G.; writing—review and editing, T.O.; visualization, K.G., T.O.; supervision, T.O.; project administration, T.O.; funding acquisition, T.O. All authors have read and agreed to the published version of the manuscript.

Funding: This research received no external funding.

Conflicts of Interest: The authors declare no conflict of interest.

References

1. Bramerdorfer, G. Tolerance analysis for electric machine design optimization: Classification, modeling and evaluation, and example. *IEEE Trans. Magn.* **2019**, *55*, 1–9. [CrossRef]
2. Orosz, T.; Rassõlkin, A.; Kallaste, A.; Arsénio, P.; Pánek, D.; Kaska, J.; Karban, P. Robust Design Optimization and Emerging Technologies for Electrical Machines: Challenges and Open Problems. *Appl. Sci.* **2020**, *10*, 6653. [CrossRef]
3. Sizov, G.Y.; Ionel, D.M.; Demerdash, N.A.O. A review of efficient FE modeling techniques with applications to PM AC machines. In Proceedings of the 2011 IEEE Power and Energy Society General Meeting, Detroit, MI, USA, 24–28 July 2011; pp. 1–6. [CrossRef]
4. Bramerdorfer, G.; Tapia, J.A.; Pyrhönen, J.J.; Cavagnino, A. Modern Electrical Machine Design Optimization: Techniques, Trends, and Best Practices. *IEEE Trans. Ind. Electron.* **2018**, *65*, 7672–7684. [CrossRef]
5. Karban, P.; Pánek, D.; Orosz, T.; Doležel, I. Semi-Analytical Solution for a Multi-Objective TEAM Benchmark Problem. *Period. Polytech. Electr. Eng. Comput. Sci.* **2021**, *65*, 84–90. [CrossRef]
6. Kuczmann, M. Overview of the Finite Element Method. *Acta Tech. Jaurinensis* **2015**, *8*, 347–383. [CrossRef]
7. Varga, T.; Király, A.; Abonyi, J. Improvement of PSO Algorithm by Memory-Based Gradient Search—Application in Inventory Management. In *Swarm Intelligence and Bio-Inspired Computation*; Elsevier: Amsterdam, The Netherlands, 2013; pp. 403–422.
8. Del Vecchio, R.M.; Poulin, B.; Feghali, P.T.; Shah, D.M.; Ahuja, R. *Transformer Design Principles: With Applications to Core-Form Power Transformers*; CRC Press: Boca Raton, FL, USA, 2017.
9. Ma, B.; Zheng, J.; Zhu, J.; Wu, J.; Lei, G.; Guo, Y. Robust design optimization of electrical machines considering hybrid random and interval uncertainties. *IEEE Trans. Energy Convers.* **2020**, *35*, 1815–1824. [CrossRef]
10. Testing Electromagnetic Analysis Methods (T.E.A.M.). Available online: https://www.compumag.org/wp/team/ (accessed on 1 June 2021).
11. TEAM Workshop Problem 35- Multi-Objective Pareto Optimization of a Solenoid. Available online: https://www.compumag.org/wp/wp-content/uploads/2021/07/problem-35.pdf (accessed on 1 June 2021).
12. Di Barba, P.; Mognaschi, M.E.; Lowther, D.A.; Sykulski, J.K. A benchmark TEAM problem for multi-objective Pareto optimization of electromagnetic devices. *IEEE Trans. Magn.* **2018**, *54*, 1–4. [CrossRef]
13. Hornak, J.; Trnka, P.; Kadlec, P.; Michal, O.; Mentlik, V.; Sutta, P.; Csanyi, G.M.; Tamus, Z.A. Magnesium oxide nanoparticles: Dielectric properties, surface functionalization and improvement of epoxy-based composites insulating properties. *Nanomaterials* **2018**, *8*, 381. [CrossRef] [PubMed]
14. Sun, S.; Zeng, H.; Robinson, D.B.; Raoux, S.; Rice, P.M.; Wang, S.X.; Li, G. Monodisperse mfe2o4 (m = fe, co, mn) nanoparticles. *J. Am. Chem. Soc.* **2004**, *126*, 273–279. [CrossRef]
15. Dennis, C.L.; Ivkov, R. Physics of heat generation using magnetic nanoparticles for hyperthermia. *Int. J. Hyperth.* **2013**, *29*, 715–729. [CrossRef]
16. Daukaev, K.; Rassolkin, A.; Kallaste, A.; Vaimann, T.; Belahcen, A. A review of electrical machine design processes from the standpoint of software selection. In Proceedings of the 2017 IEEE 58th International Scientific Conference on Power and Electrical Engineering of Riga Technical University (RTUCON), Riga, Latvia, 12–13 October 2017; pp.1–6.
17. Pánek, D.; Karban, P.; Doležel, I. Comparison of Simplified Techniques for Solving Selected Coupled Electroheat Problems. *COMPEL-Int. J. Comput. Math. Electr. Electron. Eng.* 2019, 6p.
18. Pánek, D.; Orosz, T.; Kropík, P.; Karban, P.; Doležel, I. Reduced-Order Model Based Temperature Control of Induction Brazing Process. In Proceedings of the 2019 Electric Power Quality and Supply Reliability (PQ), Kärdla, Estonia, 12–15 June 2019; 4p.
19. Lucía, O.; Maussion, P.; Dede, E.J.; Burdío, J.M. Induction Heating Technology and Its Applications: Past Developments, Current Technology, and Future Challenges. *IEEE Trans. Ind. Electron.* **2014**, *61*, 2509–2520. [CrossRef]
20. Di Barba, P.; Dughiero, F.; Forzan, M.; Sieni, E. Improved solution to a multi-objective benchmark problem of inverse induction heating. *Int. J. Appl. Electromagn. Mech.* **2015**, *49*, 279–288. [CrossRef]
21. Di Barba, P.; Forzan, M.; Sieni, E. Multiobjective design optimization of an induction heating device: A benchmark problem. *Int. J. Appl. Electromagn. Mech.* **2015**, *47*, 1003–1013. [CrossRef]
22. Pólik, Z.; Kuczmann, M. RF inductor development by using the FEM. *Acta Tech. Jaurinensis* **2010**, *3*, 99–110.
23. Di Barba, P.; Dughiero, F.; Forzan, M.; Lowther, D.A.; Mognaschi, M.E.; Sieni, E.; Sykulski, J.K. A benchmark TEAM problem for multi-objective Pareto optimization in magnetics: The time-harmonic regime. *IEEE Trans. Magn.* **2019**, *56*, 1–4. [CrossRef]
24. Di Barba, P.; Mognaschi, M.E.; Lozito, G.M.; Salvini, A.; Dughiero, F.; Sieni, I. The benchmark TEAM problem for multi-objective optimization solved with CFSO. In Proceedings of the 2018 IEEE 4th International Forum on Research and Technology for Society and Industry (RTSI), Palermo, Italy, 10–13 September 2018; pp. 1–5.
25. Wolpert, D.H.; Macready, W.G. No free lunch theorems for optimization. *IEEE Trans. Evol. Comput.* **1997**, *1*, 67–82. [CrossRef]

26. Mirjalili, S.; Dong, J.S.; Sadiq, A.S.; Faris, H. Genetic algorithm: Theory, literature review, and application in image reconstruction. In *Nature-Inspired Optimizers*; Springer: Berlin/Heidelberg, Germany, 2020; pp. 69–85.
27. Seo, M.; Ryu, N.; Min, S. Sensitivity analysis for multi-objective optimization of the benchmark team problem. *IEEE Trans. Magn.* **2019**, *56*, 1–4. [CrossRef]
28. Karban, P.; Pánek, D.; Orosz, T.; Petrášová, I.; Doležel, I. FEM based robust design optimization with Agros and Ārtap. *Comput. Math. Appl.* **2021**, *81*, 618–633. doi: 10.1016/j.camwa.2020.02.010. [CrossRef]
29. Deb, K.; Pratap, A.; Agarwal, S.; Meyarivan, T. A fast and elitist multiobjective genetic algorithm: NSGA-II. *IEEE Trans. Evol. Comput.* **2002**, *6*, 182–197. [CrossRef]
30. Di Barba, P. Multi-objective wind-driven optimisation and magnet design. *Electron. Lett.* **2016**, *52*, 1216–1218. [CrossRef]
31. Mognaschi, M. Micro biogeography-inspired multi-objective optimisation for industrial electromagnetic design. *Electron. Lett.* **2017**, *53*, 1458–1460. [CrossRef]
32. Sieni, E.; Di Barba, P.; Forzan, M. Migration NSGA: Method to improve a non-elitist searching of Pareto front, with application in magnetics. *Inverse Probl. Sci. Eng.* **2016**, *24*, 543–566. [CrossRef]
33. Meeker, D. Finite element method magnetics. *FEMM* **2010**, *4*, 162.
34. Kiss, G.M.; Kaska, J.; de Oliveira, R.A.H.; Rubanenko, O.; Tóth, B. Performance Analysis of FEM Solvers on Practical Electromagnetic Problems. *arXiv* **2020**, arXiv:2009.04399.
35. Pánek, D.; Orosz, T.; Karban, P. Artap: Robust design optimization framework for engineering applications. In Proceedings of the Third International Conference on Intelligent Computing in Data Sciences ICDS2019, Marrakech, Morocco, 28–30 October 2019; 4p.
36. Karban, P.; Mach, F.; Kůs, P.; Pánek, D.; Doležel, I. Numerical solution of coupled problems using code Agros2D. *Computing* **2013**, *95*, 381–408. [CrossRef]
37. Kuczmann, M.; Szücs, A.; Kovács, G. Transformer Model Identification by Ārtap. *Period. Polytech. Electr. Eng. Comput. Sci.* **2021**, *65*, 123–130. [CrossRef]
38. Shewchuk, J.R. Triangle: Engineering a 2D quality mesh generator and Delaunay triangulator. In *Workshop on Applied Computational Geometry*; Springer: Berlin/Heidelberg, Germany, 1996; pp. 203–222.

Article

A Multi-Objective Design Optimization for a Permanent Magnet Synchronous Machine with Hairpin Winding Intended for Transport Applications

Mohammad Soltani *, Stefano Nuzzo, Davide Barater and Giovanni Franceschini

Department of Engineering Enzo Ferrari, University of Modena and Reggio Emilia, 41125 Modena, Italy; stefano.nuzzo@unimore.it (S.N.); davide.barater@unimore.it (D.B.); giovanni.franceschini@unimore.it (G.F.)
* Correspondence: mohammad.soltani@unimore.it

Citation: Soltani, M.; Nuzzo, S.; Barater, D.; Franceschini, G. A Multi-Objective Design Optimization for a Permanent Magnet Synchronous Machine with Hairpin Winding Intended for Transport Applications. *Electronics* **2021**, *10*, 3162. https://doi.org/10.3390/electronics10243162

Academic Editors: Tamás Orosz, David Pánek, Anton Rassõlkin and Miklos Kuczmann

Received: 25 November 2021
Accepted: 15 December 2021
Published: 18 December 2021

Publisher's Note: MDPI stays neutral with regard to jurisdictional claims in published maps and institutional affiliations.

Copyright: © 2021 by the authors. Licensee MDPI, Basel, Switzerland. This article is an open access article distributed under the terms and conditions of the Creative Commons Attribution (CC BY) license (https://creativecommons.org/licenses/by/4.0/).

Abstract: Nowadays, interest in electric propulsion is increasing due to the need to decarbonize society. Electric drives and their components play a key role in this electrification trend. The electrical machine, in particular, is seeing an ever-increasing development and extensive research is currently being dedicated to the improvement of its efficiency and torque/power density. Among the winding methods, hairpin technologies are gaining extensive attention due to their inherently high slot fill factor, good heat dissipation, strong rigidity, and short end-winding length. These features make hairpin windings a potential candidate for some traction applications which require high power and/or torque densities. However, they also have some drawbacks, such as high losses at high frequency operations due to skin and proximity effects. In this paper, a multi-objective design optimization is proposed aiming to provide a fast and useful tool to enhance the exploitation of the hairpin technology in electrical machines. Efficiency and volume power density are considered as main design objectives. Analytical and finite element evaluations are performed to support the proposed methodology.

Keywords: hairpin windings; electrical machines; multi-objective optimizations; optimization

1. Introduction

Due to the ever-more stringent emission and efficiency requirements, there is currently a wide interest in the research and development of more electric vehicles. Traction applications are pushing the boundaries for high speed and power density with innovations in cores, magnets, and winding designs [1]. However, while higher speeds mean higher power for a given torque, they also result in additional losses in cores and windings, thus lowering the overall efficiency, and in structural challenges relative to the rotating components. Additionally, the relative distribution of these losses highly depends on the type of converter used to supply the machine.

In high power density traction applications, hairpin windings are widely spreading and currently seeing an ever-increasing interest in several documents [2–5]. In comparison to windings with round conductors, the end-winding length is shortened and, consequently, the DC copper loss is reduced [6]. Besides this end winding feature, the flat and "massive" shape of each hairpin leg reduces the DC copper loss compared to their round-wound counterpart. Hairpin windings achieve a higher fill factor compared to the round winding, thus obtaining higher current density and peak torque. In addition, in a series production context, a fully automated manufacturing process is possible, potentially reducing the associated costs [7].

On the other hand, being a recent technology, not much research is available on the design optimization of machines equipping this type of winding, whereas several studies focusing on optimization techniques have been proposed for electrical machines featuring random windings. For example, in [8], the analysis, design, and optimization of a permanent magnet synchronous motor (PMSM) intended for a campus patrol electric vehicle were presented. Its optimization objectives included minimization of voltage harmonic content and torque ripple. The optimum stator inductances and resistance of a PMSM were calculated in [9] using a particle swarm optimization (PSO) method. Furthermore, the maximization of the flux-weakening region was pursued in [10], where a surface-mounted PMSM was optimized. In [11], the torque ripple of a PMSM under both transient state and steady-state conditions was minimized through an analytical solution. A multi-physics optimization program based on a multi-objective genetic algorithm was developed in [12], to achieve a trade-off solution among the electromagnetic, mechanical, and thermal aspects.

Regarding hairpin windings, a design optimization was carried out in [13], where the aim of the optimization study was that of reducing the torque ripple, while little attention was given to the most critical challenge of hairpin windings, i.e., the high copper losses at high-frequency operation. This is due to skin and proximity effects, where the feeding alternating current flows in a fraction of the conductor's cross section. These phenomena exacerbate at high frequency operations and result in an increase of the effective conductor resistance (and, thus, of losses) [3].

A simple motor design for traction applications was introduced in [14], but with no optimization strategy being implemented. In [15], an induction motor equipping hairpin winding was optimized aiming at a low cost, rare-earth free design. However, the number of hairpin layers in the slot was kept fixed, thus limiting the degrees of freedom of the design optimization. Additional work has been recently published on hairpin windings, but they focus either on modelling aspects (e.g., AC loss estimation [2]) or preliminary calculations [6] or sensitivity analyses [16].

Considering all the above, in this paper, the aim is to use dedicated optimization strategies for the design of an electrical machine with hairpin windings intended for a race car application. As a case study to investigate the above concepts, the surface mounted PMSM "roughly" designed in [17] is considered. The design achieved in [17] is based on a random winding stator, thus the initial aim of this work is to transform the random winding into a hairpin one, while the second step is to move from a "rough" machine design to an optimal one. To this purpose, two objective functions were selected: maximization of the volume power density and minimization of the power losses. These are indeed the most critical and conflicting figures to achieve when hairpin windings are involved. Before implementing the optimization process, first a sensitivity analytical study is carried out on the number of poles and slots per pole per phase. This led to define a starting machine design which is used to validate the analytical sizing approach through the finite element (FE) methodology. Once validated, the analytical tool is firstly used to perform a study on the parameters mostly affecting the selected objectives, and then to run the optimization to achieve an optimal solution. The use of the analytical sizing equations ensures a limited computation burden compared to numerical-based (e.g., FE) approaches.

2. Preliminary Design Process

2.1. Assumptions and Constraints

In [17], the whole propulsion system of a Formula SAE [18] car was designed, with a detailed focus on the propulsion motor being the case study of this paper. The selection of the system architecture, i.e., a two-motor layout implemented onto the rear non-steering axle, was based upon budget considerations. Additional constraints, such as the overall dimensions of the chassis and those imposed by the race regulations were accounted for. When it came to the motor torque-speed usage during an endurance event, the resulting reduced flux-weakening region led to select the popular surface-mounted PMSM layout as the most suitable for this application, also considering lower production costs in a customized case, compared to interior PM or synchronous reluctance machine layouts.

The Formula SAE car project must meet a series of technical constraints imposed by the regulation. These are summarized as follows:

- The diameter of the wheels must be ≥203.2 mm.
- The maximum power P required from the battery must not exceed 80 kW.
- The maximum allowed DC-link voltage V_{DC} must not exceed 600 V.
- There are no limitations concerning the number and the type of electric motors.

A summary of the choices done in [17] is listed in Table 1. These are used as starting points for re-designing the motor with hairpin conductors and applying an optimization strategy on it.

Table 1. Design choices and requirements.

Parameter	Condition
Motor topology	Surface-mounted PM
Motor's location	Rear-axle
Maximum torque to wheels	600 Nm
Reduction ratio	10
Motor rated torque	30 Nm
Base speed	12,740 rpm

The main design parameters of the machine obtained in [17], used as a benchmark here, are listed in Table 2. These are used as starting conditions for the analytical sizing tool implemented as the basis for the multi-objective optimization, and whose equations are reported in the next subsection.

Table 2. Motor design parameters.

Parameter	Value
Mechanical power P	40 kW
Line-to-line Voltage V	540 V
Surface current density J	13 A/mm^2
Airgap flux density B_{ag}	0.85 T
Maximum tooth flux density B_t	1.6 T
Maximum yoke flux density B_y	1.4 T
Linear current density A	70 A/mm
Targeted efficiency	95%

2.2. Machine Sizing Equations

The design process is initialized by defining some basic machine performance requirements, such as output power, speed, voltage, and desired efficiency [19]. The values of such input parameters are listed in Table 2. The second step is that of making some assumptions on the core materials and the cooling system, which are listed in Table 3, where also the main parameters used during the design process are described.

Table 3. Design choices and symbols.

Parameter	Value
Core material	M330-50A
PM material	N28AH
Cooling system	Natural convention
Stator winding	Distributed, full-pitch, single layer

Table 3. Cont.

Parameter	Symbol
Fill factor	k_{ff}
Outer rotor diameter [mm]	D
Axial length [mm]	L
PM span [deg]	α_{PM}
Number of phases	m
Number of slots-per-pole-per-phase	q
Pole pair number	p

Core materials and cooling system allow defining magnetic and electric loadings and the maximum flux density values allowed in the various parts of the motor. Assuming a number of phases m equal to 3, the slot number is calculated as $Q = q \cdot m \cdot 2p$, and the number of turns per phase as $N = z_q \cdot q \cdot p$. Given the type of winding structure initially assumed, short pitch factor k_{cp} is equal to 1, while the distribution factor k_d is calculated using (1), where β is the slot pitch angle. The winding factor k_w is given by the product of k_{cp} and k_d [19].

$$k_d = \frac{\sin\left(\frac{q \cdot \beta}{2}\right)}{q \cdot \sin\left(\frac{\beta}{2}\right)} \quad (1)$$

Having preliminarily selected the D/L ratio, the starting point for the motor sizing is the torque expression given in (2). In (2) B is the RMS value of the fundamental harmonic B_{max} of the airgap flux density, which is obtained from (3) using the Fourier series decomposition of a square wave waveform that has amplitude B_{ag}. A is the RMS value of the linear current density. Equation (2) permits to find the values of D and L. Then, hypothesizing in the PMs the same flux density as in the airgap leveraging on Gauss' law, (4) can be used to determine the thickness l_m of the PMs. This means that the PMs are initially sized to meet the no-load requirements. In (4), B_r and μ_r are the residual flux density and relative permeability of the PMs [19].

$$T = \frac{\pi}{2} D^2 \, L \, B \, A \quad (2)$$

$$B_{max} = \frac{4 B_{ag}}{\pi} \cdot \sin\left(\frac{p \, \alpha_{PM}}{180} \cdot \frac{\pi}{2}\right), \quad (3)$$

$$l_m = \frac{\mu_r l_g}{\frac{B_r}{B_{ag}} - 1}, \quad (4)$$

The total area $S_{\text{all slots}}$ to be dedicated to the three machine phases can be calculated using (5). Yoke thickness W_y and tooth width W_t can be calculated using (6) and (7), respectively. In (6), Φ_p is the physical flux per pole and B_y the maximum yoke flux density, whereas in (7) B_{avg} is the average airgap flux density, λ_s is the stator slot pitch and B_t is the maximum yoke flux density [19].

$$A = \frac{J \cdot S_{\text{all slots}} \cdot k_{ff}}{\pi D} \quad (5)$$

$$W_y = \frac{\Phi_p}{2 B_y L} \quad (6)$$

$$W_t = \frac{B_{avg} \cdot \lambda_s}{B_t} \quad (7)$$

2.3. Power Losses

Besides these design aspects, the most crucial factor to consider when designing an electrical machine with hairpin windings is the AC Joule losses. In random windings with stranded conductors, the AC losses can be neglected in the first approximation. In contrast, in hairpin windings, AC losses need to be carefully considered and determined. The DC resistance R_{DC} of a machine phase depends on the total length of one coil L_c, the number of turns in series N and parallel paths per phase, the cross-sectional area of the conductor S_c and the conductivity of the conductive material σ_c. Considering a uniform current distribution at any frequency in stranded conductors, the losses associated with the DC resistance are the only contribution to Joule losses. On the other hand, in hairpin conductors, skin and proximity effects and the ensuing AC losses are usually determined through the ratio between R_{AC} and R_{DC} [6]. For each layer k in the slot, this ratio (k_{Rk}) is determined using (8), where φ, ψ and ξ are expressed as in (9)–(11). In (11), h_{c0} and b_c are the height and width of the conductors, respectively, while b is the slot width, ω is the supply frequency, and μ_0 is the permeability of vacuum.

$$k_{Rk} = \varphi(\xi) + k(k-1)\psi(\xi) \tag{8}$$

$$\varphi(\xi) = \xi \frac{\sinh 2\xi + \sin 2\xi}{\cosh 2\xi - \cos 2\xi} \tag{9}$$

$$\psi(\xi) = 2\xi \frac{\sinh \xi - \sin \xi}{\cosh \xi + \cos \xi} \tag{10}$$

$$\xi = h_{c0}\sqrt{\frac{1}{2}\omega\mu_0\sigma_c\frac{b_c}{b}} \tag{11}$$

Regarding iron losses, materials' suppliers usually give the loss density in W/kg, at specific frequency and flux density values. This includes both eddy current and hysteresis losses. Analytically, iron losses can be found by dividing the magnetic circuit of the machine into n sections, in which the flux density is constant. Once the masses $m_{Fe,n}$ of the different n sections are calculated from the volume density, the losses $P_{Fe,n}$ in these parts can be approximated as in (12). Here, $k_{Fe,n}$ are "loss" coefficients that, for a synchronous machine, can be imposed equal to 2 in the teeth and 1.6 in the yoke; P_{10} is the loss density at 1 T; $\widehat{B_n}$ is the maximum flux density in the n-th section [19]. The total power losses are determined using (13), where $P_{Cu_{DC}}$ and $P_{Cu_{AC}}$ are the DC and AC copper losses, respectively.

$$P_{Fe} = \sum_n k_{Fe,n} P_{10} \left(\frac{\widehat{B_n}}{1T}\right)^2 m_{Fe,n}, \tag{12}$$

$$P_{Tot\_losses} = P_{Fe} + P_{Cu_{DC}} + P_{Cu_{AC}} \tag{13}$$

2.4. Power Density

For the sake of completeness, the formula for the calculation of the volume power density is reported in (14). This is found through the ratio between the output power P and the machine volume Vol, which is defined once the main dimensions are all calculated.

$$P_{Density} = \frac{P_{out}}{Vol} \tag{14}$$

3. Optimization Process

As mentioned in Section 1, there are two objectives, i.e., the maximization of the volume power density (see (14)) and minimization of power losses (see (13)), which is equivalent to maximizing the efficiency. There are four input variable parameters, i.e., pole pair number, slot per pole per phase number, conductors' number in the slots (N), and motor's axial length. Additionally, several constraints must be met for the optimization process. Therefore, a Multi-Objective Evolutionary Algorithm (MOEA) could be used, which needs to set the weight of the input parameters based on their effect on the two objectives, and a starting point for initializing the first population. Using the equations introduced in

Section 2, a sensitivity analysis is first carried out to understand the dependence of the two objectives on the four variable parameters.

The MOEA expects a single fitness value with which to perform the selection. Additional processing is sometimes required to transform MOEA solutions' fitness vectors into a scalar. Its sequential task decomposition includes initialized population, fitness evaluation, which has a sub-level as vector transformation, recombination, mutation, and selection [20]. Figure 1 shows these decomposition tasks in five sections which has the main loop for selecting the data between the third and fifth levels.

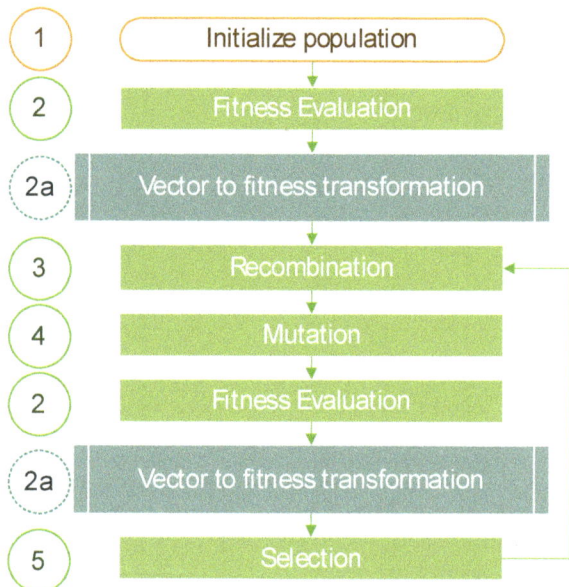

Figure 1. Sequential task decomposition for MOEA.

Regarding the constraints, first, the tooth width is imposed greater than 1.6 mm for structural reasons. Secondly, the loss density B_{10} at 1 T used in (12) for iron loss calculation is updated during optimization as it depends on frequency. Thirdly, to make the evaluation of the optimization objectives consistent, the inverse of the power density is considered, so that both the objectives must be minimized. Assuming to keep the frequency lower than 1 kHz as per [17], the maximum pole number should not exceed 8. Due to the dimensional limitations in terms of length and axial diameter, as well as the constraint on the tooth width, the maximum q is kept lower than 8. The axial length is varied between 10 mm and 100 mm. With an axial length higher than 100 mm the motor's diameter becomes less than 325 mm, resulting in a tooth width < 1.6 mm even with q = 1. The last constraint is on the maximum RMS value of the line-to-line voltage (see Table 2), which is limited by the maximum battery voltage (see Section 2.1). Another constrained value is the number of conductors per slot, which must be necessarily even due to the hairpin winding characteristics. A summary of the constraints is listed in (15)–(18).

$$2 \leq 2p \leq 8 \tag{15}$$

$$1 \leq q \leq 8 \tag{16}$$

$$10 \text{ mm} \leq L \leq 100 \text{ mm} \tag{17}$$

$$V_{L-L} \leq 540 \text{ V} \tag{18}$$

4. Results

4.1. Preliminary Sensitivity Analysis and Validation of the Analytical Model

Before using the analytical model for optimization purposes, it needs to be validated against the more accurate FE method. Once validated, it can be safely used for optimizations, thus saving computation time as opposed to FE. An initial sensitivity analysis could be carried out varying the number of poles and slots per pole per phase while keeping the other parameters constant. The sensitivity analysis results are illustrated in Figure 2, where power losses and volume power density are taken as indicators to suitably select q and p. The best solution is achieved with $p = 4$ and $q = 2$. The selected p-q combination represents the best trade-off in terms of maximum power density and minimum power losses. In fact, only two machines (referred to as "A" and "B" in the figure) achieve higher power density values, but these feature much larger losses (by 8.9% and 23.9%, respectively).

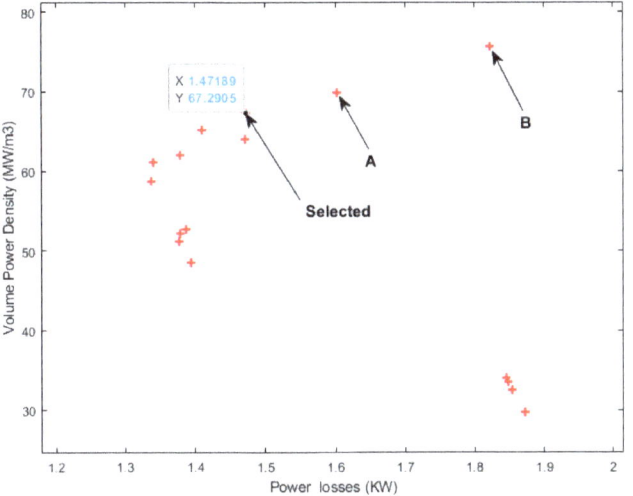

Figure 2. Preliminary sensitivity analysis.

The dimensions analytically obtained are used to build the machine geometry and a corresponding model within the FE-based software MagNet. Figure 3 shows the FE model of the motor, enriched with a flux density map and field lines distribution. Figure 4 plots the output torque obtained with the currents in phase with the corresponding back electromotive forces, with an average value equal to 30.1 Nm being obtained. This matches well the torque value of 30 Nm assumed in the analytical sizing. Besides the torque, the analytical and FE no-load voltage and flux density values in the various parts of the motor are compared. Figure 5 shows a comparison between the fundamental harmonic of the line-to-line voltage (red line) obtained from FE simulations and the corresponding sinusoidal waveform assumed for the analytical sizing (in green), with an error lower than 1% being achieved. For completeness, the FE voltage waveform evaluated via FE is also observed in Figure 5. In addition, Figure 6 illustrates the flux densities in the airgap and the main iron parts of the motor, with the blue lines referring to FE results and the red text relative to the analytical assumptions (see Table 2). Good matching is observed, with an error ranging from 3% to 8%, thus allowing to conclude that the analytical sizing equations, although suitable for preliminary sizing only, can be safely used for optimization purposes.

In the next subsection, the effect of some machine parameters on power density and power losses are investigated before proceeding with the optimization. This study allows weighting any of the input parameters in the multi-objective optimization process which will be the focus of Section 4.3.

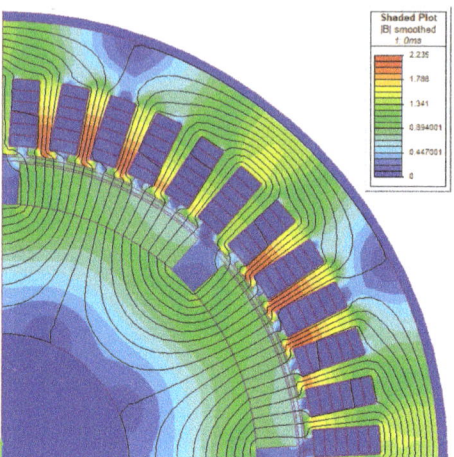

Figure 3. FE one pole pair model of the motor with the hairpin winding, highlighting flux density map (T) and field lines distribution at full-load operation.

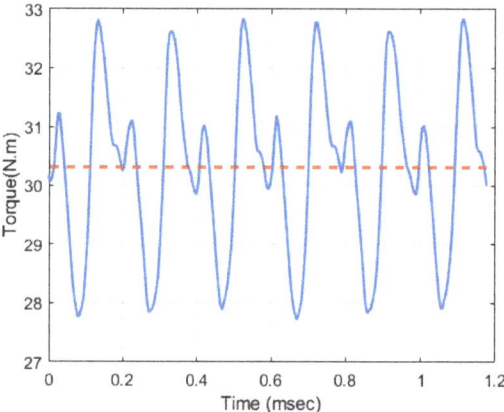

Figure 4. Output torque (in blue) and its average value (in red) obtained via FE analysis.

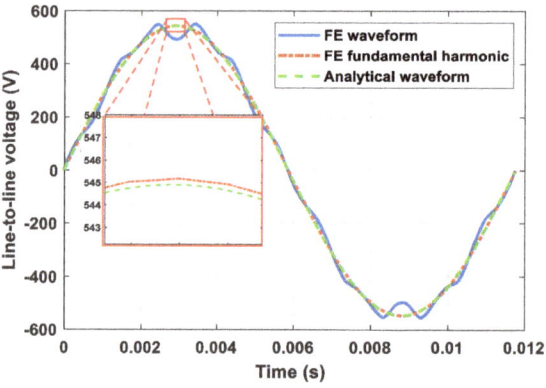

Figure 5. FE no-load line-to-line voltage (in blue) and its fundamental harmonic (in red) vs. analytical no-load line-to-line voltage (in green).

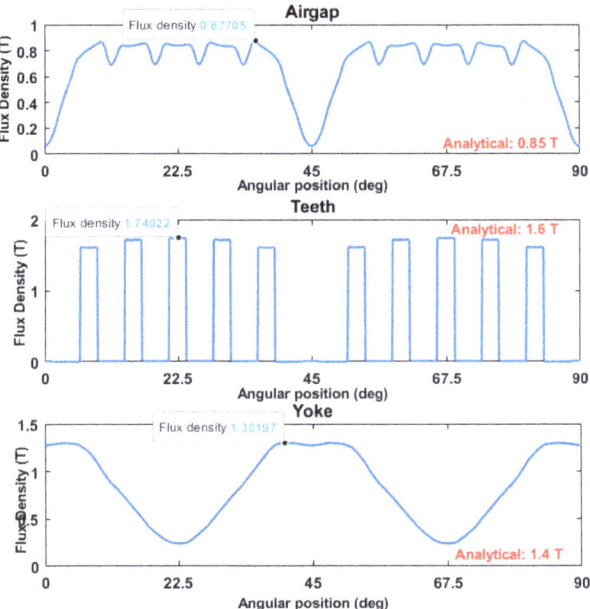

Figure 6. Comparison in terms of flux density in the airgap, teeth, and yoke.

4.2. Effective Parameters

Considering the analytical equations reported in Section 2.2, it is clear that several parameters can be utilized to achieve the main design objectives of this work, i.e., power density maximization and power losses minimization. Thus, a sensitivity analysis is performed. While the results of this study can vary depending on the power range, the geometrical and magnetic features, the airgap thickness, etc., of the PMSM motor under analysis, for the case study considered in this paper the sensitivity study can provide useful information for a first exploration of weight allocation during optimization. Assuming the hairpin motor of the previous section as the benchmark, the parameters used for the sensitivity study are normalized over the corresponding values of the benchmark machine. Figures 7 and 8 show the total power losses and volume power density for the four input parameters, i.e., pole pair number, slot per pole per phase number, conductor per slot number, and axial length. These parameters are changed "1-by-1" in this first exploration. All the curves meet at 1 p.u., corresponding to the benchmark machine. All the parameters have a non-negligible effect on both power losses (Figure 7) and power density (Figure 8). According to the methodology described in [20], the weight of each input parameter to be imposed in the optimization can be found through these figures. Using a coefficient equal to 1 for N, the pole pair number, the slot per pole per phase number and the axial length feature coefficients equal to 1.38, 1.1 and 1.15, respectively.

4.3. MOEA Results and Comparison

Regarding the mentioned sequential task decomposition of the optimization method (see Figure 1), before any mutation, the constraints (15)–(18) should be carefully considered. After running the optimization algorithm using 500 generations and 50 individuals per generation, the Pareto front shown in Figure 9 is finally obtained, where the last 50 designs are observed. Every sequential task of the optimization process shown in Figure 1 has been implemented in Matlab environment.

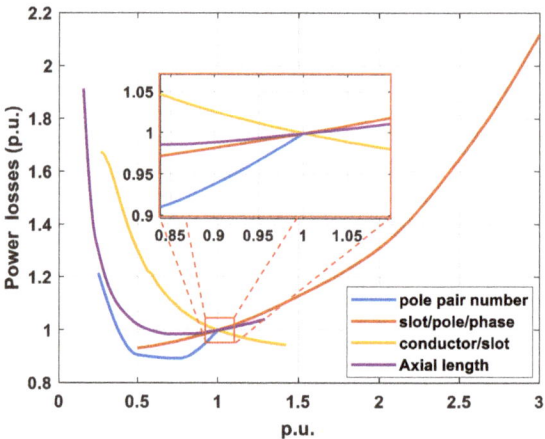

Figure 7. Effect of the input parameters on the total power losses.

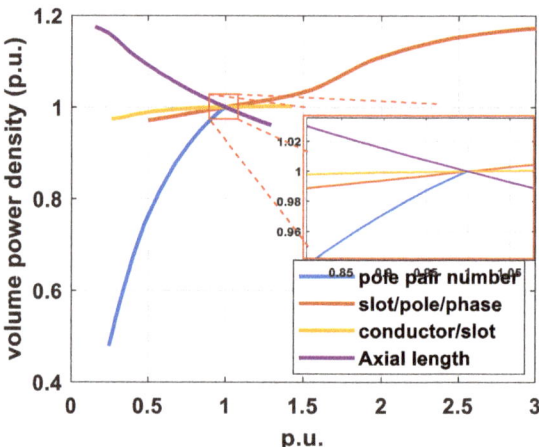

Figure 8. Effect of the input parameters on the volume power density.

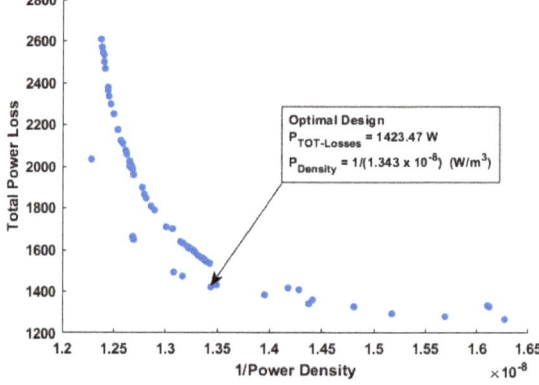

Figure 9. The final Pareto front with the final optimum point.

The optimal machine design is also highlighted in Figure 9, and its geometry is illustrated in Figure 10b, whereas in Figure 10a the machine design resulting from the first sensitivity analysis is shown for the sake of comparison. Table 4 compares the analytical results obtained for the motor with round winding designed in [17], the motor with hairpin winding resulting from the first sensitivity analysis, and the optimum one. With a focus on the motors with hairpin windings, the main indexes such as efficiency, volume power density, volume torque density, and power losses have been improved by 0.15%, 10.55%, 12.3%, and 3.4%, respectively. For completeness, the full-load output torque of the optimum motor obtained using FE is reported in Figure 11, with the mean value being highlighted in red and equal to 30.2 Nm.

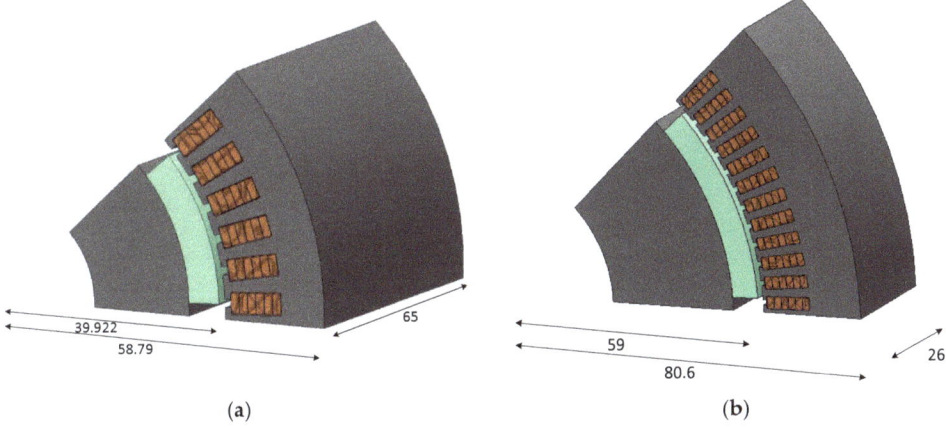

Figure 10. Comparison between the geometries of (**a**) the first analyzed motor and (**b**) the optimal motor.

Table 4. Summarizing comparison among the benchmark motor [17], the hairpin motor obtained through the first sensitivity analysis and the optimum hairpin motor.

Parameters	Round Winding	Hairpin 1st Design	Hairpin Optimal Design	Improvement
pole number	6	8	8	-
slot/pole/phase	1	2	4	-
axial length	65	65	26	-
conductors/slot	11	6	6	-
rotor radius	45	39.922	59	-
Tooth width	10	2	1.635	-
Yoke thickness	14	7.7	13.35	-
outer radius	85	58.79	80.6	-
Fill factor	60%	85%	85%	-
Peak current (A)	140	80.56	63.7	-
Torque ripple (%)	16%	17%	8.97%	9.03%
Power loss (kW)	2	1.47	1.42	10.55%,
Efficiency	95.2%	96.45%	96.6%	0.15%
volume power density (MW/m^3)	16.75	67.3	74.4	12.3%
volume torque density (kNm/m^3)	13.21	49.65	55.76	3.4%

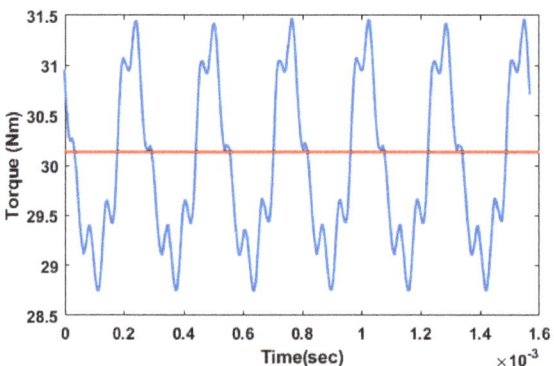

Figure 11. Output torque of the optimum motor.

5. Conclusions

In this paper, a fast and accurate optimization tool was introduced for optimal exploitation of hairpin technologies in electrical machines intended for traction applications. The optimization tool is aimed at maximizing power density and efficiency, which are key figures for the application at hand. In addition, given the challenges featured by hairpin conductors at high-frequency operations, these two objectives are rather conflicting, thus making the machine design complex. The optimization strategy, based first on a "one-by-one" sensitivity study and then on the application of a multi-objective evolutionary algorithm, proved that these two objectives can be pursued and achieved simultaneously, with excellent performance enhancement being obtained.

As a benchmark case study, a surface-mounted PMSM equipping random windings and previously designed for a Formula SAE car was considered. Therefore, the first exercise consisted of replacing the random winding with hairpin conductors. A preliminary sizing was first carried out based on the requirements of the application at hand. Then, the analytical sizing tool was validated against FE evaluations, with a maximum error of ≈8%, thus making the analytical equations a safe means for the optimization procedure. A sensitivity analysis was performed to suitably weight the optimization input parameters and, finally, the optimization algorithm was run. The optimal motor, which was selected for comparative purposes against the benchmark motor with random windings and a non-optimal hairpin motor, showed very promising results and significant performance improvements. In particular, the main indexes such as efficiency, volume power density, and power losses, were improved by 0.15%, 10.55%, and 3.4%, respectively.

Author Contributions: Conceptualization, M.S. and S.N.; methodology, M.S. and S.N.; software, M.S.; validation, M.S., S.N. and D.B.; formal analysis, M.S.; investigation, M.S.; resources, M.S.; data curation, M.S.; writing—original draft preparation, M.S.; writing—review and editing, S.N.; visualization, M.S.; supervision, S.N., D.B. and G.F.; project administration, D.B. and G.F.; funding acquisition, S.N., D.B. and G.F. All authors have read and agreed to the published version of the manuscript.

Funding: This research received no external funding.

Conflicts of Interest: The authors declare no conflict of interest.

References

1. Zhao, Y.; Li, D.; Pei, T.; Qu, R. Overview of the rectangular wire windings AC electrical machine. *CES Trans. Electr. Mach. Syst.* **2019**, *3*, 160–169. [CrossRef]
2. Arzillo, A.; Nuzzo, S.; Braglia, P.; Franceschini, G.; Barater, D.; Gerada, D.; Gerada, C. An Analytical Approach for the Design of Innovative Hairpin Winding Layouts. In Proceedings of the International Conference on Electrical Machines (ICEM), Gothenburg, Sweden, 23–26 August 2020; pp. 1534–1539.

3. Nuzzo, S.; Barater, D.; Gerada, C.; Vai, P. Hairpin Windings: An Opportunity for Next-Generation E-Motors in Transportation. *IEEE Ind. Electron. Mag.* **2021**, 2–10. [CrossRef]
4. Islam, S.; Husain, I.; Ahmed, A.; Sathyan, A. Asymmetric Bar Winding for High-Speed Traction Electric Machines. *IEEE Trans. Transp. Electrif.* **2019**, *6*, 3–15. [CrossRef]
5. Scuiller, F.; Zahr, H.; Semail, E. Maximum Reachable Torque, Power and Speed for Five-Phase SPM Machine With Low Armature Reaction. *IEEE Trans. Energy Convers.* **2016**, *31*, 959–969. [CrossRef]
6. Soltani, M.; Nuzzo, S.; Barater, D.; Franceschini, G. Considerations on the Preliminary Sizing of Electrical Machines with Hairpin Windings. In Proceedings of the 2021 IEEE Workshop on Electrical Machines Design, Control and Diagnosis (WEMDCD), Modena, Italy, 8–9 April 2021; pp. 46–51.
7. Popescu, M.; Goss, J.; Staton, D.A.; Hawkins, D.; Chong, Y.C.; Boglietti, A. Electrical Vehicles—Practical Solutions for Power Traction Motor Systems. *IEEE Trans. Ind. Appl.* **2018**, *54*, 2751–2762. [CrossRef]
8. Sun, X.; Shi, Z.; Lei, G.; Guo, Y.; Zhu, J. Analysis and Design Optimization of a Permanent Magnet Synchronous Motor for a Campus Patrol Electric Vehicle. *IEEE Trans. Veh. Technol.* **2019**, *68*, 10535–10544. [CrossRef]
9. Hernandez, O.S.; Morales-Caporal, R.; Rangel-Magdaleno, J.; Peregrina-Barreto, H.; Hernandez-Perez, J.N. Parameter Identification of PMSMs Using Experimental Measurements and a PSO Algorithm. *IEEE Trans. Instrum. Meas.* **2015**, *64*, 2146–2154. [CrossRef]
10. Dang, L.; Bernard, N.; Bracikowski, N.; Berthiau, G. Design Optimization with Flux Weakening of High-Speed PMSM for Electrical Vehicle Considering the Driving Cycle. *IEEE Trans. Ind. Electron.* **2017**, *64*, 9834–9843. [CrossRef]
11. Feng, G.; Lai, C.; Kar, N.C. An Analytical Solution to Optimal Stator Current Design for PMSM Torque Ripple Minimization With Minimal Machine Losses. *IEEE Trans. Ind. Electron.* **2017**, *64*, 7655–7665. [CrossRef]
12. Zhao, W.; Wang, X.; Gerada, C.; Zhang, H.; Liu, C.; Wang, Y. Multi-Physics and Multi-Objective Optimization of a High Speed PMSM for High Performance Applications. *IEEE Trans. Magn.* **2018**, *54*, 1–5. [CrossRef]
13. Jung, D.S.; Kim, Y.H.; Lee, U.H.; Lee, H.D. Optimum Design of the Electric Vehicle Traction Motor Using the Hairpin Winding. In Proceedings of the 2012 IEEE 75th Vehicular Technology Conference (VTC Spring), Yokohama, Japan, 6–9 May 2012. [CrossRef]
14. Xue, S.; Michon, M.; Popescu, M.; Volpe, G. Optimisation of Hairpin Winding in Electric Traction Motor Applications. In Proceedings of the IEEE International Electric Machines & Drives Conference (IEMDC), Hartford, CT, USA, 17–20 May 2021; pp. 1–7. [CrossRef]
15. Riviere, N.; Villani, M.; Popescu, M. Optimisation of a High Speed Copper Rotor Induction Motor for a Traction Application. In Proceedings of the IECON 2019—45th Annual Conference of the IEEE Industrial Electronics Society, Lisbon, Portugal, 14–17 October 2019; Volume 1, pp. 2720–2725. [CrossRef]
16. Preci, E.; Gerada, D.; Degano, M.; Buticchi, G.; Gerada, C.; Nuzzo, S.; Barater, D. Hairpin Windings: Sensitivity Analysis and Guidelines to Reduce AC Losses. In Proceedings of the 2021 IEEE Workshop on Electrical Machines Design, Control and Diagnosis (WEMDCD), Modena, Italy, 8–9 April 2021; pp. 82–87. [CrossRef]
17. Devito, G.; Nuzzo, S.; Barater, D.; Franceschini, G.; Papini, L.; Bolognesi, P. Design of the Propulsion System for a Formula SAE racing car based on a Brushless Motor. In Proceedings of the IEEE Workshop on Electrical Machines Design, Control and Diagnosis (WEMDCD), Modenta, Italy, 8–9 April 2021; pp. 318–324.
18. Formula SAE Rules 2021 Version 1.0. Available online: www.fsaeonline.com/cdsweb/gen/DocumentResources.aspx (accessed on 19 November 2021).
19. Pyrhonen, J.; Jokinen, T.; Hrabovcova, V. *Design of Rotating Electrical Machines*; John Wiley & Sons Ltd.: Chichester, UK, 2013.
20. Coello, C.A.C.; Lamont, B.G.; Van Veldhuizen, A. *Evolutionary Algorithms for Solving Multi-Objective Problems*; Springer: New York, NY, USA, 2007; Volume 5.

Article

Analytical Study and Comparison of Electromagnetic Characteristics of 8-Pole 9-Slot and 8-Pole 12-Slot Permanent Magnet Synchronous Machines Considering Rotor Eccentricity

Hoon-Ki Lee, Tae-Kyoung Bang, Jeong-In Lee, Jong-Hyeon Woo, Hyo-Seob Shin, Ick-Jae Yoon and Jang-Young Choi *

Department of Electrical Engineering, ChungNam National University, Daejeon 34134, Korea; lhk1109@cnu.ac.kr (H.-K.L.); bangtk77@cnu.ac.kr (T.-K.B.); lji477@cnu.ac.kr (J.-I.L.); dnwhd0@cnu.ac.kr (J.-H.W.); shs1027@cnu.ac.kr (H.-S.S.); ijyoon@cnu.ac.kr (I.-J.Y.)
* Correspondence: choi_jy@cnu.ac.kr; Tel.: +82-042-821-7601

Citation: Lee, H.-K.; Bang, T.-K.; Lee, J.-I.; Woo, J.-H.; Shin, H.-S.; Yoon, I.-J.; Choi, J.-Y. Analytical Study and Comparison of Electromagnetic Characteristics of 8-Pole 9-Slot and 8-Pole 12-Slot Permanent Magnet Synchronous Machines Considering Rotor Eccentricity. *Electronics* **2021**, *10*, 2036. https://doi.org/10.3390/electronics10162036

Academic Editors: Tamás Orosz, Davide Astolfi, David Pánek, Anton Rassõlkin and Miklos Kuczmann

Received: 27 July 2021
Accepted: 19 August 2021
Published: 23 August 2021

Publisher's Note: MDPI stays neutral with regard to jurisdictional claims in published maps and institutional affiliations.

Copyright: © 2021 by the authors. Licensee MDPI, Basel, Switzerland. This article is an open access article distributed under the terms and conditions of the Creative Commons Attribution (CC BY) license (https://creativecommons.org/licenses/by/4.0/).

Abstract: In this study, a magnetic field is analyzed using an analytical method and compared with the electromagnetic characteristics of 8-pole 9-slot and 8-pole 12-slot permanent magnet synchronous machines considering rotor eccentricity. The magnetic flux density and back electromotive force (EMF) are derived using perturbation theory and electromagnetic theory. First, the Fourier modeling of a permanent magnet is performed through magnetization modeling, and two analysis regions are set based on several assumptions for applying the analytical method. Accordingly, the governing equations of the analysis regions are derived in the form of Poisson and Laplace equations. In addition, the undefined coefficients of the general solutions are calculated through general solutions and appropriate boundary conditions, and the magnetic flux density and back EMF of the air gap region are derived based on the definition of the magnetic vector potential. The results obtained using the analytical method are compared with the finite element method and experimental results. In addition, we perform a torque analysis considering rotor eccentricity and analyze the torque ripple based on rotor eccentricity for two cases involving the pole/slot combination.

Keywords: PMSM; analytical method; perturbation theory; torque; torque ripple; rotor eccentricity

1. Introduction

Permanent magnet synchronous machines (PMSMs) are becoming popular as a key technology for applications such as home appliances, industrial tools, and electric vehicles because of their high efficiency, high power density, and low maintenance cost; in addition, interest in resolving motor malfunction has increased. Data provided in [1–3] indicate that 41% of motor faults are bearing faults, 37% are stator faults, 10% are rotor faults, and 12% are other faults. One of the main causes of malfunction is rotor eccentricity, wherein the center of the rotor axis deviates from the center of the stator, resulting in a non-uniform air gap. Static eccentricity, which is a type of rotor eccentricity, is a condition where the position of the minimum radial air gap is fixed [2–5]. This can be caused by stator core ovality, incorrect positioning of the stator core, or bearing at commissioning or following a repair, and its level does not change over time. Furthermore, the magnetic flux density in the air gap is an important characteristic of the machine performance. Therefore, the impact of rotor eccentricity on the magnetic field distribution must be analyzed for predicting the characteristics of PMSMs [6,7]. The finite element method (FEM) and analytical methods are employed to design PMSMs or perform characteristic analysis. The FEM is a numerical process that can be performed using a commercial tool [8]. However, it is necessary to learn to use each commercial tool, which is disadvantageous as the experience of the designer is necessitated for an accurate analysis. In the analytical method, electromagnetic field characteristics are analyzed using Maxwell's equation. Magnetization modeling is applied to the design of the machine using the Fourier series and partial differential equations derived using the magnetic vector potential. It must be preceded by deriving a solution that considers various boundary conditions. Several studies are being conducted because the analytical method can rapidly predict the characteristic variation based on the design parameters [9].

The magnetic field is analyzed using an analytical method and compared with the electromagnetic characteristics of 8-pole 9-slot and 8-pole 12-slot PMSMs considering rotor eccentricity. The magnetic flux density and back-electromotive force (EMF) are derived using perturbation theory and electromagnetic theory. The results obtained using the analytical method are compared with the FEM and experimental results. In addition, we performed a torque analysis based on rotor eccentricity and analyzed the torque ripple based on rotor eccentricity for two cases involving the pole/slot combination.

2. Electromagnetic Analysis of a PMSM Using Analytical Method

2.1. Analytical Model

Figure 1 shows the analysis models of 8-pole 9-slot and 8-pole 12-slot PMSMs. First, the analysis regions are defined for applying the analytical method, and the governing equations are derived using electromagnetic theory regarding each region. The magnetic flux density can be derived through the general solutions of the defined governing equations and the boundary conditions of each region. To apply the analytical method, the analysis model is simplified to the slotless model, the relative permeability of the iron core is infinite, the relative permeability of the permanent magnets (PMs) is equal to that of air, and the eddy effect is disregarded to apply the analytical method. Figure 2 shows the simplified model for applying the analytical method. The analysis regions are classified as an air gap region (Region I) and PM region (Region II), where rotor eccentricity is determined based on the stator coordinate (r,θ), and rotor coordinate (ξ,ψ). O_s and O_r are the centers of the stator and rotor, respectively; R_s, R_m, and R_r are the radii of the stator inner, PM surface, and rotor inner, respectively. The relationship between the parameters of the r-θ coordinate and ξ-ψ coordinate is organized based on Taylor' expansion, as follows [9].

$$\begin{aligned}\xi &= r - \varepsilon \cos(\theta - \phi) + O(\varepsilon^2) \\ \psi &= (\theta - wt) + \frac{\varepsilon}{r}\sin(\theta - \phi) + O(\varepsilon^2),\end{aligned} \qquad \varepsilon = ec \times g \qquad (1)$$

where r is the length from the stator center to the observation point, ε is the length of rotor eccentricity, ec is the eccentricity ratio, and g is the nominal air gap length. $O(\varepsilon^2)$ is the second order of the perturbation term. Only the first-order term of the perturbation term is considered, and the second-order term is disregarded in this study, since rotor eccentricity is usually small in comparison to the air gap length.

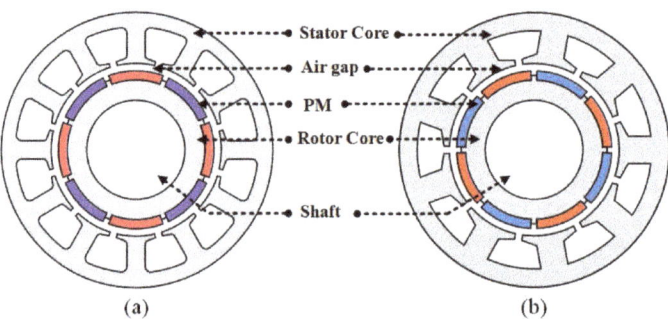

Figure 1. Analysis model: (**a**) 8 pole, 12 slot; (**b**) 8 pole, 9 slot.

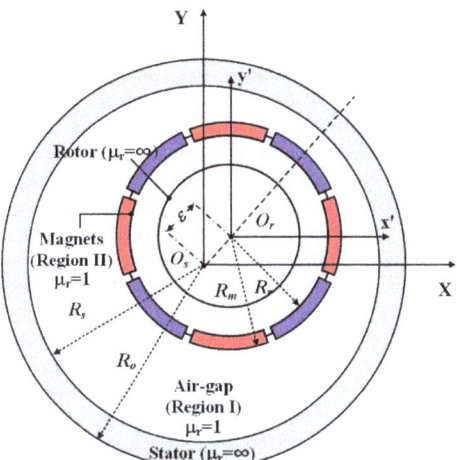

Figure 2. Simplified model for using analytical method.

2.2. Magnetic Field Analysis Using Analytical Method

To derive the magnetic flux density for PMs, Fourier modeling must be performed. Fourier modeling for PMs is expressed as follows:

$$\mathbf{M} = \sum_{n=1,3,5\cdots}^{\infty} M_{rn} \cos(np\theta)\mathbf{i}_r + M_{\theta n} \sin(np\theta)\mathbf{i}_\theta \tag{2}$$

where **M** is the magnetization vector, M_{rn} and $M_{\theta n}$ are Fourier coefficients of the radial component and tangential component of the r- and θ-direction, respectively. n and p are the space harmonic order and number of pole pairs, respectively. Rotor eccentricity can be treated as one of kind of perturbation phenomenon. Perturbation theory is necessitated to consider rotor eccentricity. Perturbation theory is a theory that expresses the solution of a problem that cannot be solved analytically as a Taylor series of parameters that can be considered extremely small. When this is applied to the magnetic vector potential, it is expressed as follows [9]:

$$\begin{aligned} A_{z1}(r,\theta,\varepsilon) &= A_{z1}^{(0)}(r,\theta) + \varepsilon A_{z1}^{(1)}(r,\theta) + \varepsilon^2 A_{z1}^{(2)}(r,\theta) + \cdots \\ A_{z2}(r,\theta,\varepsilon) &= A_{z2}^{(0)}(r,\theta) + \varepsilon A_{z2}^{(1)}(r,\theta) + \varepsilon^2 A_{z2}^{(2)}(r,\theta) \cdots \end{aligned} \tag{3}$$

where A_{z1} and A_{z2} are the magnetic vector potential of Region I and II, respectively. $A_{zn}^{(0)}$ and $A_{zn}^{(1)}$ are the zeroth and first orders of perturbation, respectively. $A_{zn}^{(0)}$ occurs when the rotor is not eccentric. $A_{zn}^{(1)}$ is generated by the rotor eccentricity effect without PMs or current excitation. The reason why even the first term is considered is that more accurate results can be derived when the second term is considered, but the calculation process becomes complicated, and reliable results can be obtained even when only the first term is considered. Therefore, the governing equation for each region is expressed as Poisson and the Laplace equations.

$$\nabla^2 \mathbf{A}_{z1}^{(0)} = \frac{\partial^2 A_{z1}^{(0)}}{\partial r^2} + \frac{1}{r}\frac{\partial A_{z1}^{(0)}}{\partial r} - \frac{q^2}{r^2}A_{z1}^{(0)} = 0 \tag{4}$$

$$\frac{\partial^2 A_{z2}^{(0)}}{\partial r^2} + \frac{1}{r}\frac{\partial A_{z2}^{(0)}}{\partial r} - \frac{q^2}{r^2}A_{z2}^{(0)} = -\mu_0 \nabla \times \mathbf{M} \tag{5}$$

$$\frac{\partial^2 A_{z1}^{(1)}}{\partial r^2} + \frac{1}{r}\frac{\partial A_{z1}^{(1)}}{\partial r} - \frac{q^2}{r^2}A_{z1}^{(1)} = 0 \tag{6}$$

$$\frac{\partial^2 A_{z2}^{(1)}}{\partial r^2} + \frac{1}{r}\frac{\partial A_{z2}^{(1)}}{\partial r} - \frac{q^2}{r^2} A_{z2}^{(1)} = 0 \tag{7}$$

The general solution of each region is derived from the Cauchy–Euler equation. The general solutions of each analysis region can be obtained as follows:

$$\mathbf{A}_{z1}^{(0)} = \sum_{n=1,3,5\cdots}^{\infty} \left(A_1 r^{np} + B_1 r^{-np}\right) \sin(np\theta) \; \mathbf{i}_z \tag{8}$$

$$\mathbf{A}_{z2}^{(0)} = \sum_{n=1,3,5\cdots}^{\infty} \left(A_2 r^{np} + B_2 r^{-np} + \frac{\mu_0 r n p M_n}{(np)^2 - 1}\right) \sin(np\theta) \; \mathbf{i}_z \tag{9}$$

$$\mathbf{A}_{z1}^{(1)} = \varepsilon \sum_{n=1,3,5\cdots}^{\infty} \begin{array}{l}\left(W_1 r^{np-1} + X_1 r^{-np+1}\right) \sin[(np-1)\theta + \phi] \\ +\left(Y_1 r^{np+1} + Z_1 r^{-np-1}\right) \sin[(np+1)\theta - \phi]\end{array} \; \mathbf{i}_z \tag{10}$$

$$\mathbf{A}_{z2}^{(1)} = \varepsilon \sum_{n=1,3,5\cdots}^{\infty} \begin{array}{l}\left(W_2 r^{np-1} + X_2 r^{-np+1}\right) \sin[(np-1)\theta + \phi] \\ +\left(Y_2 r^{np+1} + Z_2 r^{-np-1}\right) \sin[(np+1)\theta - \phi]\end{array} \; \mathbf{i}_z \tag{11}$$

The effect of the rotor eccentricity can be observed at the rotor yoke surface and the interface between the PMs and air gap in the r-θ coordinate. In the ξ-ψ coordinate, the radius corresponding to the surface and interface are R_r and R_m, respectively. By applying $\rho = R_r$ and R_m in Equation (1), the following equations can be obtained:

$$f_{R_r}(r,\theta,\varepsilon) = r - \varepsilon \cos(\theta - \phi) - R_r \tag{12}$$

$$f_{R_m}(r,\theta,\varepsilon) = r - \varepsilon \cos(\theta - \phi) - R_m \tag{13}$$

The normal direction vector of the rotor core surface and PM surface can be derived by applying the gradient (∇) to Equations (12) and (13).

$$\mathbf{n}_{R_m} = \nabla f_{R_m} = \mathbf{i}_r + \frac{\varepsilon}{r}\sin(\theta - \phi)\mathbf{i}_\theta \tag{14}$$

$$\mathbf{n}_{R_s} = \nabla f_{R_s} = \mathbf{i}_r + \frac{\varepsilon}{r}\sin(\theta - \phi)\mathbf{i}_\theta \tag{15}$$

The boundary conditions can be derived using Equations (14) and (15) and electromagnetic theory. The boundary conditions at the rotor core surface and PM–air gap interface can be expressed as follows:

$$\mathbf{n}_{R_r} \times \mathbf{H}_2 = 0 \tag{16}$$

$$\mathbf{n}_{R_m} \times (\mathbf{H}_1 - \mathbf{H}_2) = 0 \tag{17}$$

$$\mathbf{n}_{R_m} \cdot (\mathbf{B}_1 - \mathbf{B}_2) = 0 \tag{18}$$

The boundary conditions of the zeroth and first order can be derived by applying $\nabla \times \mathbf{A} = \mathbf{B}$ to Equation (3) and substituting it into Equations (16)–(18). A_1, B_1, A_2, B_2, W_1, X_1, Y_1, Z_1, W_2, X_2, Y_2, and Z_2 of Equations (8)–(11) can be calculated using the derived boundary conditions. The magnetic flux density of the r- and θ-directions can be express as follows [6]:

$$\mathbf{B}_r = \frac{1}{r}\frac{\partial \mathbf{A}}{\partial \theta}, \; \mathbf{B}_\theta = -\frac{\partial \mathbf{A}}{\partial r} \tag{19}$$

The zeroth order of the perturbation term implies no rotor eccentricity, and the first-order term refers to the amount of change in magnetic flux density based on rotor eccentricity; therefore, the final magnetic flux density is the sum of the zeroth- and first-order magnetic flux density. The magnetic flux density considering rotor eccentricity can be expressed as:

$$\mathbf{B} = \mathbf{B}^{(0)} + \varepsilon \mathbf{B}^{(1)} \tag{20}$$

2.3. Back-EMF

To obtain the back-EMF, the magnetic flux linking the coil must be determined as follows [10]:

$$\Phi_{coil,(1,\cdots,Q)} = \int_{-\theta_c/2}^{\theta_c/2} \mathbf{B} \cdot d\mathbf{S} \quad , \qquad E(t) = -N_c \frac{d(\Phi_1 + \cdots + \Phi_Q)}{dt} \qquad (21)$$

where $\mathbf{B}$ is the magnetic flux density vector in the stator surface region, and $d\mathbf{S}$ is an element of the coil surface area vector. Q is the slot number/phase. θ_c denotes the mechanical angle per slot. The back-EMF can be obtained using Faraday's law. N_c is the number of turns in each coil. Figure 3 is an example explaining the calculation of the back-EMF of the 8-pole 9-slot. The back-EMFs in other coils of the same phase are not necessarily similar because of the eccentricity. They must be calculated individually by performing an appropriate shift.

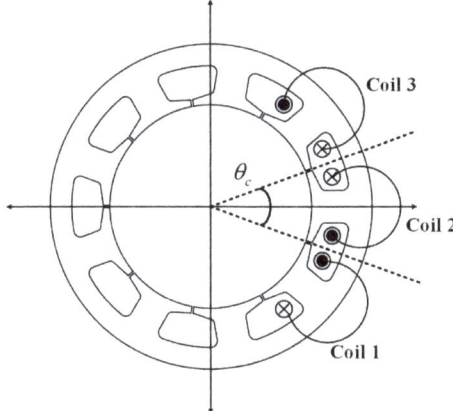

Figure 3. Winding distribution of 8-pole 9-slot.

3. Results and Discussion

Figure 4 shows the experimental set. Table 2 shows the design specifications. The stator and rotor were made of 50PN470, whereas the permanent magnet was made of N42SH; the experiment was performed at room temperature. The servo motor was installed on the opposite side of the test motor to measure the back-EMF. Figure 5a shows the magnetic flux density in the air gap when no eccentricity occurred, and Figure 5b is the variation in the magnetic flux density according to rotor eccentricity. Figure 6 shows the magnetic flux density in the air gap when 25% rotor eccentricity occurred. A 25% eccentricity is based on nominal air gap length. Since the air gap of the analysis model is 4 mm, it means that 1 mm eccentricity occurs. The analytical results were verified by comparing them with the FEM results. FEM analysis was performed using ANSYS Electronics 2020R2. It was confirmed that the results agreed well. Figure 7 is the mesh plot of non-simplified analysis models. Non-simplified model in Figures 8 and 9 are the slotted models. FEM analysis and experiments are performed using slotted models. Figure 8a,b show the back-EMFs of the 8-pole 9-slot PMSM when no rotor eccentricity and 25% rotor eccentricity occurred, respectively. The analytical results of the back-EMFs of the 8-pole 9-slot PMSM were compared with the FEM and experimental results. It was observed that the results exhibited good agreement with each other. In the 8-pole 9-slot model, the winding arrangement distributed asymmetrically to one side, as shown in Figure 8b; therefore, if eccentricity occurs, the result of the unbalanced back-EMF can be confirmed. Figure 9a,b show the back-EMF of the 8-pole 12-slot PMSM based on rotor eccentricity. As shown in Figure 9b, the winding arrangement of the 12-slot stator was distributed symmetrically. Consequently, the effect of rotor eccentricity was nullified, and the results of the cases with and without rotor eccentricity were compared. Tables 1 and 3 summarize the analysis results. The error of the analytical results is confirmed to be within 5%. Figure 10a, b show the results of the output torque and torque ripple analysis based on the eccentricity of the 8-pole 9-slot and 8-pole 12-slot PMSMs. When comparing those PMSMs, it was observed that the cogging torque of the 8-pole 12-slot PMSM was larger than that of the 8-pole 9-slot PMSM; therefore, the torque ripple ratio of the 8-pole 12-slot PMSM was larger than that of the 8-pole 9-slot under a low input current. However, in the 8-pole 9-slot model, the increasing rate of the torque ripple based on eccentricity was larger than that of the 8-pole 12-slot owing to the asymmetric winding arrangement. Under the low output power condition, the 8-pole 9-slot PMSM indicated a sinusoidal back-EMF, resulting in a small torque ripple ratio in the output torque. However, as the output power increased, the 8-pole 12-slot PMSM was less affected by the rotor eccentricity.

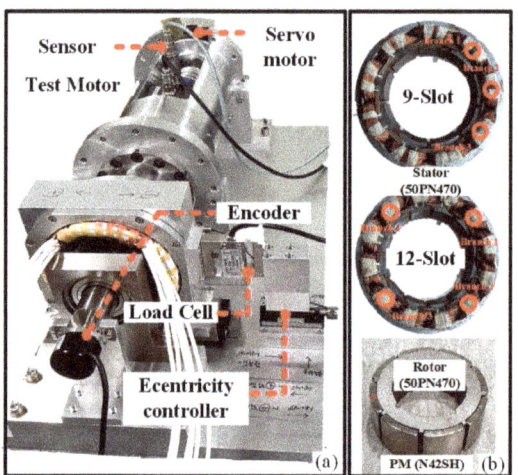

Figure 4. Experimental set: (**a**) experiment configuration; (**b**) manufactured model.

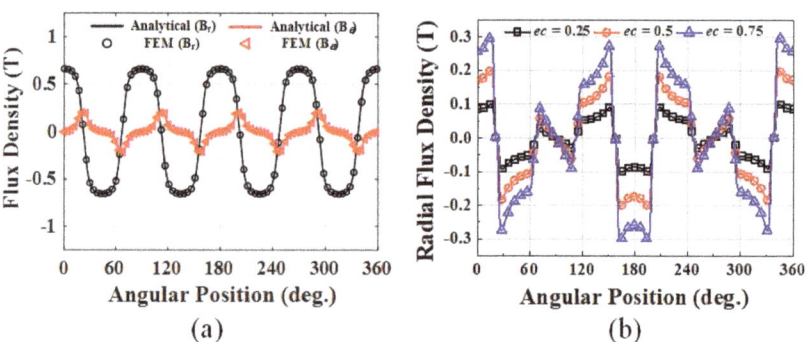

Figure 5. Flux density: (**a**) without rotor eccentricity; (**b**) variation in radial flux density according to rotor eccentricity.

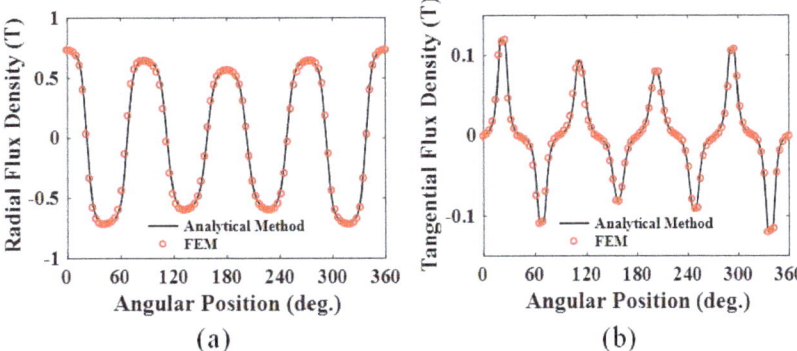

Figure 6. Flux density with 25% rotor eccentricity at the air gap: (**a**) radial flux density; (**b**) tangential flux density.

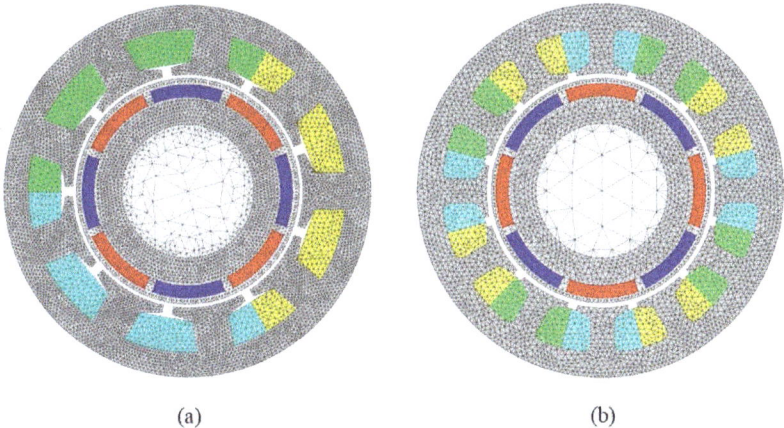

Figure 7. Mesh plot of analysis models: (**a**) 8−pole 9−slot; (**b**) 8−pole 12−slot.

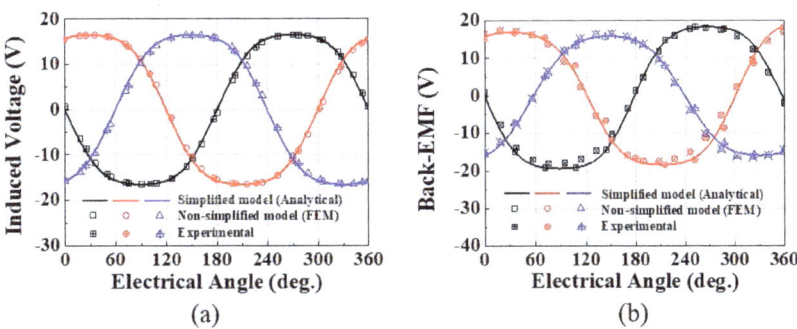

Figure 8. Back−EMF of 8−pole 9−slot PMSM: (**a**) without rotor eccentricity; (**b**) with 25% eccentricity.

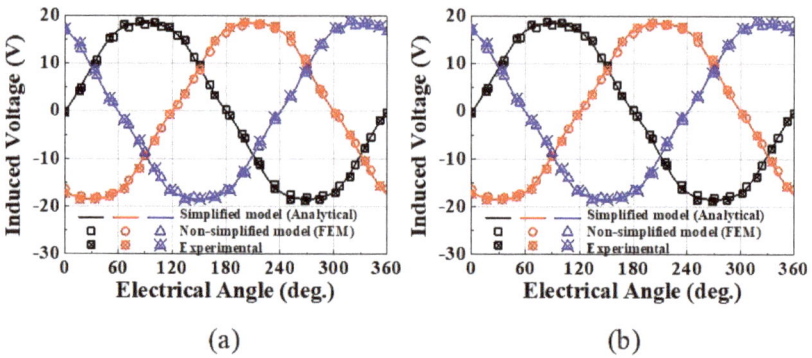

Figure 9. Back-EMF of 8−pole 12-slot PMSM: (**a**) without rotor eccentricity; (**b**) with 25% eccentricity.

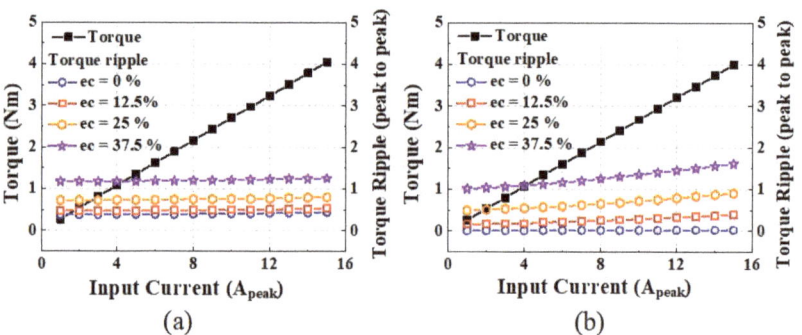

Figure 10. Torque characteristics: (**a**) 8−pole 12−slot and (**b**) 8−pole 9−slot.

Table 1. Analysis results of back-EMF without rotor eccentricity.

Parameter	Analytical		FEM		Measurement	
	8p9s	8p12s	8p9s	8p12s	8p9s	8p12s
Number of meshes	-	-	31,496	30,541	-	-
Analysis time (s)	0.11	0.12	11	23	-	-
Back-EMF (V_{max})	17.63	18.45	17.52	18.35	17.68	19.05
Error (%)	0.28	3.14	0.9	3.67	-	-

Table 2. Design specification of analysis model.

Parameter	Value	Unit
Number of slots/poles	9/8, 12/8	mm
Outer radius of stator	75	mm
Inner radius of stator	47	mm
Outer radius of rotor	43	mm
Thickness of PMs	5	mm
Axial length	30	mm
Magnet remanence	1.27	T
Rated speed	1000	Rpm
Pole arc ratio	0.9	

Table 3. Analysis results of back-EMF with 25% rotor eccentricity.

Parameter	Analytical		FEM		Measurement	
	8p9s	8p12s	8p9s	8p12s	8p9s	8p12s
Number of meshes	-	-	31,839	33,910	-	-
Analysis time (s)	0.11	0.12	12	25	-	-
Back-EMF (V_{max})	18.36	18.45	18.2	18.35	18.6	19.04
Error (%)	1.29	3.1	2.15	3.62	-	-

4. Conclusions

In this study, we performed a magnetic field analysis based on rotor eccentricity using an analytical method, and the torque characteristics of a two pole/slot combination were compared. Based on perturbation theory and electromagnetic theory, the magnetic flux density and back-EMF in the air gap region were derived, and the analytical result was verified by comparing it with the FEM and the experimental results. Both models with slotted and simplified models without slots were analyzed using the FEM. We conformed that even if the magnetic flux density is predicted as slotless and the back-EMF is derived using it, a slotted model can obtain similar results. Subsequently, torque analysis was performed based on rotor eccentricity to analyze the variation in the torque ripple for the two pole/slot combinations. The analysis results from this study will benefit the design of motors.

Author Contributions: J.-Y.C.: conceptualization, review and editing; H.-K.L.: analysis, original draft preparation; T.-K.B.: magnetic field calculation; J.-I.L.: derivation of governing equation; J.-H.W.: experiment; H.-S.S.: torque analysis; I.-J.Y.: review and editing. All authors have read and agreed to the published version of the manuscript.

Funding: This work was supported by the Basic Research Laboratory (BRL) of the National Research Foundation (NRF-2020R1A4A2002021) funded by the Korean government.

Data Availability Statement: The data presented in this study are available on request from the corresponding author.

Conflicts of Interest: The authors declare no conflict of interest.

References

1. Goktas, T.; Zafarani, M.; Lee, K.W.; Akin, B.; Sculley, T. Comprehensive Analysis of Magnet Defect Fault Monitoring Through Leakage Flux. *IEEE Trans. Magn.* **2017**, *53*, 1–10. [CrossRef]
2. Prieto, M.D.; Espinosa, A.G.; Ruiz, J.R.; Urresty, J.C.; Ortega, J.A. Feature extraction of demagnetization faults in PMSMs based on box-counting fractal dimension. *IEEE Trans. Ind. Electron.* **2011**, *58*, 1594–1605. [CrossRef]
3. Hyun, D.; Hong, J.; Lee, S.B.; Kim, K.; Wiedenbrug, E.J.; Teska, M.; Nandi, S.; Chelvan, I.T. Automated Monitoring of Airgap Eccentricity for Inverter-Fed Induction Motors Under Standstill Conditions. *IEEE Trans.* **2011**, *47*, 1257–1266.
4. Park, Y.; Fernandez, D.; Lee, S.B.; Hyun, D.; Jeong, M.; Kommuri, S.K.; Cho, C.; Reigosa, D.; Briz, F. On-line detection of rotor eccentricity for PMSMs based on Hall-effect field sensor measurements. In Proceedings of the 2017 IEEE Energy Conversion Congress and Exposition (ECCE), Cincinnati, OH, USA, 1–5 October 2017; pp. 4678–4685.
5. Thomson, W.; Barbour, A. On-line current monitoring and application of a finite element method to predict the level of static airgap eccentricity in three-phase induction motors. *IEEE Trans. Energy Convers.* **1998**, *13*, 347–357. [CrossRef]
6. Amirat, Y.; Benbouzid, M.E.H.; Bensaker, B.; Wamkeue, R. Condition monitoring and fault diagnosis in wind energy conversion systems: A review. In Proceedings of the IEEE PEMDC Conference, Antalya, Turkey, 3–5 May 2007.
7. Lu, B.; Li, Y.; Wu, X.; Yang, Z. A review of recent advances in wind turbine condition monitoring and fault diagnosis. No. 24026. In Proceedings of the IEEE Conference on Power Electronics and Machines in Wind Applications (PEMWA), Lincoln, NE, USA, 24–26 June 2009; pp. 1–7.
8. Yang, W.; Tavner, P.J.; Wilkinson, M. Wind Turbine Condition Monitoring and Fault Diagnosis Using Both Mechanical and Electrical Signatures. In Proceedings of the 2008 IEEE/ASME International Conference on Advanced Intelligent Mechatronics, Xi'an, China, 2–5 July 2008; pp. 1296–1301. [CrossRef]
9. Kim, U.; Lieu, D.K. Magnetic field calculation in permanent magnet motors with rotor eccentricity: Without slotting effect. *IEEE Trans. Magn.* **1998**, *34*, 2242–2252. [CrossRef]
10. Rahideh, A.; Korakianitis, T. Analytical open-circuit magnetic field distribution of slotless brushless permanent magnet machines with rotor eccentricity. *IEEE Trans. Magn.* **2011**, *47*, 4791–4808. [CrossRef]

Article

On the Optimal Selection of Flux Barrier Reconfiguration for a Five-Phase Permanent Magnet Assisted Synchronous Reluctance Machine for Low-Torque Ripple Application

Hamidreza Ghorbani [1], Mohammadreza Moradian [1,2,*] and Mohamed Benbouzid [3,*]

[1] Department of Electrical Engineering, Najafabad Branch, Islamic Azad University, Najafabad P.O. Box 8514143131, Iran; hamid.r.ghorbani@sel.iaun.ac.ir
[2] Smart Microgrid Research Center, Najafabad Branch, Islamic Azad University, Najafabad P.O. Box 8514143131, Iran
[3] Institut de Recherche Dupuy de Lôme (UMR CNRS 6027), University of Brest, 29238 Brest, France
* Correspondence: moradian@iaun.ac.ir (M.M.); mohamed.benbouzid@univ-brest.fr (M.B.)

Abstract: This paper aims to investigate the reconfigurations of rotor flux barriers for a five-phase Permanent Magnet Assisted Synchronous Reluctance Machine (PMASynRM). To precisely study the performance of the proposed configurations, a conventional PMASynRM with double-layer flux barriers is included in the study. Since the novel rotor schemes consume the same amount of rare-earth magnets, steel sheet materials, and copper wire, resulting in no extra manufacturing costs, the optimal reconfiguration should be determined, providing developed electromagnetic characteristics. Thus, all the proposed models are designed and analyzed under the same condition. The Lumped Parameter Model (LPM) is exported to the Finite Element Method (FEM) for precise analysis to reach developed torque and lower values of torque ripple. Based on the FEM results the model presenting the lowest torque fluctuations is selected as the optimal model and dynamically investigated. According to the results, in comparison with the conventional model, the introduced rotor designs provide a much lower value of torque fluctuations with a desirable amount of electromagnetic torque and power. In addition, the optimal model presents high values of power factor and efficiency, making it a vital alternative for low-torque ripple high-speed operations with no extra cost to the implementation process.

Keywords: Finite Element Method; Lumped Parameter Model; Permanent Magnet Synchronous Reluctance Motor; rotor flux barrier; torque development

1. Introduction

Electric Synchronous Motors (SyncM) are widely used in industrial applications due to their electromagnetic characteristics such as robustness [1], noticeable torque/power density [2,3], and efficient performance [3–6]. These types of electric motor can be categorized into (i) surface mounted Permanent Magnet Synchronous Motor (SPMSM), (ii) Interior Mounted Permanent Magnet Synchronous Motor (IPMSM), (iii) Permanent Magnet Assisted Synchronous Reluctance Motor (PMASynRM) [6]. Among these types of PMSM, the PMASynRM has attracted a huge number of investigators to study the characteristics [6–9], apply optimization processes [10–13], and perform enhancement for different applications such as electric vehicular systems [4,14–16]. Therefore, a large number of studies are devoted to introducing new branches of structural design for PMSM [4,15,17–22]. A novel dual rotor PMASynRM is introduced in [4] in which toroidal winding is applied to fully utilize electromagnetic torque (PM torque and reluctance torque). Based on the results of the Finite Element Method (FEM), the proposed configuration presents robustness through irreversible demagnetization. Wang et al., presented a new SynRM composed of grain-oriented and non-oriented silicon steels [17]. Accordingly, employing a reasonable rotor design, the results demonstrate torque improvement and significant torque ripple reduction. Liu et al., presented a novel modular PMASynRM structure that is composed of two axially combined rotor modules [18]. According to detailed reported analysis results, the new proposed motor structure provides higher values of power factor along with lower torque ripple and eddy current losses compared with conventionally known IPM and PMASynRM structures. A new hybrid PMASynRM with sandwiched magnets is investigated by Zhao et al., to study torque, efficiency, power factor, and torque ripple enhancements [19]. Applying FEM to the proposed design, the results exhibit highly improved torque density, power factor, and efficiency along with a great decline in value of torque ripple. Cai et al., reviewed recent research on electric powertrains for new electric vehicles [20]. Based on the results, this study presents efficiency, speed, size, reliability, control simplicity, and performance comparison for Direct Current (DC) motor, Induction Motor (IM), PMSM, so that it is found that although the PMSM requires a complicated control system, it presents best electromagnetic performance, high efficiency, and more reliability. Cui et al., presented a novel PMSM with an optimized air-gap for a high-power electric motorcycle. The results show improvements in torque and efficiency by asymmetric structural design optimization providing a wide range of speed and performance control. Tawfiq et al., in [23] present the investigation of a 3-phase SyncRM while transferring the machine to a 5-phase SyncRM. It has been obtained after optimization and investigating of the proposed 5-phase SyncRM that in an increasing rate of the rotor speed, the produced torque and efficiency increased significantly up to 33% and 3.5% respectively, in comparison with the 3-phase structure. In addition, in terms of one-phase faulty situation the 5-phase model works at 98.84% of it 3-phase machine's electromagnetic torque while the 3-phase model only works at about 45% of its rated torque with a high torque ripple value of 228%. Thus, a 5-phase SyncRM not only provides better torque and efficiency performance particularly in sensitive applications such as military and propulsion systems, it also brings about higher reliability under faulty situations.

Although a three-phase system is widely applied to electrical machines, due to developments of power electronics devices, the necessity of having a limited number of phases dismissed and multiphase drive systems can be applied to supply and control electrical machines. A five-phase system can be used as the drive system in PMASynRM, which brings advantages as (i) higher torque, (ii) higher efficiency, (iii) reduction of DC-Link harmonics, and (iv) reliability [23–29]. Moreover, it has been investigated in [8] that while the 3-phase inverter fed Multiphase SynRM would not utilize the full capacity of kVA of the inverter, the multiphase system would provide higher usage of the inverter power. Hence, the multiphase SyncRMs bring about higher torque density and efficiency along with lower values of financial issues. Because the utilization of a multiphase system provides investigators with the elimination of high price PM materials along with lower expenditure on lower price/kVA for inverter technology. Hence, along with better performance, multiphase SyncRMs are a vital alternative particularly for financially sensitive applications such as electric vehicle technologies and home appliances.

As the cost of the rare-earth magnets and steel sheet vary, this paper aims to study novel reconfigurations of rotor flux barriers in a five-phase permanent magnet assisted synchronous reluctance motor that consumes the same volume of steel and PMs compared with a conventional PMASynRM. Due to changes that are made in the FB arc direction, concerning the mathematical rotor design criteria, the chance of local saturation in the iron rib, flux islands, and the corresponding losses can be reduced. Consequently, it results in higher efficiency and power factor, as well as lower torque fluctuations. To aim the torque/power enhancements for the introduced schemes, the Lumped Parameter Model (LPM) of the models are utilized in a 2D Finite Element Analysis (FEA). The models are initially investigated using the corresponding LPM; then, by consideration of the stator current and the current phase angle as the optimization variables, the torque performance is calculated to result in hundreds of operational data points. Afterward, the optimal model, presenting developed torque with the lowest torque ripple is selected and analyzed dynamically. All models are designed using the same values of design parameters and analyzed under the same condition. In Section 2, the structural design data, the calculation methods, and a short mathematical review are presented. The analysis reports are illustrated in Section 3, while Section 4 held some conclusions.

2. Material and Methods

2.1. Proposed Design Scheme

A conventional PMASynRM with novel reconfigurations of rotor flux barriers (FBs) is introduced and investigated in this study. A double-layer FB scheme with inset PMs is considered for all the proposed models. A five-phase full pitch distributed winding is applied to the proposed 40-Slot 8-Pole prototypes (the ratio of the number of stator slots per number of rotor poles per machine phases equals 1). Figures 1–3 illustrate the proposed models, structural scheme and winding pattern, and the corresponding winding factor and magneto-motive force (MMF), respectively. According to Figure 1, a conventional double-layer FB PMASynRM (Model-I) is considered in this study in order to compare the performance of the proposed models (Model-II to Model-V) more precisely. The FBs and PMs in the Model-II are reversed in arc direction, the Model-III consists of FBs that are reversed interchangeably one-by-one, and the FBs of the Model-IV interchanged two-by-two and four-by-four in the Model-V. In other words, the Model-III to -V is the combination of the Model-I and -II. The design scheme differentiations, an overview of the system equations, and the conducted numerical methods (as shown in the evaluation procedure in Figure 4) are described in the following subsections. Accordingly, the d-q axes magnetic equivalent circuit (MEC) is evaluated for the LPM and then exported to the FEM to analyze the performance of the machines. Firstly, the steady-state performance at rated speed and nominal stator current is calculated to determine the torque performance and the back electromotive force (Back-EMF). Afterward, the torque enhancement is sensitively analyzed for each model with respect to the stator current amplitude and phase angle variations. Finally, the best-performed model, which produces desirable values of torque density with a lower amount of fluctuations is selected and dynamically studied. To achieve the goal of this paper, the proposed machines are designed and investigated under the same condition using the reported design parameters in Table 1 and the ambient temperature of 40 °C. Thus the proposed schemes consume similar amounts of manufacturing material and require the same steel cutting, resulting in the same value of the machine's mass and finalized implementation costs, when transforming from the PMASynRM to the Model-V.

Table 1. Design Constrains.

Parameter	Sym.	Value	Unit
Number of Phases	m	5	-
Number of Stator Slots	N_S	40	-
Number of Rotor Poles	N_P	8	-
Rated Speed	n_r	5	krpm
Input Current	I_n	15	A
DC Bus Voltage	V_{DC}	400	V
Stator Outer Diameter	D_{SO}	160	mm
Stator Inner Diameter	D_{SI}	90	mm
Rotor Outer Diameter	D_{RO}	89.15	mm
Shaft Diameter	D_{Sh}	29	mm
Stack Length	L_m	90	mm
PM Arc	L_{PM}	35	°Mech.
Air-Gap Length	L_g	0.85	mm
Steel Material	-	M800-50A	-
PM Material	-	N42SH	-
PM Mass	-	0.5	kg
Steel Laminations Mass (Rotor & Stator)	-	11.16	kg
Copper Wire Mass (AWG 18)	-	3.35	kg
Total Mass (Excluding the Shaft)	-	15	kg

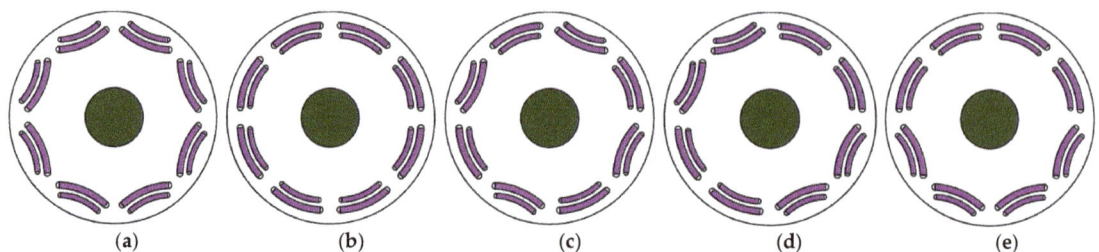

Figure 1. Proposed Models: (**a**) Model-I (PMASynRM), (**b**) Model-II, (**c**) Model-III, (**d**) Model-IV and (**e**) Model-V.

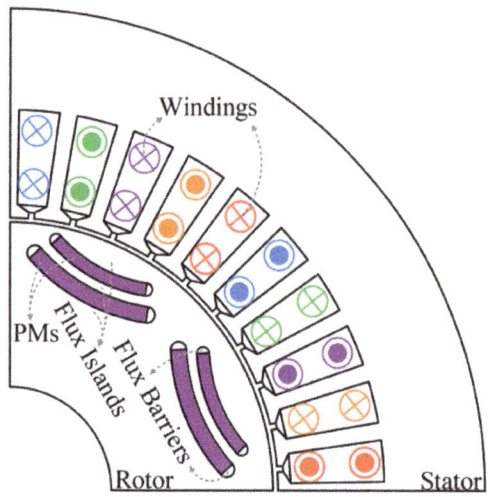

Figure 2. PMASynRM Structural Design and Winding Pattern.

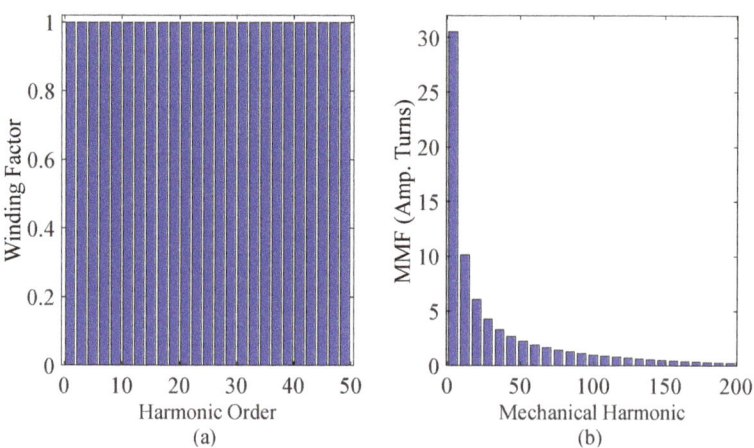

Figure 3. Winding: (**a**) Factor, (**b**) MMF.

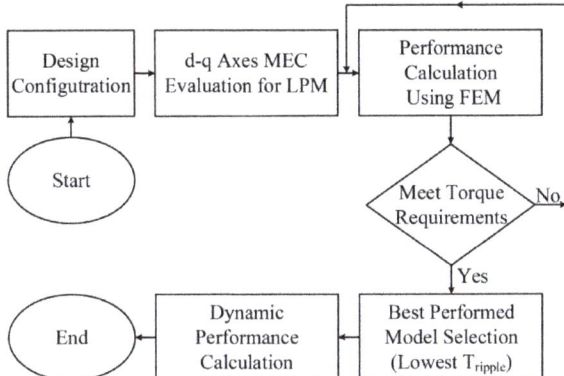

Figure 4. Evaluation Procedure.

2.2. Design Differentiation

The proposed models in this study are designed based on a conventional PMASynRM, shown in Figure 1a. The overall view of the proposed models is similar, whereas the changes that occurred in the flux barrier arc direction caused changes in some design parameters. Figure 5 depicts the major rotor design parameters, in which the W_{bk}, W_{ij}, and W_{rib} are the flux barriers, flux islands, and the iron rib width for $k = [1,2]$, $j = [1,2]$ (due to the utilization of two layers of flux barrier, the value of W_{i3} is excluded in this study). Transforming the arc face direction from the rotor design of the Model-I to the Model-II made changes in the value of the W_{ij} in which $W_{i1} > W'_{i1}$. Although by applying such transformation the $\sum W_{ij} = \sum W'_{ij}$, however, the value of the W_{rib} is not equal to the that of the W'_{rib}, so that in comparison with the Model-II with $W'_{rib} = W'_{i1}$, the Model-I has $W_{rib} < W_{i1}$. This study is aimed to investigate this transformation by proposing four different configuration models shown in Figure 1. Accordingly, this paper not only investigates the transformed W_{rib} model (Model-II), but also three models, which are the combination of the Model-I and Model-II are considered for investigation. Based on the design optimization procedures expressed in [17,30], K, the ratio of barrier width to the total rotor width, can be expressed as:

$$K = \frac{\sum_{k=1}^{2} W_{bk}}{\sum_{\substack{j=1 \\ k=[1,2]}}^{2} (W_{bk} + W_{ij})} \qquad (1)$$

In order to maximize torque and minimize torque ripple, the value of K should be limited to 0.5–0.55. Below 0.5, the machine faces a decline in torque production due to heavy magnetic flux leakages and for the greater values of K, due to the saturation of flux islands, the torque fluctuations increase significantly [30]. It has been investigated in [31,32] that the best performance is achievable if the FB island's width is different in each layer. However, there can be different schemes and reconfigurations that provide the same values for the mentioned criteria in [30–32], and such a statement has not been studied before. Hence, five reconfigurations are introduced and analyzed in this study by utilizing the reported parameter values in Table 2, the value of 0.47 and 0.54 are considered for K and K' respectively, to reduce torque ripple and develop torque performance of the proposed models as it has been addressed in [17,30–32]. Moreover, as it has been asserted in [32], two different values are assumed for the W_{i1} with one particular W_{i2} to achieve better performance.

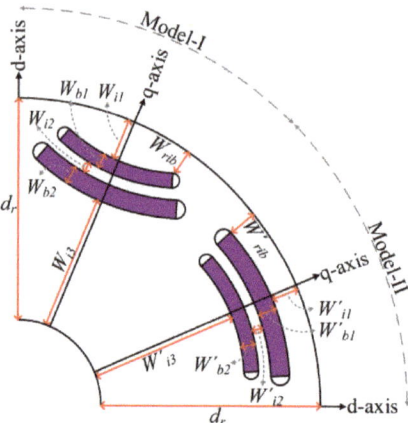

Figure 5. Main Design Parameters of the Rotor.

Table 2. Rotor Design Parameters.

Model/Parameter	K	W_{b1}	W_{b2}	W_{i1}	W_{i2}	W_{rib}	d_r	Unit
Model-I	0.47	3	4	6	2	3	30	mm
Model-II	0.54			4		4		

2.3. System Equations Review

The phasor diagram of a PMASynRM with respect to the rotor reference frame is shown in Figure 6a, considering the steady-state condition. Generally, the torque in an m-phase SynRM can be expressed as Equation (2) where X_d, X_q, L_d, L_q, I_d, and I_q are the d and q axes reactance, inductance, and currents respectively [28,29].

$$T_e = \frac{m}{2} \frac{N_P}{2} \left[(L_d - L_q) I_d I_q \right] \quad (2)$$

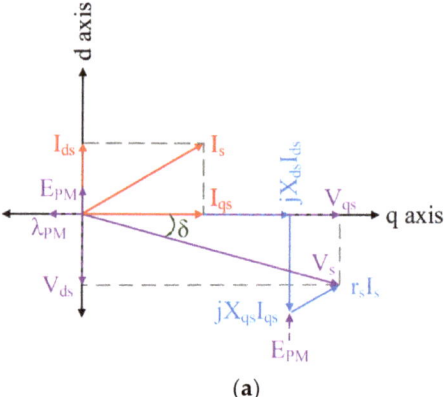

(a)

Figure 6. Cont.

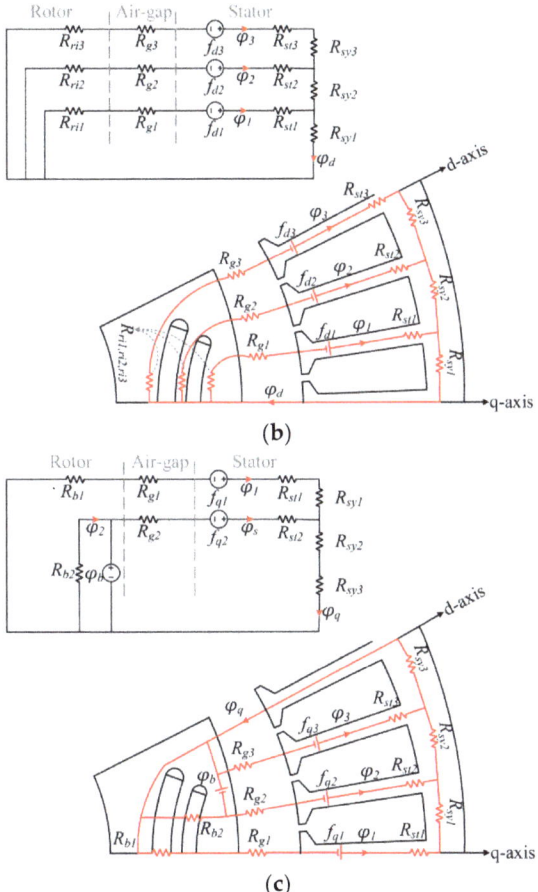

Figure 6. PMASynRM: (**a**) Phasor Diagram, (**b**) d-axis MEC, and (**c**) q-axis MEC.

In terms of a PMASynRM, the PM flux linkage (λ_{PM}) should be included in Equation (2). Considering a five-phase drive system, the stator phase voltage (V_s) and d-q axes voltages (V_d and V_q respectively) can be defined with the phase resistance, stator current as r_s, I_s, air-gap flux linkage vector of the stator, the rotor angular speed, permeability of the air as Λ_s, ω_r, μ_0, air-gap length and radius, machine stack length as l_g, r_g, and finally magnetomotive force (MMF) harmonics of the stator and rotor, stator current phase angle as L, $f_{s,h}$, $f_{r,h}$, and γ_d. (See Equations (3)–(8)) [33,34].

$$V_s = r_s I_s + \frac{d\Lambda_s}{dt} = \begin{bmatrix} v_{as} & v_{bs} & v_{cs} & v_{ds} & v_{es} \end{bmatrix}^T \tag{3}$$

$$I_s = \begin{bmatrix} I_{as} & I_{bs} & I_{cs} & I_{ds} & I_{es} \end{bmatrix}^T \tag{4}$$

$$\Lambda_s = \begin{bmatrix} \Lambda_{as} & \Lambda_{bs} & \Lambda_{cs} & \Lambda_{ds} & \Lambda_{es} \end{bmatrix}^T \tag{5}$$

$$V_d = -\omega_r(L_q I_q - \lambda_{PM}) \quad , \quad V_q = \omega_r(L_d I_d) \tag{6}$$

$$T_e = \frac{5}{2} \frac{N_P}{2} [\lambda_{PM} I_d + (L_d - L_q) I_d I_q] \tag{7}$$

$$T_{ripple} = \frac{N_P}{2} \frac{\mu_0}{l_g} r_g L \pi \sum_{\substack{h = 6n \mp 1 \\ n = 1,2,3,\ldots}} (h f_{s,h} f_{r,h} \sin((h \pm 1)\omega_c t \pm \gamma_d)) \quad (8)$$

2.4. LPM: Lumped Parameter Model

A complete machine design knowledge is required to define the major flux paths and the machine's model in the LPM, in which the magnetic saturations and other nonlinear effects are directly determined utilizing the steel sheet materials in the FEA. To determine the parameters of the motor, d-q axes MEC of the proposed models are developed as shown in Figure 6. The PM flux is oriented along the q-axis and the d-axis is aligned 90[E. Deg.] to the q-axis. The MEC, which is shown in Figure 6 is developed with two flux barriers filled with inset PMs, in which φ_d and φ_q are the d-q axes flux linkages, φ_g is the air-gap flux linkage, φ_M represents the PM flux linkage, φ_b is the saturation flux corresponding to the PM flux sources, f_d and f_q are the d-q axes magnetic potentials, and R_r, R_b, R_g, R_{st} and R_{sy} are the reluctances of the rotor islands, rotor flux barriers, air-gap, and stator core reluctances respectively. It should be noted that in comparison with the FEA, although solving such a nonlinear equation requires much smaller time steps, we have exported the LPM models to the FEM for detailed analysis results. As the stator reluctances are far lower than the air-gap reluctance, the proposed MEC in Figure 6 can be mathematically defined as:

- d-axis (Figure 6b):

$$R_{sy} + R_{st} \langle\langle R_g \rightarrow \begin{cases} \varphi_1 = \frac{f_{d1}}{R_{g1}+R_{ri1}} \\ \varphi_2 = \frac{f_{d2}}{R_{g2}+R_{ri2}} \\ \varphi_3 = \frac{f_{d3}}{R_{g3}+R_{ri3}} \end{cases} \quad (9)$$

$$\varphi_d = \varphi_1 + \varphi_2 + \varphi_3 \quad (10)$$

$$L_d = \frac{\varphi_d}{i_d} \quad (11)$$

- q-axis (Figure 6c):

$$R_{sy} + R_{st} \langle\langle R_g \rightarrow \begin{cases} \varphi_1 = \frac{f_{q1}}{R_{g1}+R_{b1}} \\ \varphi_s = \frac{f_{q2}+R_{b2}\varphi_b}{R_{g2}+R_{b2}} \end{cases} \quad (12)$$

$$\varphi_d = \varphi_1 + \varphi_s \quad (13)$$

$$L_d = \frac{\varphi_q}{i_q} \quad (14)$$

2.5. FEM: Finite Element Method

One of the most common numerical methods used to design, analyze, optimization and performance evaluation of electrical machines is the FEM. A 2D-FEM is applied in this study to calculate the torque developments, torque fluctuations, electromagnetic power, line-to-line Back-EMF, air-gap flux density, efficiency, and power factor with respect to the stator current phase angle, stator current amplitude, and rotor speed variations, for the proposed models of five-phase PMASynRM. The corresponding LPM models of the proposed configurations, shown in Figure 6b,c, are exported to the conducted FEA of this study for a more detailed electromagnetic (E-Magnetic) characteristic analysis.

3. E-Magnetic FEM Results

In the following subsections, the conducted FEM analysis results are comparatively reported. First, the models are studied by applying the nominal current of 15 A operating at 5 kRPM of rotor speed. Then, the torque performance (average torque and torque ripple) of each model is sensitively investigated to determine the best-performed model, producing the lowest value of the torque ripple, with regard to the stator current specifications (Phase angle and Amplitude) variation. Finally, the torque, power, Back-EMF, air-gap flux density, efficiency, and power factor of the candidate model are studied considering a wide range of speeds.

3.1. Steady-State Analysis at Rated Current and Nominal Speed

The steady-state operational behavior of the proposed models is illustrated in Figure 7 in which, Figure 7a,c,d depict the comparative torque performance (average torque, cogging torque, and torque ripple respectively). The Model-I and -II exhibit higher torque fluctuations; however, the Model-II produces the maximum average torque. The other models present a much lower value of cogging torque with desirable values of average torque (the value is in between that of the Model-I and -II), in which the Model-V provides the lowest T_{Cog}, and the Model-III presents the lowest T_{Ripple}. Figure 7b displays the Line-to-Line Back-EMF produced by the proposed models. Accordingly, Model-I and -II produce the minimum and maximum peak values, whereas the other models present medium levels of L-L Back-EMF. Figure 8 demonstrates the reluctance and PM torque comparison along with the harmonic behavior of the proposed structure. Accordingly, it can be seen from Figure 8a,b that there is a tradeoff between the reluctance part of the torque and the magnet part as they move in the opposite direction while reconfiguration occurred. However, the overall produced torque remained the same and approximately equal to 11.5 Nm for all of the proposed models. Based on the presented harmonic results in Figure 8c,d, the Model-I and -II suffer from high order torque and back-EMF harmonics, while Model-III to -V benefit from lower amplitudes of high order harmonics and consequently better performance is presented by them. The flux density distribution map for the proposed models is shown in Figure 9. It can be derived from Figure 9 that except for the local saturation in iron ribs, the total distributed flux density is desirable, causing a low probability of power losses, local saturation, and the chance of overheating under the nominal operational conditions. However, in comparison with the Model-I, the Model-II provides less local saturations. Based on Figure 9a,b and Equation (8), as the harmonics contents of the MMF of the rotor increase, a higher torque ripple will occur. In other words, in comparison with the Model-I and -II with the highest and lowest local saturations respectively, the local saturation in the Model-III to -V reduced due to the reconfiguration. Thus, a higher torque ripple with a lower value of torque is shown by the Model-I, and the highest torque and lower values of torque ripple are presented by the Model-II to -V, while the Model-III to -V provides a value of torque between that of the Model-I and -II. Thus, a noticeable torque sacrifice is prevented by reducing local saturations in the Model-III to -V and consequently provides better torque ripple performance. Also, as illustrated in Figure 8a,b, Model-V presents a wider range of operations in terms of the rotor speed. The calculated electromagnetic characteristics of the proposed models are reported in Table 3.

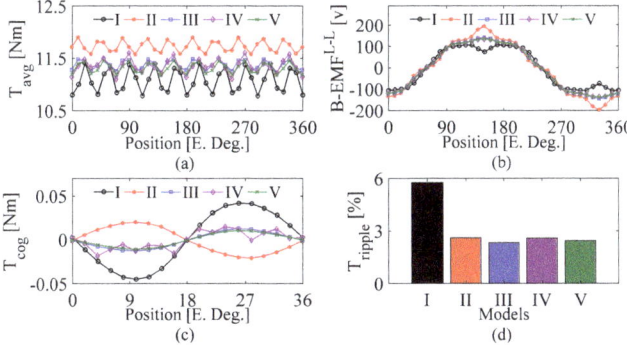

Figure 7. FEA results at rated current: (**a**) Average Torque, (**b**) L-L Back-EMF, (**c**) Cogging Torque and (**d**) Torque Ripple.

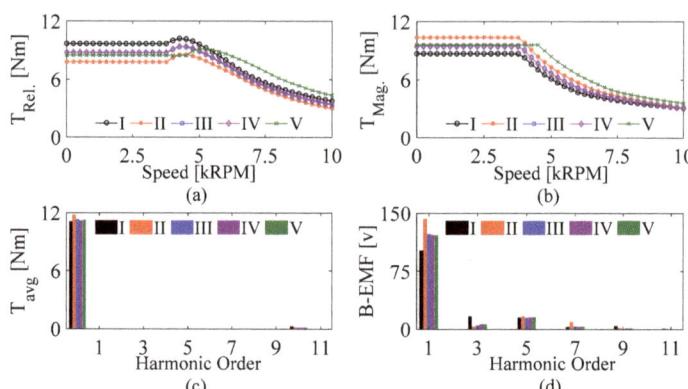

Figure 8. FEA results at rated current: (**a**) Reluctance Torque, (**b**) PM Torque, (**c**) T_{avg} Harmonics, and (**d**) Back-EMF Harmonics.

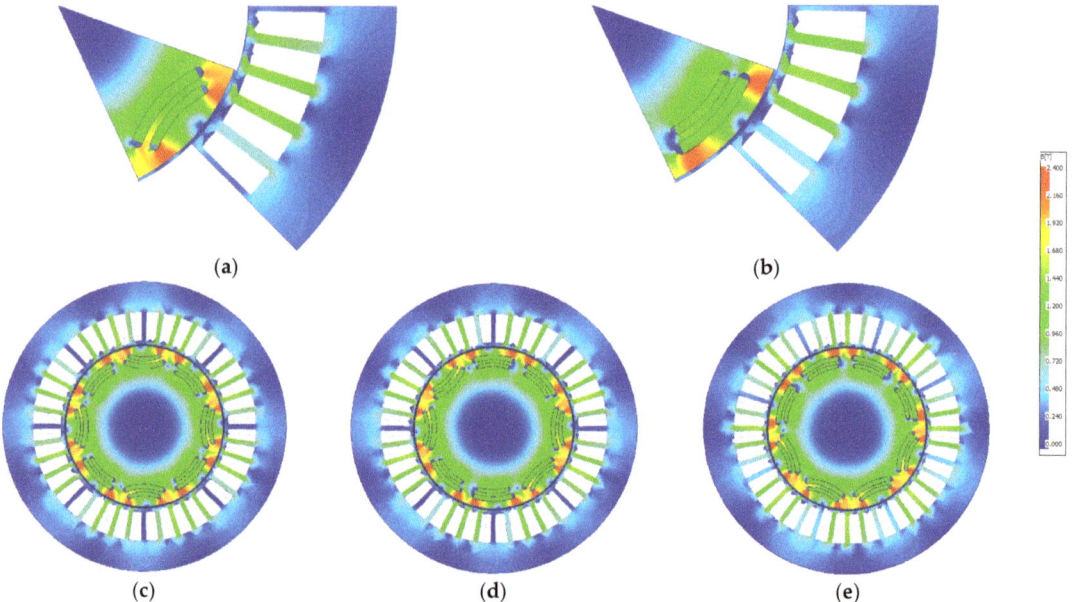

Figure 9. Flux Density Distribution Map: (**a**) Model-I (PMSynRM), (**b**) Model-II, (**c**) Model-III, (**d**) Model-IV and (**e**) Model-V.

Table 3. FEA Results at Rated Speed and Current.

Parameter	Unit	I	II	III	IV	V
T_{avg}	Nm	11.02	11.6	11.4	11.37	11.35
T_{Cog}	Nm	0.1	0.05	0.025	0.035	0.022
T_{Ripple}	%	5.9	2.95	2.8	2.93	2.85
η	%	93.8	94.75	93.94	94.2	94.1
PF	-	0.65	0.77	0.71	0.71	0.71
L_d	mH	6.07	5.944	6.03	5.99	6
L_q	mH	11.04	10.87	10.98	10.97	10.97

3.2. Optimization

Concerning the stator current phase angle (X_1) and amplitude (X_2) variations, the results achieved from the 2D-FEM, related to the average torque and torque ripple study, are illustrated in Figures 10–14. It can be seen that the presented average torque is similar for all the proposed rotor schemes with some slight differences at the minimum and maximum variable extremes. However, higher values of average torque are determined for the Model-II to -V in comparison with the proposed PMASynRM model. In terms of torque ripple, as expected from the steady-state section, the Model-I and -II present high values of torque ripple (increased along with increasing values of X_1 and X_2), while others benefit from much lower value (begins with higher values but decline as X_1 increased). Hence, the Model-V, which presents lower values of T_{Ripple} with respect to the variation of applied parameters is selected as the optimal model for Low-T_{Ripple} applications. Moreover, to precisely obtain the advantages of this candidate model to operate at a wide range of speed the following dynamic analysis is performed. Table 4. reports the T_{max} and $T_{ripple-min}$ values for the proposed structures during variation of stator current amplitude and phase angle.

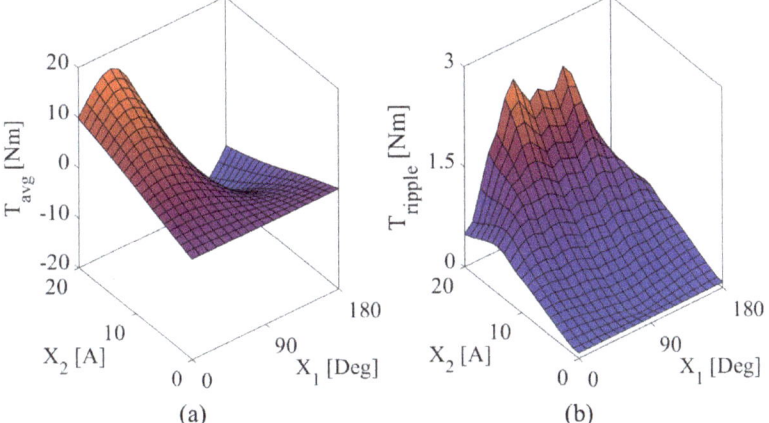

Figure 10. FEA results for torque performance of the PMASynRM: (**a**) Average Torque, and (**b**) Torque Ripple.

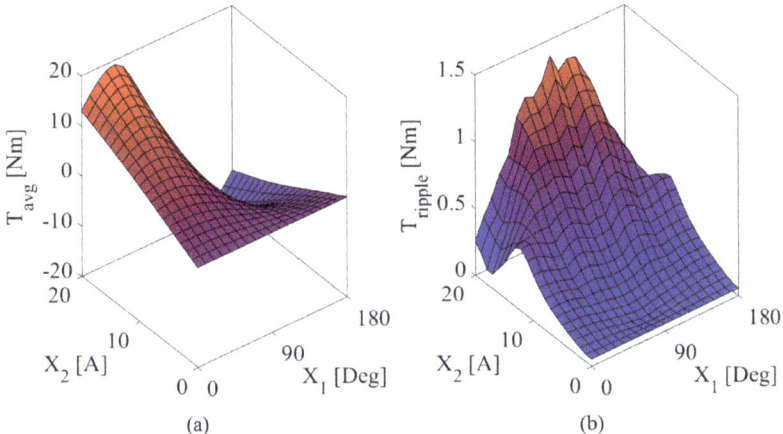

Figure 11. FEA results for torque performance of the Model-II: (**a**) Average Torque, and (**b**) Torque Ripple.

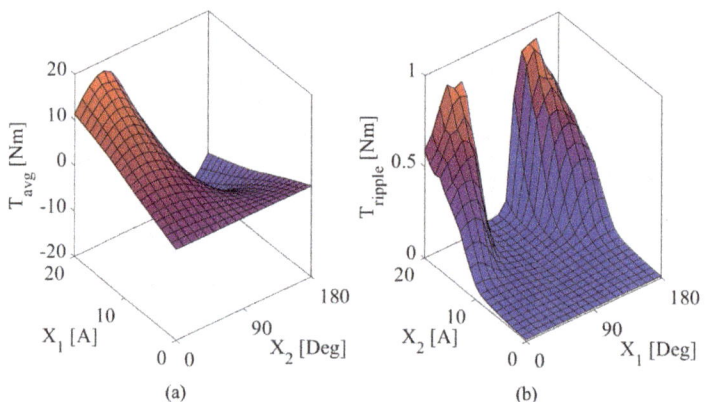

Figure 12. FEA results for torque performance of the Model-III: (**a**) Average Torque, and (**b**) Torque Ripple.

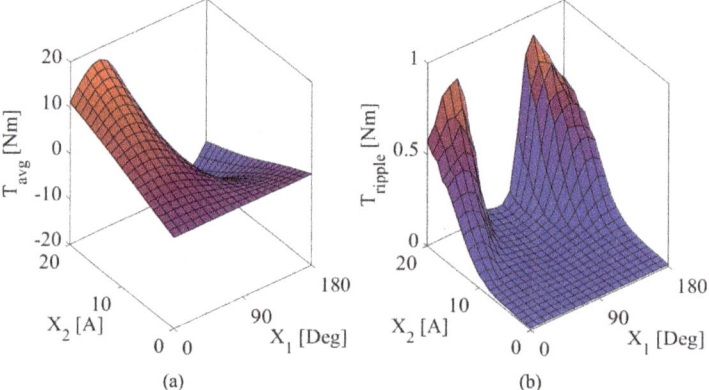

Figure 13. FEA results for torque performance of the Model-IV: (**a**) Average Torque, and (**b**) Torque Ripple.

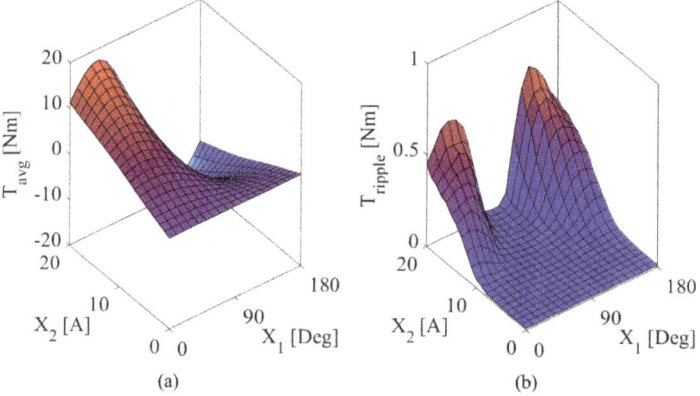

Figure 14. FEA results for torque performance of the Model-V: (**a**) Average Torque, and (**b**) Torque Ripple.

Table 4. Optimization summarized reports.

	Model-I	Model-II	Model-III	Model-IV	Model-V
T_{max} [Nm]	16.5	18.13	17.66	17.6	17.7
T_{ripple} [Nm]	1.77	0.8	0.85	0.83	0.6
X1 [Deg]	40	40	40	40	40
X2 [A]	20	20	20	20	20

3.3. Optimal Rotor Scheme

Based on the illustrated results of the performed sensitivity analysis in the previous subsection, the Model-V is selected to be studied under dynamic performance. Figure 15 demonstrated the performance of the Model-V under dynamic analyzes. Figure 15a,b show the average air-gap flux density (B_g) and L-L Back-EMF of the Model-V, operating at desired values up to 0.4 T and over 500 v respectively, at a maximum stator current amplitude of 20 A. The efficiency and power factor map of the Model-V are illustrated in Figure 15c,d respectively. Accordingly, high values of efficiency are observed at constant torque region for up to 5 kRPM of speed. Higher values of power factor are observed when the candidate model operates at the constant power region for more than 5 kRPM. Overall, the selected Model-V present higher values of torque/power density, efficiency, power factor, and Back-EMF with a much lower amount of torque fluctuations in comparison with the conventional PMASynRM, which make this model a vital alternative, applicable for Low-T_{Ripple} applications, operating in a wide range of speed up to 10 kRPM.

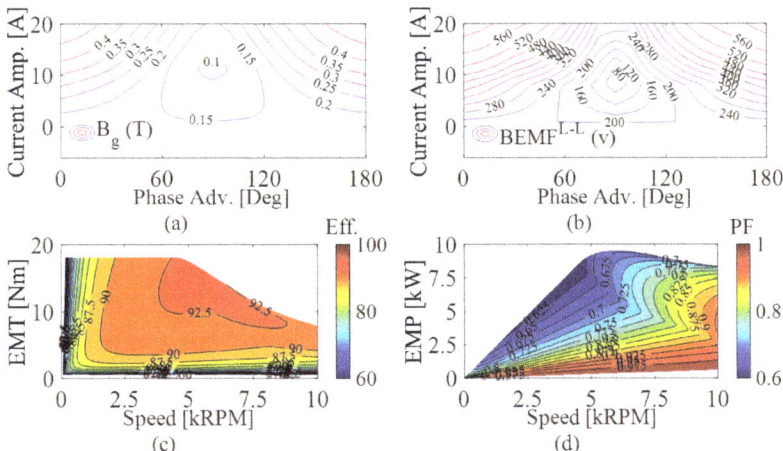

Figure 15. Dynamic Performance Results of the Model-V: (**a**) B_g, (**b**) L-L Back-EMF, (**c**) Efficiency Map, and (**d**) Power Factor Map.

4. Conclusions

The goal of this paper is to introduce and study novel rotor flux barrier reconfigurations for a five-phase PMASynRM, in which a conventional PMASynRM is considered to observe the benefits of the presented rotor schemes. The models are designed in following the formerly investigated rotor design criteria so that although the proposed structures are designed considering the same design parameter values, the flux barrier scheme has been reconfigured, and consequently results in different performances. An LPM conducted to a 2D FEM is applied to the proposed models under the steady-state condition at rated current and speed. Based on the FEM results, the maximum torque, minimum T_{Cog}, and T_{Ripple} are presented by the Model-II, Model-V, and Model-III respectively compared to the PMASynRM. Higher local saturations in the Model-I resulted in high order MMF harmonic contents and therefore increased the torque ripple. To minimize the torque reduction in the

Model-III to -V, their scheme is considered the combination of the Model-I and -II, which led to a desirable performance without a noticeable torque reduction. Since the goal of this paper is to investigate torque development, particularly the torque ripple reduction, by performing a sensitivity analysis, including stator current phase angle (X_1) and amplitude (X_2), the proposed machines provide similar average torque performance with respect to the variation of these parameters. However, the torque ripple highly decreased in Model-III to -V with an increasing value of X_2 up to $90^{E. \text{ Deg.}}$, while Model-I and -II suffer from high values of T_{Ripple} (increased along with increasing values of X_1 and X_2). Overall, the Model-V, which provides high values of torque density along with a much lower amount of torque ripple is selected as the optimal rotor scheme for five-phase PMASynRM. To obtain the advantages of the optimal model, it is studied under the dynamic condition for a wide range of operational speeds. As a result, the optimal model operates at high values of constant torque, power, efficiency, and power factor with desirable values of Line-to-Line Back-EMF and air-gap flux density. Hence, the optimal model is applicable for Low-T_{Ripple} High-Speed applications with no extra manufacturing costs when transforming from a conventional PMASynRM rotor scheme to the Model-V.

Author Contributions: Conceptualization, H.G. and M.M.; software, H.G. and M.M.; validation, M.M., and M.B.; writing—original draft preparation, H.G.; writing—review and editing, M.M., and M.B.; supervision, M.M., and M.B. All authors have read and agreed to the published version of the manuscript.

Funding: This research received no external funding.

Conflicts of Interest: The authors declare no conflict of interest.

References

1. Li, J.; Wang, K. A Novel Spoke-Type PM Machine Employing Asymmetric Modular Consequent-Pole Rotor. *IEEE ASME Trans. Mechatron.* **2019**, *24*, 2182–2192. [CrossRef]
2. Heidari, H.R.; Andriushchenko, E.; Rassolkin, A.; Kallaste, A.; Vaimann, T.; Demidova, G.L. Comparison of Synchronous Reluctance Machine and Permanent Magnet-Assisted Synchronous Reluctance Machine Performance Characteristics. In Proceedings of the 27th International Workshop on Electric Drives: MPEI Department of Electric Drives 90th Anniversary (IWED), Moscow, Russia, 27–30 January 2020. [CrossRef]
3. Moradian, M.R.; Soltani, J.; Najjar-Khodabakhsh, A.; Arab Markadeh, G.R. Adaptive Torque and Flux Control of Sensorless IPMSM Drive in the Stator Flux Field Oriented Reference Frame. *IEEE Trans. Ind. Inform.* **2019**, *15*, 205–212. [CrossRef]
4. Moradian, M.R.; Soltani, J.; Benbouzid, M.; Najjar-Khodabakhsh, A. A Parameter Independent Stator Current Space-Vector Reference Frame-Based Sensorless IPMSM Drive Using Sliding Mode Control. *Energies* **2021**, *14*, 2365. [CrossRef]
5. Ghorbani, H.R.; Majidi, B. Power Density Optimization through Optimal Selection of PM properties in a PM-SyncRM Using FEM Analysis. In Proceedings of the 2019 10th International Power Electronics, Drive Systems and Technologies Conference (PEDSTC), Shiraz, Iran, 12–14 February 2019. [CrossRef]
6. Ghorbani, H.; Moradian, M. Torque pulsation reduction in five-phase PMASyncRMs. *J. Power Electron.* **2021**, 1–10. [CrossRef]
7. Krichen, M.; Elbouchikhi, E.; Benhadj, N.; Chaieb, M.; Benbouzid, M.; Neji, R. Motor Current Signature Analysis-Based Permanent Magnet Synchronous Motor Demagnetization Characterization and Detection. *Machines* **2020**, *8*, 35. [CrossRef]
8. Agarlita, S.; Ursu, D.; Tutelea, L.; Boldea, I.; Fahimi, B. BLDC multiphase reluctance machines: A revival attempt with 2D FEM investigation and standstill tests. In Proceedings of the IEEE Energy Conversion Congress and Exposition, Denver, CO, USA, 15–19 September 2013. [CrossRef]
9. Maroufian, S.S.; Pillay, P. Design and Analysis of a Novel PM-Assisted Synchronous Reluctance Machine Topology with AlNiCo Magnets. *IEEE Trans. Ind. App.* **2019**, *55*, 4733–4742. [CrossRef]
10. Chen, K.; Yu, W.; Wen, C. Rotor Optimization for Synchronous Reluctance Motors. *CES Trans. Electr. Mach. Syst.* **2019**, *3*, 279–284. [CrossRef]
11. Jurca, F.N.; Inte, R.; Martis, C. Optimal rotor design of novel outer rotor reluctance synchronous machine. *Electr. Eng.* **2020**, *102*, 107–116. [CrossRef]
12. Inte, R.A.; Jurca, F.N.; Martis, C. Design and Analysis of Outer Rotor Permanent Magnet Assisted Synchronous Reluctance Machine with Concentrated Winding for Small Electric Propulsion. In Proceedings of the AEIT International Annual Conference (AEIT), Florence, Italy, 18–20 September 2019. [CrossRef]
13. Mohanarajah, T.; Nagrial, M.; Rizk, J.; Hellany, A. A Novel Method to Optimize Permanent Magnet Assisted Synchronous Reluctance Machines. *Electr. Power Comp. Syst.* **2020**, *48*, 933–944. [CrossRef]

14. Zeraoulia, M.; Benbouzid, M.; Diallo, D. Electric Motor Drive Selection Issues for HEV Propulsion Systems: A Comparative Study. *IEEE Trans. Veh. Tech.* **2006**, *55*, 1756–1764. [CrossRef]
15. Aryasomayajula, S.B.; Banerjee, R.; Sensarma, P. Effect of Magnets and Diamagnetic Material on Performance of SynRM with Novel Rotor Structure. In Proceedings of the National Power Electronics Conference (NPEC), Tiruchirappalli, India, 13–15 December 2019. [CrossRef]
16. Hezzi, A.; Elghali, S.B.; Bensalem, Y.; Zhou, Z.; Benbouzid, M.; Abdelkrim, M.N. ADRC-Based Robust and Resilient Control of a 5-Phase PMSM Driven Electric Vehicle. *Machines* **2020**, *8*, 17. [CrossRef]
17. Wang, S.; Ma, J.; Liu, C.; Wang, Y.; Lei, G.; Guo, Y.; Zhu, J. Design and performance analysis of a novel synchronous reluctance machine. *Int. J. Appl. Electromagn. Mech.* **2020**, *63*, 249–265. [CrossRef]
18. Liu, Z.; Hu, Y.; Wu, J.; Zhang, B.; Feng, G. A Novel Modular Permanent Magnet-Assisted Synchronous Reluctance Motor. *IEEE Access* **2021**, *9*, 19947–19959. [CrossRef]
19. Zhao, W.; Shen, H.; Lipo, T.A.; Wang, X. A New Hybrid Permanent Magnet Synchronous Reluctance Machine with Axially Sandwiched Magnets for Performance Improvement. *IEEE Trans. Energy Convers.* **2018**, *33*, 4. [CrossRef]
20. Cai, W.; Wu, X.; Zhou, M.; Liang, Y.; Wang, Y. Review and Development of Electric Motor Systems and Electric Powertrains for New Energy Vehicles. *Automot. Innov.* **2021**, *4*, 3–22. [CrossRef]
21. Cui, W.; Hu, B.; Pan, T. A Novel PMSM with Optimized Asymmetric Eccentric Air-Gap for High-Power Electric Motorcycle. *Electr. Power Compon. Syst.* **2019**, *47*, 1854–1863. [CrossRef]
22. Momen, F.; Rahman, K.; Son, Y. Electrical Propulsion System Design of Chevrolet Bolt Battery Electric Vehicle. *IEEE Tran. Ind. App.* **2018**, *55*, 376–384. [CrossRef]
23. Tawfiq, K.B.; Ibrahim, M.N.; El-Kholy, E.E.; Sergeant, P. Performance Improvement of Existing Three Phase Synchronous Reluctance Machine: Stator Upgrading to 5-Phase with Combined Star-Pentagon Winding. *IEEE Access* **2020**, *8*, 143569–143583. [CrossRef]
24. Toliyat, H.A.; Waikar, S.P.; Lipo, T.A. Analysis and simulation of five-phase synchronous reluctance machines including third harmonic of air gap MMF. *IEEE Trans. Industry App.* **1998**, *34*, 332–339. [CrossRef]
25. Shen, J.-X.; Lin, Y.-Q.; Sun, Y.; Qin, X.-F.; Wan, W.-J.; Cai, S. Permanent Magnet Synchronous Reluctance Machines with Axially Combined Rotor Structure. *IEEE Tran. Magn.* **2021**. [CrossRef]
26. Mohammadi, A.; Mirimani, S.M. Design of a Novel PM-Assisted Synchronous Reluctance Motor Topology Using V-Shape Permanent Magnets for Improvement of Torque Characteristic. *IEEE Tran. Energy Convers.* **2021**. [CrossRef]
27. Korman, O.; Degano, M.; Nardo, M.D.; Gerada, C. A Novel Flux Barrier Parametrization for Synchronous Reluctance Machine. *IEEE Tran. Energy Convers.* **2021**. [CrossRef]
28. Wang, K.; Zhu, Z.Q.; Ombach, G.; Koch, M.; Zhang, S.; Xu, J. Optimal slot/pole and flux-barrier layer number combinations for synchronous reluctance machines. In Proceedings of the Eighth International Conference and Exhibition on Ecological Vehicles and Renewable Energies (EVER), Monte Carlo, Monaco, 27–30 March 2013. [CrossRef]
29. Scmidt, E.; Brandl, W. Comparative finite element analysis of synchronous reluctance machines with internal rotor flux barriers. In Proceedings of the IEEE International Electric Machines and Drives Conference (IEMDC), Cambridge, MA, USA, 17–20 June 2001. [CrossRef]
30. Wang, Y.; Ionel, D.; Dorrell, D.G.; Stretz, S. Establishing the power factor limitations for synchronous reluctance machines. *IEEE Trans. Magn.* **2015**, *51*, 8111704. [CrossRef]
31. Bianchi, N.; Bolognani, S.; Bon, D.; Pre, M.D. Torque harmonic compensation in a synchronous reluctance motor. *IEEE Trans. Energy Convers.* **2008**, *23*, 466–473. [CrossRef]
32. Moghaddam, R.; Gyllensten, F. Novel high-performance SynRM design method: An easy approach for a complicated rotor topology. *IEEE Trans. Ind. Electron.* **2014**, *61*, 5058–5065. [CrossRef]
33. Baek, J.; Bonthu, S.S.R.; Choi, S. Design of five-phase permanent magnet assisted synchronous reluctance motor for low output torque ripple applications. *IET Electr. Power App.* **2016**, *10*, 339–346. [CrossRef]
34. Bilyi, V.; Bilyi, D.; Oleg, M.; Dajaku, G.; Gerling, D. Synchronous reluctance machine with multiphase stator cage winding. In Proceedings of the 20th International Conference on Electrical Machines and Systems (ICEMS), Sydney, Australia, 11–14 August 2017. [CrossRef]

Article

Power Quality Monitoring Strategy Based on an Optimized Multi-Domain Feature Selection for the Detection and Classification of Disturbances in Wind Generators

David A. Elvira-Ortiz [1], Juan J. Saucedo-Dorantes [1], Roque A. Osornio-Rios [1], Daniel Morinigo-Sotelo [2] and Jose A. Antonino-Daviu [3,*]

[1] HSPdigital CA-Mecatronica Engineering Faculty, Autonomous University of Queretaro, San Juan del Rio 76806, Mexico; delvira@hspdigital.org (D.A.E.-O.); jsaucedo@hspdigital.org (J.J.S.-D.); raosornio@hspdigital.org (R.A.O.-R.)

[2] Research Group HSPdigital-ADIRE, Institute of Advanced Production Technologies (ITAP), University of Valladolid, 47011 Valladolid, Spain; daniel.morinigo@eii.uva.es

[3] Instituto Tecnológico de la Energía, Universitat Politècnica de València (UPV), Camino de Vera s/n, 46022 Valencia, Spain

* Correspondence: joanda@die.upv.es

Abstract: Wind generation has recently become an essential renewable power supply option. Wind generators are integrated with electrical machines that require correct functionality. However, the increasing use of non-linear loads introduces undesired disturbances that may compromise the integrity of the electrical machines inside the wind generator. Therefore, this work proposes a five-step methodology for power quality disturbance detection in grids with injection of wind farm energy. First, a database with synthetic signals is generated, to be used in the training process. Then, a multi-domain feature estimation is carried out. To reduce the problematic dimensionality, the features that provide redundant information are eliminated through an optimized feature selection performed by means of a genetic algorithm and the principal component analysis. Additionally, each one of the characteristic feature matrices of every considered condition are modeled through a specific self-organizing map neuron grid so they can be shown in a 2-D representation. Since the SOM model provides a pattern of the behavior of every disturbance, they are used as inputs of the classifier, based in a softmax layer neural network that performs the power quality disturbance detection of six different conditions: healthy or normal, sag or swell voltages, transients, voltage fluctuations and harmonic distortion. Thus, the proposed method is validated using a set of synthetic signals and is then tested using two different sets of real signals from an IEEE workgroup and from a wind park located in Spain.

Keywords: artificial intelligence; electrical machines; optimization techniques; self-organizing map; power quality; wind generation

1. Introduction

Modern society is experiencing a series of challenges in matters of power generation associated with the use of fossil fuels in the power generation process. This situation has led to an increase in greenhouse gas emissions, which has caused severe air pollution problems [1]. Moreover, fossil fuels are non-renewable resources that have become increasingly depleted in recent years, resulting in a rise in their prices [2,3]. To deal with these problems, power generation has started using use renewable sources as fuels (such as sunlight and wind); in fact, nearly one-third of the global electricity demand is fulfilled only with the use of renewable energies [4]. Among all the renewable energies, wind energy among the most widely spread, because it is mature from a technological point of view, it presents a competitive levelized cost of energy (LCOE) and it is relatively easy to obtain an important amount of energy by means of this renewable resource [5]. Nonetheless, the use of wind energy implies some important challenges. For instance, the amount of generated energy is location-specific, and a study of the wind conditions in the location is required to properly select the wind turbine and to guarantee that energy production is sufficient to represent monetary earns [6]. Also, the policies regarding wind generation are different from one country to another [7]. Additionally, wind generators are complex systems that combine mechanical, electric, and electronic devices to transform wind energy into electricity, and they must provide a robust, reliable, and high-quality power supply. Maintaining this high-quality supply is a challenge due to the large amount of non-linear loads that are used nowadays. These non-linear loads introduce a high number of harmonics that contaminate the power grid and cause waveform distortion. An electric grid that presents power quality (PQ) issues generates damages in domestic loads and leads to unexpected stops at industrial facilities that will translate into financial losses. In this sense, the electric generator becomes of great importance in any wind turbine. Therefore, in order to optimally design a wind generator, it is necessary to develop strategies that allow determining the existence of failures that compromise the quality of the generated energy. PQ problems cause erratic operation of electronic controllers and computer data loss [8]. They also lead to the inappropriate operation of relays, programmable logic controllers, and computers. Therefore, the methodologies for disturbance detection allow for improving the design of wind generators and preventing the malfunctioning of their components.

PQ monitoring has been widely explored, and several techniques have been developed to determine the presence of waveform distortion or power quality disturbances (PQD) in electrical signals. To properly perform this identification, it is important to carry out a feature extraction that provides information regarding the occurrence of any event. One of the most common techniques for this feature extraction is the Fourier transform (FT) [9,10], which delivers good results in the evaluation of stationary disturbances such as harmonic distortion. However, the conventional FT-based methodologies present some important drawbacks, such as the existence of spectral leakage and the fact that this technique cannot be applied in the analysis of transient disturbances. Moreover, the FT cannot provide temporal information related to the occurrence of the PQD. To overcome the issues related with the FT, some other time-frequency transforms have been explored, for instance, the short-time Fourier transform [11], S-transform [12]; the wavelet transform [13]; empirical mode decomposition (EMD) [14]; and the Hilbert Huang transform [15], among others. These techniques are able to detect not only stationary PQD but also non-stationary PQD; furthermore, they provide accurate information associated with the time when the disturbance occurs. However, these time-frequency techniques demand a higher computational effort and lose accuracy in frequency information, since they work with modes that contain a group of frequencies instead of a single frequency component. Also, they suffer from mode mixing, so the information regarding a specific PQD can appear in more than one mode, hindering the disturbance identification. This is why some other works prefer to extract features like high-order statistics (HOS) directly in the time domain [16]. The use of HOS features presents some interesting advantages; for instance, the insensitivity to Gaussian noise and the low computational burden. On the other hand, HOS are highly sensitive to window size, and the use of a different number of samples of the same signal may lead to different results, especially when the PQD is short. Finally, it is important to mention that all the aforementioned techniques can be implemented to work along with artificial intelligence techniques such as artificial neural networks (ANN) [17], fuzzy logic-based classifiers [8], support vector machines [18], genetic algorithms (GA) [19], and even with some deep learning approaches [20]. This combination of strategies allows for performing an automatic classification of the founded PQD accurately. Yet, the number of extracted features in all the aforementioned approaches can be high, and many of them do not deliver important information regarding the existence of a specific disturbance. Thus, it is necessary to develop strategies to perform a proper feature selection. Specifically speaking of power quality in grids with injection of wind energy, it has been reported that the disturbances that more commonly appear are harmonic distortions, notch, voltage swell/sag, momentary interruptions, and voltage fluctuations [21]. To deal with these issues, some wind generators incorporate distribution static compensators [22] or passive and active filters [23,24]. These devices are intended to suppress the presence of harmonics and to work as reactive power compensators, and the PQ of the grid improves as a result of their action. Since, in this field, attention is focused on the development of devices for mitigating PQ issues, there is a lack of methodologies for the detection and identification of disturbances. Nonetheless, the development of techniques for PQ analysis can work along with the devices for PQ issues mitigation, because they can estimate the features required for tuning the filters and compensators used in wind turbines. Additionally, information from PQ monitoring allows for improvement in the design of blades, mechanical transmission systems, electric generators, in order to obtain a more reliable and robust machine.

Indeed, several methodologies have been reported for carrying out optimal feature selection in order to discard redundant information. Thus, some optimization techniques, like k-means [25] and bio-inspired algorithms [26], are used to set a model that describes the behavior of the PQD and select the features that better describe such behavior. In this way, it is possible to reduce the required computational effort and to increase the efficiency of the results. Also, in recent years, the use of dimensionality reduction techniques such as the linear discriminant analysis (LDA) [27] and principal component analysis (PCA) has been explored [28] for dealing with a complex set of features and reducing it to a three-dimensional or two-dimensional view. Additionally, with the use of these techniques, it is possible to maximize the distance between clusters, making the classification process more efficient and accurate. The aforementioned works use features in only one domain (time, frequency, or time-frequency); therefore, they are prone to experience difficulties when dealing with disturbances that exhibit similar behaviors in the analyzed domain. Hence, in [29], a multi-domain feature extraction for discerning between PQD with similar behavior is proposed; then, using an autoencoder, a dimensionality reduction is performed to facilitate the classification process. The problem with the multi-domain feature extraction is that the number of features to be considered highly increases. In this sense, using an optimization technique for feature selection may be helpful for reducing the effort required in the dimensionality reduction process. In terms of wind turbines, these methodologies have been used for the detection of failures in the components of the mechanism. For instance, in [30], PCA is used along with Hoteling's T2 method to assess the condition of the electric generator in a wind turbine. On the other hand, in [31], different variables such as active power, wind speed, rotor velocity, and blade angle are measured in a wind power installation. A generalized regression neural network ensemble for single imputation is used for feature extraction in all the measured variables and then, a feature reduction is performed using PCA. Finally, the wavelet-based probability density function is implemented, with the aim of identifying blade failures. Although these works deal with the identification of undesired conditions in wind turbines, they only consider the condition of the machine, and the PQ is left aside. It is important to pay more attention in the detection of PQD, since considering them is helpful for the general design of the wind generation system.

Thereby, the main contribution of this work relies in the proposal of a strategy for optimal feature selection that allows for modeling electric signals through statistical features in different domains that are used to better characterize the behavior of a PQD. The proposed methodology considers as a first step the implementation of a multi-domain feature extraction. Since the resultant number of features is high, a GA–PCA optimization is carried out to eliminate those features that provide redundant information. Then, a feature learning stage is implemented. In this step, self-organizing maps (SOM) are used to obtain a model of the PQD in the time, frequency and time-frequency domains. Finally, the SOM models obtained in every domain are used as inputs of a softmax layer ANN that works as the classifier. In the present work, both stationary and non-stationary disturbances are considered. Among the wide variety of PQD, only the following are considered: harmonics and voltage fluctuations for the stationary disturbances; and voltage sag, voltage swell, and transients (impulsive and oscillatory) for the non-stationary disturbances. These disturbances are selected because their appearance is common in grids that include renewable resources such as wind generation. The training and validation of the proposed strategy are performed using a set of synthetic signals that are modeled to be a reliable representation of electrical signals containing PQD. Then, the methodology is tested using two different groups of real signals. The first set is provided by the IEEE 1159.3 working group, whereas the second one corresponds to a series of measurements taken in a real wind farm located in northern Spain. As previously mentioned, the existence of PQD can produce a malfunction of the components of the machine; therefore, this methodology aims to be a tool for detecting PQD and improving the reliability of the wind turbine by preventing its failure. In this way, the designers and manufacturers of wind turbines can consider the existence of PQD during the entire production process in order to improve the quality, not only of the power supply, but of the entire generation system.

2. Theoretical Background

2.1. Self-Organizing Maps

The self-organizing map (SOM) is a novel unsupervised machine learning technique, whose main purpose consists of performing a non-liner projection of a high-dimensional input data set into a low-dimensional space. SOM is based in a neural network that requires a pre-defined number of neurons to resemble and map the data distribution of the input space. The use of SOM presents an interesting advantage against other methodologies for PQ monitoring, and due to its capability for automatically adjusting to different data topologies, the SOM may be used as a learning algorithm for mapping an input feature space and model that can be considered the normal behavior, and then identifying patterns that differ from this normality and classifying them according to the topological characteristics of the data input [32].

An SOM model is composed of two main layers of neurons as it is presented in Figure 1; the input layer is composed of N neurons, where each one represents an input variable of the input feature space; through the input layer, the received information is transmitted to the output layer. The output layer comprises predefined M neurons and, in this layer, aims to automatically adapt the input feature space in order to obtain a characteristic pattern map. Each neuron of the grid in the output layer represents a matching unit (MU). Normally, the neurons in the output layer are arranged in the form of a two-dimensional map, which is also known as the resulting SOM neuron grid. As Figure 1 shows, the connections between the two layers of the SOM network are always forward; that is, the information of the input feature space is propagated from the input layer to the output layer. Thus, each input neuron i is connected to each of the output neurons j by a weight ω_{ji}; in this way, the output neurons are associated with a vector of weights W_j that is called the reference vector or codebook, since it constitutes the prototype or average vector of the category represented by the output neuron j. Thus, the SOM model defines a projection from a high-dimensional data space into a two-dimensional neuron grid map of neurons [32–34].

The SOM learning process can be described by two main steps as follows: step (i) A vector x is randomly selected from the input feature space and its distance or similarity to the vectors m_j, in the codebook, is calculated, using, for example, the Euclidean distance (1):

$$\| x - m_j \| = \min_j \{ x - m_j \} \tag{1}$$

Once the closest vector or BMU (best matching unit) has been found, the rest of the vectors in the codebook are updated. Step (ii) the BMU and its neighbors, in the topological sense, move close to the vector x in the input feature space. The magnitude of this attraction is described by the learning rate, which is also known as the topological error ($\overline{E}_t$). As the learning process proceeds and new vectors are assigned to the neuron grip map, the learning rate gradually decreases towards zero; consequently, the neighborhood radius also decreases. The update or learning rule for the given reference vector i is defined by (2):

$$m_j(t+1) = \begin{cases} m_j(t) + \alpha(t)\left[x(t) - m_j(t)\right] & j \in N_c(t) \\ m_j(t) & j \notin N_c(t) \end{cases} \quad (2)$$

where, t is the discrete-time index for the variables, $\alpha(t) \in [0,1]$ is a scalar that defines the relative size of the learning step, and $N_c(t)$ specifies the neighborhood around the winner in the map array.

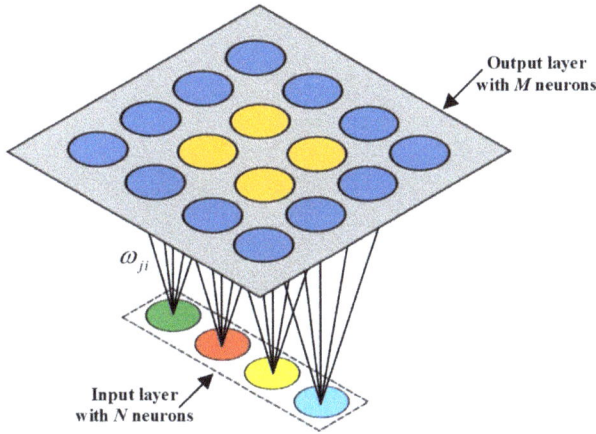

Figure 1. Schematic representation of a SOM structure, its construction and the two main characteristic layers.

Then, steps i and ii are repeated until the training process ends. The number of training steps must be pre-defined a priori to calculate the convergence rate of the neighborhood function and the learning rate. Once the training is finished, the resulting neuron grip map is ordered in a topological sense: n topologically close vectors are applied in n adjacent neurons or even in the same neuron. Moreover, to determine whether the resulting SOM neuron grid has been properly adapted to the input feature space during the training process, as measures of quality of the maps, the precision of the projection and the preservation of the topology are considered. The projection precision measure describes how neurons adapt or respond to input feature space. Usually, the number of data points is greater than the number of neurons, and the precision error is always different from 0. To calculate the precision of the projection, the mean quantization error ($\overline{E}_q$) over the complete input feature space is estimated as (3):

$$\overline{E}_q = \frac{1}{N} \sum_{i=1}^{N} \| x_i - m_c \| \quad (3)$$

Also, as aforementioned, the topology preservation measure describes how the SOM neuron grid preserves the topology of the input feature space. This measurement considers the structure of the neuron grid map, i.e., on an oddly twisted map, and the topographic error is large even if the precision error is small. Thus, the topological error, $\overline{E}_t$, can be calculated by following (4):

$$\overline{E}_t = \frac{1}{N} \sum_{i=1}^{N} u(x_k) \quad (4)$$

where, $u(x_k)$ is equal to 1 if the first and second BMUs of x_k are not close to each other, otherwise, $u(x_k)$ is equal to 0.

An additional advantage of using SOM to model an input feature space is that SOM performance is qualitatively measured in terms of the $\overline{E}_q$, that also provides information regarding the detection of unknown events that do not match with the topology of input feature space used to create a SOM neuron grid model. In Figure 2a–c, general and visual descriptions that depict the learning procedure performed to model a SOM neuron grid are shown.

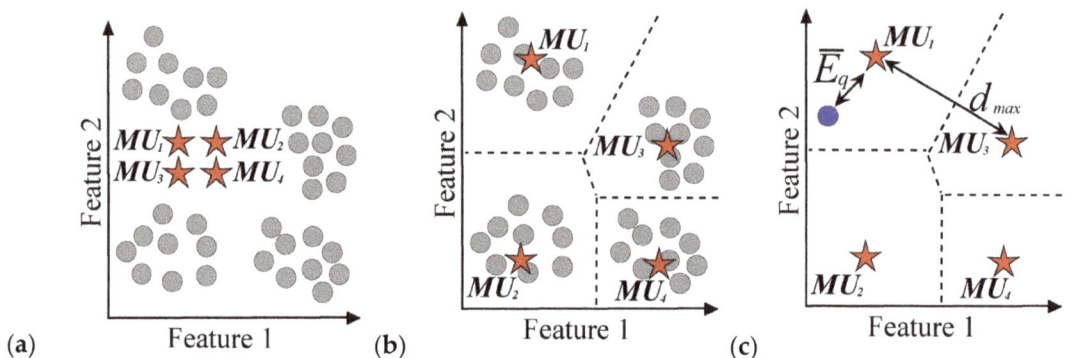

Figure 2. Representation of the self-organizing mapping procedure in a 2-dimensional input and output spaces. (**a**) Input feature space, ◯, and a randomly initialized 2 × 2 neuron grid, ★. (**b**) Resulting training procedure, where, the dotted lines represent the assigned memberships regions of the matching units considering Euclidian distances. The maximum distance between MUs, $dmax$, corresponds with MU_1 and MU_3. (**c**) Assessment of a new input data sample, ●. Assignation to MU_1 as closest matching unit with the corresponding individual quantization error $\overline{E}_q$.

2.2. Power Quality Definitions

The term power quality is used for defining a wide variety of electromagnetic phenomena that occur at a certain time and location on the power system. These phenomena result in the parameters that describe an electrical signal, like frequency and amplitude, deviating from the ideal values, causing waveform distortions. According to the IEEE standard 1159–2019 [35], voltage sag and voltage swell are RMS variations. The former occurs when RMS voltage decreases to a value between 0.1 pu and 0.9 pu; the latter is represented by an increment of the RMS voltage to values above 1.1 pu. The same standard defines a transient event as a disturbance that is undesirable but momentary in nature. These events are classified into two categories: impulsive and oscillatory. A sudden nonpower frequency change from the nominal condition that is unidirectional in polarity is known as impulsive transient; in contrast, when an electrical signal presents a sudden nonpower frequency change in the steady-state condition that includes both positive and negative polarity values, then it is said that an oscillatory transient has occurred. Additionally, voltage fluctuations are defined as systematic variations of the signal envelope causing the peak value of the voltage signal to oscillate between 0.95 pu and the 1.05 pu. Finally, harmonics are sinusoidal components that are integer multiples of the fundamental frequency (usually 50 Hz or 60 Hz). When harmonics are combined with the fundamental component, they produce a waveform distortion that is evaluated using a quantity called the total harmonic distortion (THD). The IEEE standard 519–2014 [36] establishes that the THD level must remain under the 8% in grids that handle voltages lower than 1.0 kV. All the aforementioned disturbances can be mathematically modeled, and Table 1 shows the equations that describe them.

The parameters in Table 1 are described in detail as follow: A is the amplitude of the fundamental component; f_{fc} is the frecuency of the fundamental component; k is the discrete number of sample; ϕ is the phase angle in radians; α represents an amplitude deviation; k_1 is the sample where the disturbance begins; k_2 is the sample where the disturbance ends; ψ corresponds to the amplitude of the transients, f_{fl} is the frequency of the voltage fluctuations; M is te total number of harmonics; and A_h is the amplitude of every single harmonic.

Table 1. Mathematical models used in the generation of the synthetic signals for the 6 different conditions.

Condition	Mathematical Model	Parameter Description
Healthy	$x_{hlt}(k) = A\sin(2\pi f_{fc}k + \phi) + \eta(k,\sigma)$ [1]	$-\frac{\pi}{12} \leq \phi \leq \frac{\pi}{12}$
Voltage sag	$x_{sag}(k) = -\alpha A[u(k-k_1) - u(k-k_2)]\sin(2\pi f_{fc}k + \phi) + \eta(k,\sigma)$ [2]	$0.1 \leq \alpha \leq 0.9$ $k_1 < k_2$ $-\frac{\pi}{12} \leq \phi \leq \frac{\pi}{12}$
Voltage swell	$x_{swell}(k) = \alpha A[u(k-k_1) - u(k-k_2)]\sin(2\pi f_{fc}k + \phi) + \eta(k,\sigma)$	$0.1 \leq \alpha \leq 0.3$ $k_1 < k_2$ $-\frac{\pi}{12} \leq \phi \leq \frac{\pi}{12}$
Transients	$\begin{aligned}x_{tr}(k) &= A\Big[\sin(2\pi f_{fc}k + \phi) \\ &\quad -\psi\Big(e^{-750(k-k_1)} - e^{-344(k-k_1)}\Big)(u(k-k_1) - u(k-k_2))\Big] \\ &\quad + \eta(k,\sigma)\end{aligned}$	$0.222 \leq \psi \leq 1.11$ $k_b = k_a + 8$ $-\frac{\pi}{12} \leq \phi \leq \frac{\pi}{12}$
Voltage fluctuation	$x_{fl}(k) = \alpha A\sin(2\pi f_{fl}k + \phi)\sin(2\pi f_{fc}k + \phi) + \eta(k,\sigma)$	$1 \leq f_{fl} \leq 30$ $0 < \alpha \leq 0.1$ $-\frac{\pi}{12} \leq \phi \leq \frac{\pi}{12}$
Harmonics	$x_{har}(k) = A\sin(2\pi f_{fc}k + \phi) + \sum_{h_n=2}^{M} A_h \sin(2\pi h_n f_{fc}k + \phi) + \eta(k,\sigma)$	$5 \leq M \leq 50$ $0.012 \leq A_h \leq 0.1$ $-\frac{\pi}{12} \leq \phi \leq \frac{\pi}{12}$

[1] The term $\eta(k,\sigma)$ represents additive Gaussian noise with zero mean and standard deviation $0.05 \leq \sigma \leq 0.1$.
[2] $u(\ )$ is the step function.

3. Methodology

As mentioned, in the design of electric machines such as wind generators, it is important to consider the identification of failures and situations that compromise the quality of the power supply and, therefore, the integrity of the loads attached to the grid. In this regard, Figure 3 presents the flowchart of the proposed strategy that focuses on the identification and classification of PQD through an optimal multi-domain feature selection. The methodology has been designed to follow a step-by-step scheme to make its comprehension and application easier. A total of five stages compounds the PQ monitoring strategy: database, multi-domain feature estimation, optimized feature selection, feature learning and classification, where this final stage delivers the PQ disturbance detection as output. Every step is described in detail in the following subsections.

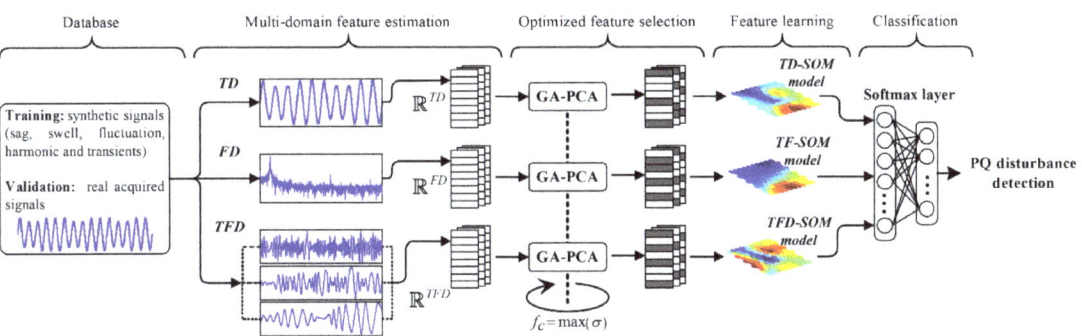

Figure 3. Diagram of the proposed methodology based on an optimized multi-domain feature selection for the detection and classification of disturbances.

3.1. Database

This work considers the use of synthetic and real signals. The former are used in the training process whereas the latter are used for validating the results of the proposed strategy.

The synthetic signals are generated with the purpose of representing six different conditions of electrical signals: a healthy signal (i.e., a signal without any disturbance), a voltage sag, a voltage swell, transients (impulsive and oscillatory), voltage fluctuations, and harmonic distortion. Considering the definitions stated by the IEEE standard 1159–2019, the mathematical models presented in Table 1 are used for generating the set of synthetic signals.

Before continuing, it is important to address some facts. For instance, all the parameters presented in the third column of Table 1 are randomly generated considering the range of values established in the same table. Also, the term f_{fc}, which represents the frequency of the fundamental component, is considered as 50 Hz. Moreover, for the case of harmonics, the number of harmonics and the amplitude of harmonicas is randomly selected, but in all the cases, a THD value higher than 8% must be accomplished to consider those cases with unacceptable harmonic distortion. Additionally, the model presented for the description of transients corresponds to an impulsive transient. Although impulsive and oscillatory transients are different and they can be described with different parameters, for the sake of simplicity, in this work, it is considered that an oscillatory transient can be expressed as an impulsive transient that appears more than one time with different values; therefore, the classifier will detect both disturbances only as transients. Also, it is considered that all the signals are generated using a sampling frequency of 8 kHz and with a duration of 300 ms. Finally, 100 signals per condition are generated to obtain a total of 600 elements that will be used in the following stages of the training process.

Regarding the real signals, these are taken from two different data sets. A first data set is provided by the IEEE 1159.3 working group [37], and it consists of a series of voltage and current signals, recorded from different real locations, with diverse PQD. The data set is formed by over 300 signals, but to validate the correct performance of the proposed strategy, only 3 cases are presented: transients, a voltage sag, and a voltage swell. In these signals, it is considered that the fundamental frequency is 60 Hz, and the signals are acquired at different sampling rates. For instance, the signal with the transients is acquired at a sampling rate of 15,360 Hz, whereas the signals with voltage sag and voltage swell are acquired considering a sampling frequency of 7680 Hz. The second set of real signals is acquired from a 30-MW wind park located in northern Spain. A proprietary data acquisition system (DAS) is used for collecting and storing electrical signals. This DAS is based on field-programmable gate array (FPGA) technology and it is able to acquire data from 7 channels simultaneously. The sampling rate of these signals is 8 kHz and the fundamental frequency is 50 Hz. At this location, a total of 4 different cases are presented: one for a healthy signal, another one for voltage sag, one more for transients, and, finally, one for harmonic distortion. Both sets of real signals are used to assess the performance of the proposed strategy under real conditions. However, the proposed methodology aims to be a tool for wind turbine designers; therefore, the results obtained with the second set of real signals come to be of great importance for validating the reliability of this strategy.

3.2. Multi-Domain Feature Estimation

It has been previously addressed that for PQD that present similar behaviors, a multi-domain approach may be helpful for obtaining better classification. Thus, h the use of three different domains is proposed here: time domain (TD), frequency domain (FD), and time-frequency domain (TFD). However, before performing any feature estimation, it is necessary to perform an amplitude normalization of the electrical signal; such normalization is carried out considering the nominal RMS value of the voltage signal. Therefore, all the amplitude values are dimensionless and expressed as *per unit* (pu). This consideration is implemented because the data sets that are used in this work consider signals from different grids and, therefore, have different nominal amplitudes. Nevertheless, by performing this normalization, the proposed methodology is able to properly work, even for signals with different nominal amplitude values.

In the case of the TD feature estimation, the 15 statistical features summarized in Table 2 are calculated for every signal. Therefore, the dimensionality of this space is set as TD = 15 and a feature matrix composed by statistical time domain features is obtained, $\mathbf{TD} \in \mathbb{R}^{TD}$. In the case of the FD analysis, first, it is necessary to compute the fast Fourier transform (FFT) of each normalized signal to obtain its representative spectrum. Then, the 14 statistical features presented in Table 3 are estimated over the signal spectrum. Hence, the dimensionality of this new space is FD = 14 and a representative FD-dimensional feature matrix, $\mathbf{FD} \in \mathbb{R}^{FD}$, is obtained. At this point, it is important to address the fact that the statistical features are estimated over the amplitude values of the signal spectrum. Since the signals have been previously normalized, it is expected that the fundamental component presents an amplitude of 1 pu in a healthy condition, and any variation from this value will be related with the existence of a disturbance. Moreover, since only the amplitude values of the spectrum are considered, the proposed methodology can be applied in any signal, regardless the value of the fundamental frequency. This turns to be one of the main advantages of the proposed approach, because it can be applied in 60 Hz grids and also in 50 Hz grids without requiring any modification. Finally, to carry out the TFD feature estimation, a preprocessing of the normalized signals is required prior to feature estimation. This preprocessing task consists of performing a signal decomposition, and the EMD technique is used for this purpose. The result of applying the EMD over the voltage signals is a set of sub-signals that show the main oscillatory modes of the original signal and that are called intrinsic mode functions (IMF). An important drawback of the EMD technique lies in the fact that it is not possible to have a priori knowledge of the IMF that can be obtained from a particular signal. Moreover, when the EMD is applied over two different signals, it is possible that a different number of IMF is obtained from each signal. To consider that a signal provides significant information in the TFD, only those signals that deliver 3 or more IMFs after applying the EMD are considered; the rest are discarded. Once the preprocessing task has been applied, the set of 15 statistical features presented in Table 2 are individually estimated over the three first resulting IMFs. So, for this last space, the dimensionality turns out to be TFD = 45, and, as in the previous cases, it is possible to obtain a TFD-dimensional feature matrix, $\mathbf{TFD} \in \mathbb{R}^{TFD}$. As in the previous cases, the feature estimation is performed over the amplitude values of every IMF; therefore, the methodology is insensitive to variations in the value of the fundamental frequency, and it can be applied in both 60 Hz and 50 Hz grids.

Table 2. Proposed set of statistical features for the characterization of the available signals during the processing in the time-domain analysis, where, $x(i)$ is a sample for $i = 1, 2, \ldots, N$, and N is the number of points for each acquired signal.

Statistical Time-Domain Feature	Mathematical Equation
Mean	$T_1 = \frac{1}{N} \cdot \sum_{i=1}^{N} |x_i|$
Maximum value	$T_2 = max(x)$
Root mean square	$T_3 = \sqrt{\frac{1}{N} \cdot \sum_{i=1}^{N} (x_i)^2}$
Square root mean	$T_4 = \left(\frac{1}{N} \cdot \sum_{i=1}^{N} \sqrt{|x_i|} \right)^2$
Standard deviation	$T_5 = \sqrt{\frac{1}{N} \cdot \sum_{i=1}^{N} (x_i - T_1)^2}$
Variance	$T_6 = \frac{1}{N} \cdot \sum_{i=1}^{n} (x_i - T_1)^2$
RMS shape factor	$T_7 = \frac{T_3}{\frac{1}{N} \cdot \sum_{i=1}^{N} |x_i|}$
SRM shape factor	$T_8 = \frac{T_4}{\frac{1}{N} \cdot \sum_{i=1}^{N} |x_i|}$

Table 2. *Cont.*

Statistical Time-Domain Feature	Mathematical Equation
Crest factor	$T_9 = \frac{T_2}{T_3^2}$
Latitude factor	$T_{10} = \frac{T_2}{T_4^2}$
Impulse factor	$T_{11} = \frac{T_2}{\frac{1}{N} \cdot \sum_{i=1}^{N} |x_i|}$
Skewness	$T_{12} = \frac{\sum\left[(x_i - T_1)^3\right]}{T_5^3}$
Kurtosis	$T_{13} = \frac{\sum\left[(x_i - T_1)^4\right]}{T_5^4}$
Fifth moment	$T_{14} = \frac{\sum\left[(x_i - T_1)^5\right]}{T_5^5}$
Sixth moment	$T_{15} = \frac{\sum\left[(x_i - T_1)^6\right]}{T_5^6}$

Table 3. Proposed set of statistical features for the characterization of frequency spectra estimated from each available signal during its processing in the frequency-domain analysis, where $s(k)$ is a spectrum for $j = 1, 2, \ldots, M$, and M is the number of lines with f_j as the frequency value of the jth spectrum line.

Statistical Feature	Mathematical Equation
Mean	$F_1 = \frac{1}{M} \cdot \sum_{j=1}^{M} s(j)$
Variance	$F_2 = \frac{1}{M-1} \cdot \sum_{j=1}^{M} (s(j) - F_1)^2$
Third moment	$F_3 = \frac{1}{M\left(\sqrt{F_2}\right)^3} \cdot \sum_{j=1}^{M} (s(j) - F_1)^3$
Fourth moment	$F_4 = \frac{1}{M\left(\sqrt{F_2}\right)^2} \cdot \sum_{j=1}^{M} (s(j) - F_1)^4$
Grand mean	$F_5 = \frac{\sum_{j=1}^{M} f_j \, s(j)}{\sum_{j=1}^{M} s(j)}$
Standard deviation 1	$F_6 = \sqrt{\frac{\sum_{j=1}^{M} (f_j - F_5)^2 \, s(j)}{M}}$
C factor	$F_7 = \sqrt{\frac{\sum_{j=1}^{M} f_j^2 \, s(j)}{\sum_{j=1}^{M} s(j)}}$
D factor	$F_8 = \sqrt{\frac{\sum_{j=1}^{M} f_j^4 \, s(j)}{\sum_{j=1}^{M} f_j^2 \, s(j)}}$
E factor	$F_9 = \frac{\sum_{j=1}^{M} f_j^2 \, s(j)}{\sqrt{\sum_{j=1}^{M} s(j) \, \sum_{j=1}^{M} f_j^4 \, s(j)}}$
G factor	$F_{10} = \frac{F_6}{F_5}$
Third moment 1	$F_{11} = \frac{\sum_{j=1}^{M} (f_j - F_5)^3 \, s(j)}{M \, F_6^3}$
Fourth moment 1	$F_{12} = \frac{\sum_{j=1}^{M} (f_j - F_5)^4 \, s(j)}{M \, F_6^4}$
H factor	$F_{13} = \frac{\sum_{j=1}^{M} (f_j - F_5)^{1/2} \, s(j)}{M \, \sqrt{F_6}}$
J factor	$F_{14} = \frac{(F_7 + F_8)}{F_1}$

At this point, it is important to mention that, in the case of the training process, every synthetic signal is generated with a duration of 300 ms, and the feature estimation is performed over the complete signal. In the case of the real signals, they present different durations: if the length of the real signal is less or equal to 300 ms, the feature extraction is carried out over the complete signal; if the length of the signal is more than 300 ms, the signal is divided in windows of 300 ms and the statistical features are extracted for every window. Moreover, this proposed approach is intended to be applied offline, even with the real signals.

3.3. Optimized Feature Selection

Considering the three proposed domains (TD, FD and TFD), a total of 74 statistical features are estimated. This is a considerable number of features, and there is no guarantee that all of them provide valuable information regarding the PQD behavior. This is why it is necessary to perform an optimization in the feature selection process. For this purpose, the fusion of two different techniques, GA and PCA, is proposed. GA is a heuristic search algorithm based in Darwin's natural selection. This technique has been widely used for solving optimization problems because of its ability for minimizing estimation errors. GA requires an objective function that will be the one in charge of defining the goodness of fit (GOF) in the optimization task. In this work, the objective function for the GA is directly stated by the PCA, a mathematical procedure that allows performing a reduction in the dimensionality of a problem, preserving the variability of the data. To assess the variability that has been preserved by the PCA, the data variance is used, and it is precisely this value of the parameter that will be used for the GA to perform the optimization task. The complete optimized feature selection is carried out following the procedure proposed in [38] and illustrated in Figure 4 as described below:

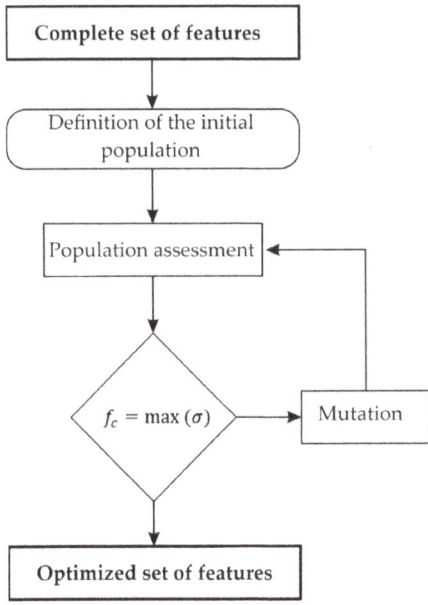

Figure 4. Flow chart for the GA implementation.

Stage 1: Definition of the initial population. It is considered that the population that will be held by the GA is composed of a logical vector that counts with a total of 74 chromosomes, where every chromosome represents each one of the statistical features previously estimated. A chromosome takes a value of zero if the statistical feature that represents is not considered in the evaluation process, and it takes a value of one if the statistical feature is being considered in the analysis. Thus, the initial population is randomly generated by considering that at least one of the elements contained in the logical vector has to be selected to be evaluated; also, more than one element can be evaluated. Once this task has been fulfilled, the procedure goes to stage 2.

Stage 2: Population assessment. At this point, the fitness function of the GA must be selected to assess the performance of each individual. In this particular case, the fitness function is defined in terms of the accumulation of the data variance. This cumulative variance is calculated using the PCA, and the fitness function comprises the cumulative variance of the two and three first principal components. In this sense, the optimization problem that must be solved by the GA consists of searching for the specific statistical features that maximize the cumulative data variance delivered by the PCA. Once the whole population is evaluated, the condition of best features obtained is analyzed; therefore, the next stage is 4.

Stage 3: Generation of a new population. The GA has two operations that allow to generate a new population preserving the values that positively contribute to reach the optimization goal. These operations are the crossover and the mutation. Here, the common single-point crossover operator and the roulette wheel selection are in charge of generating this new population. In this way, it is possible to take the chromosomes of the previous population that present the highest fitting values (higher data variance), and keep them for the new population. Also, to prevent stagnation and to provide the new population with fitness variability, the mutation operation is applied using a Gaussian distribution. Next, the new population has to be evaluated; thus, the algorithm continues in stage 2.

Stage 4: Stop criteria. There are two different constrains that determine if the GA must finish its execution. The first one occurs when the optimization problem is solved and the GA finds the features that reach the highest maximization of the data variance; the second one consists on reaching a maximum number of generations (iterations). When one of the stop criteria is reached, the GA delivers the optimized set of features and the iterative process finishes; otherwise, the process is iteratively repeated until one of the stop criteria is reached. If the stop criteria are not met, then the algorithm continues in stage 3.

The described procedure is applied to each domain separately; therefore, three optimized feature sets are obtained: one for the TD, other for the FD and a third one for the TFD. Then, the feature learning step only receives the sets of features that reached the maximum cumulative variance. Therefore, as a result of the optimized feature selection, the dimensionality of each one of the domains has been reduced. This situation is helpful for the next steps in order to obtain a better characterization of each disturbance.

3.4. Feature Learning

The feature learning stage is performed by means of using the SOM unsupervised algorithm, and the objective of this stage lies in modeling those selected sets of features that better characterize each of the evaluated conditions for the three domains of analysis, TD, FD and TFD. In this regard, different SOM neuron grids are generated, as many feature matrices are available, where there exist three available feature matrices that characterize each one of the evaluated conditions. Therefore, several SOM neuron grids are generated with a pre-defined number of neurons, i.e., defined with 100 neurons over a 10×10 grid, and then each one of the available feature matrices is subjected to the feature learning. Thereby, the resulting SOM neuron grids may represent each one of the different evaluated conditions (healthy or normal, sag or swell voltages, transients like impulsive and oscillatory, voltage fluctuations and harmonic distortion) and the original d-dimensional space of the input feature spaces are then represented into a 2-dimensional neuron grid. Once the feature learning is carried out, for each SOM neuron grid model, the pre-defined neurons known as matching unit (MU) are adapted to the input feature spaces or characteristic feature matrices preserving the topological properties that represent a high-performance feature characterization of the assessed conditions.

3.5. Classification

The idea of performing an optimized feature selection and then the modeling of the disturbances under evaluation is to carry out the classification process as simply as possible. In sense, the use of a simple softmax layer neural network to perform the multicategory classification is proposed. Therefore, the input layer of the neural network receives the three SOM neuron grid models for each one of the studied conditions and the output layer of the softmax network is composed of six neurons representing six different categories that correspond to each one of the conditions under test; that is; healthy or normal, sag or swell voltages, transients, voltage fluctuations and harmonic distortion. This approach is based on a probability function and the category with the highest probability is delivered as result. These probabilities are calculated using the mathematical expression shown in (5).

$$P(x \in C_m) = \frac{e^{W_m A}}{\sum_{l=1}^{N} e^{W_l A}} \quad (5)$$

where x is the input matrix with the SOM neuron grid models, C_m is the m-th category, W_m is the weight for the m-th neuron, A is the activation of the m-th neuron, and N is the number of categories.

The purpose of this block is to determine if an electrical signal presents a PQD; therefore, the output of the classifier is the PQ disturbance detection between the healthy or normal, sag or swell voltages, transients, voltage fluctuations and harmonic distortion conditions and it allows for determining whether or not a signal is contaminated. When a specific signal is introduced as input of the proposed methodology, it follows the complete described scheme, and the signal is classified in one of the 6 categories: healthy, sag, swell, transients, fluctuations or harmonics. It is important to mention that the IEEE standard 1159–2019 states that a transient is an event that is undesirable but momentary in nature and it classifies a transient event into two categories: impulsive and oscillatory. Since it has been mentioned that, in this work, both the impulsive transient and the oscillatory transient are treated as only one type of PQD, when one of these disturbances is detected, the classifier delivers *transients* as output, indicating that it can be impulsive or oscillatory.

In the design of a specific electric machine, such as wind generators, it is expected that the delivered electric signals can be classified as healthy; otherwise, it is an indicator of some problem that must be corrected in the design or the operation of the machine. Hence, the PQ disturbance detection allows for taking actions to improve the design of the complete system and increase the reliability of the same.

4. Results and Discussions

4.1. Database and Multi-Domain Feature Estimation

The proposed PQ monitoring strategy, which allows for the identification of six different electrical conditions of electrical signals (healthy or normal, sag or swell voltages, transients, voltage fluctuations and harmonic distortion), is developed under Matlab 2020a software by means of using and programming the pre-loaded functions, and also, by means of using the SOM Toolbox for Matlab [39]. Thus, the proposed PQ monitoring strategy is designed and trained by taking into account only synthetic signals and then evaluated by analyzing two different datasets of real signals where the first dataset belongs to the IEEE 1159.3 working group [37] and the second one belongs to real signals are acquired from a 30-MW wind park located in northern Spain.

Hence, regarding the proposed method, a set of synthetic signals is generated as above described in order to produce different electrical signals that fulfill to the corresponding standard definitions; thereby, the generated synthetic signals belong to a normal condition or healthy condition, and five different disturbances such as sag, swell, fluctuation, harmonic and impulsive. In this regard, each synthetic signal was generated during 100 s by considering a sampling frequency of 8 kHz and 50 Hz as the fundamental frequency. In Figure 5a–f, are shown different electrical signals that are synthetically generated and that belong to evaluated conditions: healthy or normal, sag or swell voltages, transients, voltage fluctuations and harmonic distortion, respectively.

Subsequently, each one of the synthetic signals is characterized by means of applying a multi-domain feature estimation that leads to the signal characterization in three different domains, that is, TD, FD and TFD. Hence, aiming to achieve the multi-domain feature estimation and to obtain a consecutive set of samples, each synthetic signal was segmented into 333 equal parts of approximately 0.3 s that comprises around 15 cycles. In this sense, the multi-domain feature estimation is individually applied to each available signal and for the TD is estimated a set of 15 statistical time-domain features from each segmented part; as a result, a characteristic TD feature matrix that is composed of 15 statistical features with 333 consecutive samples is obtained. For the FD, the fast Fourier transform is computed from each segmented part and then a set of 14 statistical features is calculated from each resulting frequency spectra; as a result, a characteristic FD feature matrix that comprises 14 statistical features with 333 consecutive samples is generated. For the TFD, each segmented part is analyzed through the empirical mode decomposition technique in order to perform the signal decomposition. Then, the first three resulting intrinsic mode functions are separately characterized by a set of 15 statistical time-domain features; as a result, a characteristic TFD feature matrix that is formed by 45 statistical features with 333 samples is obtained. Consequently, each evaluated condition is characterized by three different feature matrices that contain significant information represented in three different domains, TD, FD and TFD.

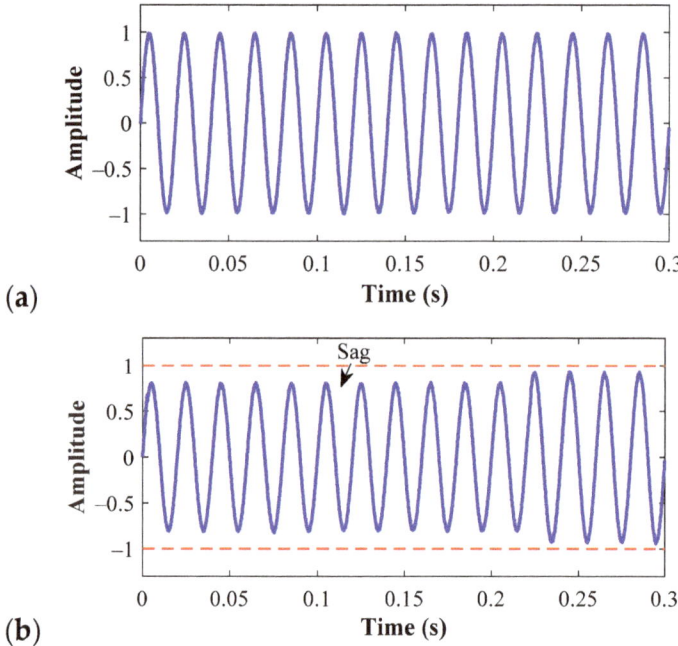

Figure 5. *Cont.*

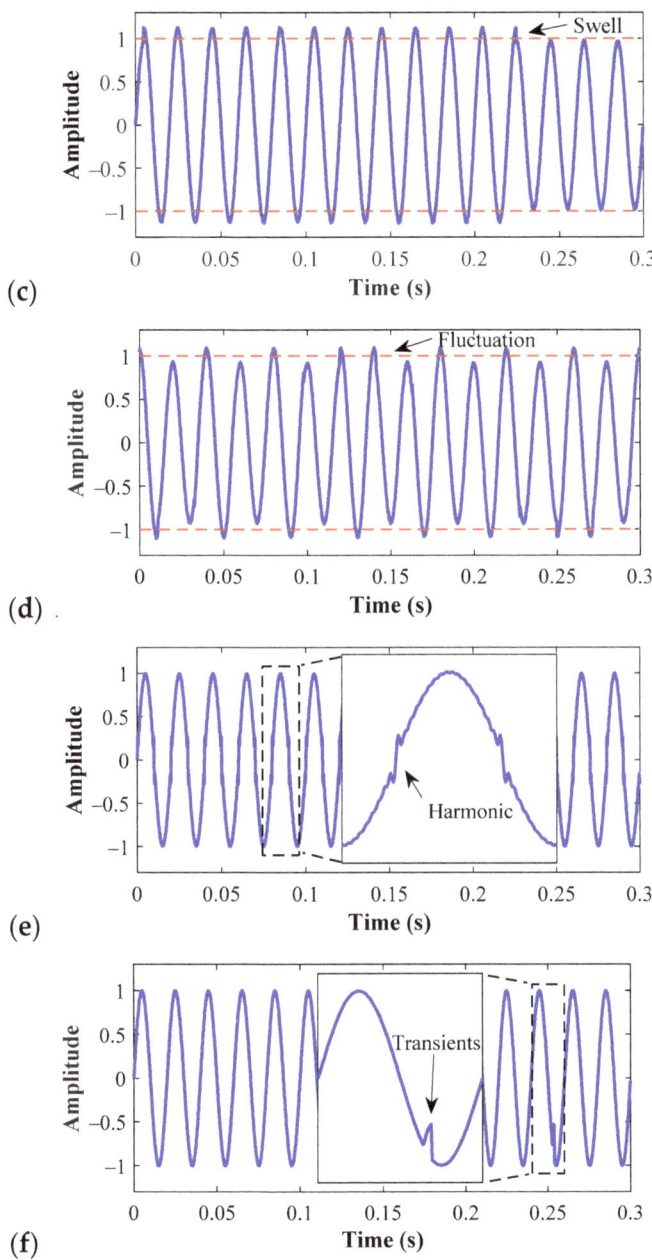

Figure 5. Set of different electrical signals that are synthetically generated and that belong to evaluated conditions: (**a**) healthy or normal, (**b**) sag voltage, (**c**) swell voltage, (**d**) voltage fluctuations, (**e**) harmonic distortion and (**f**) transients.

4.2. Optimized Feature Selection

Afterward, the optimized feature selection stage is carried out and applied to each evaluated condition. Specifically, such optimized feature selection is individually performed to each characteristic feature matrix, aiming to select and retain those features that are more significant and that better represent each of the analyzed domains, TD, FD and TFD. In this regard, the feature selection searching structure is designed based on a GA–PCA approach that evaluates the combination of different features and estimates the cumulative data variance in the first two PCs by means of the PCA. The combination of features is performed by the GA and the feature selection stops by two criteria: (i) maximization of the fitness function (achieve the maximum data variance) and (ii) reach the maximum number of generations. For this application, all combinations of selected features reached maximum data variance higher than 95%; thus, since the optimize feature stage is individually applied to each evaluated condition for each analyzed domain, in Table 4 the results obtained by the GA–PCA searching structure are summarized. As shown in Table 4, for each evaluated condition, a specific subset of features is selected. From these selected subsets of features, it must be highlighted that each evaluated condition is represented by a meaningful subset of features; i.e., for the TD, the voltage sag is characterized by the features number 3 and 11 that correspond with the *RMS* and the *impulse factor*, the voltage fluctuation is characterized by the features number 5 and 15 which correspond with the *standard deviation* and the *fifth moment*; whereas the harmonic distortion is well-characterized by the features number 2, 3, 5 and 14 that are the *maximum* value, the RMS, the *standard deviation* and the *sixth moment*; additionally, it should be mentioned that the statistical features lead to a high-performance characterization of studied electrical disturbances because of the capability of modeling trends and changes in signals. Although the feature selection is individually applied to each assessed condition, the final subsets of selected features are composed by including all the selected features for each analyzed domain. That is, for the TD, the optimal selected features are the subset consisting of 9 features which numbers are 2, 3, 4, 5, 7, 11, 12, 14 and 15. Accordingly, the optimal subsets of features are composed by 9 features for the TD, 8 features for the FD and 16 features for the TFD, precisely, from the original set of 74 features are selected 33 of them.

Table 4. Resulting feature selection achieved by the GA–PCA selection structure applied to each evaluated condition for each analyzed domain with TD = 15, FD = 14 and TFD = 45, where, $\mathbf{TD} \in \mathbb{R}^{TD}$, $\mathbf{FD} \in \mathbb{R}^{FD}$ and $\mathbf{TFD} \in \mathbb{R}^{TFD}$.

Condition	Domain of Analysis		
	TD	FD	TFD
Normal	2, 12	3, 10	18, 19, 20, 21, 33, 34, 35, 36, 39
Sag	3, 11	3, 6	4, 15, 24
Swell	4, 5	12, 14	8, 32
Fluctuation	5, 15	4, 6	15, 31
Harmonic	2, 3, 5, 14	4, 5	21, 26
Transients	4, 7	2, 12	21, 35
Selected features	2, 3, 4, 5, 7, 11, 12, 14, 15	2, 3, 4, 5, 6, 10, 12, 14	4, 8, 15, 18, 19, 20, 21, 24, 26, 31, 32, 33, 34, 35, 36, 39

To validate the optimal feature selection procedure, the characteristic features matrices for all considered conditions in the FD are analyzed through the PCA technique. That is, the original 14 statistical features from FD are subjected to a linear transformation and are projected into a 2-d feature space to visualize the data distribution; thus, in Figure 6a, different clusters that represent all the considered conditions are projected. On the other hand, the PCA technique is also used to analyze the data distribution for all considered conditions by taking into account only the subset of selected features for the FD (features number 2, 3, 4, 5, 6, 10, 12, 14); thereby, in Figure 6b, different clusters are projected for all considered conditions and as it is appreciated an improved class separation is achieved by analyzing those selected features for the FD.

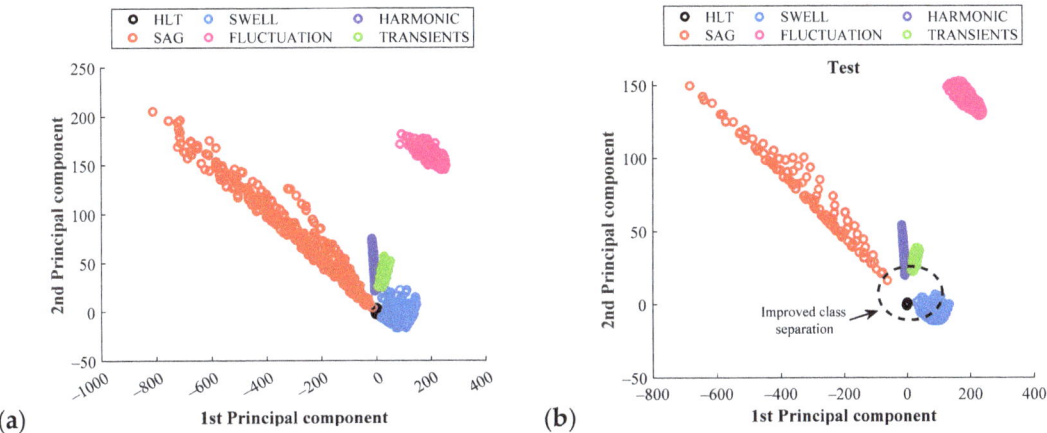

Figure 6. 2-*d* visual representation of the data distribution for all the assessed conditions achieved by the PCA technique during the analysis of each characteristic feature matrices for: (**a**) the estimated features for FD and (**b**) the subset of selected features for FD.

4.3. Feature Learning

Subsequently, the feature learning stage is performed by generating as many SOM as many feature matrices are available, where the $N = 100$ number of predefined neurons, in a 10×10 grid, are randomly initialized and then automatically adapts to the corresponding input feature space under evaluation. As a result, for each one of the studied conditions, three SOM neuron grid models containing its topology are obtained. The advantage of using SOM neuron grids is that a self-adaptation to data distribution of input feature space is achieved. Also, such modeling allows for retaining the topology of the modeled data for the evaluated conditions: healthy or normal, sag or swell voltages, transients, voltage fluctuations and harmonic distortion. In this sense, during the feature learning procedure, the quantization error ($\overline{E}_q$) and the topological error ($\overline{E}_t$) are measured and, as above mentioned, the $\overline{E}_q$ depicts the accuracy of the data representation, and this value is achieved as the mean distance from each available measurement to its BMU; whereas, the $\overline{E}_t$ allows assessing the topology preservation of the data. For both values, $\overline{E}_q$ and $\overline{E}_t$, achieving small values is desired. Table 5 summarizes the achieved errors, $\overline{E}_q$ and $\overline{E}_t$, during the feature learning of the characteristic feature matrices for each considered condition by taking into account the subsets of selected features for each corresponding domain of analysis and, also under a fusion approach where three domains of analysis are considered together for the learning process. As it can be seen in Table 5, for the TD, the conditions of healthy, flicker and impulsive show $\overline{E}_t$ values near to zero describing a high preservation of the data topology; meanwhile, for the conditions of sag, swell and harmonics the $\overline{E}_t$ values are around 0.3 ± 0.15, approximately. Although for some evaluated conditions are obtained $\overline{E}_t$ values around or near to 0.5, the modeled SOM neuron grids may show an excellent performance shows due to precision errors being small.

Table 5. Achieved values of $\overline{E}_q$ and $\overline{E}_t$ resulting from the feature learning procedure performed by the proposed SOM neuron grid models.

Condition	Domain of Analysis						Fusion Approach (TD+TF+TFD)	
	TD		FD		TFD			
	$\overline{E}_q$	$\overline{E}_t$	$\overline{E}_q$	$\overline{E}_t$	$\overline{E}_q$	$\overline{E}_t$	$\overline{E}_q$	$\overline{E}_t$
Healthy	1.2730	0.0259	0.7889	0.0144	1.7646	0.0202	3.4177	0.0115
Sag	9.8701	0.2075	9.9301	0.3862	81.85	0.3833	114.533	0.0951
Swell	3.1649	0.3084	4.0235	0.1095	34.135	0.3919	52.741	0.2421
Flicker	3.9299	0.0922	2.8075	0.2911	4.7213	0.1758	15.105	0.0403
Harmonics	1.0924	0.5043	0.6608	0.2824	31.6633	0.3343	37.2256	0.2911
Transients	1.3996	0.0720	1.1745	0.0403	485.131	0.6455	483.8992	0.6023

In order to interpret and to understand the results of the feature learning procedure, all the SOM neuron grid models are projected into a 2-d space by means of the T-SNE technique. In Figure 7a–c, are shown such 2-d representations that are carried out by considering all evaluated conditions but they are performed separately for each analyzed domain, TD, FD and TFD, respectively. As can be appreciated, most of the clusters that appear in Figure 7a,b are almost well-separated among them; notwithstanding, it is observed in Figure 7a that the sag, swell and fluctuations conditions appear very close to each other. This situation is more or less expected, since the behavior in the TD of these three disturbances is very similar: they present amplitude variations in the peak values of the voltage signal. Hence, if only the TD analysis is used, it is prone to failure in the identification of these types of disturbances. This situation is corrected when the FD is used and the sag, swell and healthy signals are now clearly separated (see Figure 7b). However, in the FD, the harmonic and transients conditions are overlapped. Again, this result can be explained by the fact that high harmonic contamination causes a severe waveform distortion and introduces unexpected peaks that may be considered as periodic transients. The worst cluster separation appears in the TFD (see Figure 7c), where a severe cluster overlapping is observed. In this case, the overlap among clusters can be associated with the use of the EMD, because this technique may suffer mode mixing and the behavior of a disturbance can be observed in more than one IMF. On the other hand, although the clusters of Figure 7c appear overlapped among them, the consideration of all SOM neuron grid models from TF, FD and TFD may lead to clear separation between all considered classes, remembering that each class represents a PQD. This statement is considered in this proposed approach, thereby, a 2-d visual representation is also performed by the T-SNE technique by analyzing the three domains of analysis, TD, FD and TFD, for all considered conditions; thus, in Figure 8 different clusters that appear clearly separated among them are shown. Then, even though some disturbances may have similar behaviors in one domain, they are different in other domains, and by using a multi-domain approach it is possible to differentiate every disturbance in a better way. It should be mentioned regarding Figure 8 that the contribution of different SOM neuron grids that are modeled through statistical features in different domains leads to a high-performance characterization of data that represents the evaluated conditions.

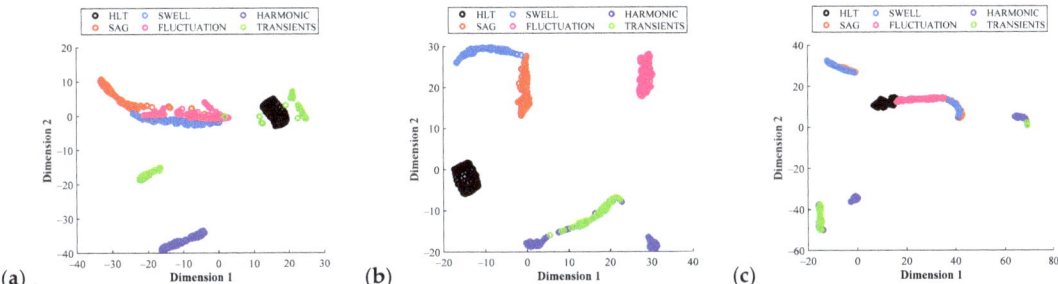

Figure 7. 2-*d* visual representation of the data distribution performed by the T-SNE technique over the resulting SOM neuron grid models for all considered conditions when analyzing: (**a**) SOM neuron grids models for TD, (**b**) SOM neuron grids models for FD and (**c**) SOM neuron grids models for TFD.

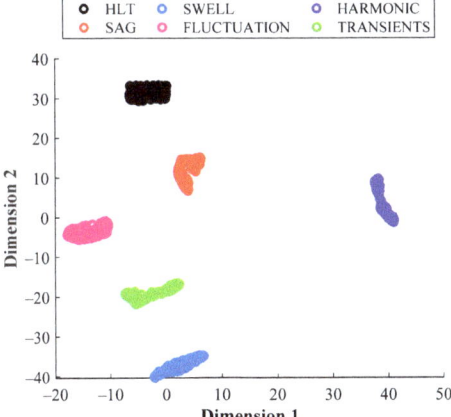

Figure 8. 2-*d* visual representation of the data distribution performed by the T-SNE technique over the resulting SOM neuron grid models for all considered conditions when analyzing all SOM neuron grid models from the three analyzed domains, TD, FD and TFD.

4.4. Evaluation and Classification of Synthetic Signals

Lastly, to provide the automatic fault diagnosis and to detect the occurrence of PQ disturbances, all the feature spaces mapped into different SOM neuron grid models are concatenated under a feature fusion approach and then evaluated under a single softmax layer that is proposed to achieve the PQ disturbance diagnosis. In Table 6, the global classification rations achieved by the proposed softmax layer during the training and test are summarized; as it is possible to appreciate, low-performance classification ratios are estimated when each one of the analyzed domains is individually evaluated through the proposed softmax layer. On the other side, when the three analyzed domains are considered under the fusion approach, a high-performance classification ratio is accomplished, leading to proper detection and identification of electrical disturbances that may suddenly appear; besides, the signal characterization through different domains contribute to the estimation of meaningful and discriminant patterns that specifically characterizes a specific electrical disturbance.

Table 6. Resulting feature selection achieved by the GA–PCA selection structure applied to each evaluated condition for each analyzed domain.

Feature Domain	Global Classification Ratio	
	Training	Test
TD	78.7%	79.3%
FD	82.8%	84.0%
TFD	55.8%	52.7%
Fusion approach (TD+TF+TFD)	100%	100%

Moreover, despite the fact that the proposed PQ detection approach manages as many models as evaluated conditions, each model is focused on the characterization of a particular pattern that describes each one of the assessed electrical conditions and leads to a high capability of response for its detection. Such capability of response may be calculated in terms of the computational burden, thereby, over an Intel Core i7-4770K @3.50GHz CPU, the execution of the proposed algorithm in Matlab 2020a takes less than 350 ms for all evaluated conditions.

4.5. Evaluation and Classification of Real Signals

Finally, in order to validate the effectiveness of the proposed PQ detection approach, different real signals are analyzed through the proposed strategy in order to search and identify the occurrence of disturbances. In this sense, as previously mentioned, two different experimental datasets are analyzed, the first is the dataset provided by the IEEE 1159.3 working group and, the second one belongs to real signals that are acquired from a 30-MW wind park located in northern Spain. Different PQ disturbances were identified after analyzing these datasets through the proposed method, thus, the first parameter to take into account for the detection of events is the abrupt change in the $\overline{E}_q$ value of the SOM neuron grid that represents the normal condition. In this sense, it is important to recall that the SOM is a technique for novelty detection, i.e., it informs when something different from the "normal" behavior occurs. In this particular case, the normality represents a healthy signal; therefore, the SOM delivers an alert when a PQD is found in the electric signal. To demonstrate this situation, the signal presented in Figure 9a is analyzed with the proposed methodology. By making a zoom to the region squared in Figure 9a, it is possible to observe that a voltage swell is present in the signal (see Figure 9b). In Figure 10, the achieved $\overline{E}_q$ for the SOM of the six conditions (PQD) are presented when the signal with the voltage swell is analyzed. Figure 10a represents the value of the SOM model for the healthy signal; Figure 10b is the value of the SOM model for the sag condition; Figure 10c is the value of the SOM model for the swell condition; Figure 10d is the value of the SOM model for the fluctuation condition; Figure 10e is the value of the SOM model for the harmonics condition and; Figure 10f is the value of the SOM model for the transients condition. All the graphics shown in Figure 10 are the qualitative representations of the achieved $\overline{E}_q$ during the analysis of a real signal. From Figure 10a,b,d–f it is possible to appreciate that an abrupt increase appears for the sample number 100; a situation that indicates that the normal condition has changed, i.e., a PQD has been detected. However, in this case, the fact that the $\overline{E}_q$ presents a raising in its value implies that the detected disturbance do not correspond with the one that has been modeled by this specific SOM. On the other hand, in Figure 10c such $\overline{E}_q$ value presents a decrease since the evaluated sample has similar topological properties with the SOM neuron grid that models the swell condition. This is a correct performance and identification of the PQD because, as observed in Figure 9b, a swell condition appears in the signal.

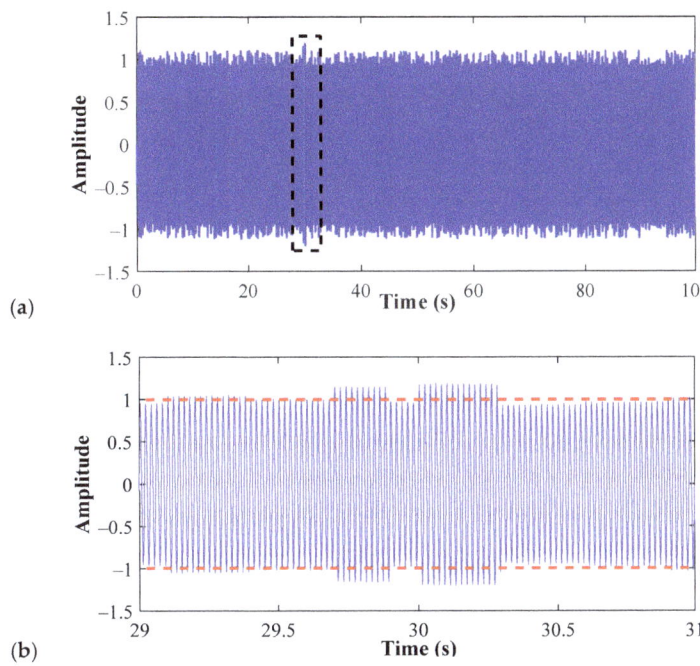

Figure 9. Real signal analyzed through the proposed PQ detection strategy: (**a**) representation of 100 s of the analyzed signal and (**b**) zoom over the near area where the detection of swell is presented.

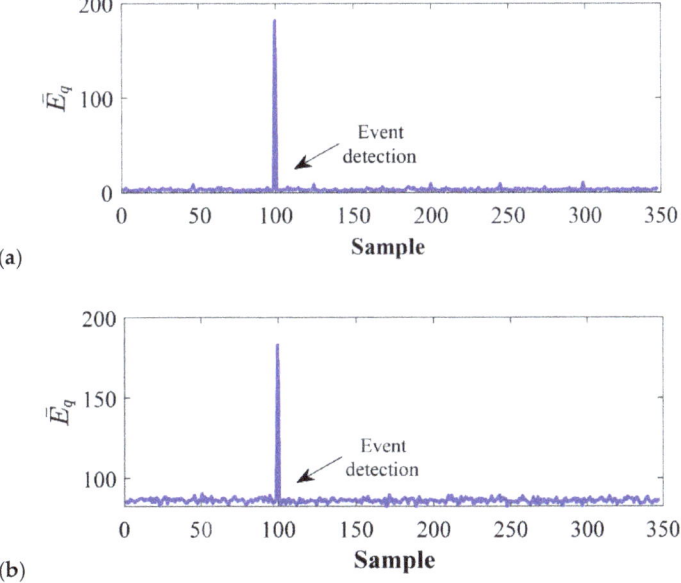

Figure 10. *Cont.*

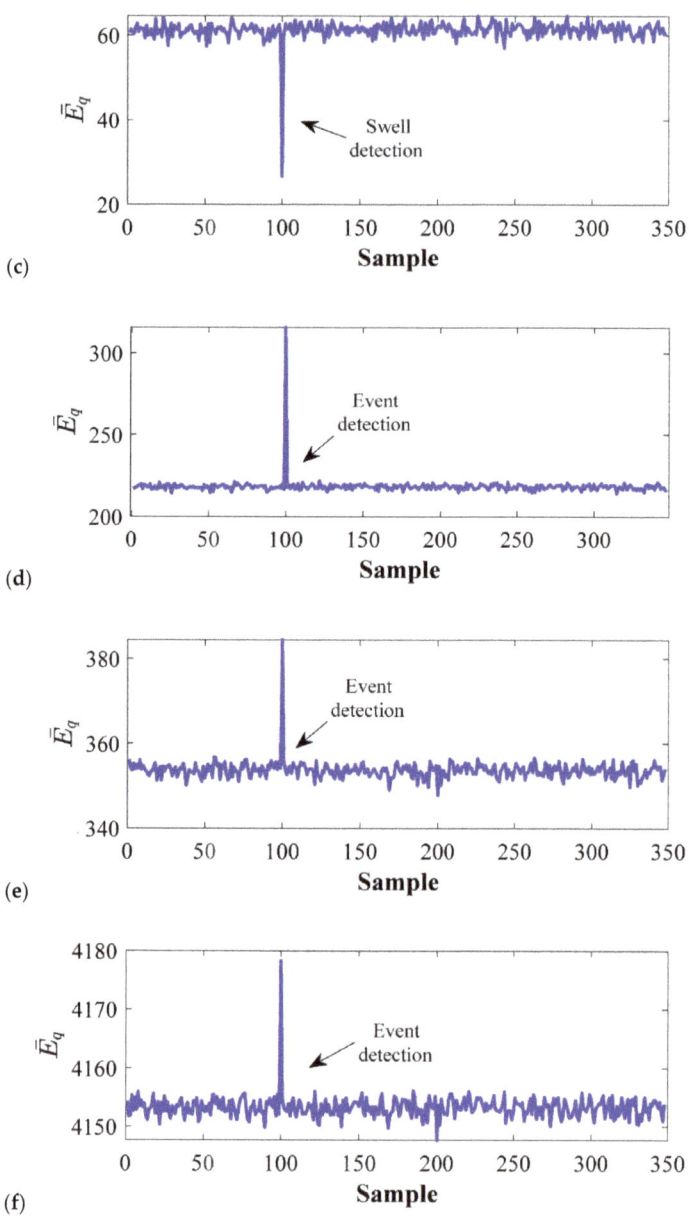

Figure 10. Achieved quantization error, $\overline{E}_q$, during the assessment of a real signal over the SOM neuron grids that models the conditions of: (**a**) normal condition, (**b**) sag, (**c**) swell, (**d**) fluctuation, (**e**) harmonic and (**f**) transients.

5. Conclusions

Due to the recent issues associated with air pollution and the scarcity of fossil fuels, renewable sources are an attractive alternative for energy generation. Therefore, it is necessary to properly design the electric machines that are used in this type of generation to ensure a robust and reliable power supply. One of the issues that must be considered in the design of electric generators used in wind turbines is that the PQ remains within acceptable levels; thus, the methodologies for detecting disturbances in electric signals are of great interest in this area.

The results reported in this work show that when only one individual domain (time, frequency or time-frequency) is used for PQ analysis, the classification of the disturbances in the grid presents a low performance. This situation relies on the fact that there are many disturbances that present similar behaviors in a given domain. Nevertheless, it has been demonstrated that when the multi-domain approach is implemented, the classification results are improved, because the similitudes that exist in one domain do not appear in a different one. However, when a multidomain approach is used, the number of features that describe a singular PQD considerably grows. Hence, the detection and classification tasks become more complicated and require of a high computational effort. In this sense, the proposed methodology proved that there are features that do not provide important information and, therefore, they can be discarded to reduce the dimensionality of the problem and to facilitate the classification task. Although that optimized feature selection may seem trivial, it is important to perform a proper selection of the features and be careful of not losing the features that provide relevant information. Thus, it is necessary to count with an indicator of the goodness of the selection. Additionally, it is important to carry out this task in an ordinated way to ensure the obtaining of a good result. In this sense, GA provides this structured feature searching, whereas the PCA brings the indicator of the goodness of the selection. Moreover, to make the classification task even simpler, SOM proved to be effective in the modeling of PQD, since they provide a 2-dimensional representation that is different for each disturbance. Finally, it is important to recall that the methodology is trained using synthetic signals; however, the approach is robust enough to also work with real signals. The proposed methodology allowed for detecting a series of PQD that occurred in a wind farm, proving effective in the detection of anomalies associated with wind generation. Then, by finding the existence of PQD that can produce a malfunction of the components of the machine, the proposed methodology aims to be a tool for detecting PQD and improving the reliability of the wind turbine by preventing the failure of any of its components. Moreover, having a priori knowledge of the disturbances related to wind generators, it is possible to take into consideration the design stage to prevent the appearance of these issues. Finally, if the disturbance appears when the machine is already working, with the proposed methodology, it is possible to take actions for corrective maintenance in order to ensure the proper working of all the grid elements.

Author Contributions: Conceptualization, D.A.E.-O. and R.A.O.-R.; methodology, J.J.S.-D., D.A.E.-O. and J.A.A.-D.; validation, D.A.E.-O., and J.J.S.-D.; formal analysis, J.J.S.-D. and R.A.O.-R.; investigation, J.A.A.-D. and D.M.-S.; resources, J.A.A.-D.; data curation, D.A.E.-O. and D.M.-S.; writing—original draft preparation, D.A.E.-O. and J.J.S.-D.; writing—review and editing, J.J.S.-D., R.A.O.-R. and J.A.A.-D.; visualization, D.A.E.-O. and D.M.-S.; supervision, D.M.-S., R.A.O.-R. and J.A.A.-D.; project administration, R.A.O.-R. and J.A.A.-D.; funding acquisition, J.A.A.-D. All authors have read and agreed to the published version of the manuscript.

Funding: This research was partially funded by FONDEC-UAQ 2020 FIN202011 project. It was also supported by the Spanish 'Ministerio de Ciencia Innovación y Universidades' and FEDER program in the framework of the 'Proyectos de I+D de Generación de Conocimiento del Programa Estatal de Generación de Conocimiento y Fortalecimiento Científico y Tecnológico del Sistema de I+D+i, Subprograma Estatal de Generación de Conocimiento' (ref: PGC2018-095747-B-I00).

Data Availability Statement: Publicly available datasets were analyzed in this study. This data can be found here: [https://grouper.ieee.org/groups/1159/3/docs.html (accessed on 22 December 2021)].

Conflicts of Interest: The authors declare no conflict of interest.

References

1. Shahbaz, M.; Raghutla, C.; Chittedi, K.R.; Jiao, Z.; Vo, X.V. The effect of renewable energy consumption on economic growth: Evidence from the renewable energy country attractive index. *Energy* **2020**, *207*, 118162. [CrossRef]
2. Kirsch, S. Running out? Rethinking resource depletion. *Extr. Ind. Soc.* **2020**, *7*, 838–840. [CrossRef]
3. Kalair, A.; Abas, N.; Saleem, M.S.; Kalair, A.R.; Khan, N. Role of energy storage systems in energy transition from fossil fuels to renewables. *Energy Storage* **2021**, *3*, e135. [CrossRef]
4. REN 21. *Renewables 2021 Global Status Report*; REN21 Secretariat: Paris, France, 2021; ISBN 978-3-948393-03-8.
5. Nazir, M.S.; Alturise, F.; Alshmrany, S.; Nazir, H.; Bilal, M.; Abdalla, A.N.; Sanjeevikumar, P.; Ali, Z.M. Wind generation forecasting methods and proliferation of artificial neural network: A review of five years research trend. *Sustainability* **2020**, *12*, 3778. [CrossRef]
6. Ueckerdt, F.; Brecha, R.; Luderer, G. Analyzing major challenges of wind and solar variability in power systems. *Renew. Energy* **2015**, *81*, 1–10. [CrossRef]
7. Liu, D.; Liu, Y.; Sun, K. Policy impact of cancellation of wind and photovoltaic subsidy on power generation companies in China. *Renew. Energy* **2021**, *177*, 134–147. [CrossRef]
8. Mahela, O.P.; Khan, B.; Alhelou, H.H.; Siano, P. Power quality assessment and event detection in distribution network with wind energy penetration using stockwell transform and fuzzy clustering. *IEEE Trans. Ind. Inform.* **2020**, *16*, 6922–6932. [CrossRef]
9. Liu, H.; Hu, H.; Chen, H.; Zhang, L.; Xing, Y. Fast and flexible selective harmonic extraction methods based on the generalized discrete Fourier transform. *IEEE Trans. Power Electron.* **2018**, *33*, 3484–3496. [CrossRef]
10. Hou, R.; Wu, J.; Song, H.; Qu, Y.; Xu, D. Applying directly modified RDFT method in active power filter for the power quality improvement of the weak power grid. *Energies* **2020**, *13*, 4884. [CrossRef]
11. Dhoriyani, S.L.; Kundu, P. Comparative Group THD Analysis of Power Quality Disturbances using FFT and STFT. In Proceedings of the 2020 IEEE First International Conference on Smart Technologies for Power, Energy and Control (STPEC), Nagpur, India, 25–26 September 2020; The Institute of Electrial and Electronics Engineers: Nagpur, India, 2020.
12. Shamachurn, H. Assessing the performance of a modified S-transform with probabilistic neural network, support vector machine and nearest neighbour classifiers for single and multiple power quality disturbances identification. *Neural Comput. Appl.* **2019**, *31*, 1041–1060. [CrossRef]
13. Eristi, B.; Yildirim, O.; Eristi, H.; Demir, Y. A new embedded power quality event classification system based on the wavelet transform. *Int. Trans. Electr. Energy Syst.* **2018**, *28*, e2597. [CrossRef]
14. Malik, H.; Kaushal, P.; Srivastava, S. A hybrid intelligent model for power quality disturbance classification. *Appl. Artif. Intell. Tech. Eng.* **2019**, *697*, 55–63.
15. Sahani, M.; Dash, P.K. Automatic power quality events recognition based on Hilbert Huang transform and weighted bidirectional extreme learning machine. *IEEE Trans. Ind. Inform.* **2018**, *14*, 3849–3858. [CrossRef]
16. Nagata, E.A.; Ferreira, D.D.; Bollen, M.H.; Barbosa, B.H.; Ribeiro, E.G.; Duque, C.A.; Ribeiro, P.F. Real-time voltage sag detection and classification for power quality diagnostics. *Measurement* **2020**, *164*, 108097. [CrossRef]
17. Das, S.R.; Ray, P.K.; Mohanty, A. Improvement of power quality using hybrid active filter with artificial intelligence techniques. In *Applications of Computing, Automation and Wireless Systems in Electrical Engineering*, 1st ed.; Springer: Singapore, 2019; pp. 393–402.
18. Yılmaz, A.; Küçüker, A.; Bayrak, G.; Ertekin, D.; Shafie-Khah, M.; Guerrero, J.M. An improved automated PQD classification method for distributed generators with hybrid SVM-based approach using un-decimated wavelet transform. *Int. J. Electr. Power Energy Syst.* **2022**, *136*, 107763. [CrossRef]
19. Singh, U.; Singh, S.N. Optimal feature selection via NSGA-II for power quality disturbances classification. *IEEE Trans. Ind. Inform.* **2017**, *14*, 2994–3002. [CrossRef]
20. Sahani, M.; Dash, P.K.; Samal, D. A real-time power quality events recognition using variational mode decomposition and online-sequential extreme learning machine. *Measurement* **2020**, *157*, 107597. [CrossRef]
21. Rostami, M.; Lotfifard, S. optimal remedial actions in power systems considering wind farm grid codes and UPFC. *IEEE Trans. Ind. Inform.* **2019**, *16*, 7264–7274. [CrossRef]
22. Hussain, J.; Hussain, M.; Raza, S.; Siddique, M. Power quality improvement of grid connected wind energy system using DSTATCOM-BESS. *Int. J. Renew. Energy Res.* **2019**, *9*, 1388–1397.
23. Kececioglu, O.F.; Acikgoz, H.; Yildiz, C.; Gani, A.; Sekkeli, M. Power quality improvement using hybrid passive filter configuration for wind energy systems. *J. Electr. Eng. Technol.* **2017**, *12*, 207–216. [CrossRef]
24. Sahoo, B.; Routray, S.K.; Rout, P.K. Repetitive control and cascaded multilevel inverter with integrated hybrid active filter capability for wind energy conversion system. *Eng. Sci. Technol. Int. J.* **2019**, *22*, 811–826. [CrossRef]
25. Erişti, H.; Yıldırım, Ö.; Erişti, B.; Demir, Y. Optimal feature selection for classification of the power quality events using wavelet transform and least squares support vector machines. *Int. J. Electr. Power Energy Syst.* **2013**, *49*, 95–103. [CrossRef]

26. Chamchuen, S.; Siritaratiwat, A.; Fuangfoo, P.; Suthisopapan, P.; Khunkitti, P. High-Accuracy power quality disturbance classification using the adaptive ABC-PSO as optimal feature selection algorithm. *Energies* **2021**, *14*, 1238. [CrossRef]
27. Liu, Y.; Jin, T.; Mohamed, M.A.; Wang, Q. A Novel Three-Step Classification Approach Based on Time-Dependent Spectral Features for Complex Power Quality Disturbances. *IEEE Trans. Instrum. Meas.* **2021**, *70*, 1–14. [CrossRef]
28. Shen, Y.; Abubakar, M.; Liu, H.; Hussain, F. Power quality disturbance monitoring and classification based on improved PCA and convolution neural network for wind-grid distribution systems. *Energies* **2019**, *12*, 1280. [CrossRef]
29. Gonzalez-Abreu, A.-D.; Delgado-Prieto, M.; Osornio-Rios, R.-A.; Saucedo-Dorantes, J.-J.; Romero-Troncoso, R.-D.-J. A Novel Deep Learning-Based Diagnosis Method Applied to Power Quality Disturbances. *Energies* **2021**, *14*, 2839. [CrossRef]
30. Wang, Y.; Ma, X.; Qian, P. Wind turbine fault detection and identification through PCA-based optimal variable selection. *IEEE Trans. Sustain. Energy* **2018**, *9*, 1627–1635. [CrossRef]
31. Rezamand, M.; Kordestani, M.; Carriveau, R.; Ting, D.S.K.; Saif, M. A new hybrid fault detection method for wind turbine blades using recursive PCA and wavelet-based PDF. *IEEE Sens. J.* **2019**, *20*, 2023–2033. [CrossRef]
32. Rui, H.; Weihao, H.; Nuri, G.; Pengfei, L.; Qi, H.; Zhe, C. High resolution wind speed forecasting based on wavelet decomposed phase space reconstruction and self-organizing map. *Renew. Energy* **2019**, *140*, 17–31.
33. Dipak, K.M.; Sourav, D.; Chiranjib, K.; Nirmal, K.R.; Sivaji, C. Self-organizing feature map based unsupervised technique for detection of partial discharge sources inside electrical substations. *Measurement* **2019**, *147*, 106818.
34. Saucedo-Dorantes, J.J.; Delgado-Prieto, M.; Romero-Troncoso, R.J.; Osornio-Rios, R.A. Multiple-fault detection and identification scheme based on hierarchical self-organizing maps applied to an electric machine. *Appl. Soft Comput.* **2019**, *81*, 105497. [CrossRef]
35. IEEE. Recommended Practice for Monitoring Electric Power Quality. In *IEEE Standard 1159–2019*; The Institute of Electrial and Electronics Engineers: New York, NY, USA, 2019.
36. IEEE. Recommended Practice and Requirements for Harmonic Control in Electric Power Systems. In *IEEE Standard 519–2014*; The Institute of Electrial and Electronics Engineers: New York, NY, USA, 2014.
37. IEEE P1159.3 On-Line Documents. Available online: https://grouper.ieee.org/groups/1159/3/docs.html (accessed on 22 December 2021).
38. Saucedo-Dorantes, J.J.; Jaen-Cuellar, A.Y.; Delgado-Prieto, M.; Romero-Troncoso, R.J.; Osornio-Rios, R.A. Condition monitoring strategy based on an optimized selection of high-dimensional set of hybrid features to diagnose and detect multiple and combined faults in an induction motor. *Measurement* **2021**, *178*, 109404. [CrossRef]
39. Vatanen, T.; Osmala, M.; Raiko, T.; Lagus, K.; Sysi-Aho, M.; Orešič, M.; Honkela, T.; Lähdesmäki, H. Self-organization and missing values in SOM and GTM. *Neurocomputing* **2015**, *147*, 60–70. [CrossRef]

Article

The Structural and Dielectric Properties of $Bi_{3-x}Nd_xTi_{1.5}W_{0.5}O_9$ (x = 0.25, 0.5, 0.75, 1.0)

Sergei V. Zubkov [1,*], **Ivan A. Parinov** [2,*] **and Yulia A. Kuprina** [1,*]

[1] Research Institute of Physics, Southern Federal University, Stachki Ave., 194, 344090 Rostov-on-Don, Russia
[2] I. I. Vorovich Mathematics, Mechanics and Computer Sciences Institute, Southern Federal University, 344090 Rostov-on-Don, Russia
* Correspondence: svzubkov61@mail.ru (S.V.Z.); parinov_ia@mail.ru (I.A.P.); kyprins@rambler.ru (Y.A.K.)

Abstract: A new series of layered perovskite-like oxides $Bi_{3-x}Nd_xTi_{1.5}W_{0.5}O_9$ (x = 0.25, 0.5, 0.75, 1.0) was synthesized by the method of high-temperature solid-state reaction, in which partial substitution of bismuth (Bi) atoms in the dodecahedra of the perovskite layer (*A*-positions) by Nd atoms takes place. X-ray structural studies have shown that all compounds are single-phase and have the structure of Aurivillius phases (APs), with close parameters of orthorhombic unit cells corresponding to space group $A2_1am$. The dependences of the relative permittivity $\varepsilon/\varepsilon_0$ and the tangent of loss $tg\sigma$ at different frequencies on temperature were measured. The piezoelectric constant d_{33} was measured for $Bi_{3-x}Nd_xTi_{1.5}W_{0.5}O_9$ (x = 0.25, 0.5, 0.75) compounds of the synthesized series.

Keywords: Aurivillius phases; $Bi_{3-x}Nd_xTi_{1.5}W_{0.5}O_9$; activation energy E_a; Curie temperature T_C

Citation: Zubkov, S.V.; Parinov, I.A.; Kuprina, Y.A. The Structural and Dielectric Properties of $Bi_{3-x}Nd_xTi_{1.5}W_{0.5}O_9$ (x = 0.25, 0.5, 0.75, 1.0). *Electronics* 2022, 11, 277. https://doi.org/10.3390/electronics11020277

Academic Editors: Tamás Orosz, David Pánek, Anton Rassõlkin and Miklos Kuczmann

Received: 8 December 2021
Accepted: 13 January 2022
Published: 16 January 2022

Publisher's Note: MDPI stays neutral with regard to jurisdictional claims in published maps and institutional affiliations.

Copyright: © 2022 by the authors. Licensee MDPI, Basel, Switzerland. This article is an open access article distributed under the terms and conditions of the Creative Commons Attribution (CC BY) license (https://creativecommons.org/licenses/by/4.0/).

1. Introduction

In 1949, while studying the Bi_2O_3-TiO_2 system, V. Aurivillius established the formation of an oxide: $Bi_4Ti_3O_{12}$ with a perovskite-type structure [1]. Then, within two years, he obtained several more oxides with a similar structure [2,3]. However, at the first stage, V. Aurivillius limited himself to studying only the structure of the compounds obtained. Only ten years later G. Smolenskiy, V. Isupov and A. Agranovskaya [4] discovered the ferroelectric properties of Bi_2PbNbO_9, which belongs to this class of compounds. Subsequently, several tens of Aurivillius phases were obtained, and almost all of them turned out to be ferroelectrics [5–10]. Aurivillius phases (APs) form a large family of bismuth-containing layered perovskite type compounds, with the chemical composition described by the general formula $A_{m-1}Bi_2B_mO_{3m+3}$. The crystal structure of the APs consists of alternating $[Bi_2O_2]^{2+}$ layers separated by *m* perovskite-like layers $[A_{m-1}B_mO_{3m+1}]^{2-}$, where *A* are ions with large radii (Bi^{3+}, Ca^{2+}, Gd^{3+}, Sr^{2+}, Ba^{2+}, Pb^{2+}, Na^+, K^+, Y^{3+}, Ln^{3+} (lanthanides)) and have dodecahedral coordination, while the *B*-positions inside oxygen octahedra are occupied by strongly charged ($\geq 3^+$) cations with a small radius (Ti^{4+}, Nb^{5+}, Ta^{5+}, W^{6+}, Mo^{6+}, Fe^{3+}, Mn^{4+}, Cr^{3+}, Ga^{3+}, etc.). The value of *m* is determined by the number of perovskite layers $[A_{m-1}B_mO_{3m+1}]^{2-}$ located between the fluorite-like layers $[Bi_2O_2]^{2+}$ and can take integer or half-integer values in the range 1–5 (Figure 1).

If *m* is a half-integer number, then in the lattice, there are alternative perovskite layers with *m* differing by 1. For example, at *m* = 1.5, the lattice has an equal number of layers with *m* = 1 and *m* = 2. The value *m* = 1 corresponds, for example, to the compound Bi_2WO_6, *m* = 2 corresponds to Bi_2PbNbO_9, *m* = 3 corresponds to $Bi_4Ti_3O_{12}$, *m* = 4 corresponds to $Bi_4CaTi_4O_{15}$, *m* = 5 corresponds to $Bi_4Sr_2Ti_5O_{18}$.

Positions *A* and *B* can be occupied by the same or by several different atoms. Atomic substitutions in positions *A* and *B* have a significant effect on the electrophysical characteristics of the APs. In particular, there are large changes in the values of dielectric constants, conductivity. Moreover, Curie temperature T_C can also vary within wide limits. Thus, the study of cation-substituted APs plays an important role in the creation of materials for various technological applications.

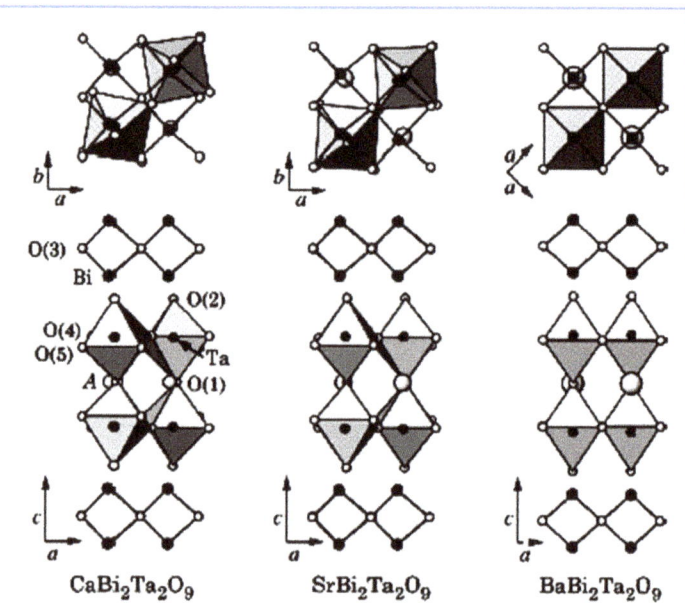

Figure 1. Crystal structure of $A\text{Bi}_2\text{Ta}_2\text{O}_9$, where A = Ca, Sr, Ba.

The structure of $\text{Bi}_2 A_{m-1} B_m \text{O}_{3m+3}$ compounds above the Curie point T_C is tetragonal and belongs to the space group $I4/mmm$. The type of space group below the Curie point T_C depends on the value of the number m. For odd m, the space group of the ferroelectric phase is $B2cb$ or $Pca2_1$, for even m, it is $A2_1am$, and for half-integer m, it is $Cmm2$ or $I2cm$.

This work considers the conditions for the existence of these compounds [11]:

$$t_1 < t = \left[(1.12 R_A + R_O)/\sqrt{2}(R_B + R_O)\right] < t_2, \qquad (1)$$

where R_A, R_B are the cation radii, R_O is the oxygen anion radius, t is the Goldschmidt tolerance factor. The boundary values of the tolerance factor, which determines the possibility of the existence of a compound belonging to the APs, are defined as $t_1 = 0.870$ and $t_2 = 0.985$. A detailed study of the regularities of changes in the Curie temperature of the Aurivillius phases on such parameters as the radii and electronegativity of the A- and B-cations, as well as on the cell parameters, was carried out in [12]. Some anomalies in the properties of layered ferroelectrics $A_{m-1}\text{Bi}_2 B_m \text{O}_{3m+3}$ were also considered [13]. In particular, it was shown that Bi_2O_2 layers have a constricting effect on the layered structure of these compounds, but the strength of such an effect decreases with an increase in the number of perovskite layers. Moreover, it was shown that the Curie temperatures pass through a maximum with increasing distortions of the pseudoperovskite cell in the perovskite-like layer, and the position of the maximum changes with a change in the number of perovskite layers m. Despite the fact that the crystal structure of the APs has been fairly well studied by various methods (X-ray powder diffraction, neutron diffraction, etc.), some aspects related to the distortion of the APs' unit cell from the "ideal" tetragonal system with the space group $I4/mmm$(139), and the reasons for such distortions, are of scientific interest. The structural features of APs, which determine the appearance of ferroelectric properties in these compounds, have also not been sufficiently clarified. Basically, this is attributed to the displacement of the B-ion (Ti^{4+}, Nb^{5+}, Ta^{5+}) from the center of the oxygen octahedron in the perovskite layers. Scientific interest in the synthesis and study of new APs is stimulated by numerous examples of their use in various electronic devices, due to their unique physical properties (piezoelectric, ferroelectric, etc.). They demonstrate low temperature coefficients of dielectric and piezoelectric losses, and low aging temperatures in addition to high Curie temperatures ($T_C \leq 965\ ^\circ C$) [14,15].

In recent years, more attention has been placed on the design and studies of new APs [16–20]. The APs, such as $SrBi_2Nb_2O_9$ (SBN), $SrBi_4Ti_4O_{15}$ (SBTi),$SrBi_2Ta_2O_9$ (SBTa), $La_{0.75}Bi_{3.25}Ti_3O_{12}$ (BLT) and so on, were accepted as excellent materials for the energy independent ferroelectric memory with small access time (FeRAM) [21–25]. Bi_3TiNbO_9 (BTNO) with $m = 2$ that consists of $(Bi_2O_2)^{2+}$ layers between which there are $(BiTiNbO_7)^{2-}$ layers [26] is a promising material for fabricating high temperature piezoelectric sensors because of their very high Curie temperature T_C (914–921 $^\circ C$) [14,15], despite the fact that the piezoelectric modulus of BTNO ceramic is fairly low ($d_{33} < 7\ pC/N$) [27]. Numerous examples [28–42] showed that replacements of atoms in A- and also in B-positions of an AP's crystal lattice led to a change in the structure, the dielectric properties and significantly influenced the polarization processes in these compounds.

The purpose of this study was to investigate the dielectric characteristics when bismuth cation (A-position) is replaced by neodymium ions of the basic composition $Bi_3Ti_{1.5}W_{0.5}O_9$. It was previously observed that the partial replacement of bismuth ions by neodymium cations in the series of perovskite-like Bi-containing oxides Bi_3TiNbO_9, Bi_3TiTaO_9 led to a significant decrease in the phase transition temperature (Curie temperature T_C) and a change in dielectric properties [43].

2. Experimental Section

Polycrystalline samples of APs were synthesized by the solid-phase reaction of the corresponding Bi_2O_3, TiO_2, Nd_2O_3, WO_3. After weighting in accordance with the stoichiometric composition and a thorough grinding of the initial compounds with the addition of ethyl alcohol, the pressed samples were calcined at a temperature of 770 $^\circ C$ for 2 h. The samples were fired in a laboratory muffle furnace in air. Then, the samples were repeatedly ground and pressed into pellets with a diameter of 10 mm and a thickness of 1.0–1.5 mm, followed by the final synthesis of APs at a temperature of 1100 $^\circ C$ (for 2 h).

The X-ray diffraction patterns were recorded on a DRON-3M diffractometer with attachment for powder diffractionand an X-ray tube BSV21-Cu with a Cu X-ray tube. The Cu $K_{\alpha1,\alpha2}$ radiation was separated from the total spectrum with the use of a Ni-filter. The X-ray diffraction patterns were measured in the range of 2θ angles from 10° to 65° with a scan step of 0.02° and an exposure (intensity registration time) of 4 s per point. The analysis of the profiles of the diffraction patterns, the determination of the positions of the lines, their indexing (hkl), and the refinement of the unit cell parameters were performed by using the PCW 2.4 program [44]. For dielectric permittivity and electrical conductivity measurements, on flat surfaces of samples of APs, in the form of disks with a diameter of 10 mm and a thickness of approximately 1 mm, electrodes were deposited, using an Ag-paste annealed at a temperature of 700 $^\circ C$ (for 1 h). The temperature and frequency dependences of the dielectric characteristics were measured using an E7-20 immittance meter in the frequency range from 100 kHz to 1 MHz and at temperatures in the range from room temperature to 900 $^\circ C$. All the samples were poled in an oil bath at 125 $^\circ C$ under 35 kV/cm for 30 min.

3. Results and Discussion

Powder X-ray diffraction patterns of all investigated solid solutions $Bi_{3-x}Nd_xTi_{1.5}W_{0.5}O_9$ ($x = 0.25, 0.5, 0.75, 1.0$) correspond to single-phase APs with $m = 2$, and do not contain additional reflections isostructural to the known perovskite-like oxide $Bi_3Ti_{1.5}W_{0.5}O_9$. It was found that all synthesized APs crystallize in an orthorhombic system with a unit cell space group $A2_1am$(36). The diffraction patterns of all the compounds correspond to the

APs with $m = 2$. Figure 2 shows the experimental powder X-ray diffraction patterns of the studied compounds.

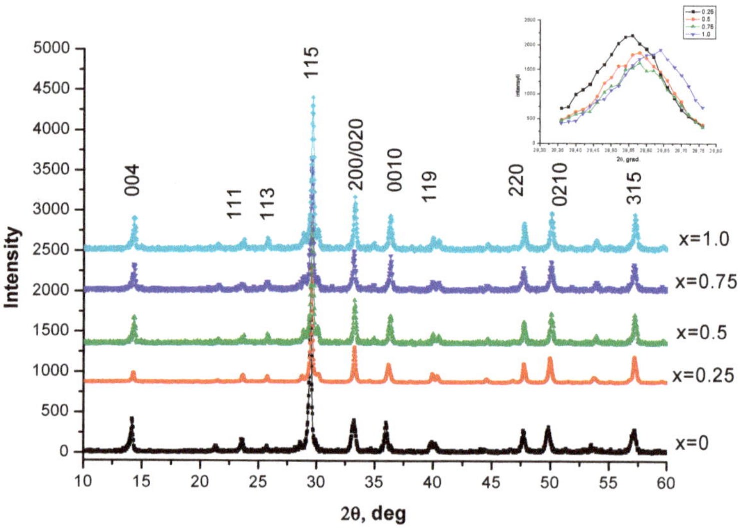

Figure 2. Experimental curve of the X-ray powder diffraction patterns of the $Bi_{3-x}Nd_xTi_{1.5}W_{0.5}O_9$ (x = 0.0, 0.25, 0.5, 0.75, 1.0) compounds.

According to the data of X-ray diffraction, the parameters of the unit cell and the volume of the unit cell were determined; they are given in Table 1.

Table 1. Unit cell parameters a_0, b_0, c_0, V, a_t is the parameter of the tetragonal period, c' is the octahedron height along axis c, $\delta c'$ is the deviation of the unit from the cubic shape, δb is the rhombic distortion.

Compounds	a_0, Å	b_0, Å	c_0, Å	V, Å^3	c', Å	a_t, %	$\delta c'$, %	δb_0, %
$Bi_{2.75}Nd_{0.25}Ti_{1.5}W_{0.5}O_9$	5.3861	5.3742	24.8572	719.51	3.7586	3.8043	−1.2	−0.2
$Bi_{2.5}Nd_{0.5}Ti_{1.5}W_{0.5}O_9$	5.3916	5.3742	24.8421	719.81	3.7263	3.8063	−2.1	−0.3
$Bi_{2.25}Nd_{0.75}Ti_{1.5}W_{0.5}O_9$	5.3977	5.3875	24.8388	722.31	3.7258	3.8131	−2.28	−0.18
$Bi_2NdTi_{1.5}W_{0.5}O_9$	5.4013	5.3903	24.8388	723.17	3.7248	3.8154	−2.28	−0.2

Table 1 also shows the parameters of the orthorhombic δb_0 and tetragonal $\delta c'$ deformation; average tetragonal period a_t, coefficient of tolerance t and the average thickness of one perovskite layer c'; $c' = 3c_0/(8 + 6m)$ is the thickness of a single perovskite-like layer, m is the number of layers, $a_t = (a_0 - b_0)/2\sqrt{2}$ is the average value of the tetragonal period, a_0, b_0, c_0 are the lattice periods, $\delta c' = (c' - a_t)/a_t$ is the deviation of a cell from a cubic shape, that is a lengthening or shortening from a cubic shape, $\delta b_0 = (b_0 - a_0)/a_0$ is the rhombic deformation. The obtained unit cell parameters of the studied APs $Bi_{3-x}Nd_xTi_{1.5}W_{0.5}O_9$ samples (x = 0.25, 0.5, 0.75, 1.0) are close to those determined earlier: a = 5.4018 (2) Å, b = 5.3727 (4) Å, c = 24.9388 (1) Å [23]. In order to obtain the degree of distortion of the ideal structure of perovskite in Nd^{3+}, we determined the tolerance factor t, which is presented in Table 2.

Table 2. Dielectric characteristics of $Bi_{3-x}Nd_xTi_{1.5}W_{0.5}O_9$ (x = 0.25, 0.5, 0.75, 1.0): Curie temperature T_C, piezomodule d_{33}, tolerance factor t, relative permittivity $\varepsilon/\varepsilon_0$, activation energy E_n.

Compounds	T_C, °C	d_{33}, pC/N	t	$\varepsilon/\varepsilon_0$(T) (at 100 kHz)	$E_1/E_2/E_3$, eV
$Bi_{2.75}Nd_{0.25}Ti_{1.5}W_{0.5}O_9$	681	10	0.9778	1000	0.67/0.29/0.06
$Bi_{2.5}Nd_{0.5}Ti_{1.5}W_{0.5}O_9$	637	5	0.9745	500	0.77/0.31/0.1
$Bi_{2.25}Nd_{0.75}Ti_{1.5}W_{0.5}O_9$	617	3.5	0.9713	550	0.65/0.21
$Bi_2NdTi_{1.5}W_{0.5}O_9$	165	0	0.9681	160	-

The tolerance factor t was introduced by Goldschmidt [45] as a geometric criterion that determines the degree of stability and distortion of the crystal structure:

$$t = (R_A + R_O)/\left[\sqrt{2}(R_B + R_O)\right], \quad (2)$$

where R_A and R_B are the radii of cations in positions A and B, respectively; R_O is the ionic radius of oxygen. Values of tolerance factors t for the samples under study are shown in Table 2. In this work, the tolerance coefficient t was calculated taking into account the Shannon ionic radii for the corresponding coordination numbers (CN) (O^{2-} (CN = 6) R_O = 1.40 Å, Nd^{3+} (CN = 6) R_{Nd3+} = 1.27 Å, W^{6+} (CN = 6) R_{W6+} = 0.6 Å, Ti^{4+} (CN = 6) R_{Ti} = 0.605 Å). Shannon [46] did not provide the ionic radius of Bi^{3+} for coordination with CN = 12. Therefore, its value was determined from the ionic radius with CN = 8 (R_{Bi} = 1.17 Å) multiplied by an approximation factor of 1.179, then for Bi^{3+}(CN = 12) we got R_{Bi} = 1.38 Å.

In addition to the results of structural studies, temperature dependences of the relative permittivity ε and the loss tangent $tg\sigma$ were obtained at various frequencies. Figure 3 shows the temperature dependences of the relative permittivity $\varepsilon(T)$ and the dielectric loss tangent for Nd^{3+} $Bi_{3-x}Nd_xTi_{1.5}W_{0.5}O_9$ (x = 0.25, 0.5, 0.75, 1.0) at a frequency from 100kHz to 1 MHz.

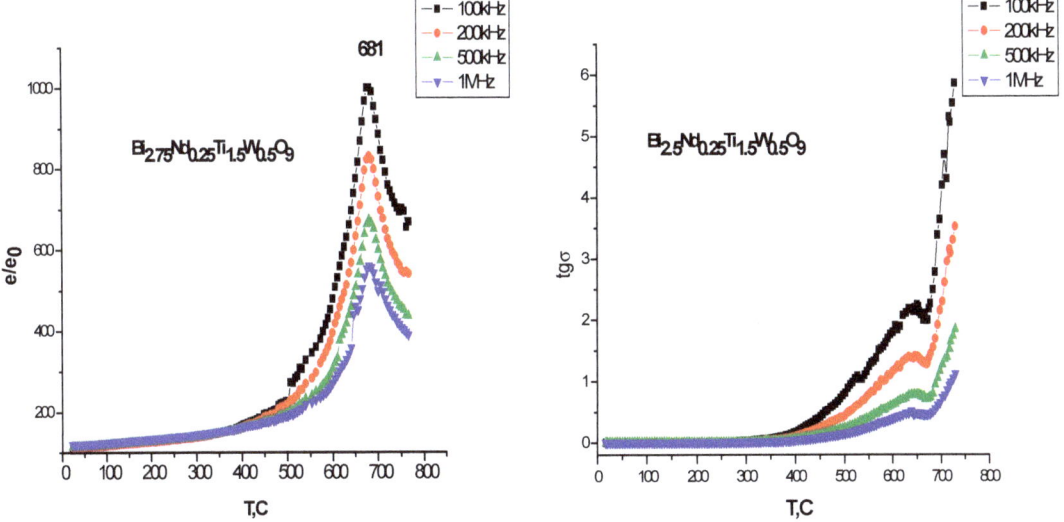

Figure 3. Cont.

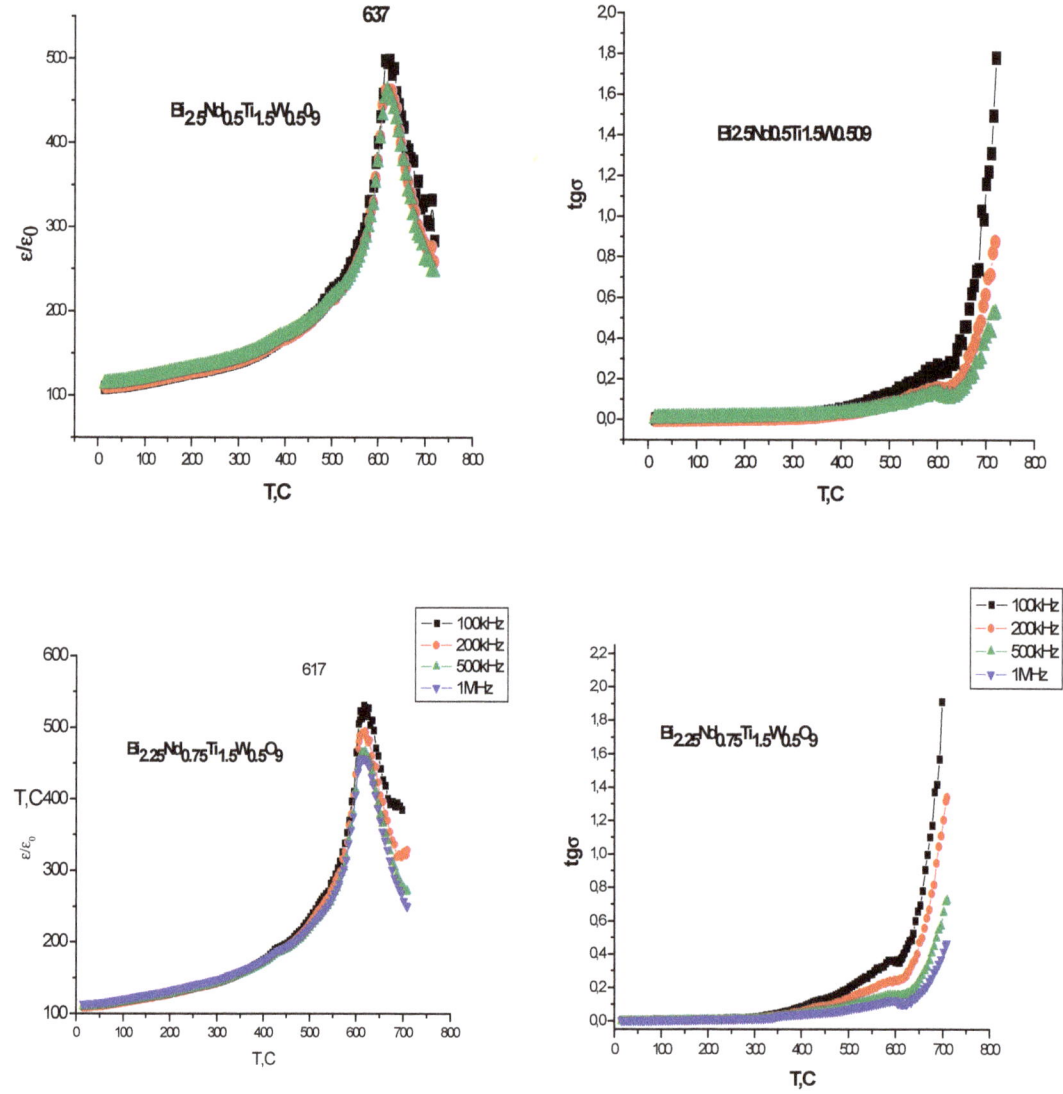

Figure 3. *Cont.*

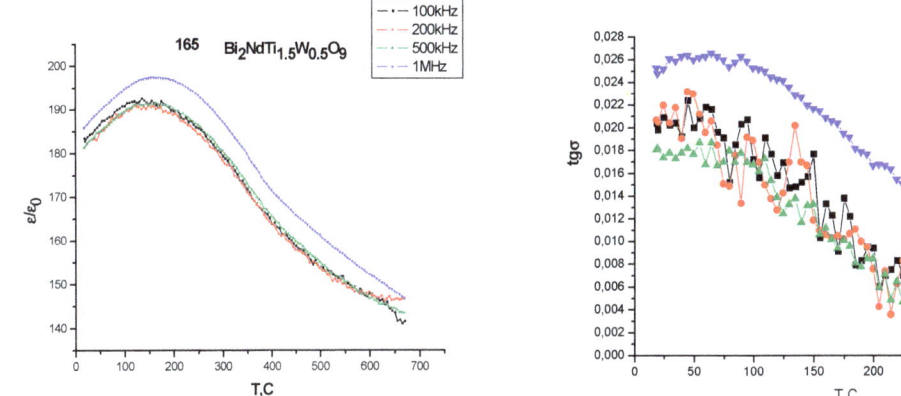

Figure 3. Temperature dependences of the relative permittivity $\varepsilon/\varepsilon_0$ and loss tangent tgσ for APs $Bi_{3-x}Nd_xTi_{1.5}W_{0.5}O_9$ (x = 0.25, 0.5, 0.75, 1.0) at a frequency from 100 kHz to 1 MHz: $Bi_{2.75}Nd_{0.25}Ti_{1.5}W_{0.5}O_9$, $Bi_{2.5}Nd_{0.5}Ti_{1.5}W_{0.5}O_9$, $Bi_{2.25}Nd_{0.75}Ti_{1.5}W_{0.5}O_9$, $Bi_2NdTi_{1.5}W_{0.5}O_9$.

For $Bi_{3-x}Nd_xTi_{1.5}W_{0.5}O_9$ (x = 0.25, 0.5, 0.75), the $\varepsilon(T)$ dependences are clearly pronounced. The intensity $\varepsilon(T)$ in the range of 0.25–0.75 drops almost two times, while the dielectric loss decreases almost ten times. The temperature dependence of the relative permittivity $\varepsilon/\varepsilon_0$ for the AP $Bi_{3-x}Nd_xTi_{1.5}W_{0.5}O_9$ (x = 1.0) at a frequency from 100 kHz to 1 MHz has a strongly diffuse transition, which is usually typical of ferroelectric relaxors. The obtained values of the activation energy E_a of charge carriers in $Bi_{3-x}Nd_xTi_{1.5}W_{0.5}O_9$ (x = 0.25, 0.5, 0.75) at frequency of 100 kHz are presented in Table 2.

The activation energy E_a was determined from the Arrhenius equation:

$$\sigma = (A/T)\exp[-E_a/(kT)], \qquad (3)$$

where σ is the electrical conductivity, k is a Boltzmann's constant, and A is a constant, E_a is the activation energy. A typical dependence of lnσ on $1/(kT)$ (at a frequency of 100 kHz), which was used to determine the activation energies E_a, is shown in Figure 4 for the APs$Bi_{3-x}Nd_xTi_{1.5}W_{0.5}O_9$ (x = 0.25, 0.5, 0.75). All three of these compounds $Bi_{3-x}Nd_xTi_{1.5}W_{0.5}O_9$ (x = 0.25, 0.5, 0.75) have different temperature ranges in Figure 4, in which the activation energies E_a have significantly different behavior. If for the first two compounds x = 0.25, 0.5, three regions of the activation energy E_a of charge carriers are observed, then we observe only two regions for the compound x = 0.75. In the low-temperature range, the electrical conductivity is predominantly determined by impurity defects with very low activation energies of the order of a few hundredths of an electron-volt. For the $Bi_{3-x}Nd_xTi_{1.5}W_{0.5}O_9$ (x = 0.5, 0.75) compounds, we do not observe a region with a clearly pronounced impurity conductivity.

At the same time, we observe for these compounds a decrease in the dielectric loss tangent and, as a consequence, a decrease in the conductivity. The decrease in the conductivity can be attributed to a decrease in oxygen vacancies.

Figure 5 shows the dependence of the unit cell parameters a, b, c on the parameter x. As seen from Figure 5, parameter a and b increase, while parameter c decreases for the entire series of compounds. It should also be noted that, despite the decrease in the thickness c' of the perovskite layer, the volume of the unit cell V increases. The change in the unit cell parameters a, b, c, V and APs $Bi_{3-x}Nd_xTi_{1.5}W_{0.5}O_9$ (x = 0.25, 0.5, 0.75, 1.0) is associated, among other things, with the difference in radii in the ions in position A, which have a dodecahedral layer, where position A is occupied by Bi^{3+} ions (R_{Bi3+} = 1.38 Å [46]) and replaced by Nd^{3+} ions with a much smaller radius (R_{Nd3+} = 1.27 Å [46]).

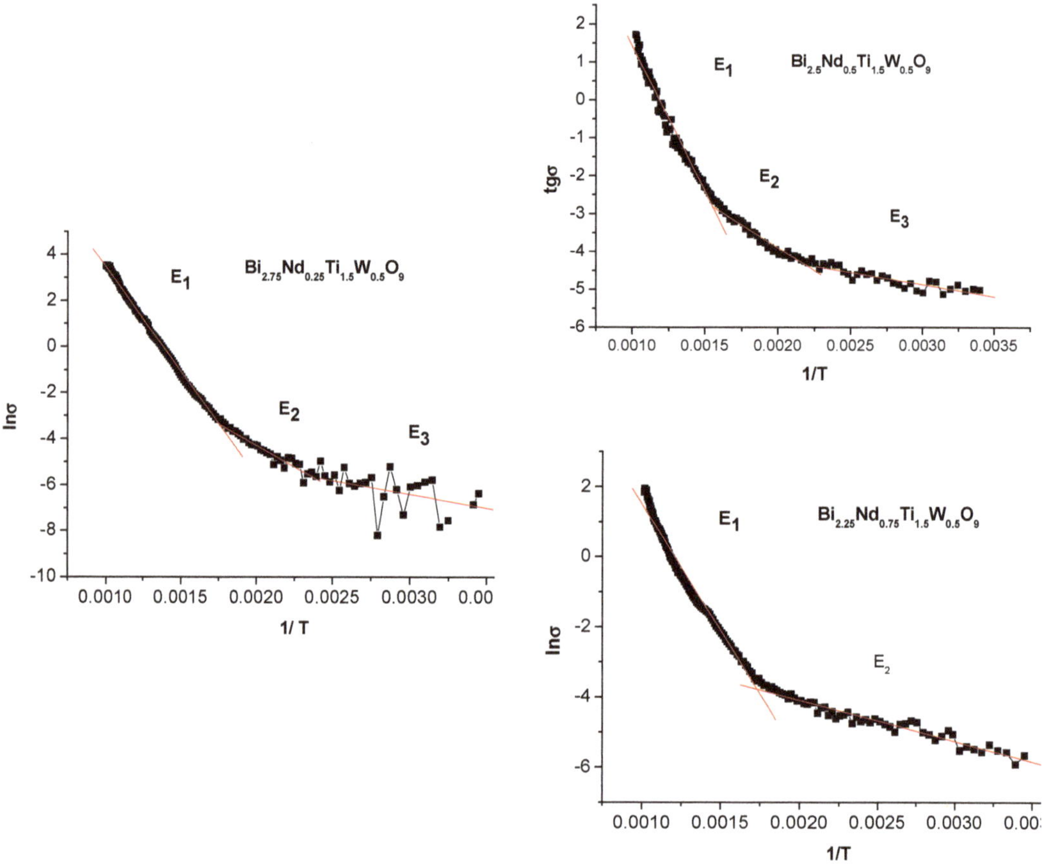

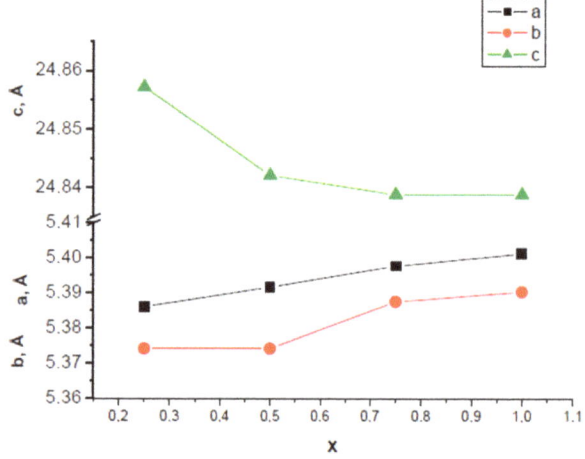

Figure 4. Dependence of $\ln\sigma$ on $1/T$ for the $Bi_{3-x}Nd_xTi_{1.5}W_{0.5}O_9$ (x = 0.25, 0.5, 0.75) sample.

Figure 5. Dependences of the unit cell parameters *a, b, c* of the synthesized $Bi_{3-x}Nd_xTi_{1.5}W_{0.5}O_9$ (x = 0.25, 0.5, 0.75, 1.0) on the parameter x.

It should be noted that the observed increase in the unit cell volume at x = 0.25–1.0 is associated only with a change in the unit cell parameters b and a, while the parameter c decreases. At the same time, if the parameter b changes almost linearly, then the parameter a has a non-linear dependence. It can be assumed that such a situation is possible if the neodymium ion has an ellipsoidal shape with a constant semi-major axis.

In Table 2, we can see the piezoelectric constant d_{33} for the $Bi_{3-x}Nd_xTi_{1.5}W_{0.5}O_9$ (x = 0.25, 0.5, 0.75). For the $Bi_{3-x}Nd_xTi_{1.5}W_{0.5}O_9$ (x = 1.0), the piezoelectric constant d_{33} could not be measured.

4. Conclusions

Series of layered bismuth perovskite oxides $Bi_{3-x}Nd_xTi_{1.5}W_{0.5}O_9$ (x = 0.25, 0.5, 0.75, 1.0) were synthesized by the solid-state method. The X-ray structural studies performed in our work showed that all the compounds obtained have single-phase with an orthorhombic crystal lattice (space group A2$_1$am, Z = 36). An analysis of the details of the AP-structure showed that an increase in the neodymium concentration x from 0.25 to 1.0 and a partial replacement of bismuth ions with neodymium ions lead to a decrease in the dielectric loss tangent and a decrease in $\varepsilon/\varepsilon_0$. For the entire series of synthesized compounds, the parameter c (thickness of the perovskite layer) decreases with an increase in neodymium cations. At the same time, the volume of the unit cell increases with decreasing c due to an increase in parameters a and b. Isovalent substitutions of Bi^{3+} ions by Nd^{3+} ions lead to a decrease in oxygen vacancies and leakage current and, accordingly, to a decrease in the dielectric loss tangent. Replacement of Bi^{3+} ions with Nd^{3+} ions, which have an ionic radius less than the ionic radius of bismuth, leads to a decrease in the Curie temperature T_C. This effect is observed only upon doping with neodymium ions. The temperature dependences $\varepsilon/\varepsilon_0(T)$ in $Bi_{3-x}Nd_xTi_{1.5}W_{0.5}O_9$ (x = 0.25, 0.5, 0.75) exhibit a high-temperature anomaly associated with the Curie temperature T_C, which corresponds to the transition from the paraelectric phase to ferroelectric. For $Bi_{2.75}Nd_{0.25}Ti_{1.5}W_{0.5}O_9$ the piezoelectric constant is 10 pC/N and tgσ < 1 at 1 MHz. Elements $Bi_{3-x}Nd_xTi_{1.5}W_{0.5}O_9$ (x = 0.25, 0.5, 0.75, 1.0) of the synthesized series can become the basis for creating new lead-free piezo-ferroelectric materials.

Author Contributions: S.V.Z.—original draft preparation, writing—review and editing, investigation; I.A.P.—review and validation, conceptualization; Y.A.K.—X-ray investigation. All authors have read and agreed to the published version of the manuscript.

Funding: This research was funded by Southern Federal University, grant No. 21-19-00423.

Acknowledgments: The equipment of SFedU was used. The authors acknowledge the support by Southern Federal University, grant No. 21-19-00423 of the Russian Science Foundation.

Conflicts of Interest: The authors declare no conflict of interest.

References

1. Aurivillius, B. Mixed Bismuth Oxides with Layer Lattices: I. Structure Type of $CaBi_2B_2O_9$. *Arkiv Kemi* **1949**, *54*, 463–480.
2. Aurivillius, B. Mixed Bismuth Oxides with Layer Lattices: II. Structure Type of $Bi_4Ti_3O_{12}$. *Arkiv Kemi* **1949**, *58*, 499–512.
3. Aurivillius, B. Mixed Bismuth Oxides with Layer Lattices: III. Structure Type of $BaBi_4Ti_4O_{15}$. *Arkiv Kemi* **1950**, *37*, 512–527.
4. Smolensky, G.A.; Isupov, V.A.; Agranovskaya, A. New ferroelectric $PbBi_2Nb_2O_9$. *FTT* **1959**, *1969*. (In Russian)
5. Ismayilzade. X-ray study of the structure of some new ferroelectrics with a layered structure. *Izv. AN SSSR* **1960**, *24*, 1198–1202. (In Russian)
6. Aurivillius, B. Ferroelectricity in the compound $BaBi_4Ti_5O_{18}$. *Phys. Rev.* **1962**, *12*, 6893–6896.
7. Subbarao, E.C. Crystal chemistry of mixed bismuth oxides with layer-type structure. *Am. Ceram. Soc.* **1962**, *45*, 166. [CrossRef]
8. Subbarao, E.C. Ferroelectricity in Mixed Bismuth Oxides with Layered-Type Structure. *Chem. Phys.* **1961**, *34*, 695.
9. Subbarao, E.C. A Family of Ferroelectric Bismuth Compounds. *Phys. Chem. Solids* **1962**, *23*, 665–676. [CrossRef]
10. Subbarao, E.C. Ferroelectricity in $BiTi_3O_{12}$ and its solid solutions. *Phys. Rev.* **1961**, *122*, 804–807. [CrossRef]
11. Isupov, V.A. Crystal chemical aspects of the bismuth–containing layered compounds of the $A_{m-1}Bi_2B_mO_{3m-3}$ type. *Ferroelectrics* **1996**, *189*, 211–217. [CrossRef]
12. Reznichenko, L.A.; Razumovskaya, O.N.; Shilkina, L.A.; Dergunova, N.V. On the relationship between the Curie temperature and the crystal-chemical characteristics of ions included in Bi-containing compounds. *Inorg. Mater.* **1996**, *32*, 474–481. (In Russian)

13. Isupov, V.A. Anomalies in the properties of layered ferroelectrics $Bi_2A_{m-1}B_mO_{3m+3}$. *Inorg. Mater.* **2006**, *421*, 353–1359. (In Russian)
14. Zubkov, S.V.; Vlasenko, V.G. Crystal structure and dielectric properties of layered perovskite-like solid solutions $Bi_{3-x}Y_xTiNbO_9$ (x = 0.0, 0.1, 0.2, 0.3) with high Curie temperature. *Phys. Solid State* **2017**, *59*, 2325. [CrossRef]
15. Zubkov, S.V.; Shevtsova, S.I. Crystal Structure and Dielectric Properties of Layered Perovskite-Like Solid Solutions $Bi_{3-x}Lu_xTiNbO_9$ (x = 0, 0.05, 0.1) with High Curie Temperature. *Adv. Mater.* **2020**, 173–182. [CrossRef]
16. Zarubin, I.A.; Vlasenko, V.G.; Shuvaev, A.T. Structure and dielectric properties of $Bi_5Sr(TiNb_3)1-xB_xO_{18}$ (0 < x ≤ 0.25; B = Sb, V, Re) layered perovskite-like solid solutions. *Inorg. Mater.* **2009**, *45*, 555.
17. Vlasenko, V.G.; Shuvaev, A.T.; Zarubin, I.A.; Vlasenko, E.V. Dielectric relaxation in layered oxides of the Aurivillius phase family. *Phys. Solid State* **2010**, *52*, 744. [CrossRef]
18. Gai, Z.G.; Zhao, M.L.; Su, W.B.; Wang, C.L.; Liu, J.; Zhang, J.L. Influences of ScTa co-substitution on the properties of Ultra-high temperature Bi_3TiNbO_9-based piezoelectric ceramics. *J. Electroceramic* **2013**, *31*, 143–147. [CrossRef]
19. Bekhtin, M.A.; Bush, A.A.; Kamentsev, K.E.; Segalla, A.G. Preparation and dielectric and piezoelectric properties of Bi_3TiNbO_9, $Bi_2CaNb_2O_9$, and $Bi_{2.5}Na_{0.5}Nb_2O_9$ ceramics doped with various elements. *Inorg. Mater.* **2016**, *52*, 557. [CrossRef]
20. Zhang, Z.; Yan, H.; Dong, X.; Wang, Y. Preparation and electrical properties of bismuth layer-structured ceramic Bi_3NbTiO_9 solid solution. *Mater. Res. Bull.* **2003**, *38*, 241. [CrossRef]
21. Ando, A.; Kimura, M.; Sakabe, Y. Piezoelectric Properties of Ba and Ca Doped $SrBi_2Nb_2O_9$ Based Ceramic Materials. *Appl. Phys.* **2003**, *42*, 520.
22. Hou, R.Z.; Chen, X.M. Synthesis and Dielectric Properties of Layer-structured Compounds $A_{n-3}Bi_4Ti_nO_{3n+3}$ (A = Ba, Sr, Ca) with n > 4. *Mater. Res.* **2005**, *20*, 2354. [CrossRef]
23. Hou, R.Z.; Chen, X.M. La^{3+} Substitution in Four-layers Aurivillius Phase $SrBi_4Ti_4O_{15}$. *Solid State Commun.* **2004**, *130*, 469. [CrossRef]
24. Noguchi, Y.; Miwa, I.; Goshima, Y.; Miyayama, M. Defect Control for Large Remanent Polarization in Bismuth Titanate Ferroelectrics Doping Effect of Higher-Valent Cations. *Appl. Phys.* **2000**, *39*, 1259. [CrossRef]
25. Yao, Y.Y.; Song, C.H.; Bao, P.; Su, D.; Lu, X.M. Doping effect on the dielectric property in bismuth titanate. *Appl. Phys.* **2004**, *95*, 3126. [CrossRef]
26. Newnham, R.E.; Wolfe, R.W.; Dorrian, J.F. Structural basis of ferroelectricity in the bismuth titanate family. *Mater. Res. Bull.* **1971**, *6*, 1029–1039. [CrossRef]
27. Moure, A.; Pardo, L.; Alemany, C.; Millan, P.; Castro, A. Piezoelectric ceramics based on Bi_3TiNbO_9 from mechanochemically activated precursors. *Eur. Ceram.* **2001**, *21*, 1399. [CrossRef]
28. Zubkov, S.V.; Vlasenko, V.G.; Shuvaeva, V.A. Structure and dielectric properties of solid solutions $Bi_7Ti_{4+x}W_xNb_{1-2x}O_{21}$ (x = 0–0.5). *Phys. Solid State* **2015**, *57*, 900.
29. Rajashekhar, G.; Sreekanth, T.; Ravikiran, U. Dielectric properties of Na and Pr doped $SrBi_4Ti_4O_{15}$ceramics. *Mater. Today* **2020**, *33*, 5467–5470.
30. Zubkov, S.V.; Vlasenko, V.G.; Shuvaeva, V.A.; Shevtsova, S.I. Structure and dielectric properties of solid solutions $Bi_7Ti_{4+x}W_xTa_{1-2x}O_{21}$ (x = 0–0.5). *Phys. Solid State* **2016**, *58*, 42. [CrossRef]
31. Rizwana; Sarah, P. Dielectric, Ferroelectric and Piezoelectric Properties of $Sr_{0.8}Na_{0.1}Nd_{0.1}Bi_4Ti_4O_{15}$ Prepared by Sol Gel and Solid State Technique. *Ferroelectrics* **2014**, *467*, 181–193. [CrossRef]
32. Fang, W.; Zhao, H.; Jia, T.; Fu, Q.; Xu, C.; Tao, H.; Weng, J.; Wang, S.; Ma, Z. Effects of La and Ni doping on ferroelectric and photocatalytic properties of Aurivillius $Bi_7Ti_3Fe_3O_{21}$. *Solid-State Electron.* **2021**, *186*, 108170. [CrossRef]
33. Dahake, K.; Jain, P.; Subohi, O. Impedance spectroscopy, dielectric, ferroelectric and electrical transport properties of Ba-doped Bi_3TiNbO_9 ceramics. *J. Mater. Sci. Mater. Electron.* **2021**, *32*, 26770. [CrossRef]
34. Xi, J.; Xing, J.; Chen, H.; Zhang, F.; Chen, Q.; Zhang, W.; Zhu, J. Crystal structure and electrical properties of Li/Mn co-doped NBT-based Aurivilliustype ceramics. *Alloys Compd.* **2021**, *868*, 159216. [CrossRef]
35. Rehman, F.; Li, J.-B.; Ahmad, I.; Jin, H.B.; Ahmad, P. Dielectric relaxation and electrical properties of $Bi_{2.5}Nd_{0.5}Nb_{1.5}Fe_{0.5}O_9$ ceramics. *Mater. Chem. Phys.* **2019**, *226*, 100. [CrossRef]
36. Bartkowska, J.A.; Bochenek, D. Dielectric relaxation of manganese modified $Bi_6Fe_2Ti_3O_{18}$ Aurivillius type ceramics. *Arch. Metall. Mater.* **2019**, *64*, 221.
37. Cheng, Z.X.; Wang, X.L. A way to enhance the magnetic moment of multiferroic bismuth Ferrite. *J. Phys. D* **2010**, *43*, 242001. [CrossRef]
38. Sengupta, P.; Sadhukhan, P.; Ray, A.; Mal, S.; Singh, A.; Ray, R.; Bhattacharyya, S.; Das, S. Influence of activation energy on charge conduction mechanism and giant dielectric relaxation of sol-gel derived $C_3H_7NH_3PbBr_3$ perovskite; Act as high performing UV photodetector. *Alloys Compd.* **2021**, *892*, 162216. [CrossRef]
39. Zdorovets, M.; Kozlovskiy, A.; Arbuz, A.; Tishkevich, D.; Zubar, T.; Trukhanov, A. Phase transformations and changes in the dielectric properties of nanostructured perovskite-like LBZ composites as a result of thermal annealing. *Ceram. Int.* **2020**, *46*, 14460. [CrossRef]
40. Long, C.; Chang, Q.; Wu, Y.; He, W.; Li, Y.; Fan, H. New layer-structured ferroelectric polycrystalline materials, $Na_{0.5}Nd_xBi_{4.5-x}Ti_4O_{15}$: Crystal structures, electrical properties and conduction behaviors. *Mater. Chem. C* **2015**, *3*, 8852.

41. Sengupta, P.; Sadhukhan, P.; Ray, A.; Ray, R.; Bhattacharyya, S.; Das, S. Temperature and frequency dependent dielectric response of $C_3H_7NH_3PbI_3$: A new hybrid perovskite. *J. Appl. Phys.* **2020**, *127*, 204103. [CrossRef]
42. Kozlovskiy, A.L.; Kenzhina, I.E.; Zdorovets, M.V.; Saiymova, M.; Tishkeviche, D.I.; Trukhanov, S.V.; Trukhanov, A.V. Synthesis, phase composition and structural and conductive properties of ferroelectric microparticles based on $ATiOx$ (A = Ba, Ca, Sr). *Ceram. Int.* **2019**, *45*, 17236. [CrossRef]
43. Zubkov, S.V. Structure and dielectric properties of solid solutions $Bi_{7-2x}Nd_{2x}Ti_4NbO_{21}$ (x = 0.0, 0.2, 0.4, 0.6, 0.8, 1.0). *Adv. Dielectr.* **2021**, *11*, 2160018. [CrossRef]
44. Kraus, W.; Nolze, G. *PowderCell for Windows, Version 2.3*; Federal Institute for Materials Research and Testing: Berlin, Germany, 1999.
45. Goldschmidt, V.M. *Geochemische Verteilungsgesetze der Elemente*; Norske: Oslo, Norway, 1927.
46. Shannon, R.D. Revised Effective Ionic Radii and Systematic Studies of Interatomic Distances in Halides and Chalcogenides. *Acta Crystallogr. Sect. A* **1976**, *32*, 751. [CrossRef]

Article

Assessment of Thermophysical Performance of Ester-Based Nanofluids for Enhanced Insulation Cooling in Transformers

Suhaib Ahmad Khan [1], Mohd Tariq [1,*], Asfar Ali Khan [1], Basem Alamri [2] and Lucian Mihet-Popa [3,*]

1. Department of Electrical Engineering, Zakir Husain College of Engineering and Technology, Aligarh Muslim University, Aligarh 202002, India; suhaib.zhcet@gmail.com (S.A.K.); asfaralikhan@gmail.com (A.A.K.)
2. Department of Electrical Engineering, College of Engineering, Taif University, Taif 21944, Saudi Arabia; b.alamri@tu.edu.sa
3. Faculty of Information Technology, Engineering and Economics, Oestfold University College, 1757 Halden, Norway
* Correspondence: tariq.ee@zhcet.ac.in (M.T.); lucian.mihet@hiof.no (L.M.-P.)

Citation: Khan, S.A.; Tariq, M.; Khan, A.A.; Alamri, B.; Mihet-Popa, L. Assessment of Thermophysical Performance of Ester-Based Nanofluids for Enhanced Insulation Cooling in Transformers. *Electronics* **2022**, *11*, 376. https://doi.org/10.3390/electronics11030376

Academic Editors: Tamás Orosz, David Pánek, Anton Rassölkin and Miklos Kuczmann

Received: 4 December 2021
Accepted: 21 January 2022
Published: 26 January 2022

Publisher's Note: MDPI stays neutral with regard to jurisdictional claims in published maps and institutional affiliations.

Copyright: © 2022 by the authors. Licensee MDPI, Basel, Switzerland. This article is an open access article distributed under the terms and conditions of the Creative Commons Attribution (CC BY) license (https://creativecommons.org/licenses/by/4.0/).

Abstract: Nanotechnology provides an effective way to upgrade the thermophysical characteristics of dielectric oils and creates optimal transformer design. The properties of insulation materials have a significant effect on the optimal transformer design. Ester-based nanofluids (NF) are introduced as an energy-efficient alternative to conventional mineral oils, prepared by dispersing nanoparticles in the base oil. This study presents the effect of nanoparticles on the thermophysical properties of pure natural ester (NE) and synthetic ester (SE) oils with temperature varied from ambient temperature up to 80 °C. A range of concentrations of graphene oxide (GO) and TiO_2 nanoparticles were used in the study to upgrade the thermophysical properties of ester-based oils. The experiments for thermal conductivity and viscosity were performed using a TC-4 apparatus that follows Debby's concept and a redwood viscometer apparatus that follows the ASTM-D445 experimental standard, respectively. The experimental results show that nanoparticles have a positive effect on the thermal conductivity and viscosity of oils which reduces with an increase in temperature.

Keywords: upgraded insulant; ester oil-based nano fluids; thermal conductivity; relative viscosity; nanoparticles effect; alternative fluid; temperature change

1. Introduction

Mineral oil is traditionally used in transformers as an insulating liquid due to its excellent dielectric and heat transfer capabilities, but its operation under excessive surrounding temperatures may lead to fire explosions which are hazardous to the environment [1]. The efficient and proper working of transformers depends upon the dielectric strength and cooling functionalities of the insulating oil used [2]. Therefore, it is important to investigate the thermal and physical properties of insulating oils used in transformers and find ways to improve them or look for a better alternative.

The dielectric mineral oil plays the dual role of insulation as well as heat dissipation in power transformers that are operated at high voltages [3]. Proper functioning of transformers at high loads generally requires continuous monitoring and maintenance of the insulating oil used in transformers. It is important to analyze the properties of the insulating material to determine its useful life, which is directly related to the lifetime and optimal design of transformers [4,5]. Therefore, to analyze and improve the thermal performance of transformers, thermophysical properties such as thermal conductivity and viscosity are important to study the heat transfer characteristics and cooling functionalities of insulating oils used in transformers. The main source of heat generation in oil-immersed transformers is the loss occurring in the core and the windings. These losses are transformed into heat, which results in the dissipation of heat in the transformer tank and eventually in the increase of the temperature of insulating oil [6,7]. It is desirable to have better heat dissipation power of the insulating liquids used in transformers in order to achieve improved efficiency and better heat transfer performance. The application of nanofluids to improve transformers' cooling systems is under investigation to create optimal transformer design by improving the cooling capacity of conventional oils [8].

In the last decade considerable effort has been put into preparing nanofluids by dispersing nanoparticles into oil to determine dielectric and electrical properties [3,9]. However, researchers now are mainly concerned with measuring the thermal and physical characteristics of oils. It is reported in the literature that nanoparticle addition would greatly improve the thermal conductivity of mineral oils [10,11]. Many investigations have been performed to determine the effect of various types of nanoparticles and temperature on the thermal conductivity and viscosity of mineral oil [12], but the effect on ester-based oils still needs to be investigated. It has been reported by Zhang et al. that the addition of TiO_2 and Al_2O_3 nanoparticles would improve thermal conductivity with an increase in their concentrations [13]. However, most of the studies on the dielectric and thermal properties are related to the mineral oil-based nanofluids and limit themselves only to these properties or those of mineral oils [14,15]. Recently, considerable research has been performed to determine the effect of temperature and nanoparticle concentration on the thermophysical properties of mineral, synthetic ester and natural ester oils [16–18], but there is a need to investigate these parameters for natural and synthetic ester oils simultaneously and to compare these parameters based on the nanoparticles' effect and temperature in order to present an environment friendly alternative to mineral oil with enhanced performance [19,20].

In the present study, novel Graphene oxide and TiO_2 nanoparticles are included in the natural ester (NE) and synthetic ester (SE) oils with the aim to enhance their thermophysical properties. In addition, apart from analyzing the effect of nanoparticles on the thermophysical properties of insulating liquids, the effect of temperature has also been examined by plotting the variation of thermal conductivity and viscosity of pure ester oils as well as nanofluids against temperature. Natural ester oil is basically a vegetable oil produced from rapeseed, and synthetic ester is obtained by the treatment of alcohol with carboxylic acids to give a robust fluid [21]. The most commonly used method—called the two-step method—used to prepare nanofluid is a widely recognized method due to its low cost and better compatibility with oils [22]. Oleic acid is added as a surfactant to the the base oil to improve the long-term stability of the nanofluids that are discussed in the paper.

The main contribution of this paper is to enhance the thermophysical characteristics of ester-based nano-oils using novel graphene oxide nanoparticles that provide better cooling functionality and a longer life than the conventional insulating oils used in transformers. The purpose of developing nano-oil is to decrease power waste by improve cooling capability during transformer operation. The correlation between thermal conductivity and viscosity of natural and synthetic ester oils for a particular concentration and temperature is carried out for their better industrial application. The remaining sections are organized as follows: Section 2 discusses the nanofluid preparation, experimental technique and heat transfer performance of nanofluids. The results are presented in Section 3. Section 4 of the paper presents the conclusion.

2. Experimental Technique, Nanofluid Preparation and Heat Transfer Performance

The flow chart describing the steps involved in this section is shown in Figure 1. The transmission electron microscopy image (TEM) of TiO_2, and the scanning electron microscopy image (SEM) of Graphene oxide (GO) nanoparticles are shown in Figure 2. The experiment to determine thermal conductivity is carried out on a thermal conductivity apparatus (TC-4 model) with a temperature control unit and a nanofluid cell, and the viscosity of oils is performed on a redwood viscometer as shown in Figure 3a,b respectively. The experimental standard used to determine viscosity of oils is ASTM-D445. All the experimental testing is performed at a 230 V, 50 Hz AC supply. In the experiment, six individual samples of nano-oil are prepared by incorporating three different concentrations, i.e., 0.01, 0.03 and 0.05 wt% of each type of nanoparticles, namely TiO_2 and Graphene oxide (GO) in the pure ester-based oils. Then, these samples are tested to determine the thermal conductivity and viscosity for fresh as well as for nano- oil, for different temperatures starting from room temperature up to 80 °C at intervals of 20 °C. The thermal conductivity apparatus consists of the electronic unit, a nanofluid cell of 7 MHz frequency, and the temperature control unit, which uses the novel ultrasonic approach to test the liquids for thermal conductivity [23]. In addition, the relative viscosity is determined using a redwood viscometer apparatus that is used to test the physical parameters of pure oils and nanofluids. The temperature controller unit is used to maintain the desired temperature up to 90 °C. The properties of nanoparticles used in the study are shown in Table 1. The insulating oils used in the experiment are commercially obtained, and its properties are shown in Table 2.

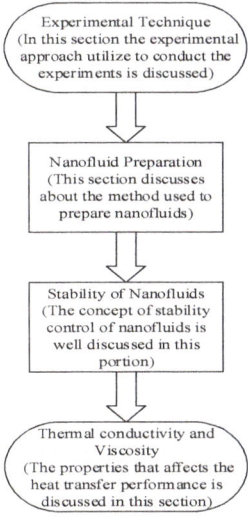

Figure 1. Flow-chart showing the steps involved in Section 2.

Table 1. Specifications of Nanoparticles.

Parameters	TiO_2	Graphene Oxide
Particle size	80–110 nm (TEM)	100–120 nm (SEM)
Density (gm/cc)	3.8	2.7
Melting point (°C)	1800	3652
Thermal conductivity (W/m·K)	8.5	18.0

Table 2. Properties of Ester-based Oils.

Parameters	Natural Ester	Synthetic Ester
Viscosity (Cst) at 40 °C	38	29
Density (gm/cm^3)	0.92	0.97
Water content (ppm)	<50 mg/kg	<50 mg/kg
Pour point (°C)	−31	−56
Breakdown Voltage (kV)	>75	>75
Thermal Conductivity (W/m·K) at 24 °C	0.16–0.17	0.14–0.15

(a) Graphene oxide (GO)

(b) TiO₂

Figure 2. TEM and SEM images of nanoparticles: (a) GO and (b) TiO_2.

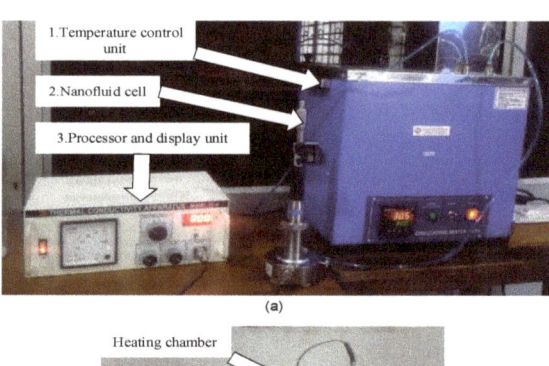

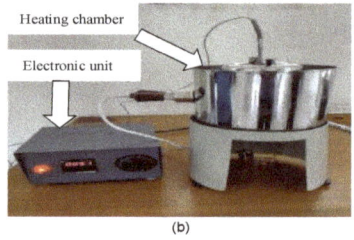

Figure 3. Experimental set-up to measure: (a) thermal conductivity and (b) viscosity of ester oils and nanofluids.

2.1. Nanofluid Preparation

The widely recognized two-step method is used to prepare the nanofluid samples as shown in Figure 4 [22,24]. The ester oils were initially filtered, and the nanoparticles were synthesized using the top-down nano-technique [25]. Oleic acid is added as a surfactant in the pure oil to improve the long term stability and dispersion stability of the prepared nano-oil samples. Magnetic stirring of the oil sample is performed for about 20–25 min to ensure removal of excess moisture and unwanted contaminants from the oils. The next step is adding nanoparticles in the base oil. Finally, the ultra-sonication process follows, which involves generation of high frequency (40 kHz) waves that disperse the nanoparticles uniformly into the base oil. In this way, the sample of nanofluids is ready for testing. The power rating of sonicator is 360 W (230 V AC, 50 Hz).

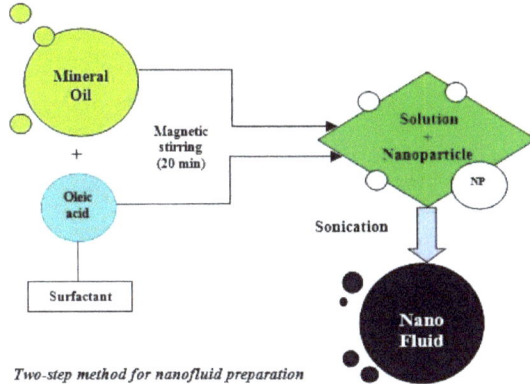

Figure 4. Two-step method for the nanofluid preparation of insulating oils.

2.2. Stability of Nanofluids

The main problem encountered in the preparation and application of nanofluids is its stability. How to improve the long term stability of nanofluid dispersions is an important concern for researchers because after the addition of nanoparticles in the base oil they may agglomerate and become an aggregate-like matter. These nanoparticles lose their size properties and, thus, limit their ability to improve the thermophysical properties of the insulating oils. In order to resolve this problem and to improve the long-term stability of the prepared nanofluid samples, surfactant is added in the form of oleic acid. The surfactant addition would introduce a repulsive force that will overcome the Van der Waals attractive force acting between the nanoparticle surfaces based on DVLO theory [26]. In this way, the nanoparticles do not agglomerate and they give stable nano-oil dispersions for longer a period of time. This concept of steric stabilization is explained by DVLO theory. Among all the prepared samples of nanofluids, the samples with 0.03 wt% concentration give stable dispersions for the nanoparticles based on the simple bottle test performed on them, which show no sedimentation even after 72 h of their preparation.

2.3. Thermal Conductivity

This is the key parameter to examine the heat transfer performance of the insulating oil. It is desirable that the oils should have a high value of thermal conductivity because liquids with high thermal conductivity absorb more heat [27]. This reduces losses and eventually improves efficiency of the power system. Thermal conductivity is determined using the TC-4 apparatus, and the measurement is conducted for the temperature range of room temperature to 80 °C. The thermal conductivity apparatus [23] follows the theory of heat conduction in liquids based on Debye's concept. In this process of measurement hydro acoustic waves are generated in the oils, and these waves are responsible for heat transfer in oils. On the basis of above heat transfer mechanism, Bridgman obtained a relation between thermal conductivity and sound velocity as given below.

$$k = 3.0 \left(\frac{N}{V}\right)^{\left(\frac{2}{3}\right)} K \cdot v_s \qquad (1)$$

where k is the thermal conductivity, v_s is the ultrasound velocity, N is Avogadro's number, V is the molar volume and K is the Boltzmann constant.

The thermal conductivity apparatus consists of three parts, namely, an electronic unit with a display to indicate the measured micrometer reading, a nanofluid cell of frequency 7 MHz and the temperature control unit to set the desired temperature. A volume of 100 mL of oil is poured into the nanofluid cell, and, then, ultrasonic waves of known frequency (7 MHz) are produced; their wavelength is measured as indicated by the micrometer display. Seven to eight iterations at each temperature are recorded and the mean value is reported. Finally, the sound velocity is measured using the relation given below,

$$v_s = \lambda \cdot f \qquad (2)$$

where v_s is the sound velocity, λ is the wavelength and f is the frequency of ultrasound waves.

After calculating the velocity of sound in nanofluids, the value of thermal conductivity for oils and nanofluids is finally determined.

2.4. Viscosity

Viscosity of insulating oil is also one of the vital parameters to understand its heat transfer characteristics. The high value of viscosity of oils will reduce its flow in the transformer and ultimately affect the heat transfer capability of oils [27]. Hence, viscosity affects the cooling functionality of insulating oils. The redwood viscometer apparatus is used for the measurement of viscosity of the pure ester-based oil and corresponding nanofluids for the temperature range of room temperature to 80 °C at intervals of 20 °C. The apparatus follows the ASTM D445 experimental standard [28], which allows the volume of liquid (50 mL) to flow through a capillary and the time to collect 50 cc of oil is recorded to determine the viscosity of the oils. The process is repeated three times to calculate the mean value. The electronic display unit is utilized to determine the viscosity of the oils.

3. Experimental Procedure and Analysis Results

The thermal conductivity is determined after calculating the velocity of sound waves as obtained from equation (2) and substituting the calculated value in equation (1). The test is performed on a 230 V, 50 Hz (AC) supply for the complete set of experiments. The value of Boltzmann's constant (K), i.e., 1.3807×10^{-23} and Avogadro's number (N), i.e., 6.023×10^{23} are used in equation (1) to determine thermal conductivity of oils. In addition, the viscosity is measured using the density of oils and the mean time to flow. Correspondingly, the graphs are plotted for thermal conductivity and viscosity of pure and nano- oils with nanoparticle concentration and temperature. The flow-chart showing the steps followed in Section 3 is shown in Figure 5.

3.1. Thermal Conductivity

The results for the thermal conductivity of pure ester oils and equivalent nanofluids (i.e., TiO_2 and GO nanofluids) with temperature and concentration variation is graphically presented as shown in Figures 6–9. The graphs clearly show that the addition of both the nanoparticles improves the thermal conductivity of ester-based oils almost for the complete temperature range, reducing with the temperature increase. As can be seen, the natural ester-based GO nanofluid shows more enhancement for thermal conductivity compared to natural esters modified by TiO_2 nanoparticles under the same nanoparticle concentration and temperature. However, synthetic ester oil has an almost similar enhancement for both GO and TiO_2 nanoparticles. At a 60 °C temperature, the thermal conductivity of

GO modified NE oil reaches a value of 0.0164 W/m·K at a concentration of 0.01 wt%, which is even higher than TiO_2 modified NE oil at a concentration of 0.05 wt% as shown in Figures 6 and 7. At a concentration of 0.05 wt%, the thermal conductivity of GO modified NE oil at 80 °C is equal to TiO_2 modified NE oil at a temperature of 40 °C as shown in Figures 8 and 9. In general, the linear declining variation is shown by ester-based oils for thermal conductivity with temperature, except for TiO_2 modified NE oil at higher temperatures. Similarly, the thermal conductivity of oils show enhancement with an increase in nanoparticle concentration except for NE at 0.05 wt% concentration and at a particular temperature.

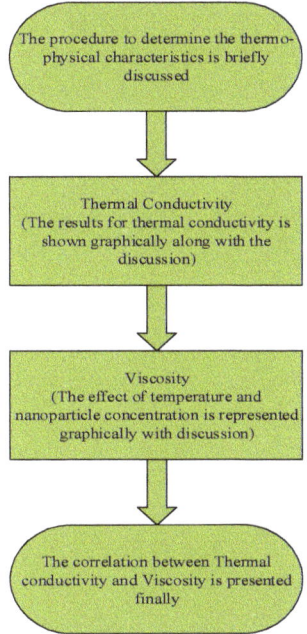

Figure 5. Flow-chart describing the procedure performed in Section 3.

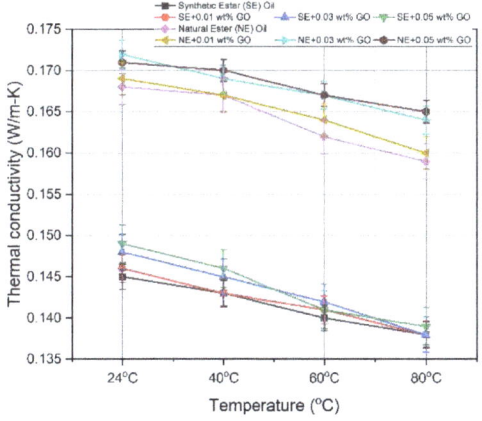

Figure 6. Thermal conductivity variation of ester oils with temperature.

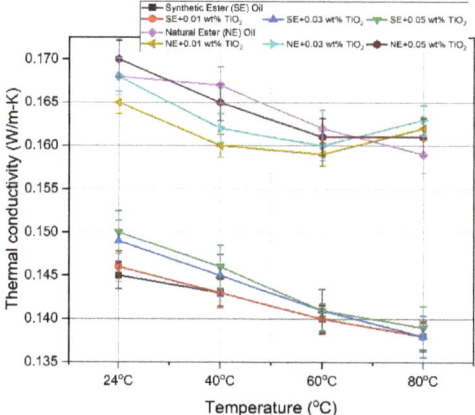

Figure 7. Thermal conductivity variation of ester oils with temperature.

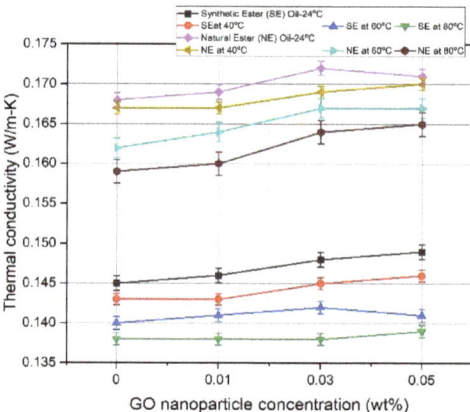

Figure 8. Thermal conductivity of ester oils versus nanoparticle concentration.

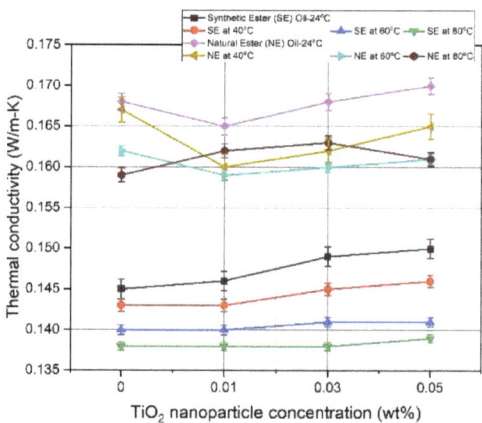

Figure 9. Thermal conductivity of ester oils versus nanoparticle concentration.

The interfacial region formed due to the addition of nanoparticles in the oils acts as the main reason for the significant improvement in thermal conductivity. The nanoparticle links with the oil molecule and further forms a bridge by linking with other nanoparticle/oil layers that will result in significant improvement [29]. Furthermore, the theory suggested by Keblinski, according to which a phonon generated in one particle will extend to surrounding particles, leads to considerable improvement at lower concentrations [30]. The high thermal conductivity of GO-based nanofluids vs. TiO_2 modified esters can be attributed to the high thermal conductivity of GO nanoparticles. The thermal conductivity of nano liquids increases as the concentration of nanoparticles increases due to the increase of Brownian motion as the collision of more particles will occur at higher concentration. Moreover, the improvement could be attributed to the interfacial region due to nanoparticle addition and ballistic phonon transport between nanoparticles. The thermal enhancement phenomena are explained based on the theories of Brownian motion of the nanoparticles in oil, conductive cover and bridges due to particle agglomeration and ballistic phonon transport [19], as shown in Figure 10.

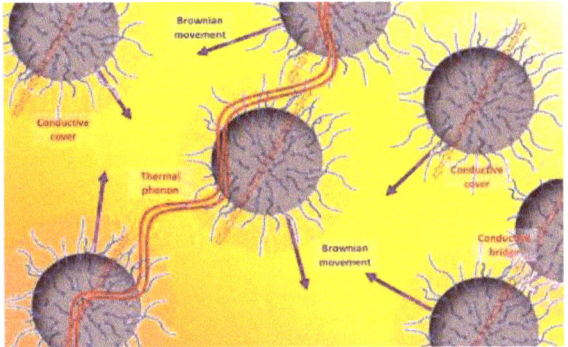

Figure 10. Thermal enhancement phenomena in nanofluids.

3.2. Viscosity

Viscosity is an important parameter to analyze the condition of insulating oils used in distribution/power transformers as it is related to the cooling functionality of oils [31]. Mineral oil should have a low viscosity value so that it can flow easily inside transformer. The measured value of viscosity of ester oils tested is presented as shown in Figures 11–14. For the graph plotted for viscosity, it is observed that, initially, at room temperature pure oils possess lower viscosity than GO and TiO_2 nanofluids, which further reduces correspondingly with temperature increase, with the exception of TiO_2 nanofluids at higher temperatures as seen in Figures 11 and 12. At 40 °C, the viscosity of NE-based GO nanofluid (NF) is lower than pure NE for higher concentration range (i.e., 0.03 and 0.05 wt%) as shown in Figure 13. Similarly, NE-based TiO_2 nanofluids (NF) show lower viscosity than pure oil even at elevated temperatures as shown in Figure 14.

In general, the viscosity of synthetic esters and their nanofluids is lower than the natural esters and their corresponding nanofluids for the entire temperature and concentration range as can be seen from Figures 11–14, which might be due to the low pour point and better oxidation stability of synthetic esters. The low viscosity of GO-based NF is due to low contamination of ester oils at high temperatures by GO nanoparticles as they have high density and form stable dispersions. A high value of viscosity is observed for the TiO_2 nanofluid due to oxidation of the TiO_2 nanoparticles at high temperature. The viscosity may rise due to presence of contaminants or due to nanoparticle aggregation with the rise in temperature [19]. In general, viscosity of nanofluids increases with nanoparticle concentration, which might be due to formation of clusters that are bonded together due to their forces, resulting in higher resistance to the flowability of nanofluids. It is observed that viscosity decreases with further addition of nanoparticles due to the self-lubricating property of these materials [32]. This effect is generally observed in graphene nanomaterials due to its very strong graphene layers. This effect develops a layer that provides lubrication and reduces friction over the surface. Moreover, this trend of lower viscosity at higher nanoparticle loading is also seen in TiO_2 nanofluids, which may be due to the lower oxidation stability of TiO_2 nanoparticles, particularly at higher temperature, which results in a loss of bonding force and decreases the resistance of nanofluids. This, hence, results in lower viscosity of the nanofluids.

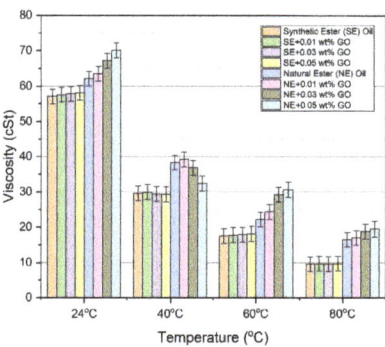

Figure 11. Viscosity variation of ester oils with temperature.

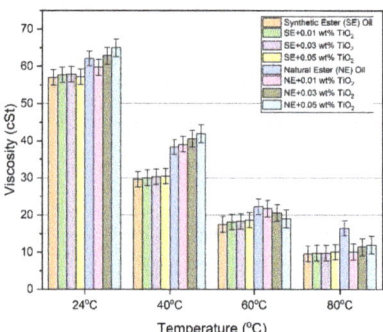

Figure 12. Viscosity variation of ester oils with temperature.

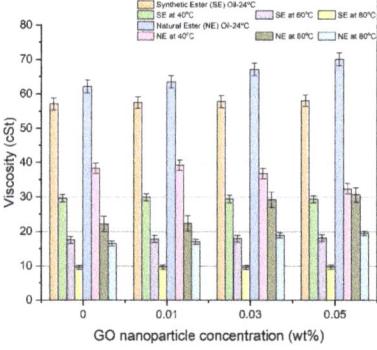

Figure 13. Viscosity of ester oils versus nanoparticle concentration.

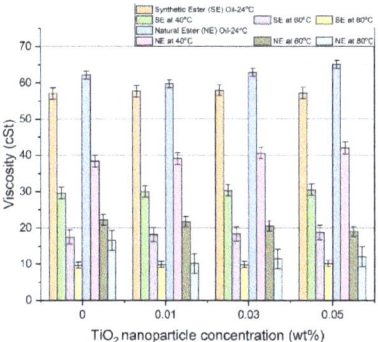

Figure 14. Viscosity of ester oils versus nanoparticle concentration.

3.3. Relation between the Two Parameters

The comparison between thermal conductivity and viscosity of ester-based oils for GO nanoparticles with temperature is performed to understand the relationship between them in affecting the cooling capability of insulating oils as shown in Figures 15 and 16. The relation shows a positive correlation as both the parameters decline linearly with temperature. However, it is important to optimize these parameters for better performance. For example, at 40 °C both the parameters give the desired results, but natural esters produce a better combination of results than synthetic esters for GO nanoparticle at 0.03 wt% concentration.

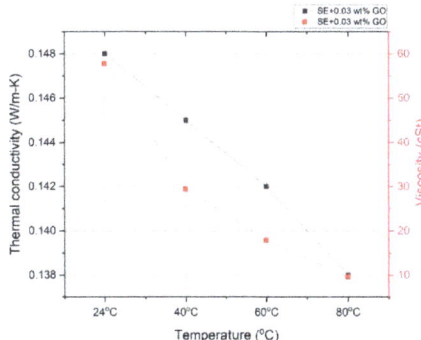

Figure 15. Correlation between thermal conductivity and viscosity for GO-based synthetic ester (SE) oil.

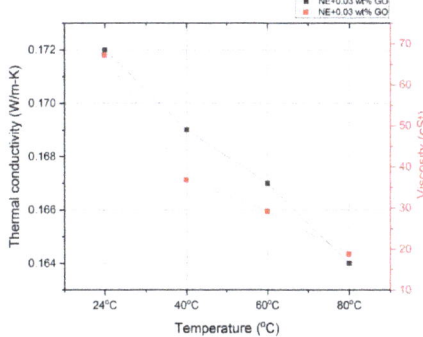

Figure 16. Correlation between thermal conductivity and viscosity for GO-based natural (NE) oil.

The key motivation of transformer oils in improving the cooling functionality of insulation is enhancing the thermal conductivity. Therefore, to obtain better cooling conditions the thermal conductivity of any desired fluid should be significantly improved, which can be achieved by the addition of nanoparticles in the base oil. However, nanoparticle loading may deteriorate the viscosity of oils, which affects the heat transport in fluids. As such, despite of the deterioration of the viscosity, efficient heat transport can be achieved with natural ester-based nanofluids due to their high thermal conductivity.

4. Conclusions

The effects of temperature and nanoparticles on the thermophysical properties of natural and synthetic ester oil and its nanofluids is experimentally observed and presented in this paper. The aim of this study is to improve the thermophysical properties of insulating liquids tested. Among the insulating oils tested, GO-based nanofluids exhibit superior thermal and physical characteristics; TiO_2 nanoparticle may get oxidized easily at high temperatures, which results in the deterioration of the TiO_2 nanofluid thermophysical characteristics. The GO nanoparticle is chemically inert, forms stable dispersions and has a lesser affinity towards oxidation at elevated temperatures. Therefore, there will be less contamination in the oil, which results in lower viscosity of the nanofluids. In addition, the GO nanoparticle has a higher surface-to-volume ratio than TiO_2 nanoparticle; as a result GO-based nanofluids exhibit higher thermal conductivity than pure ester oils and TiO_2 nanofluids.

GO nanoparticles show a maximum thermal conductivity enhancement of 3.77% for pure natural ester oil at 0.05 wt% concentration and 80 °C. Similarly, TiO_2 nanoparticle gives a maximum enhancement of 3.44% for synthetic ester oil at 0.05 wt% concentration and 24 °C. The high thermal conductivity of natural esters can be attributed to their lower oxidation rate at high temperatures than synthetic esters. However, the superior value of thermal conductivity and optimal viscosity of the GO nanofluid under high temperatures concludes that the GO-nanofluid can be a better alternative to conventional mineral oil for cooling functionality in transformers. However, nano-oil is a new area that needs to be researched more. Therefore, there are some challenges that need to be explored, which are also briefly highlighted in Table 3.

Table 3. Limitations and future work of Ester-based nanofluids.

Limitations	Future Work
Stability of Nanofluids	Stability for longer durations of time still need to be investigated.
Selection of nanoparticle type	Selection of nanoparticles that enhance thermal conductivity of ester-fluids.
Preparation of low-cost nanoparticles	Improve the preparation process with low cost.

- Stability of prepared nanofluids are investigated in the present study but stability for longer durations with respect to temperature is still need to be investigated.
- The present research shows the effect of different nanoparticles on the thermal conductivity and viscosity of ester oils. Therefore, a selection of nanoparticles with enhanced thermal conductivity should possess optimum viscosity for excellent thermophysical performance of nanofluids. Hence, the choice of nanoparticle needs to be researched.
- Most of the research used the two-step method to prepare nanofluids, which requires a high production cost. The question of how to improve the nanofluid preparation process with a reduce cost will be important research in the future.

Nano-oil and nano-oil paper insulation systems are a new area of research and, therefore, need to be investigated more either in terms of their thermal performance or insulation capabilities. Many problems related to the long-term stability of nanofluids still need to be explored as it is a challenge for their industrial application. In the future, nanofluid dispersions need to be tested more for thermal characteristics to find an even better alternative in the form of a nano-oil that can replace mineral oil for transformers.

Author Contributions: Conceptualization, S.A.K., M.T. and A.A.K.; Formal analysis, S.A.K., M.T., A.A.K., B.A. and L.M.-P.; Funding acquisition, M.T. and B.A.; Investigation, S.A.K., M.T. and A.A.K.; Methodology, S.A.K., M.T. and A.A.K.; Supervision, M.T. and A.A.K.; Validation, S.A.K. and M.T.; Writing—original draft, S.A.K. and M.T.; Writing—review & editing, A.A.K., B.A. and L.M.-P. All authors have read and agreed to the published version of the manuscript.

Funding: This research was funded in part by Taif University Researchers Supporting Project Number (TURSP-2022/278), Taif University, Taif, Saudi Arabia, in part by the Smart City Development Consultancy Project and Collaborative Research Grant Scheme [CRGS/MOHD TARIQ/01 and CRGS/MOHD TARIQ/02] projects, Department of Electrical Engineering, Aligarh Muslim University, India.

Acknowledgments: The authors also acknowledge the technical support provided by the Hardware-In-the-Loop (HIL) Lab and Dielectrics and Insulation Lab, Department of Electrical Engineering, Aligarh Muslim University, India.

Conflicts of Interest: The authors declare no conflict of interest.

References

1. Rafiq, M.; Shafique, M.; Azam, A.; Ateeq, M.; Khan, I.A.; Hussain, A. Sustainable, Renewable and Environmental-Friendly Insulation Systems for High Voltages Applications. *Molecules* **2020**, *25*, 3901. [CrossRef] [PubMed]
2. Saha, T.K.; Purkait, P. Investigation of polarization and depolarization current measurements for the assessment of oil-paper insulation of aged transformers. *IEEE Trans. Dielectr. Electr. Insul.* **2004**, *11*, 144–154. [CrossRef]
3. Du, Y.; Lv, Y.; Li, C.; Chen, M.; Zhong, Y.; Zhou, J.; Li, X.; Zhou, Y. Effect of Semiconductive Nanoparticles on Insulating Performances of Transformer Oil. *IEEE Trans. Dielectr. Electr. Insul.* **2012**, *19*, 770–776.
4. Abid, M.A.; Khan, I.; Ullah, Z.; Ullah, K.; Haider, A.; Ali, S.M. Dielectric and Thermal Performance Up-Gradation of Transformer Oil Using Valuable Nano-Particles. *IEEE Access* **2019**, *7*, 153509–153518. [CrossRef]
5. Rajnak, M.; Timko, M.; Kopcansky, P.; Paulovicova, K.; Kuchta, J.; Franko, M.; Kurimsky, J.; Dolnik, B.; Cimbala, R. Transformer oil-based magnetic nanofluid with high dielectric losses tested for cooling of a model transformer. *IEEE Trans. Dielectr. Electr. Insul.* **2019**, *26*, 1343–1349. [CrossRef]
6. Tang, W.H.; Wu, Q.H.; Richardson, Z.J. Equivalent heat circuit based power transformer thermal model. *IEE Proc.-Electr. Power Appl.* **2002**, *149*, 87–92. [CrossRef]
7. Khare, V.; Khare, C.J. Aspects of transformer in electricity generation: A review. *J. Adv. Mach.* **2018**, *3*, 1–33.
8. Olmo, C.; Méndez, C.; Ortiz, F.; Delgado, F.; Valiente, R.; Werle, P. Maghemite Nanofluid Based on Natural Ester: Cooling and Insulation Properties Assessment. *IEEE Access* **2019**, *7*, 145851–145860. [CrossRef]
9. Zhong, Y.X.; Lv, Y.Z.; Li, C.R.; Du, Y.F.; Chen, M.C.; Zhang, S.N.; Zhou, Y.; Chen, L. Insulating Properties and Charge Characteristics of Natural Ester Fluid Modified by TiO2 Semiconductive Nanoparticles. *IEEE Trans. Dielectr. Electr. Insul.* **2013**, *20*, 135–140. [CrossRef]
10. Du, B.X.; Li, X.L.; Li, J. Thermal conductivity and dielectric characteristics of transformer oil filled with BN and Fe_3O_4 nanoparticles. *IEEE Trans. Dielectr. Electr. Insul.* **2015**, *22*, 2530–2536. [CrossRef]
11. Du, B.X.; Li, X.L.; Xiao, M. High thermal conductivity transformer oil filled with BN nanoparticles. *IEEE Trans. Dielectr. Electr. Insul.* **2015**, *22*, 851–858. [CrossRef]
12. Chiesa, M.; Das, S.K. Experimental investigation of the dielectric and cooling performance of colloidal suspensions in insulating media. *Colloids Surf. A Physicochem. Eng. Asp.* **2009**, *335*, 88–97. [CrossRef]
13. Zhang, X.; Gu, H.; Fujii, M. Experimental Study on The Effective Thermal Conductivity and Thermal Diffusivity of Nanofluids. *Int. J. Thermophys.* **2006**, *27*, 569–580. [CrossRef]
14. Ahmad, F.; Khan, A.A.; Khan, Q.; Hussain, M.R. State-of-art in nano- based dielectric oil: A review. *IEEE Access* **2019**, *7*, 13396–13410. [CrossRef]
15. Primo, V.A.; Garcia, B.; Albarracin, R. Improvement of transformer liquid insulation using nanodielectric fluids: A review. *IEEE Elect. Insul. Mag.* **2018**, *34*, 13–26. [CrossRef]
16. Nadolny, Z.; Dombek, G. Electro-Insulating Nanofluids Based on Synthetic Ester and TiO_2 or C_{60} Nanoparticles in Power Transformer. *Energies* **2018**, *11*, 1953. [CrossRef]
17. Dombek, G.; Nadolny, Z.; Przybylek, P. Cooling properties of natural ester modified by nanopowders fullerene C60 and TiO_2 for high voltage insulation applications. In Proceedings of the 2017 International Symposium on Electrical Insulating Materials (ISEIM), Toyohashi, Japan, 11–15 September 2017; pp. 442–445. [CrossRef]
18. Dombek, G.; Nadolny, Z.; Marcinkowska, A. Effects of Nanoparticles Materials on Heat Transfer in Electro-Insulating Liquids. *Appl. Sci.* **2018**, *8*, 2538. [CrossRef]
19. Amin, D.; Walvekar, R.; Khalid, M.; Vaka, M.; Mubarak, N.M.; Gupta, T.C.S.M. Recent Progress and Challenges in Transformer Oil Nanofluid Development: A Review on Thermal and Electrical Properties. *IEEE Access* **2019**, *7*, 151422–151438. [CrossRef]

20. Mentlik, V.; Trnka, P.; Hornak, J.; Totzauer, P. Development of a Biodegradable Electro-Insulating Liquid and Its Subsequent Modification by Nanoparticles. *Energies* **2018**, *11*, 508. [CrossRef]
21. Khan, S.A.; Khan, A.A.; Tariq, M. Measurement of Tan-delta and DC Resistivity of Synthetic Ester Based Oil Filled with Fe_2O_3, TiO_2 and Al_2O_3 Nanoparticles. *Smart Sci.* **2021**, *9*, 216225. [CrossRef]
22. Khan, S.A.; Khan, A.A.; Tariq, M. Experimental Analysis for the Effect of Fe/Ti Oxides and Fe-Cu Nanoparticles on the Dielectric Strength of Transformer Oil. In Proceedings of the 2019 International Conference on High Voltage Engineering and Technology (ICHVET), Hyderabad, India, 7–8 February 2019; pp. 1–6.
23. Rashin, M.N.; Hemalatha, J. A novel ultrasonic approach to determine thermal conductivity in Cu-O ethylene glycol nanofluids. *J. Mol. Liq.* **2014**, *197*, 257–262. [CrossRef]
24. Ibrahim, M.E.; Abd-Elhady, A.M.; Izzularab, M.A. Effect of nanoparticles on transformer oil breakdown strength: Experiment and theory. *Sci. Meas. Technol. IET* **2016**, *10*, 839–845. [CrossRef]
25. Khan, Q.; Singh, V.; Ahmad, F.; Khan, A.A. Dielectric performance of magnetic nanoparticles-based ester oil. *IET Nanodielectr.* **2021**, *4*, 45–52. [CrossRef]
26. Huang, Z.; Li, J.; Yao, W.; Wang, F.; Wan, F.; Tan, Y.; Ali, M. Electrical and thermal properties of insulating oil-based nanofluids: A comprehensive overview. *IET Nanodielectr.* **2019**, *2*, 27–40. [CrossRef]
27. Maharana, M.; Bordeori, M.M.; Nayak, S.K.; Sahoo, N. Nanofluid based transformer oil: Effect of aging on thermal, electrical and physio-chemical properties. *IET Sci. Meas. Technol.* **2018**, *12*, 878–885. [CrossRef]
28. ASTM D445; Standard Test Method for Kinematic Viscosity of Transparent and Opaque Liquids (and Calculation of Dynamic Viscosity). Available online: https://global.ihs.com/doc_detail.cfm?document_name=ASTM%20D445&item_s_key=00018647 (accessed on 15 October 2021).
29. Kole, M.; Dey, T.K. Role of Interfacial Layer and Clustering on the Effective Thermal Conductivity of CuO-Gear Oil Nanofluids. *Exp. Therm. Fluid Sci.* **2011**, *35*, 1490–1495. [CrossRef]
30. Keblinski, P.; Phillpot, S.R.; Choi, S.U.S.; Eastman, J.A. Mechanisms of Heat Flow in Suspensions of Nano-Sized Particles (Nanofluids). *Int. J. Heat Mass. Transf.* **2001**, *45*, 855–863. [CrossRef]
31. FFernández, I.; Valiente, R.; Ortiz, F.; Renedo, C.J.; Ortiz, A. Effect of TiO_2 and ZnO Nanoparticles on the Performance of Dielectric Nanofluids Based on Vegetable Esters During Their Aging. *Nanomaterials* **2020**, *10*, 692. [CrossRef]
32. Berman, D.; Erdemir, A.; Sumant, A.V. Graphene: A new emerging lubricant. *Mater. Today* **2014**, *17*, 31–42. [CrossRef]

Article

Comparison of Mechanical and Low-Frequency Dielectric Properties of Thermally and Thermo-Mechanically Aged Low Voltage CSPE/XLPE Nuclear Power Plant Cables

Ramy S. A. Afia [1,2], Ehtasham Mustafa [2,3] and Zoltán Ádám Tamus [2,*]

[1] Department of Electrical Power and Machines Engineering, Helwan University, Helwan 11792, Egypt; ramysaad@h-eng.helwan.edu.eg

[2] Department of Electric Power Engineering, Faculty of Electrical Engineering and Informatics, Budapest University of Technology and Economics, H-1111 Budapest, Hungary; mustafa.ehtasham@vet.bme.hu

[3] Department of Electrical Engineering, Faculty of Engineering and Technology, Gomal University, Dera Ismail Khan 29050, Pakistan

* Correspondence: tamus.adam@vik.bme.hu; Tel.: +36-1-463-2780

Citation: Afia, R.S.A.; Mustafa, E.; Tamus, Z.Á. Comparison of Mechanical and Low-Frequency Dielectric Properties of Thermally and Thermo-Mechanically Aged Low Voltage CSPE/XLPE Nuclear Power Plant Cables. *Electronics* 2021, 10, 2728. https://doi.org/10.3390/electronics10222728

Academic Editor: Davide Astolfi

Received: 12 October 2021
Accepted: 4 November 2021
Published: 9 November 2021

Publisher's Note: MDPI stays neutral with regard to jurisdictional claims in published maps and institutional affiliations.

Copyright: © 2021 by the authors. Licensee MDPI, Basel, Switzerland. This article is an open access article distributed under the terms and conditions of the Creative Commons Attribution (CC BY) license (https://creativecommons.org/licenses/by/4.0/).

Abstract: During the service period of low-voltage nuclear cables, multiple stresses influence the aging of polymeric materials of cables. Thermal and radiation stresses are considered service aging factors in qualification tests, while the standards usually do not prescribe mechanical stress. CSPE/XLPE insulated nuclear cable samples were exposed to thermal and combined thermo-mechanical aging for more than 1200 h at 120 °C. The real and imaginary parts of permittivity were measured in the 200 µHz to 50 mHz range as dielectric properties. The Shore D hardness of the samples was measured to analyze the mechanical characteristics of the cable. To characterize the dielectric spectrum, derived quantities, namely central real and imaginary permittivities and real and imaginary permittivities' central frequencies were calculated. The change of dielectric spectra did not show a clear trend with aging, but the imaginary permittivity's central frequency was higher by 0.5 mHz in the case of thermo-mechanically aged samples. The Shore D hardness was also higher on the thermo-mechanically aged samples. These findings show the combined aging has a higher impact on the insulation properties. Hence, involving the mechanical stress in the aging procedure of cable qualification enables the design of more robust cables in a harsh environment.

Keywords: nuclear power plant; thermal degradation; thermal-mechanical aging; low-voltage cables; polymer degradation; dielectric spectroscopy; hardness

1. Introduction

In 2020, the built-in nuclear-generating capacity was 393 GW (electrical), and its contribution to electricity generation is expected to increase. In the highest case predictions, the world's nuclear capacity will be doubled to 792 GW by 2050, keeping its almost 5% ratio [1]. Hence, nuclear power will keep its important role in power generation for decades, and the current nuclear power plants' (NPPs') designed lifetime is potentially extended to 80 years [2]. During this long period, the safe and reliable operation of NPPs in normal service and design basis events (DBEs) require safety-related equipment performance to meet their designed requirements. The equipment qualification is the procedure when safety-related equipment performance is tested in all operational states and accident conditions [3]. Since the cabling condition plays a key role in the reliable operation of safety systems, the safety-related cables as system components are also subject to the qualification which the test procedure is described by standards [4]. More the 1000 miles of cable installed typically in a pressurized water reactor (PWR), low-voltage (LV) power cables account for only 15% of the total LV cables deployed in the NPPs [5]. Still, they are highly important as they supply motors and pumps related to nuclear safety. The structure of these cables varies with the application. These power cables are multi- or single conductors with or without shielding and have different polymeric components for core insulation, jacket, and filling material [6–9]. During operation in the NPP environment, these LV cables are exposed to numerous stresses, thermal, radiation, electrical, and mechanical, which cause degradation in these polymeric materials [10]. The electrical and thermal stresses are the prominent aging factors for the high-voltage (HV) and medium-voltage (MV) cables [11]. For the LV cables, elevated temperature and radiation could be the major factors, along with the chemical contamination and mechanical stresses in some cases [10,12].

Considering that the operational stresses affect the cables' functionality, the qualification procedure includes the simulation of aging in normal service conditions before DBE and post-DBE functionality tests. Although mechanical stress as pressing with a cable cleat, and low bending radius, can appear in operation, the standards do not prescribe any mechanical stress during the accelerated aging that simulates operation conditions [13]. Nevertheless, the bending with a low radius is used to demonstrate a lack of embrittlement and adequate flexibility after aging [4]. The impact of mechanical stress on the degradation of the polymers is well known, and numerous studies have investigated the effects of mechanical stress on the functionality of the polymer insulating materials [14]. However, as the degradation or aging of the polymeric material is a multi-factor phenomenon, thermal stress has more importance than other stresses. However, the effect of the simultaneous presence of mechanical stress and thermal stress on high-voltage cables has been investigated since the 1980s [15], the topic still has to be explored in the case of the NPPs environment.

According to the robust design principle, the product performance can be improved by minimizing performance variations caused by uncontrollable parameters (noise factors) or design variables (control factors) [16]. The robust approach is widely used in the design of NPP control systems, electrical equipment, and machines [17–23]. Hence, considering NPP cable as a product, if the mechanical stress is not prescribed as an aging parameter in qualification, this can be regarded as a noise factor and can cause uncertainty in the cable performance. If the mechanical stress is involved in the aging procedure, the performance uncertainty caused by this factor can be minimized. Therefore, the purpose of this study is to compare the mechanical and dielectric properties of cable samples subjected to thermal only and combined thermal and mechanical aging.

The subject of the investigation is a single-core cross-linked polyethylene (XLPE) insulated and chlorosulphonated polyethylene (CSPE) jacketed NPP power cable. One group of cables was only thermally and the other thermo-mechanically aged. The change of dielectric properties was measured by low-frequency dielectric spectroscopy. The reason for the application of this technique in this study is that dielectric spectroscopy as condition monitoring for NPP cables has recently become a focus of interest because of its non-destructivity. Several studies show promising results, and their future expansion is likely [11,12,24–31]. From the results of dielectric spectroscopy measurement, deducted quantities were introduced because assigning one measure to the whole low-frequency spectrum makes it easier to analyze the changing of the dielectric spectrum with aging. The mechanical properties were measured using Shore D hardness, which is a simplified indenter measurement. The indenter type measurements are widely and effectively used for the aging monitoring of NPP cables [32–34]. The results of the thermally and thermo-mechanically aged groups were compared to determine the degradation caused by combined stress over the simple thermal aging.

This paper has been organized, as Section 2 elaborates the cable sample, aging stresses, the electrical and mechanical measurement. The results of the measurement are given in Section 3. Section 4 explains the measurement results, and the concluding remarks are provided in Section 5.

2. Materials and Methods

2.1. Specimens

A Firewall III radiation-resistant Class 1E low-voltage (600 V) NPP unshielded power cable (RSCC Wire and Cable, East Granby, CT, USA) under investigation is shown in Figure 1. The cable consisted of three parts: annealed, tin-coated copper conductor with a cross-sectional area of 6 AWG (13.3 mm^2), cross-linked polyethylene (XLPE) core insulation having a thickness of 45 mils (1.143 mm), and chlorosulphonated polyethylene (CSPE) jacket with 30 mils (0.762 mm) thickness. The overall diameter of the cable was 0.34 inches (8.636 mm). Under the International Atomic Energy Agency's (IAEA's) guidelines [35] and as expressed in Figure 1, 1 cm and 3 cm of the insulation and jacket were removed from both sides of the cable sample, respectively. The cable sample was 0.5 m in length for the experiments.

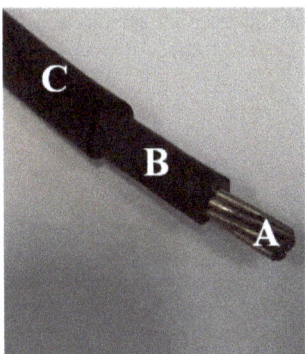

Figure 1. The LV unshielded NPP cable under consideration. A—Tin-coated copper, B—XLPE insulation, C—CSPE jacket.

2.2. Accelerated Aging

2.2.1. Thermal Aging

The cable samples were exposed to 120 °C accelerated thermal agings in an air-circulating oven for seven different periods: 176, 338, 512, 784, 912, 1056, and 1248 h. Applying these aging parameters is because the 120 °C aging temperature was also used for benchmark analysis of this cable type in the IAEA Coordinated Research Project [35]. Moreover, elongation at break data for the CSPE jacket are also available for these aging times in [35]. The cable samples in the oven are shown in Figure 2a.

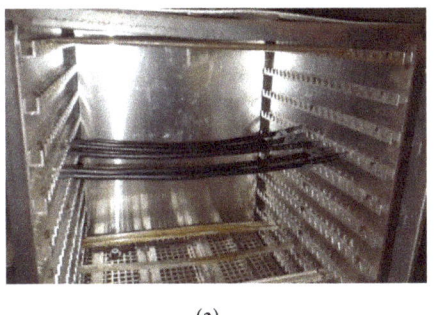

(a)   (b)

Figure 2. Cable samples in the oven for (**a**) thermal aging; (**b**) thermo-mechanical aging.

2.2.2. Thermo-Mechanical Aging

According to the IEEE standard, the cable samples were bent on a mandrel with an outer diameter of 15 cm for the thermo-mechanical (T-M) simultaneous aging [4].

Then the cable samples were placed in the air circulated oven at a temperature of 120 °C. The cables were exposed to simultaneous aging for 176, 338, 507, 779, 907, 1051, and 1243 h (Figure 2b). After each aging period, the samples were removed from the cylinder and straightened for measurements. After the measurements, the samples were bent on the cylinder again. Then, they inserted back to the aging chamber for the next round.

2.3. Dielectric Spectroscopy Measurement

Since the subject of the investigation is a single core unshielded power cable having a jacket and core insulation also, this cable structure can be considered a layered insulation arrangement. The most dominant polarization process in layered insulations is interfacial polarization, with a far lower characteristic frequency than 1 Hz. Therefore dielectric spectroscopy was carried out in the frequency range of 200 μHz to 50 mHz by investigating the complex permittivity of the material. The complex permittivity is defined by the expression:

$$\dot{\varepsilon} = \varepsilon' + j\varepsilon'', \tag{1}$$

where ε' and ε'' are defined as the real and imaginary parts of permittivity since the former depicts the strength of the dipoles in the material aligning themselves when an external electric field is applied. This part is known as permittivity characterizing the electric energy stored within the dielectric material [36,37]. The imaginary permittivity represents the losses in the material due to conduction and polarization. The dissipation factor or tan δ is the ratio of the imaginary and real parts of permittivity (tan $\delta = \varepsilon''/\varepsilon'$). Modeling a relaxation process by the Debye model, the real and imaginary parts of permittivity as a function of angular frequency can be expressed by the following equations:

$$\varepsilon'(\omega) = \varepsilon_\infty + \frac{\varepsilon_s - \varepsilon_\infty}{1 + (\frac{\omega}{\omega_0})^2}, \tag{2}$$

$$\varepsilon''(\omega) = \frac{(\varepsilon_s - \varepsilon_\infty)(\frac{\omega}{\omega_0})}{1 + (\frac{\omega}{\omega_0})^2}, \tag{3}$$

where the ε_s and ε_∞ are the permittivities at 0 and infinity frequency, at the same time, ω_0 is the characteristic angular frequency of the relaxation process. The relationship between ε_s and ε_∞ can be seen in Figure 3. As the figure shows, the imaginary part of permittivity has a peak at the characteristic frequency, i.e., loss peak. Where the imaginary part has the peak, the changing of the real part is the highest. By changing the characteristic frequency, the curves shift together. The complex permittivity also enables the determination of the conductivity of the material. However, ε'' contains the sum of resistive and dielectric losses, if the resistive part is dominant, the slope of $\varepsilon(\omega)$ is ω^{-1} and $\varepsilon''(\omega)$ is constant in the dielectric spectrum [38]. At very low frequencies (below 1 Hz), the dc conduction is the dominant part of dielectric loss in XLPE cable insulation [39].

The measurements were carried out with Omicron Dirana (Omicron Electronics Gmbh, Klaus, Austria). This equipment uses the combination of frequency-domain spectroscopy (FDS) and polarization-depolarization current (PDC) methods to determine the dielectric response. The equipment directly measures the dielectric response in the frequency domain at higher frequencies by the FDS technique. To determine the response in the lower frequency range, time-domain PDC data are recorded. Then, the PDC data are converted to the frequency domain by using discrete Fourier transformation. This technique has an important advantage, namely, it reduces the measurement time by 73% [38,40]. The accuracy of the equipment is 2% below 1 mHz for power and dissipation factor measurement and 0.5% for capacitance.

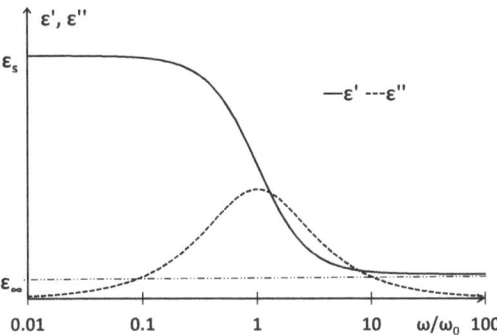

Figure 3. The relationship between real (ε') and imaginary (ε'') parts of permittivity in case of one Debye relaxation.

Since the subject of the investigation is a single core unshielded cable, the measurement of dielectric properties requires an external electrode, which was prepared by wrapping alumina foil around the cable. The voltage source, the equipment terminal, was connected to the external foil electrode through a copper strip. In contrast, the current output was connected to the internal conductor, as the measurement setup is shown in Figure 4. This connection ensures the lowest noise in the result. The cable samples were placed in the Faraday's cage connected to the guard for more noise suppression.

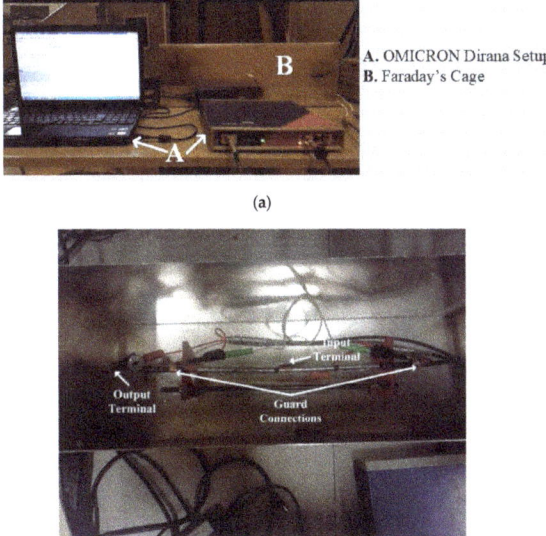

Figure 4. The test setup: (**a**) Omicron Dirana equipment; (**b**) cable sample in the Fraday's cage.

2.4. Shore D Hardness Measurement

The hardness measurement is based on the indentation depth of the indenter foot into the material applying a constant force. If the indentation is the highest, the measured value is 100, and if there is no indentation, the result is 0. In the case of the Shore D scale, the force is 4450.0 mN, the maximum penetration distance is 2.54 mm, and a 30-degree conical pressure foot is used. The Shore D hardness measurement is suitable for testing flat samples with a minimum 6 mm thickness according to the ASTMD2240-05 standard [41].

Therefore in this research, the Shore D hardness was tested as a comparative measurement to investigate the mechanical properties.

The hardness of the cable was measured at the ends and center with a total of 10 measuring points at $25 \pm 0.5\ °C$. Although the test method is suitable for the flat samples [41], with the adaption of the foot adapter, the measurement can be executed for the round surfaces. In this investigation, the Shore D hardness measures the resultant hardness of the jacket and the insulation.

3. Results

3.1. Dielectric Spectroscopy

3.1.1. Thermal Aging

The measurement result of the real part of permittivity (ε') for the thermal stress is plotted against the frequency for each period in Figure 5a. According to the general behavior of dielectrics, the ε' decrease as the frequency increase. This characteristic behavior of the ε' was the same for all the aging periods. With aging time, the ε' either decreased or remained constant at all frequencies, except at 2×10^{-2} Hz and above, where a slight increase was observed. This behavior can be explained by the comparison with the imaginary parts curves.

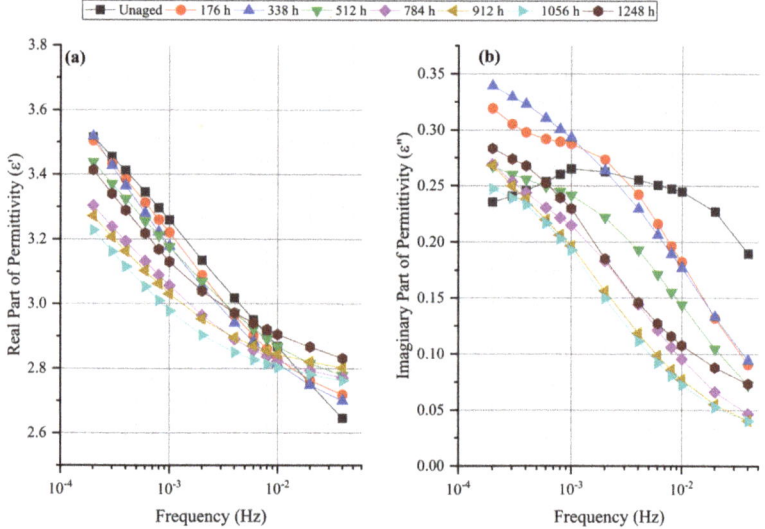

Figure 5. (a) Real and (b) imaginary parts of permittivities for thermal aging.

The results of the imaginary part of permittivity (ε'') are plotted in Figure 5b. The rearrangement of curves in the frequency range suggests that the ε'' curves shift towards a lower frequency range with aging, indicating the conductivity decrease with aging. This behavior explains the decreasing of ε'' values at the lowest frequencies. In the case of the unaged sample, the ε'' started with a certain value, then increased with the increase in frequency and reached a maximum value, and then again started to decrease. With thermal aging, the ε'' increased between 2×10^{-4} Hz and 1×10^{-3} Hz for the first two thermal aging periods, and then ε'' decreased with aging time. For frequency higher than 1×10^{-3} Hz there was a decreasing trend in the values of ε''. This behavior was observed until the sixth thermal aging period (1056 h), whereas the values increased at all frequency points.

3.1.2. Thermo-Mechanical Aging

The ε' in the case of the T-M aging is shown in Figure 6a. The behavior of the ε' against frequency was similar to the thermal stress, irrespective of the aging. In contrast, the observed impact of T-M was as the ε' increased after the first two periods for the whole frequency spectrum, while it started to decrease after the third period (507 h). A slight increase after the sixth period (1051 h) was observed, while a substantial decrease in the whole curve was noted after the seventh T-M period.

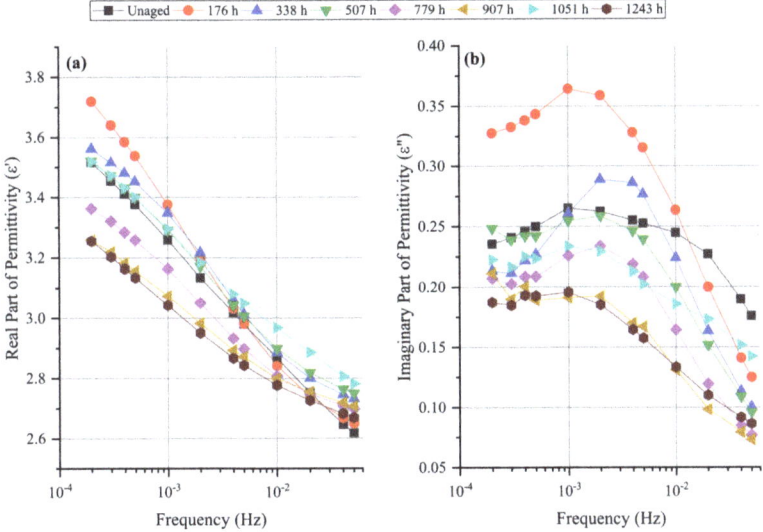

Figure 6. (a) Real and (b) imaginary parts of permittivities for thermo-mechanical aging.

The frequency plot of ε'' values is shown in Figure 6b. For almost all aging periods, ε'' started with a particular value. Then, the imaginary part of permittivity increased with frequency, reached a peak value at a specific frequency, and then declined with a further frequency increase. A noticeable increase in the values was noted in the ε'' after the first T-M period between 2×10^{-4} Hz and 1×10^{-3} Hz, while at higher frequencies, the values decreased. After a longer aging time, the ε'' decreased at all frequencies till the fifth T-M period (907 h). Like the ε', after 1051 h, the ε'' increased, which then decreased after the last aging round.

3.2. Shore D Hardness

The Shore D hardness recorded results of the cable under thermal and thermo-mechanical aging have been plotted in Figure 7. An overall increase in the hardness of the cable was also observed for thermal and thermo-mechanical aging. However, the hardness increase is higher in thermo-mechanical aging, which suggests the combined stress has a more intensive effect on the material structure, which results in higher hardness values.

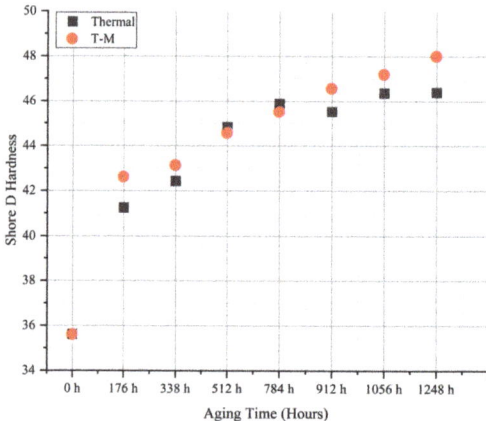

Figure 7. Shore D hardness against aging time thermal and thermo-mechanical (T-M) aging.

4. Discussion

The increase in ε' in a very-low-frequency range (below 1 Hz) is associated with the electrode polarization when the charge carriers accumulate near the electrodes, increasing the apparent value of the dielectric constant [42]. While the ε'' is a component related to the dielectric loss [43,44], one can expect that with aging, an increase in the losses will be experienced with the degradation of the polymer. Three frequencies were selected to simplify the analysis of the results: 200 µHz, 1 mHz, and 10 mHz, and the behavior of both kinds of aging were studied. The plot of the ε' and ε'' for each stress at the selected frequencies is shown in Figure 8.

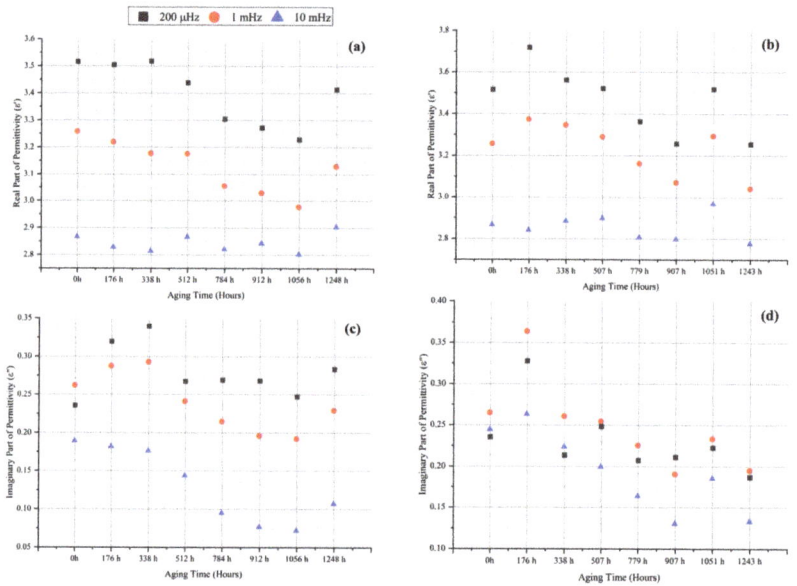

Figure 8. Real part of permittivity for (a) thermal aging, and (b) thermo-mechanical aging; imaginary part of permittivity for (c) thermal aging, and (d) thermo-mechanical aging at selected frequencies.

Under thermal aging, the ε' at the selected frequencies decreased with aging. After the last aging period, it increased, at 10 mHz, the ε' value even exceeded the unaged value.

Under T-M aging, at 200 µHz and 1 mHz, an initial increase in the ε' was observed, then the ε' started to decrease with more aging times. In contrast, different behavior is seen at 10 mHz, where the real part of permittivity dropped after the first period. Then ε' increased until the third period. More aging periods resulted in a decrease in the ε' values. A surprising behavior was observed under the T-M aging after the sixth period, where the values of the ε' increased even higher than the unaged values, which then decreased after the seventh period.

The effect of thermal stress on the ε'' caused an increase in the values for the first two periods at only 200 µHz and 1 mHz, which then declined with more aging, but at 10 mHz the values linearly decreased. The last thermal aging period resulted in a substantial increase in the values. At 200 µHz the value of ε'' remained higher than the unaged ones for all the aging periods.

While the T-M stress resulted in the increase in the ε'' after the first stress period at 1 mHz and 10 mHz, then it decreased with aging. In comparison, a clear trend was not observed at 200 µHz, where only the first and third periods affected the increase in the values higher than the unaged ones. Like the ε', the ε'' values increased at all the selected frequencies after the sixth thermal period, whereas after the seventh thermal period, the values decreased.

The loss peak frequencies are also plotted for thermal and thermo-mechanical aging (Figure 9). For an unaged cable sample, a polarization peak was observed at 1 mHz, which with aging, was shifted to 200 µHz Figure 9a. Nevertheless, the curves of Figure 5b suggest in the case of aged samples, the peak of the polarization peak should be below 200 µHz. In the case of the T-M stress, the polarization peak did not change its position after the first aging period. However, it shifted to a higher frequency of 2 mHz until the fourth aging period and then to 200 µHz after the fifth aging period, Figure 9b. At the same time, it shifted back to 1 mHz after the sixth period and remained as it for the seventh period.

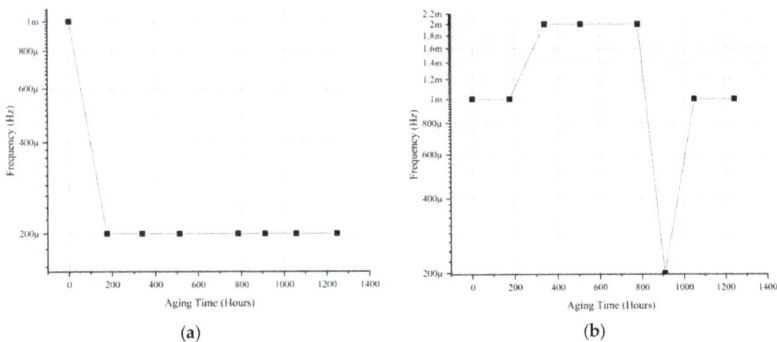

Figure 9. Shifting of the maximum value of the imaginary part of permittivity under (**a**) thermal, and (**b**) thermo-mechanical aging.

For a more detailed analysis of the dependence of real and imaginary parts of permittivity curves on aging, and similarly to [30,45], four deducted quantities have been calculated, namely the central real and imaginary parts of permittivity (*CRP* and *CIP*), and the real and imaginary permittivities' central frequencies (*RPCF* and *IPCF*). The *CRP* is calculated by summing up the multiplication of the logarithm of the frequencies by the measured ε' values at given frequencies and dividing this sum by the sum of the logarithm of the frequencies, as it can be seen in Equation (4).

$$CRP = \frac{\sum_{i=1}^{n} log_{10} f_i \varepsilon'_i(f_i)}{\sum_{i=1}^{n} log_{10} f_i} \qquad (4)$$

By changing the ε' to ε'' in Equation (4), the *CIP* can be calculated:

$$CIP = \frac{\sum_{i=1}^{n} \log_{10} f_i \varepsilon_i''(f_i)}{\sum_{i=1}^{n} \log_{10} f_i}. \quad (5)$$

The *RPCF* can be calculated as the average of the permittivity values weighted by the logarithm of the frequency:

$$RPCF = 10^{\frac{\sum_{i=1}^{n} \log_{10} f_i \varepsilon_i'(f_i)}{\sum_{i=1}^{n} \varepsilon_i'(f_i)}}. \quad (6)$$

By changing the ε' to ε'' in the Equation (6), the *IPCF* can be calculated:

$$IPCF = 10^{\frac{\sum_{i=1}^{n} \log_{10} f_i \varepsilon_i''(f_i)}{\sum_{i=1}^{n} \varepsilon_i''(f_i)}}. \quad (7)$$

These deducted quantities make spectroscopy curves evaluate easier since two numbers characterize the shifting of the curves. *CRP* and *CIP* are the characteristic values for real and imaginary permittivity changes over the frequency range of investigation. *RPCF* and *IPCF* characterise the shift of the curves in the frequency range. The change of *CRP* *RPCF* with aging is Figure 10.

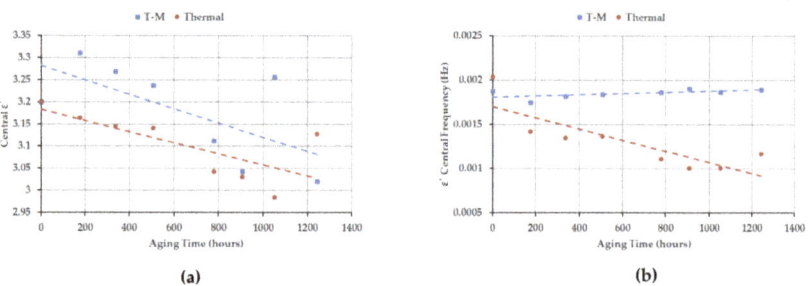

Figure 10. The calculated deducted quantities to characterize the $\varepsilon'(f)$ curves (**a**) central real part of permittivity (*CRP*); (**b**) real part of permittivity's central frequency (*RPCF*).

Figure 10a shows that *CRP* of thermally aged samples decreases with aging from the initial 3.2 below 3. However, after the last aging round, it jumps up to almost 3.15. In the case of thermo-mechanically aged samples, the *CRP* has increased over 3.3 after the first aging round. Then, it decreases. The fitted trendlines show that the real part of the permittivity for the T-M samples was higher by nearly 0.1 during the whole aging period in the investigated frequency range.

The *CRP* curve of thermally aged samples shows a monotonous decreasing trend with aging, while the *CRP* of thermo-mechanically aged samples does not change (Figure 10b). Accordingly, the curves of the real part of permittivity of thermally aged samples shift towards lower frequencies, while there is no significant change in the case of T-M samples.

In general, the *CIP* and *IPCF* values clearly show the changing of an average loss in the investigated frequency range and the changing of the average polarization peak with aging. The values of *CIP* and *IPCF* are depicted in Figure 11.

Figure 11a shows the *CIP* change with aging in case thermal and T-M aging. In both cases, the dielectric loss increases at the beginning of aging. The *CIP* increases in the first two aging periods of thermal aging. A more significant increase can be observed in the first aging period of T-M aging, then the *CIP* values decrease. By calculating the linear trend, no significant difference can be observed between thermal and T-M *CIP* values. The *IPCF* values (Figure 11b) were dropped by 0.5 mHz after the first aging round, then the *IPCF* of thermally aged samples decreased, while that of T-M samples shows a small variation, a minimal decreasing trend can be observed. The calculated linear trends suggest the *IPCF* values of T-M samples are higher 0.5 mHz at the ending of aging. The trendlines show the ε'' curves shifted towards higher frequencies in the case of T-M aging. Hence the polarisation peaks are at higher frequencies than the thermally aged samples.

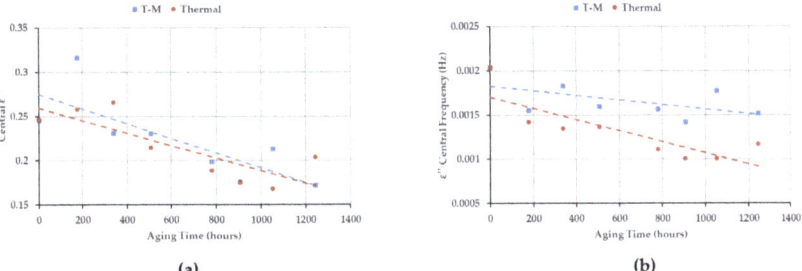

Figure 11. The calculated deducted quantities to characterize the $\varepsilon''(f)$ curves (**a**) central imaginary part of permittivity (*CIP*); (**b**) imaginary part of permittivity's central frequency (*IPCF*).

The comparison of the change in Shore D hardness of thermally and thermo-mechanically aged samples has been drawn in Figure 7. For most of the aging periods (176 h, 338 h, 912 h, 1056 h, and 1248 h), the increases in hardness were 19.7%, 21.2%, 30.8%, 32.61%, and 34.89%, respectively, for T-M in comparison to 15.78%, 19.12%, 27.82%, 30.18% and 30.26% for thermal only. Hence, the thermo-mechanical stress has resulted in more hardness of the cable than the thermal stress only.

Under the thermal stress in the presence of oxygen, it is believed that the polymer undergoes molecular structural changes due to the cross-linking, chain scission, and oxidation reactions, which occur at the same time in the crystalline and amorphous regions. The actual cause of the degradation of the polymer depends on the dominance of one of these reactions. The cross-linking reaction generates a solid network that opposes the external field's effect and restrains the dipoles' movements, which is a case opposite to the chain scission reaction.

However, a very simple cable was chosen for the experiment, from the point of view of aging, the subject of the experiment is a complex structure. It contains two layers made from different polymers; moreover, the inner XLPE is covered by the CSPE jacket. Therefore, during the accelerated aging, the XLPE insulation was not contacted directly with the air. By investigating cable jacket samples removed from commercial cables, the significant effect of diffusion-limited oxidation (DLO) on the degradation of CSPE cable jacket material has been reported at temperatures as low as 110 °C [46]. Consequently, in the case of intact cable samples, when the air contacts only the outer surface of samples, it can be assumed the CSPE jacket consumes oxygen during aging at elevated temperatures. Therefore, the oxidative degradation of the XLPE insulation was very limited; hence, cross-linking and recrystallization were the main degradation mechanisms [47].

In addition to these reactions, materials such as CSPE, which has chlorine and sulfur dioxide attached to the polyethylene backbone, undergo dehydrohalogenation. During dehydrohalogenation, the halogen atom is separated from the polymer chain and the hydrogen, resulting in double bonds in the polymer chain [48,49], resulting in increased conductivity and permittivity [50].

Under the exclusive mechanical stress, it has been reported that the polymer may experiences two stresses: tension and compression [14]. The former assists the movement of the molecular chain, which may lead to the fracture of the chain and could increase the microcavities size [51,52]. It has also been reported that this would also increase the space charges. In contrast, the compression stress acts opposite to the tension, where the molecular chains come close to each other and support the bond attraction leading to more stabilization. This also inhibits the increase in the intensity of space charges. Since in our case, the cable has been exposed to both thermal and mechanical stresses, where the inner side of the cable is under compression force and the outer side under tension force, Figure 12. Therefore, cross-linking and chain scission reactions in the presence of oxygen under thermal stress are also playing their role.

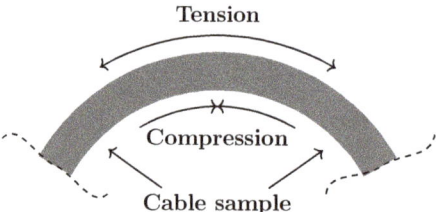

Figure 12. Tension and compression stresses on a bended cable sample.

The cable insulation's hardness increase under both types of stresses is also related to the reason that at elevated temperature, the generated small molecules due to decomposition reactions re-cross link with each other and increase the cable's hardness [47]. This phenomenon in the presence of compression stress due to mechanical aging is reinforced.

From the point of dielectric measurement view, the insulation and the jacket of non-shielded, single-core cables are considered a layered arrangement. Hence, the applied electrode arrangement (covering the cable's surface by conductive foil) can investigate only the resultant dielectric properties, i.e., the real and imaginary parts of permittivities, of the layers. Similarly, the Shore D hardness also measures the resultant hardness of both layers. Since the degradation processes also increase the hardness of the CSPE and the XLPE, the result will also be an increasing trend in thermal and T-M aging cases. However, conductivity and permittivity of CSPE increase due to thermal aging, the resultant dielectric loss and permittivity decrease in the investigated frequency range according to the change of *CIP* values. Nevertheless, degradation processes of the XLPE, namely the cross-linking and recrystallization, decrease its conductivity and permittivity [53]. Since the thickness of the XLPE insulation is higher by 50%, the resultant values of the real and imaginary parts of permittivities are significantly affected by the XLPE. The annealing effect of XLPE can cause the initial increase in CIP. The annealing effect increases the conductivity of XLPE at the beginning of thermal treatment [54].

It can be concluded that the parallel thermal-mechanical stress results in more intensive degradation of the mechanical properties of cable insulation than the thermal stress alone. Since the layered structure of jacket and insulation makes it difficult to identify the degradation processes and analyze the dielectric behavior. Further studies, including chemical analysis, are needed to reveal the degradation mechanism of single-core LV cables. This study would be beneficial to point out the importance of applying combined mechanical-thermal stressing for accelerated aging testing in the qualification procedure of NPP cables.

5. Conclusions

The main purpose of the work was to compare the dielectric behavior in-low-frequency range and Shore D hardness of thermally and thermo-mechanically aged single-core CSPE/XLPE insulated LV NPP cables. For the purpose of investigation, one group of samples was straightened, and the other one was coiled on a cylinder. Both groups of samples were aged at 120 °C for more than 1200 h. The dielectric spectrum in the 200 µHz to 50 mHz range and the Shore D hardness were measured on both groups. By analyzing the dielectric spectra, the real and imaginary parts of permittivities changed differently in both groups although, they did not show a clear trend with aging. To clarify the changes in the dielectric spectrum due to aging, derived quantities, namely, the central real and imaginary parts of permittivity and the real and imaginary permittivities' central frequency were introduced. The deducted quantities show that the real part of the permittivity of the thermo-mechanically aged samples was higher by nearly 0.1 than that of thermally aged ones during the whole aging period in the investigated frequency range. The deducted quantities show that the real part of the permittivity of the thermo-mechanically aged samples was higher by nearly 0.1 than that of thermally aged ones during the whole aging period in the investigated frequency range. At the same time, the central frequency of the real part of permittivity curves decreased by 1 mHz due to thermal aging. A similar change was not observed on thermo-mechanically aged samples.

However, the central imaginary part of permittivity did not differ significantly between the groups, the imaginary permittivity's central frequency was higher by 0.5 mHz in the case of thermo-mechanically aged samples. This suggests a higher conductivity of thermo-mechanically aged samples, which can be the result of the annealing effect. During aging, the Shore D hardness was also higher on the thermo-mechanically aged samples than the thermally aged ones. At the end of aging, the hardness of the thermo-mechanically aged samples was 34% higher than the initial value, while that of the thermally aged samples was only 30% higher.

Based on the results, it can be concluded that mechanical stress has a strong impact on the degradation of the polymeric materials of the cable in combination with the thermal stress, which is considered during the simulation of service aging of cables. These results could lead to the inclusion of mechanical stress in the aging procedure of cable qualification, enabling the design of more robust cables in a harsh environment. For the future perspective, it is intended to carry out the chemical and other electrical and mechanical tests to further elaborate and understand the impact of mechanical stress with thermal stress on the LV cable aging.

Author Contributions: Conceptualization, R.S.A.A., E.M. and Z.Á.T.; investigation R.S.A.A., E.M. and Z.Á.T.; formal analysis, E.M.; writing—original draft preparation, E.M. and Z.Á.T.; visualization, E.M.; writing—review and editing, R.S.A.A. and Z.Á.T.; supervision, Z.Á.T.; funding acquisition, Z.Á.T. All authors have read and agreed to the published version of the manuscript.

Funding: Project no. 123672 has been implemented with the support provided by the National Research, Development and Innovation Fund of Hungary, financed under the KNN_16 funding scheme.

Data Availability Statement: The data presented in this study are available on request from the corresponding author.

Conflicts of Interest: The authors declare no conflict of interest.

References

1. International Atomic Energy Agency. *Energy, Electricity and Nuclear Power Estimates for the Period up to 2050*; Number 1 in Reference Data Series; International Atomic Energy Agency: Vienna, Austria, 2021.
2. International Atomic Energy Agency. *Assessing and Managing Cable Ageing in Nuclear Power Plants*; Number NP-T-3.6 in Nuclear Energy Series; International Atomic Energy Agency: Vienna, Austria, 2012.
3. International Atomic Energy Agency. *Safety of Nuclear Power Plants: Commissioning and Operation*; Number SSR-2/2 (Rev. 1) in Specific Safety Requirements; International Atomic Energy Agency: Vienna, Austria, 2016.
4. *IEEE Standard for Qualifying Electric Cables and Splices for Nuclear Facilities*; IEEE Std 383-2015 (Revision of IEEE Std 383-2003); IEEE: New York, NY, USA, 2015; pp. 1–27. [CrossRef]
5. Subudhi, M. *Literature Review of Environmental Qualification of Safety-Related Electric Cables: Summary of Past Work*; Technical Report NUREG/CR–6384-Vol1; Brookhaven National Lab.: Upton, NY, USA, 1996; Volume 1.
6. Gazdzinski, R.; Denny, W.; Toman, G.; Butwin, R. *Aging Management Guideline for Commercial Nuclear Power Plants, Electrical Cable and Terminations*; Sandia Labs Report, SAND96-0344; Sandia National Laboratories: Albuquerque, NM, USA, 1996.
7. Bustard, L.; Holzman, P. *Low-Voltage Environmentally-Qualified Cable License Renewal Industry Report: Revision 1*; Final Report; Electric Power Research Inst.: Palo Alto, CA, USA, 1994.
8. Chailan, J.F.; Boiteux, G.; Chauchard, J.; Pinel, B.; Seytre, G. Effects of thermal degradation on the viscoelastic and dielectric properties of chlorosulfonated polyethylene (CSPE) compounds. *Polym. Degrad. Stab.* **1995**, *48*, 61–65. [CrossRef]
9. Nanda, M.; Tripathy, D. Physico-mechanical and electrical properties of conductive carbon black reinforced chlorosulfonated polyethylene vulcanizates. *Express Polym. Lett.* **2008**, *2*, 855–865. [CrossRef]
10. Mustafa, E.; Afia, R.S.A.; Tamus, Z.Á. Condition Monitoring Uncertainties and Thermal–Radiation Multistress Accelerated Aging Tests for Nuclear Power Plant Cables: A Review. *Period. Polytech. Electr. Eng. Comput. Sci.* **2020**, *64*, 20–32. [CrossRef]

11. Suraci, S.V.; Fabiani, D.; Mazzocchetti, L.; Giorgini, L. Degradation Assessment of Polyethylene-Based Material Through Electrical and Chemical-Physical Analyses. *Energies* **2020**, *13*, 650. [CrossRef]
12. Mustafa, E.; Afia, R.S.A.; Tamus, Z.Á. Application of Non-Destructive Condition Monitoring Techniques on Irradiated Low Voltage Unshielded Nuclear Power Cables. *IEEE Access* **2020**, *8*, 166024–166033. [CrossRef]
13. Plaček, V.; Kohout, T.; Kábrt, J.; Jiran, J. The influence of mechanical stress on cable service life-time. *Polym. Test.* **2011**, *30*, 709–715. [CrossRef]
14. Afia, R.S.A.; Mustafa, E.; Tamus, Z.Á. Mechanical Stresses on Polymer Insulating Materials. In Proceedings of the 2018 International Conference on Diagnostics in Electrical Engineering (Diagnostika), Pilsen, Czech Republic, 4–7 September 2018; pp. 1–4. [CrossRef]
15. Ball, E.; Holdup, H.; Skipper, D.; Vecillio, B. *Development of Crosslinked Polyethylene Insulation for UV Cables*; CIGRE Paper; CIGRE: Paris, France, 1984; Volume 21.
16. Chen, W.; Allen, J.K.; Tsui, K.L.; Mistree, F. A Procedure for Robust Design: Minimizing Variations Caused by Noise Factors and Control Factors. *J. Mech. Des.* **1996**, *118*, 478–485. [CrossRef]
17. Petkovski, D.B. *Multivariable Control Systems Design: A Case Study of Robust Control of Nuclear Power Plants*; Pergamon Press: Oxford, UK, 1987.
18. Banavar, R.; Deshpande, U. Robust controller design for a nuclear power plant using H/sub /spl infin// optimization. *IEEE Trans. Nucl. Sci.* **1998**, *45*, 129–140. [CrossRef]
19. Vajpayee, V.; Becerra, V.; Bausch, N.; Deng, J.; Shimjith, S.; Arul, A.J. Robust-optimal integrated control design technique for a pressurized water-type nuclear power plant. *Prog. Nucl. Energy* **2021**, *131*, 103575. [CrossRef]
20. Pánek, D.; Orosz, T.; Karban, P. Artap: Robust Design Optimization Framework for Engineering Applications. In Proceedings of the 2019 Third International Conference on Intelligent Computing in Data Sciences (ICDS), Marrakech, Morocco, 28–30 October 2019; pp. 1–6. [CrossRef]
21. Orosz, T.; Rassõlkin, A.; Kallaste, A.; Arsénio, P.; Pánek, D.; Kaska, J.; Karban, P. Robust Design Optimization and Emerging Technologies for Electrical Machines: Challenges and Open Problems. *Appl. Sci.* **2020**, *10*, 6653. [CrossRef]
22. Gadó, K.; Orosz, T. Robust and Multi-Objective Pareto Design of a Solenoid. *Electronics* **2021**, *10*, 2139. [CrossRef]
23. Karban, P.; Pánek, D.; Orosz, T.; Petrášová, I.; Doležel, I. FEM based robust design optimization with Agros and Ārtap. *Comput. Math. Appl.* **2021**, *81*, 618–633. [CrossRef]
24. Arvia, E.M.; Sheldon, R.T.; Bowler, N. A capacitive test method for cable insulation degradation assessment. In Proceedings of the 2014 IEEE Conference on Electrical Insulation and Dielectric Phenomena (CEIDP), Des Moines, IA, USA, 19–22 October 2014; pp. 514–517. [CrossRef]
25. Linde, E.; Verardi, L.; Fabiani, D.; Gedde, U. Dielectric spectroscopy as a condition monitoring technique for cable insulation based on crosslinked polyethylene. *Polym. Test.* **2015**, *44*, 135–142. [CrossRef]
26. Imperatore, M.V.; Fifield, L.S.; Fabiani, D.; Bowler, N. Dielectric spectroscopy on thermally aged, intact, poly-vinyl chloride/ethylene propylene rubber (PVC/EPR) multipolar cables. In Proceedings of the 2017 IEEE Conference on Electrical Insulation and Dielectric Phenomenon (CEIDP), Fort Worth, TX, USA, 22–25 October 2017; pp. 173–176. [CrossRef]
27. Sriraman, A.; Bowler, N.; Glass, S.; Fifield, L.S. Dielectric and Mechanical Behavior of Thermally Aged EPR/CPE Cable Materials. In Proceedings of the 2018 IEEE Conference on Electrical Insulation and Dielectric Phenomena (CEIDP), Cancun, Mexico, 21–24 October 2018; pp. 598–601. [CrossRef]
28. Suraci, S.V.; Fabiani, D.; Xu, A.; Roland, S.; Colin, X. Ageing Assessment of XLPE LV Cables for Nuclear Applications Through Physico-Chemical and Electrical Measurements. *IEEE Access* **2020**, *8*, 27086–27096. [CrossRef]
29. Suraci, S.V.; Fabiani, D.; Colin, X.; Roland, S. Chemical and electrical characterization of XLPE cables exposed to radio-thermal aging. In Proceedings of the 2020 IEEE 3rd International Conference on Dielectrics (ICD), Valencia, Spain, 5–31 July 2020; pp. 57–60. [CrossRef]
30. Afia, R.S.A.; Mustafa, E.; Tamus, Z.Á. Aging Mechanisms and Non-Destructive Aging Indicators of XLPE/CSPE Unshielded LV Nuclear Power Cables Subjected to Simultaneous Radiation-Mechanical Aging. *Polymers* **2021**, *13*, 3033. [CrossRef]
31. Mustafa, E.; Afia, R.S.A.; Nouini, O.; Tamus, Z.Á. Implementation of Non-Destructive Electrical Condition Monitoring Techniques on Low-Voltage Nuclear Cables: I. Irradiation Aging of EPR/CSPE Cables. *Energies* **2021**, *14*, 5139. [CrossRef]
32. Matsunami, U.; Mikami, M. Study on the ageing degradation diagnosis of electric cables based on indenter modulus method. *INSS J.* **2008**, *15*, 236–242.
33. McCarter, D.; Shumaker, B.; McConkey, B.; Hashemian, H. Nuclear power plant instrumentation and control cable prognostics using indenter modulus measurements. *Int. J. Progn. Health Manag.* **2015**, *6*. [CrossRef]
34. Hashemian, H.; Mcconkey, B.; Harmon, G.; Sexton, C. Methods for testing nuclear power plant cables. *IEEE Instrum. Meas. Mag.* **2013**, *16*, 31–36. [CrossRef]
35. International Atomic Energy Agency. *Benchmark Analysis for Condition Monitoring Test Techniques of Aged Low Voltage Cables in Nuclear Power Plants*; Number 1825 in TECDOC Series; International Atomic Energy Agency: Vienna, Austria, 2017.
36. Altındal Yerişkin, S.; Balbaşı, M.; Tataroğlu, A. Frequency and voltage dependence of dielectric properties, complex electric modulus, and electrical conductivity in Au/7% graphene doped-PVA/n-Si (MPS) structures. *J. Appl. Polym. Sci.* **2016**, *133*, 43827. [CrossRef]

37. Yıldız, D.E.; Dökme, İ. Frequency and gate voltage effects on the dielectric properties and electrical conductivity of Al/SiO2/p-Si metal-insulator-semiconductor Schottky diodes. *J. Appl. Phys.* **2011**, *110*, 014507. [CrossRef]
38. Fofana, I.; Hadjadj, Y. Electrical-Based Diagnostic Techniques for Assessing Insulation Condition in Aged Transformers. *Energies* **2016**, *9*, 679. [CrossRef]
39. Fothergill, J.C.; Dodd, S.J.; Dissado, L.A.; Liu, T.; Nilsson, U.H. The measurement of very low conductivity and dielectric loss in XLPE cables: A possible method to detect degradation due to thermal aging. *IEEE Trans. Dielectr. Electr. Insul.* **2011**, *18*, 1544–1553. [CrossRef]
40. Koch, M.; Raetzke, S.; Krueger, M. Moisture diagnostics of power transformers by a fast and reliable dielectric response method. In Proceedings of the 2010 IEEE International Symposium on Electrical Insulation, San Diego, CA, USA, 6–9 June 2010; pp. 1–5. [CrossRef]
41. American Society for Testing and Materials. *ASTM D2240-05 Standard Test Method for Rubber Property: Durometer Hardness*; ASTM: West Conshohocken, PA, USA, 2010.
42. Min, D.; Yan, C.; Huang, Y.; Li, S.; Ohki, Y. Dielectric and Carrier Transport Properties of Silicone Rubber Degraded by Gamma Irradiation. *Polymers* **2017**, *9*, 533. [CrossRef]
43. Menczel, J.D.; Prime, R.B. *Thermal Analysis of Polymers: Fundamentals and Applications*; John Wiley & Sons: Hoboken, NJ, USA, 2009.
44. Jonscher, A.K. Dielectric relaxation in solids. *J. Phys. D Appl. Phys.* **1999**, *32*, R57–R70. [CrossRef]
45. Csányi, G.M.; Bal, S.; Tamus, Z.Á. Dielectric Measurement Based Deducted Quantities to Track Repetitive, Short-Term Thermal Aging of Polyvinyl Chloride (PVC) Cable Insulation. *Polymers* **2020**, *12*, 2809. [CrossRef] [PubMed]
46. Gillen, K.T.; Assink, R.; Bernstein, R.; Celina, M. Condition monitoring methods applied to degradation of chlorosulfonated polyethylene cable jacketing materials. *Polym. Degrad. Stab.* **2006**, *91*, 1273–1288. [CrossRef]
47. Zhang, Y.; Wu, Z.; Qian, C.; Tan, X.; Yang, J.; Zhong, L. Research on Lifespan Prediction of Cross-Linked Polyethylene Material for XLPE Cables. *Appl. Sci.* **2020**, *10*, 5381. [CrossRef]
48. Mustafa, E.; Ádám, T.Z.; Afia, R.S.A.; Asipuela, A. Thermal Degradation and Condition Monitoring of Low Voltage Power Cables in Nuclear Power Industry. In *Technological Innovation for Industry and Service Systems*; Camarinha-Matos, L.M., Almeida, R., Oliveira, J., Eds.; Springer International Publishing: Cham, Switzerland, 2019; pp. 405–413.
49. York, R.J.; Ulrich, J.B.; Murphy, G.; Prather, D.G. *Mitigation of Aging in Low Voltage Power Cables in Nuclear Power Plants*; University of Tennessee: Knoxville, TN, USA, 2015.
50. Lee, J.H.; Kang, M.K.; Jeon, J.S.; Lee, S.H.; Kim, I.Y.; Park, H.S.; Shin, Y.D. A study on the properties of CSPE according to accelerated thermal aging years. *J. Electr. Eng. Technol.* **2014**, *9*, 643–648. [CrossRef]
51. Du, B.X.; Xu, H.; Li, J. Effects of mechanical stretching on space charge behaviors of PP/POE blend for HVDC cables. *IEEE Trans. Dielectr. Electr. Insul.* **2017**, *24*, 1438–1445. [CrossRef]
52. Du, B.X.; Su, J.G.; Han, T. Effects of mechanical stretching on electrical treeing characteristics in EPDM. *IEEE Trans. Dielectr. Electr. Insul.* **2018**, *25*, 84–93. [CrossRef]
53. Chi, X.; Li, J.; Ji, M.; Liu, W.; Li, S. Thermal-Oxidative Aging Effects on the Dielectric Properties of Nuclear Cable Insulation. *Materials* **2020**, *13*, 2215. [CrossRef]
54. Diego, J.A.; Belana, J.; Orrit, J.; Cañadas, J.C.; Mudarra, M.; Frutos, F.; Acedo, M. Annealing effect on the conductivity of XLPE insulation in power cable. *IEEE Trans. Dielectr. Electr. Insul.* **2011**, *18*, 1554–1561. [CrossRef]

Article

Optimization of a 3D-Printed Permanent Magnet Coupling Using Genetic Algorithm and Taguchi Method

Ekaterina Andriushchenko [1,*], Ants Kallaste [1], Anouar Belahcen [1,2], Toomas Vaimann [1,3], Anton Rassõlkin [1,3], Hamidreza Heidari [1] and Hans Tiismus [1]

[1] Department of Electrical Power Engineering and Mechatronics, Tallinn University of Technology, Ehitajate tee 5, 12616 Tallinn, Estonia; ants.kallaste@taltech.ee (A.K.); anouar.belahcen@taltech.ee (A.B.); toomas.vaimann@taltech.ee (T.V.); anton.rassolkin@taltech.ee (A.R.); haheid@taltech.ee (H.H.); hans.tiismus@taltech.ee (H.T.)
[2] Department of Electrical Engineering and Automation, Aalto University, P.O. Box 15500 Aalto, Finland
[3] Faculty of Control Systems and Robotics, ITMO University, 197101 Saint Petersburg, Russia
* Correspondence: ekandr@taltech.ee; Tel.: +372-5614-0410

Citation: Andriushchenko, E.; Kallaste, A.; Belahcen, A.; Vaimann, T.; Rassõlkin, A.; Heidari, H.; Tiismus, H. Optimization of a 3D-Printed Permanent Magnet Coupling Using Genetic Algorithm and Taguchi Method. *Electronics* **2021**, *10*, 494. https://doi.org/10.3390/electronics10040494

Academic Editor: Hamid Reza Karimi

Received: 19 January 2021
Accepted: 18 February 2021
Published: 20 February 2021

Publisher's Note: MDPI stays neutral with regard to jurisdictional claims in published maps and institutional affiliations.

Copyright: © 2021 by the authors. Licensee MDPI, Basel, Switzerland. This article is an open access article distributed under the terms and conditions of the Creative Commons Attribution (CC BY) license (https://creativecommons.org/licenses/by/4.0/).

Abstract: In recent decades, the genetic algorithm (GA) has been extensively used in the design optimization of electromagnetic devices. Despite the great merits possessed by the GA, its processing procedure is highly time-consuming. On the contrary, the widely applied Taguchi optimization method is faster with comparable effectiveness in certain optimization problems. This study explores the abilities of both methods within the optimization of a permanent magnet coupling, where the optimization objectives are the minimization of coupling volume and maximization of transmitted torque. The optimal geometry of the coupling and the obtained characteristics achieved by both methods are nearly identical. The magnetic torque density is enhanced by more than 20%, while the volume is reduced by 17%. Yet, the Taguchi method is found to be more time-efficient and effective within the considered optimization problem. Thanks to the additive manufacturing techniques, the initial design and the sophisticated geometry of the Taguchi optimal designs are precisely fabricated. The performances of the coupling designs are validated using an experimental setup.

Keywords: design optimization; genetic algorithms; Taguchi designs; electromagnetic coupling; additive manufacturing

1. Introduction

The term permanent magnet (PM) coupling or clutch refers to a device that is used to transmit torque between two shafts without mechanical contact. Torque transmission is served by the magnetic field induced by PMs placed on the driving member. Throughout the years, PM couplings have been widely employed in blowers and compressors, conveyors and pumps, and food processing equipment due to their unique qualities [1,2]. For instance, the highlighted features of the PM couplings are the ability to transmit torque through a separator and easy maintenance. Still, there are several important aspects to take into account in PM couplings design. Among these concerns, mass characteristics, transmitted torque, and their balance remain challenging.

Nowadays, the design optimization is extensively used for enhancing the performance of PM couplings. The majority of the studies on PM coupling optimization have utilized coupling dimensions as optimization parameters [3–5]. On the other hand, the optimization of coupling shapes may propose a better improvement of the device performance.

Researchers have been avoiding the optimization of coupling shapes due to the restricted abilities of conventional manufacturing techniques. Presently, additive manufacturing (AM) is considered a constructive alternative to the conventional ways of fabrication [6–9]. Being a flexible and low-material waste technique, the AM can construct geometrically intricate components. Overall, the AM techniques provide an opportunity to discover more favorable shapes of PM couplings and greatly enhance their performance.

To date, several methods have been developed to optimize the design of electrical machines and devices. The direct and indirect optimization methods (DOM and IOM), multi-level optimization methods, and robust optimization methods are the main approaches. In this study, two methodological approaches are selected: the DOM accompanied by the genetic algorithm (GA) and the Taguchi optimization method [10,11]. The DOM presents a clear and intuitive structure, since it simply utilizes a finite element model (FEM) along with the GA [12–16]. The unique features of the GA, such as the ability to obtain the global minimum, handle non-analytic formulation of optimization problems, and high flexibility, justify its popularity among researchers. This algorithm not only considerably narrows the solution space during optimization but also presents an impressive searching ability. Regardless of the great advantages of DOM-GA optimization, it often appears time-consuming [17–19]. In contrast with the DOM-GA, the Taguchi method requires a considerably lower number of calculations that significantly reduces the execution time [20]. This method takes into account the manufacturing variations of the optimization parameters within the optimization model and, consequently, reaches the high reliability of the optimization results [21–23]. However, far too little attention has been paid to the Taguchi method within the design optimization of electromagnetic devices.

This paper aims to carry out the optimization of the PM coupling shapes with the following optimization objectives: minimization of the coupling volume and maximization of the transmitted torque. Additionally, the study compares the DOM-GA and the Taguchi method in terms of the obtained optimization results and the required execution time. The importance and originality of this study is that it explores complex shapes of the PM coupling design and proposes a great improvement of the device performance. Moreover, the comparative analysis of the DOM-GA and Taguchi method should make an important contribution to the field of design optimization of electromagnetic devices.

The paper is organized as follows. First, the initial design of the PM coupling and definition of the optimization model is presented in Sections 2 and 3, respectively. It will then go on to Section 4, which is dedicated to GA optimization, and Section 5, which presents the Taguchi optimization. Next, Section 6 provides a comprehensive comparison of the applied optimization methods. Then, Section 7 describes the experimental setup and provides the test results for the initial and optimal designs of the coupling, respectively. Finally, the discussion and conclusion of the study are presented in Section 8.

2. Permanent Magnet Coupling Design

This paper considers an optimization problem of a face type PM coupling. Before proceeding to the optimization, it is important to overview the concept of the PM coupling design and operation principle. To illustrate the structure of the coupling, Figure 1 is presented. The figure shows two main components of the coupling: driving and driven members. The driving member possesses magnetic teeth, while the driven member has steel teeth. Along with the structure, Figure 1 demonstrates the main dimensions of the coupling. Additionally, Figure 1 shows the angle of deviation of the coupling members θ. To demonstrate θ, the centers of the disks C1 and C2 are specified. Table 1 lists the main parameters of the coupling geometry.

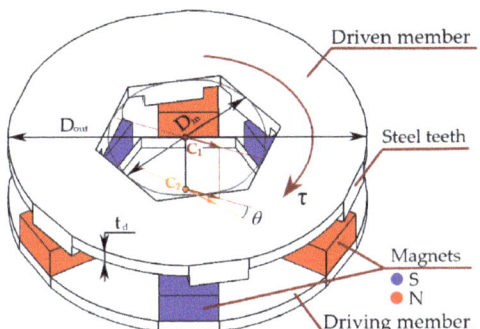

Figure 1. The initial design of the permanent magnet (PM) coupling.

Table 1. Coupling specifications.

Dimension/Materials	Value
Outer diameter D_{out}	30 mm
Inner diameter D_{in}	12.5 mm
Thickness of the disks t_d	1.2 mm
Steel teeth height	1.6 mm
Steel teeth width	5 mm
Steel teeth length	8 mm
Magnets thickness	3 mm
Magnets width	5 mm
Magnets length	8 mm
Air gap	1.5 mm

The operation concept of the PM coupling is based on the attraction efforts that appear between the magnets placed on the driving disk and the driven member made of steel. The magnetic torque induced in the driven disk depends on the angle of deviation of the coupling members θ, magnetic flux density B, and magnetic field intensity H [24]:

$$\tau = \frac{\delta \int_V \int_0^H BdHdV}{\delta \theta} \quad (1)$$

For prototyping, the steel material with 6.5% silicon content was utilized for the disks and driven member's teeth. The neodymium magnets N52 (Sintered Nd-Fe-B) were employed to provide the magnetic force.

The finite element analysis of the coupling initial design was carried out through Symcenter MagNet. According to the initial design modelling, the volume of the coupling was 2.31×10^{-6} m^3 and the maximum magnetic torque was 73.0×10^{-3} Nm. Figure 2 presents the dependence of the torque on the angle of deviation. The static simulation results and their approximation are provided. The approximation was carried out by fitting the smoothing spline within the Matlab Curve Fitting Toolbox.

It is important to notice that the magnetic torque reached its maximum when the angle of deviation of the coupling members θ was 17°. Therefore, this position was chosen for static simulations within the optimization.

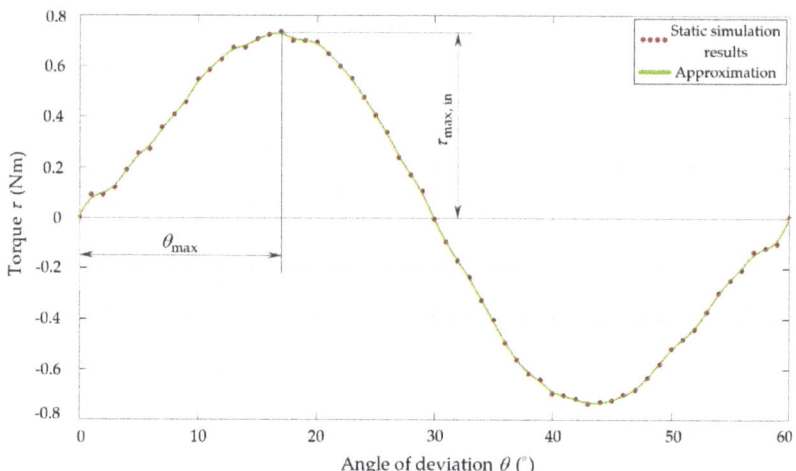

Figure 2. Magnetic torque versus angle of deviation of the initial design of the coupling.

3. Permanent Magnet Coupling Optimization Model

Figure 3 shows the distribution of the magnetic flux density obtained through the MagNet for the initial design of the coupling. It can be seen that the flux density saturation is quite low in particular areas of the coupling disks. Here, the low saturation is a sign that the material of the coupling is not utilized efficiently. Therefore, the coupling design needs to be improved to enhance the effectiveness of material usage. For this purpose, the design optimization can be employed.

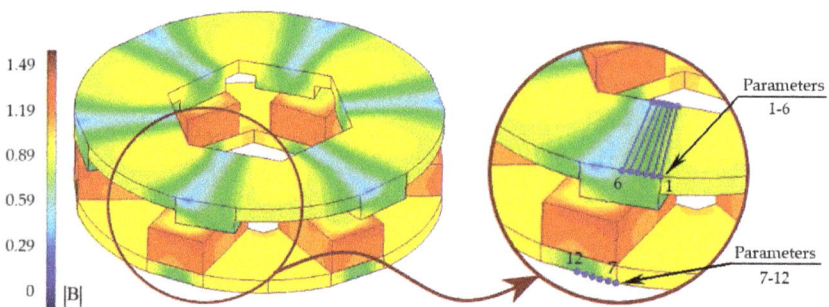

Figure 3. Initial design of the coupling with the distribution of magnetic flux density and illustration of the optimization parameters.

Many researchers have optimized PM couplings paying particular attention to the torque output and volume of the utilized materials [1,4]. Traditionally, linear dimensions, such as diameters of the disks or sizes of magnets, are chosen as optimization parameters. This might be due to the restrictions of the conventional methods of fabrication on design production.

Since AD techniques allow producing complex geometry, the search for optimal dimensions can be replaced with the search for optimal shapes. Therefore, this paper aims to obtain an optimal shape of the PM coupling disks to minimize the material usage and maximize the transmitted torque.

In solving an optimization problem, the first step is to create an optimization model, which involves defining objectives, constraints, and parameters. This study considers the optimization problem, in which the objective functions were non-analytical. More specifically, the volume and the magnetic torque were obtained using FEA within Simcenter MAGNET. The optimization problem was unconstrained. To find an optimal shape of the clutch disks, the vector of optimization parameters was formed by twelve elements, which represented geometrical locations of the points. Figure 3 shows a set of the geometrical points used as the optimization parameters. As can be noted, the points were placed within the area of low saturation of the coupling disks. Within this area, the material could be potentially removed in order to increase the effectiveness of material usage. The demonstrated set was repeated along the circumference of the coupling disks. Within the optimization, the variation of the parameters had the following limits: [0 . . . 1] mm. The disks' general thicknesses t_d were not included in the group of the optimization parameters, since they were minimized beforehand and their further reduction negatively influenced the torque.

4. Optimization Using Genetic Algorithm

4.1. Genetic Algorithm

To carry out a multi-objective optimization, an optimization model should be formulated in the following view:

$$\begin{aligned} \text{minimize } & f(x) = [f_1(x), f_2(x), \ldots, f_n(x)]^T, \\ \text{subject to } & g_i(x) \leq 0, i = \{1 \ldots m\}, \\ & h_j(x) = 0, j = \{1 \ldots p\}, \end{aligned} \quad (2)$$

where the vector $f(x)$ is formed from objective functions, and the vector x presents a set of k optimization parameters. The functions $g_i(x)$ and $h_j(x)$ are constraint functions.

In solving multi-objective problems (MOPs), the ultimate goal is to find good compromises between the objective functions. Traditionally, this goal is achieved using the concept of Pareto Optimality.

To understand the idea of the Pareto Optimality, several definitions should be presented. First, a classic definition of Pareto Optimal Solution can be expressed as follows. A solution $x \in \Omega$ is called a Pareto Optimal Solution if there is no $x' \in \Omega$ for which the objective vector $f_k(x')$ dominates $f_k(x)$. Here, Ω implies the feasible region of the optimization problem. The feasible region is an area of the parameter space, where all constraints are satisfied. Second, Pareto Dominance can be defined as follows. A vector $f_k(x)$ is said to dominate another vector $f_k(x')$ only if $f_k(x)$ is partially less than $f_k(x')$.

Essentially, the main functions of the multi-objective genetic algorithm (MOGA) are to obtain a set of Pareto Optimal Solutions (*P**). The set *P** is a set of optimal values of the optimization parameters. Mathematically, the Pareto Optimal Set can be defined as follows [19]:

$$P* := \{x \in \Omega \mid \neg \exists\, x' \in \Omega \mid f(x') \leq f(x)\}, \quad (3)$$

The second function of the MOGA is to construct the Pareto Front (*PF**). At first, many points within the feasible region should be calculated. If the number of the points is high enough, the GA finds the non-dominated points and identifies *PF**:

$$PF* := \{u = f(x) \mid x \in P*\}. \quad (4)$$

The procedure that allows the MOGA to explore the solution space is presented in Algorithm 1 [19]. The specific terms used within the MOGA procedure are the following:

- The term "gene" implies an optimization parameter;
- The term "individual" defines a set of optimization parameters;
- The term "population" presents a group of different parameter sets.

	Algorithm 1 MOGA
1:	Initialize Population;
2:	Evaluate Objective Values;
3:	Assign Rank based on Pareto Dominance;
4:	Compute Niche Count;
5:	Assign Linearly Scaled Fitness;
6:	Assign Shared Fitness;
7:	**for** i = 1 to number of Generations **do**;
8:	Tournament Selection;
9:	Single-Point Crossover;
10:	Uniform Mutation;
11:	Evaluate Objective Values;
12:	Assign Rank based on Pareto Dominance;
13:	Compute Niche Count;
14:	Assign Linearly Scaled Fitness;
15:	Assign Shared Fitness;
16:	**end.**

The first steps in the MOGA are to generate the initial population and to compute the values of optimization objectives. The next phase involves ranking based on the Pareto Dominance and assigning the fitness values using the niching technique. Fitness value expresses how "good" an individual is. It is a positive real value and, therefore, is often easier to use than the values of the objectives. The niching technique (also called the fitness sharing technique) is responsible for maintaining diversity in the population. To use the niching technique, the size of the neighborhood (niche radius) of each individual should be calculated first. Then, the linearly scaled fitness value of each individual is decreased proportionally to the number of individuals sharing the same neighborhood.

Using the obtained fitness values, the cycle of the evolutionary search starts with the following operators: selection, crossover, and mutation. The general functions of these operators are the following:

- The selection operator selects individuals from the current population based on their fitness values; the selected individuals are called "parents";
- The crossover operator is applied to the "parents" to create new individuals called "offspring";
- The mutation operator broadens the search space by making changes in the current population; then, the "offspring" and mutated individuals form a new generation.

There are many types of selection, crossover, and mutation operators. In this optimization problem, the tournament selection, single-point crossover, and uniform mutation were used. Figure 4 illustrates the basic ideas of the applied operators [19].

The tournament selection acts in the following way: first, it randomly chooses four individuals from the population, and then picks the individual with the higher fitness value for using in the next generation. As for the crossover, it takes two individuals from the current generation and combines them at a random point. The uniform mutation takes an individual and selects one or more random mutation points (genes). Then, this operator replaces the values of the selected genes with a uniform random value between the upper and lower bounds defined for this gene.

After that, the new generation is formed and assessed using fitness values. In the next step of the procedure, the algorithm checks if a stop criterion is satisfied. If it is, then the algorithm stops working. Otherwise, it continues the cycle of creating new generations.

To date, the MOGA has been integrated to different computing environments, such as Matlab and Ārtap [25–27]. In this study, the MOGA was applied through the Matlab optimization toolbox.

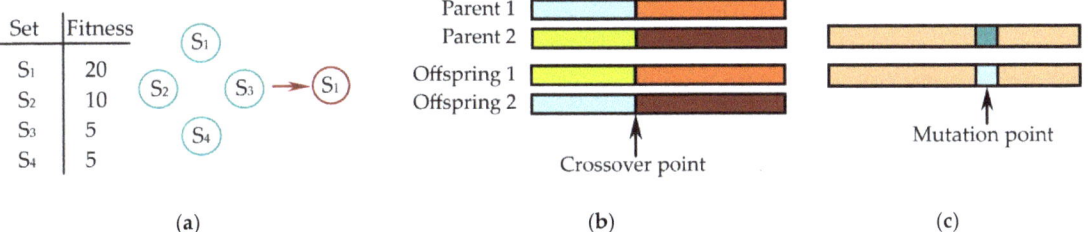

Figure 4. (a) Tournament selection; (b) single-point crossover; (c) uniform mutation.

4.2. Optimization Method

The optimization was carried out using the procedure illustrated in Figure 5. The interaction between Matlab, SolidWorks, and MagNet software programs was organized within Visual Studio as follows. The optimization cycle started with a set of parameters defined by the GA within the Matlab optimizer. Then, these parameters were used to build a 3D model using SolidWorks. Once it was complete, MagNET calculated the maximum torque and directed it together with the coupling volume to the Matlab optimizer. Using the obtained values of the objectives, the Matlab optimizer refined the parameters, and the same cycle was executed until the stop criterion had been satisfied. The number of generations and individuals defined the stop criterion. Particularly, the optimization was performed with 30 generations constituted by 50 individuals. Consequently, the cycle was repeated 1500 times.

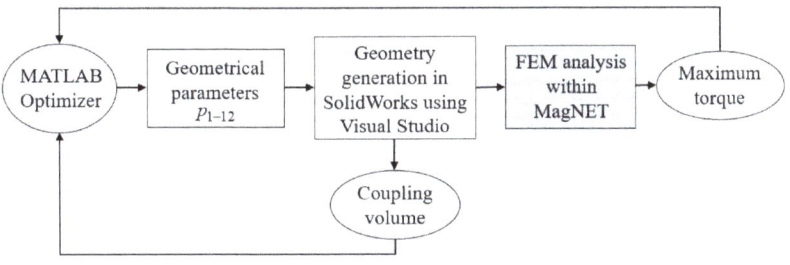

Figure 5. Optimization flowchart.

4.3. Simulation Results of the GA Optimization

The optimal design and the magnetic flux density distribution are presented in Figure 6. The figure shows that the coupling members were deeply saturated. For the driving member body, the average value of flux density |B| was near 0.83 T, and for the driven member it was slightly lower—about 0.78 T. The obtained values of the maximum magnetic torque and the volume are reported in Table 2. A significant reduction in the volume can be noticed from the table. However, no difference greater than 2% was observed in the torque value.

Overall, the GA showed constructive results; however, the execution time was quite high. Fifty hours were required to resolve the optimization problem.

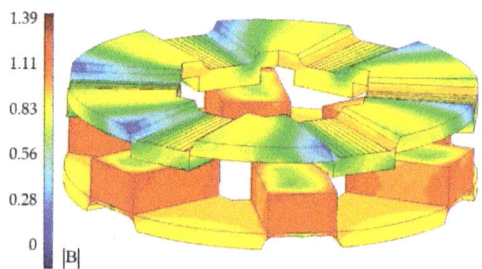

Figure 6. GA optimal design with the distribution of magnetic flux density.

Table 2. Simulation results of genetic algorithm (GA) optimization.

Objective	Initial Design	GA
τ_{max}	73.0×10^{-3} Nm	74.5×10^{-3} Nm
V	2.31×10^{-6} m^3	1.91×10^{-6} m^3

5. Optimization Using Taguchi Method

5.1. Taguchi Methodology

The Taguchi method is a statistical method that discovers the parameter space to find a design with better performance. The parameter space in Taguchi's terminology is called the orthogonal array. Essentially, the orthogonal array is a matrix that includes various combinations of optimization parameters. Each combination is called an experiment. The experiments should be carried out in a real test or simulation to obtain values of optimization objectives. A major advantage of the Taguchi method is that the procedure of forming the orthogonal array ensures the minimization of experiment quantity.

In the Taguchi method, once the orthogonal array is formed, the experiments are carried out, values of optimization objectives are obtained, and analysis of the results starts. Essentially, this analysis intends to reveal the effect of the optimization parameters and their levels on the objectives using average peak-to-peak values of the objectives.

5.2. Conducting the Taguchi Experiments

Within this study, a standard L50 orthogonal array was used. It included fifty experiments that involve eleven parameters with five levels and one parameter with two levels. The parameters and their levels are listed in Table 3.

Table 3. Optimization parameters and their levels.

Parameter	Level 1	Level 2	Level 3	Level 4	Level 5
1	0.8	1	-	-	-
2–12	0.6	0.7	0.8	0.9	1

The experiments were carried out using MagNET software. The obtained values of the magnetic torque and the volume were organized into the cost function:

$$f = \frac{\tau}{V} \quad (5)$$

To find the best combination of parameters levels, the mean values were calculated and analyzed. The mean values of the objectives and the cost function were as follows:

$$m_V = \frac{1}{50}\sum_{k=1}^{50} V_i = 1.98 \cdot 10^{-6} \text{m}^3, \quad m_\tau = \frac{1}{50}\sum_{k=1}^{50} \tau_i = 75.0 \cdot 10^{-3} \text{Nm}, \quad (6)$$

$$m_f = \frac{1}{50}\sum_{k=1}^{50} f_k = 3.79$$

Then, the average peak-to-peak values of the cost function were calculated for each factor at each level:

$$m_{ij}(f) = \frac{1}{n} \cdot \sum f(i,j), \quad (7)$$

where i is the parameter number, j is the level number, n represents the number of experiments, and $f(i,j)$ denotes the value of the objective function for experiments that involved the parameter i at the level j. Figure 7 shows the average peak-to-peak values depending on the parameters and parameters' levels.

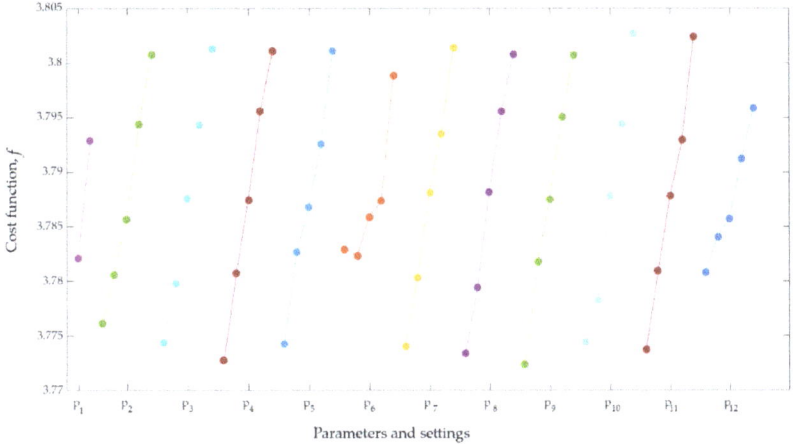

Figure 7. Parameter effects on the objective function.

As can be seen, the parameters combination $[p_{12}, p_{i5},] i = 2 \ldots 12$ gives the minimum value of the cost function. The optimal design provided the value of the magnetic torque of $75.0 \cdot 10^{-3}$ Nm and the value of the volume $1.91 \cdot 10^{-6}$ m^3.

The last step of the Taguchi optimization is the analysis of variance (ANOVA). Using the sum of squares ss, the effect of each parameter on the objective function was computed:

$$ss_{ij} = n \cdot \sum (m_{ij} - m_f)^2, \quad (8)$$

It can be seen from Table 4 that the influence of the parameters on the cost function was nearly equal. Only the parameters p_6 and p_{12} made the exception. This might be because the saturation of the disks near these points was the smallest for all the designs.

5.3. Simulation Results of the Taguchi Optimization

The optimal design of the coupling was obtained by the Taguchi method. The corresponding geometry and the magnetic flux distribution are shown in Figure 8. Closer inspection of the figure reveals that the bodies of the driving and driven member were highly saturated. For the driving member body, the average value of flux density $|B|$ was near 0.86 T, and for the driven member, it was slightly lower—about 0.8 T. Table 5 compares the magnetic torque and volume values of the initial and optimal designs. Using the Taguchi optimization method allowed us to reduce the volume by 17% and to enhance the torque by 2.2% compared to the initial value.

Table 4. Effects of different parameters on the cost function.

Variable	Sum of Squares	Factor Effect (%)	Variable	Sum of Squares	Factor Effect (%)
1	0.0001	0.5	7	0.0023	10.0
2	0.0019	8.7	8	0.0025	10.9
3	0.0023	10.1	9	0.0025	10.7
4	0.0025	11.1	10	0.0027	11.7
5	0.0021	8.9	11	0.0024	10.5
6	0.0008	3.8	12	0.0007	3.1

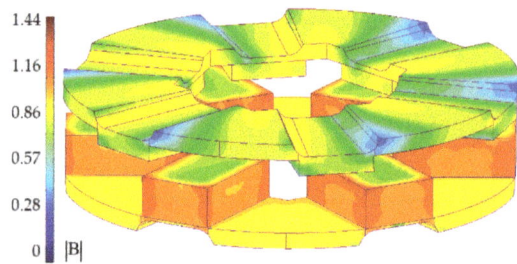

Figure 8. Taguchi optimal design with the distribution of magnetic flux density.

Table 5. Simulation results of Taguchi optimization.

Objective	Initial Design	Taguchi Design
τ_{max}	73.0×10^{-3} Nm	75.0×10^{-3} Nm
V	2.31×10^{-6} m^3	1.91×10^{-6} m^3

6. Comparison of the Simulation Results of the GA Optimization and the Taguchi Optimization

The designed PM couplings were compared in terms of the volume, magnetic torque, and magnetic torque density. The highlighted characteristics of the couplings are listed in Table 6. It is apparent from this table that the optimal designs showed a considerable improvement in the magnetic torque density—more than 20%. Similarly, the volume of the coupling disks was significantly reduced using both optimization methods. However, only a slight increase in torque was found after optimization—about 2%.

Table 6. Simulation results of GA and Taguchi optimization.

Objective	Initial Design	GA Design	Taguchi Design
τ_{max}	73.0×10^{-3} Nm	74.5×10^{-3} Nm	75.0×10^{-3} Nm
V	2.31×10^{-6} m^3	1.91×10^{-6} m^3	1.91×10^{-6} m^3
τ_{max}/V	31.6 kN·m/m^3	39.0 kN·m/m^3	39.3 kN·m/m^3

The 3D models of the initial and optimal designs are presented in Figure 9. Additionally, Table 7 provides the thickness values of the disks at the optimization parameters points locations. A comparison of the GA and Taguchi designs reveals that the obtained geometry and volume of the PM coupling were identical. Similarly, the maximum value of the magnetic torque, as well as the magnetic torque density, were quite close for both designs.

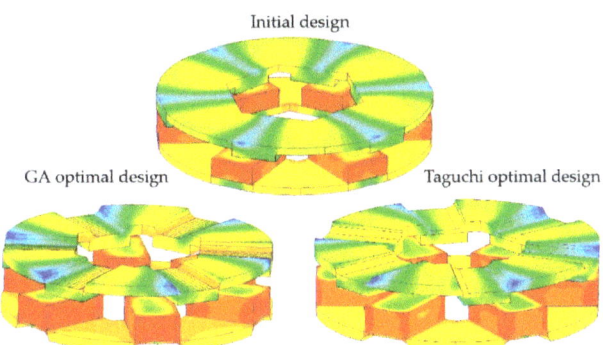

Figure 9. Comparison of initial and optimal design geometries.

Table 7. Discs thicknesses values for initial and optimal designs.

Parameter Number	Initial Design	GA Design	Taguchi Design
1	1.2 mm	0.21 mm	0.2 mm
2	1.2 mm	0.2 mm	0.2 mm
3	1.2 mm	0.2 mm	0.2 mm
4	1.2 mm	0.2 mm	0.2 mm
5	1.2 mm	0.4 mm	0.2 mm
6	1.2 mm	0.2 mm	0.2 mm
7	1.2 mm	0.5 mm	0.2 mm
8	1.2 mm	0.2 mm	0.2 mm
9	1.2 mm	0.2 mm	0.2 mm
10	1.2 mm	0.2 mm	0.2 mm
11	1.2 mm	0.2 mm	0.2 mm
12	1.2 mm	0.6 mm	0.2 mm

To provide a more comprehensive comparison of the coupling designs, the dependence of the magnetic torque on the deviation angle θ was explored. Figure 10 illustrates the approximated results of the simulations. As can be seen from the figure, the torque curves of the optimal and initial designs were quite close. Yet, the variation of the torque in the Taguchi design was more stable in the region of θ change from 0° to 5°.

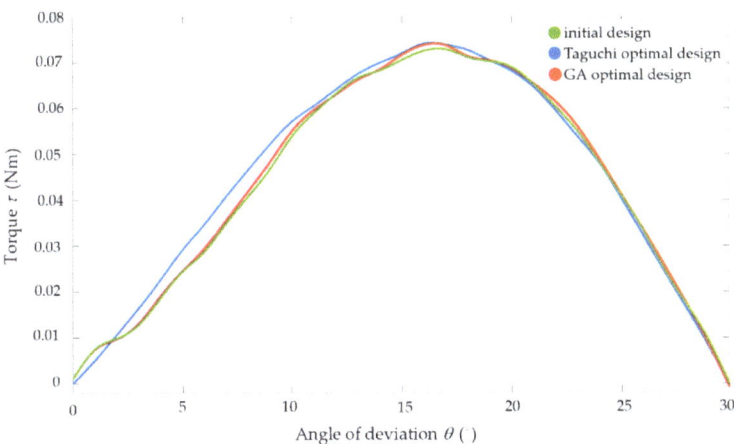

Figure 10. Comparison of three designs in terms of magnetic torque versus angle of deviation.

Moreover, the Taguchi optimization method was considerably more effective in terms of time consumption. Particularly, the GA optimization was performed within 50 hours, while the Taguchi method required just 1.5 hours of calculations. Therefore, these results taken together indicate that the Taguchi optimization had better performance compared to the GA in the scope of PM coupling optimization.

7. Experimental Setup
7.1. Test Bench

To validate the performance of the coupling, an experimental setup was designed. First, the initial design of the coupling was printed from electrical steel with 6.5% silicon content by selective laser melting printing [28]. Similarly, the Taguchi optimal design was manufactured. Three-dimensional printed prototypes are presented in Figure 11.

(a) (b)

Figure 11. (a) Prototype of the initial design of the coupling; (b) prototype of the optimized design on the coupling.

The second step was to construct a test bench with an adjustable air gap and ability to measure the torque in various relative positions of the coupling members. Figure 12 illustrates the experimental design of the coupling together with the designed setup for the test. The driving and driven disks were inserted into two shafts which hold them in a certain position. The shafts were supported by a pair of angular contact ball bearings. The bed components were designed in such a way that the air gap could be regulated. Particularly, the following values of the air gap could be selected: 1, 1.5, 2 . . . 3.

Moreover, a mechanism was proposed to vary the angle of deviation between the driving and driven member. As shown in Figure 12, the mechanism included three elements: two disks with holes and one stick. The green disk was placed on the driving member shaft and could be rotated. The beige disk was placed on the support and fixed. The green disk was divided into 36 sectors with the step of 10°. The beige disk was divided into 12 sectors with the step of 11°. In each sector of both disks, a hole was placed to adjust the angle θ with the step 1° using the stick. All components were printed from PLA material using a 3D-printing machine.

The implemented setup was prepared for measuring the torque on the driven member shaft. Utilizing the scale provided the measurement basis for the setup (see Figure 13). In this test, the rotation of the driving member shaft induced torque on the driven member shaft. The last one had the arm, which was in contact with the scales. Essentially, the scales here acted as a measuring device of the force produced by the arm F_R. This force had a particular relation with the torque described by Equation (9).

$$\tau = F_R \times r,$$
$$r = r \cdot \sin(\varphi), \ F_R = mg, \ \varphi = \pi/2 \Rightarrow \tau = F_R \cdot r, \quad (9)$$

where the constant r is the length of the arm, θ represents the angle of deviation between coupling members, and φ implies for the angle between vectors r and F_R.

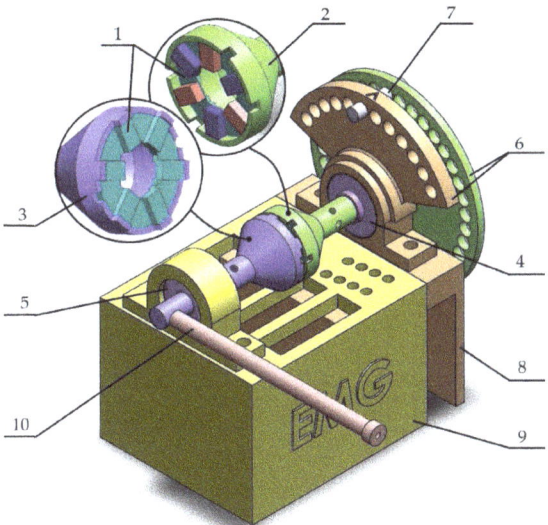

Figure 12. First view of the experimental setup. 1—PM coupling; 2—driving member shaft; 3—driven member shaft; 4 and 5—bearings; 6—mechanism for the angle θ variation; 7—stick for fixing the angle θ; 8 and 9—bed components; 10—arm.

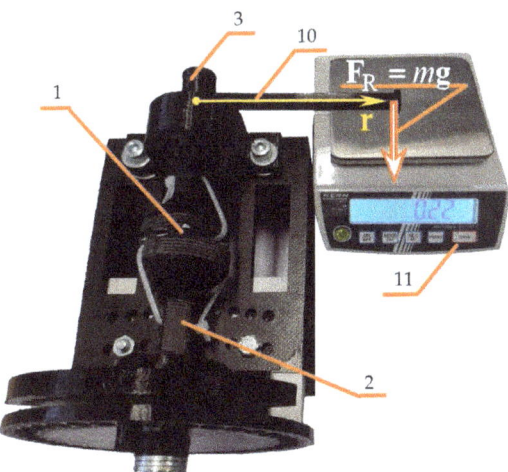

Figure 13. The measurement setup.

7.2. Experimental Results

To certify the optimization results, the initial and optimal designs were tested and compared. Each design was tested four times, and the means of the torque values were used for further analysis. Figure 14 provides the experimental data on the initial and optimal designs together with the data approximation. Particularly, the graph shows the relation of the torque, induced on the driven member shaft, and the angle θ. It can be seen that the curves were quite close within the change of the deviation angle from 0° to 17°. Yet, there was a slight difference in torque values of initial and optimal designs at the point of the torque maximum ($\theta = 17°$).

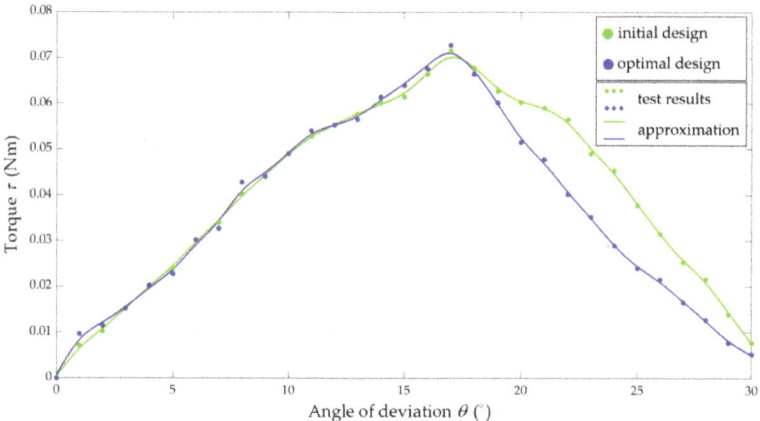

Figure 14. Test results for the initial and optimal designs of the coupling.

Additionally, Figure 15 summarizes the results obtained from the simulation and the experiments. The figure shows that the simulation and test curves were adjacent within the change of θ from 0° to 7°. However, around $\theta = 7° \ldots 17°$, the torque, obtained from the test, was slightly lower. Moreover, it should be noted that the experimental curves appeared to be steep which indicated the rapid torque change. An explanation might be that the measured torque was not only dependent on the coupling design but also experienced the influence from the setup structure and the bearings. Additionally, the accuracy of the scales, used for measuring the torque, was not high enough.

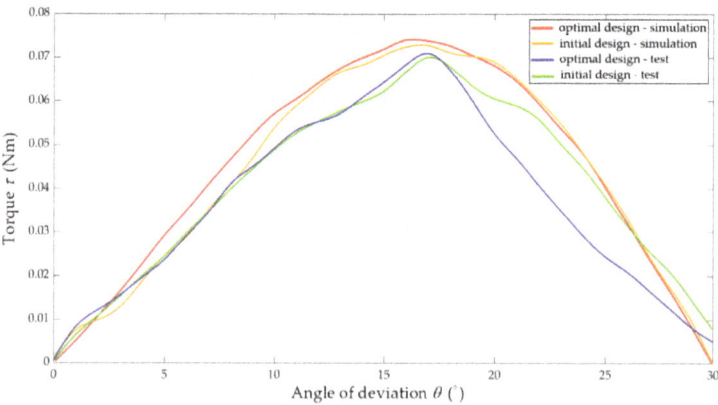

Figure 15. Comparison of simulation and experimental results for the initial and optimal designs of the coupling.

To provide a comprehensive comparison of the designs, Table 8 presents the torque-to-volume ratio according to the experiment. The table demonstrates that the optimal design achieved considerably higher performance compared to the initial design. Particularly, the difference in the torque-to-volume ration was above 20%.

Table 8. Test results of GA and Taguchi optimization.

Specification	Initial Design	Taguchi Design
τ_{max}	71.0×10^{-3} Nm	72.0×10^{-3} Nm
V	2.31×10^{-6} m^3	1.91×10^{-6} m^3
τ_{max}/V	30.7 kN·m/m^3	37.7 kN·m/m^3

8. Discussion and Conclusions

This study presented the optimization of the PM coupling shapes with the following objectives: minimization of the coupling volume and maximization of the transmitted torque. For this optimization problem, two methodological approaches were employed: the DOM accompanied by the GA and Taguchi optimization method. The results of the PM coupling optimization using both approaches were impressive. The DOM and the Taguchi method led to identical geometry and the same reduction in the coupling volume. Consequently, the increase in the magnetic torque density was also quite high for both optimized designs.

Compared to the DOM-GA, the key advantage of the Taguchi method was the significant reduction in the execution time. Taking into account that the obtained results of the optimization by both methods were the same, the overall performance of the Taguchi method optimization was concluded to be higher. However, the major limitation of the Taguchi approach is the incapability to solve multi-objective problems with a high number of the optimization parameters and complex relations between the optimization objectives, constraints, and parameters. Therefore, the findings of this study are not generalizable to all optimization problems. Still, considering the obtained results, the Taguchi optimization method offers a reasonable alternative to the time-consuming DOM-GA for certain optimization problems.

Another portion of this study was dedicated to the performance validation of the initial and Taguchi optimal design of the coupling. For this purpose, the experimental setup was constructed, and both designs were tested. The experiments showed that the couplings achieved relatively similar torque values, while the torque density was improved. These experiments confirmed that the coupling design obtained from the Taguchi optimization had a comparable performance with the simulation results. Yet, to obtain a better accuracy of the torque measurements, further experimental tests need to be carried out using more precise measurement devices.

This study suggests that the capabilities of the Taguchi optimization method can be examined within the optimization of other electromagnetic devices. For example, further research will focus on the design optimization of a switched reluctance motor using the Taguchi optimization method.

Author Contributions: Conceptualization, methodology, software, validation, formal analysis, and writing—original draft preparation, E.A.; writing—review and editing, resources, and funding acquisition, A.K.; project administration, A.B. and T.V.; supervision, A.B., T.V., A.R., and H.H.; investigation, data curation, and visualization, H.H., H.T., and A.R. All authors have read and agreed to the published version of the manuscript.

Funding: The research was supported by the Estonian Research Council under grant PSG137 "Additive Manufacturing of Electrical Machines".

Data Availability Statement: Data are contained within the article.

Conflicts of Interest: The authors declare no conflict of interest.

References

1. El-Wakeel, A.S. Design optimization of PM couplings using hybrid Particle Swarm Optimization-Simplex Method (PSO-SM) Algorithm. *Electr. Power Syst. Res.* **2014**, *116*, 29–35. [CrossRef]
2. Andriushchenko, E.; Kaska, J.; Kallaste, A.; Belahcen, A.; Vaimann, T.; Rassõlkin, A. Design Optimization of Permanent Magnet Clutch with Ārtap Framework. *TechRxiv* **2021**, in press.
3. Charpentier, J.F.; Lemarquand, G. Optimal design of cylindrical air-gap synchronous permanent magnet couplings. *IEEE Trans. Magn.* **1999**, *35*, 1037–1046. [CrossRef]
4. Hornreich, R.M.; Shtrikman, S. Optimal design of synchronous torque couplers. *IEEE Trans. Magn.* **1978**, *14*, 800–802. [CrossRef]
5. Zhang, B.; Wan, Y.; Li, Y.; Feng, G. Optimized design research on adjustable-speed permanent magnet coupling. In Proceedings of the IEEE International Conference on Industrial Technology, Cape Town, Western Cape, South Africa, 25–28 February 2013; pp. 380–385.
6. Buchanan, C.; Gardner, L. Metal 3D printing in construction: A review of methods, research, applications, opportunities and challenges. *Eng. Struc.* **2019**, *180*, 332–348. [CrossRef]
7. Frazier, W.E. Metal additive manufacturing: A review. *J. Mat. Eng. Perform.* **2014**, *23*, 1917–1928. [CrossRef]
8. Zhang, Z.Y.; Jhong, K.J.; Cheng, C.W.; Huang, P.W.; Tsai, M.C.; Lee, W.H. Metal 3D printing of synchronous reluctance motor. In Proceedings of the IEEE International Conference on Industrial Technology, Taipei, Taiwan, 14–17 March 2016; pp. 1125–1128.
9. Wrobel, R.; Mecrow, B. A Comprehensive Review of Additive Manufacturing in Construction of Electrical Machines. *IEEE Trans. Energy Convers.* **2020**, *35*, 1054–1064. [CrossRef]
10. Lei, G.; Zhu, J.; Guo, Y.; Liu, C.; Ma, B. A review of design optimization methods for electrical machines. *Energies* **2017**, *10*, 1962. [CrossRef]
11. Duan, Y.; Ionel, D.M. A review of recent developments in electrical machine design optimization methods with a permanent magnet synchronous motor benchmark study. In Proceedings of the IEEE Energy Conversion Congress and Exposition: Energy Conversion Innovation for a Clean Energy Future, ECCE 2011, Rostock, Germany, 24–26 August 2011; pp. 3694–3701.
12. López-Torres, C.; Espinosa, A.G.; Riba, J.R.; Romeral, L. Design and optimization for vehicle driving cycle of rare-earth-free SynRM based on coupled lumped thermal and magnetic networks. *IEEE Trans. Veh. Technol.* **2018**, *67*, 196–205. [CrossRef]
13. Babetto, C.; Bacco, G.; Bianchi, N. Synchronous Reluctance Machine Optimization for High-Speed Applications. *IEEE Trans. Energy Convers.* **2018**, *33*, 1266–1273. [CrossRef]
14. Cupertino, F.; Pellegrino, G.; Gerada, C. Design of synchronous reluctance motors with multiobjective optimization algorithms. *IEEE Trans. Ind. Appl.* **2014**, *50*, 3617–3627. [CrossRef]
15. Pellegrino, G.; Cupertino, F.; Gerada, C. Automatic Design of Synchronous Reluctance Motors Focusing on Barrier Shape Optimization. *IEEE Trans. Ind. Appl.* **2015**, *51*, 1465–1474. [CrossRef]
16. Andriushchenko, E.A.; Kallaste, A.; Belahcen, A.; Heidari, H.; Vaimann, T.; Rassõlkin, A. Design Optimization of Permanent Magnet Clutch. In Proceedings of the International Conference on Electrical Machines (ICEM), Gothenburg, Sweden, 23–26 August 2020.
17. Jensen, M.T. Reducing the Run-Time Complexity of Multiobjective EAs: The NSGA-II and Other Algorithms. *IEEE Trans. Evol. Comput.* **2003**, *7*, 503–515. [CrossRef]
18. Smith, J.E.; Fogarty, T.C. Operator and parameter adaptation in genetic algorithms. *Soft Comput.* **1997**, *1*, 81–87. [CrossRef]
19. Lamont, G.B.; Coello, C.A.C.; Van Veldhuizen, D.A. *Evolutionary Algorithms for Solving Multi-Objective Problems*; Springer: New York, NY, USA, 2007.
20. Hwang, C.C.; Lyu, L.Y.; Liu, C.T.; Li, P.L. Optimal design of an SPM motor using genetic algorithms and Taguchi method. *IEEE Trans. Magn.* **2008**, *44*, 4325–4328. [CrossRef]
21. Sorgdrager, A.; Wang, R.J.; Grobler, A. Taguchi method in electrical machine design. *SAIEE Africa Res. J.* **2017**, *108*, 150–164. [CrossRef]
22. Yang, B.Y.; Hwang, K.Y.; Rhee, S.B.; Kim, D.K.; Kwon, B.I. Optimization of novel flux barrier in interior permanent magnet-type brushless dc motor based on modified Taguchi method. *J. Appl. Phys.* **2009**, *105*, 07F106. [CrossRef]
23. Ashabani, M.; Mohamed, Y.A.R.I.; Milimonfared, J. Optimum design of tubular permanent-magnet motors for thrust characteristics improvement by combined taguchineural network approach. *IEEE Trans. Magn.* **2010**, *46*, 4092–4100. [CrossRef]
24. Ferreira, C.; Vaidya, J. Torque analysis of permanent magnet coupling using 2d and 3d finite elements methods. *IEEE Trans. Magn.* **1989**, *25*, 3080–3082. [CrossRef]
25. Panek, D.; Orosz, T.; Karban, P. Artap: Robust Design Optimization Framework for Engineering Applications. In Proceedings of the 3rd International Conference on Intelligent Computing in Data Sciences, ICDS 2019, Marrakech, Morocco, 28–30 October 2019.
26. Kaska, J.; Orosz, T.; Karban, P.; Dolezel, I.; Pechanek, R.; Panek, D. Optimization of Reluctance Motor with Printed Rotor. In Proceedings of the COMPUMAG 2019—22nd International Conference on the Computation of Electromagnetic Fields, Paris, France, 15–19 July 2019.
27. Karban, P.; Pánek, D.; Orosz, T.; Petrášová, I.; Doležel, I. FEM based robust design optimization with Agros and Ārtap. *Comput. Math. Appl.* **2020**, *81*, 618–633. [CrossRef]
28. Tiismus, H.; Kallaste, A.; Vaimann, T.; Rassolkin, A.; Belahcen, A. Axial Synchronous Magnetic Coupling Modeling and Printing with Selective Laser Melting. In Proceedings of the 2019 IEEE 60th International Scientific Conference on Power and Electrical Engineering of Riga Technical University (RTUCON), Riga, Latvia, 7–9 October 2019; pp. 1–4.

Article

A Computationally Efficient Model Predictive Current Control of Synchronous Reluctance Motors Based on Hysteresis Comparators

Wagner Benjamim, Imed Jlassi * and Antonio J. Marques Cardoso

CISE—Electromechatronic Systems Research Centre, University of Beira Interior, Calçada Fonte do Lameiro, P-6201-001 Covilhã, Portugal; wagner.benjamim@ubi.pt (W.B.); ajmcardoso@ieee.org (A.J.M.C.)
* Correspondence: jlassi-imed@hotmail.fr

Abstract: Model predictive current control (MPCC) has recently become a powerful advanced control technology in industrial drives. However, current prediction in MPCC requires a high number of voltage vectors (VVs) synthesizable by the converter, thus being computationally demanding. Accordingly, in this paper, a computationally efficient MPCC of synchronous reluctance motors (SynRMs) that reduces the number of VVs used for prediction is proposed. By making the most of the simplicity of hysteresis current control (HCC) and integrating it with the MPCC scheme, only four out of eight predictions are needed to determine the best VV, dramatically reducing algorithm computations. The experimental results show that the execution time can be shortened by 20% while maintaining the highest control efficiency.

Keywords: model predictive control; hysteresis current control; execution time; synchronous reluctance motors

1. Introduction

Synchronous reluctance motors (SynRMs) have, in recent years, attracted much attention due to their high-efficiency output and nature of their construction denoted by the lack of expensive magnetic materials, thus cheapening the overall cost whilst increasing in robustness. These benefits have made the SynRM a strong contender against other established electric motors in the market, namely, permanent magnet synchronous motors (PMSMs) and induction motors (IMs) [1–4].

In order to achieve high control performance and efficiency from the SynRM drive, a suitable control technique is required. The finite-control-set model predictive control (MPC) has recently gained attention and notoriety [5–18]. It has distinguished itself from conventional control techniques, such as vector and direct control strategies, due to its ability to deal straightforwardly and intuitively with multi-objective control and integrate nonlinearities and constraints into a predefined cost function while providing a fast dynamic response and superior performance.

Although advantageous, MPC demands a high computational burden due to all the voltage vectors (VVs) combinations of the power converter being used for prediction and evaluation [15]. For example, 8 VVs are used to predict and evaluate the cost function of a two-level voltage source inverter (2L-VSI). Furthermore, 16 VVs are used in a two-level back-to-back converter (2L-BTB). In addition, 32 and 64 VVs are needed for 5- and 6-leg converters, respectively. On the other hand, 27 and 125 VVs are required for MPC of 3L-VSI/matrix converter and 5L-VSI, respectively.

The sampling time for MPC algorithms has been reported in the literature to be 50 µs for the 2L-VSI and 2L-BTB [16] and 100 µs for the 5-leg converter [17]. A sampling time of 65 µs is required for matrix converters [19]. In turn, sampling times of 52 µs and 93 µs are needed for 3L-VSI and 5L-VSI, respectively [20].

Accordingly, with the increase in the complexity of the converter, the quantity of feasible VVs increases; therefore, the computation effort rises. Thus, high sampling times are required, producing large current ripples and reducing the overall drive efficiency. Consequently, costly digital processors are needed to keep up with the computational demand, thereby affecting the cost-effectiveness of MPC and subsequently slowing its widespread acceptance in the industry.

To deal with the issues previously mentioned, some predictive control strategies have recently been proposed. MPC is combined with a graphical approach to reduce the computation effort [21]. In [22], a control scheme based on a predefined voltage reference is implemented to predict only one VV in a 2L-VSI. In [23,24], deadbeat control is paired with MPC to select three out of the eight predictions in 2L-VSI- and 2L-BTB-fed PMSMs, respectively. Furthermore, the same approach can be seen in [25], resulting in less computational power being used. However, the graphical approach used in [21] is not intuitive and straightforward and the deadbeat control algorithms used in [23–25] are complex and highly dependent on system parameters, being sensitive to parameter uncertainty.

Alternatively to complex MPC schemes, hysteresis-based control techniques are simple in both concept and implementation. For instance, in [26], direct torque control (DTC) and direct power control (DPC) were applied to permanent magnet synchronous generator (PMSG) drives, with results showing that the execution time is considerably lower than that of direct MPC. Consequently, given its straightforwardness, fast dynamic response and low parameter dependency, direct control techniques could present themselves as a solution, conferring significant advantages when paired with MPC techniques. In [27–29], a reduction in the candidate VVs and computation was achieved by reformulating new DTC switching tables and combining them with direct MPC. In [30], new DTC and DPC switching tables were combined with direct the MPC of a 2L-BTB-fed PMSG, significantly reducing the number of candidates from 16 to 6 VVs and requiring less computation. DTC-based MPC has also been proposed in [19,31] for matrix-converter-fed PMSMs. Furthermore, regarding the multilevel converters, a decrease in execution time was obtained by minimizing the number of VVs in 3L-VSI through the estimation of the position and deviation of the stator flux relative to its reference [32], an analysis of the voltage reference vector [33] or, a branch-and-bound approach [34]. For the 3L-BTB-fed PMSG, again, the deadbeat based on system parameters is employed to reduce the candidate VVs, successfully decreasing the algorithm execution time [35].

Unfortunately, the solutions presented so far, although promising, still show some significant disadvantages, with most of the computationally efficient MPC methods being based on either a DTC switching table or deadbeat concept that, due to their need for system parameters, add further parameter dependency on the already heavily dependent predictive algorithm schemes, amplifying the adverse effects of a model-based predictive approach.

MPC solutions require sophisticated algorithms to achieve superior efficiency at the expense of computational effort. The literature survey shows a substantial shortage of research into a practical and easy MPC scheme that offers attractive characteristics such as simplicity, high control performance and low computational effort. On the other hand, hysteresis current control (HCC) bears a far more straightforward approach, both practically and conceptually, displaying a zero-parameter dependency on the system's model and less significant computational cost requirements.

However, to the authors' knowledge, a less computationally demanding MPCC based on HCC, which aims to obtain superior control performance, has not yet been reported in the literature. Accordingly, this paper intends to solve the issues mentioned earlier, thus proposing a combination of HCC–MPCC for SynRM drives with enhanced control performance and robustness in the form of less parameter dependence in the HCC while being low in both complexity and computational burden. As a result, the number of required VVs was effectively reduced from eight to four VVs; consequently, a low computational time was achieved, requiring less sampling time and enhancing the control performance. The proposed control algorithm was tested and validated by intensive experimental results.

2. Proposed HCC–MPCC of the VSI

The proposed control scheme HCC–MPCC intends to reduce the computational burden of the classical predictive scheme whilst maintaining an excellent control performance by combining the benefits of HCC with MPCC, thus also equipping the proposed control scheme with the robustness and simplicity derived from the HCC and superior control performance derived from MPCC. Ultimately, a lower execution time was achieved using 4 VVs for prediction and evaluation instead of all 8 available VVs of the VSI whilst maintaining good control performance with minor current ripples.

2.1. VV Selection from HCC

HCCs, also known as bang–bang controllers, are among the most straightforward and intuitive control types. They work by directly controlling the motor phase currents whilst displaying their already mentioned benefits, such as robustness, simplicity, excellent dynamic response limited merely by the switching speed and the load time constant and independence of system parameters, making it attractive for this paper's intended purposes. The following expression summarizes the operation principle of an HCC:

$$S_x = \begin{cases} 1 \; if \; i_x^* > i_x + \frac{B_{hys}}{2} \\ 0 \; if \; i_x^* < i_x - \frac{B_{hys}}{2} \end{cases} \quad x \in \{a, b, c\} \tag{1}$$

where S_x denotes the switching state of the upper semiconductor in the inverter arm of each phase, while the lower semiconductor takes the state complementary to the upper semiconductor; i_x and i_x^* are the actual current and the reference, respectively, where the subscript "x" denotes the phase and B_{hys} denotes a defined hysteresis band.

The HCC control strategy is focused on the utilization of three hysteresis comparators to generate the converter gate signals, where each comparator has, as an input, the error between the measured current and its reference in the corresponding phase. The controllers then use the error in each phase to maintain their values within a defined hysteresis band B_{hys}, such that, if the error crosses the upper band limit, the upper semiconductor is turned ON and the lower semiconductor is turned OFF. Conversely, if the error crosses the lower band limit, the upper semiconductor is turned OFF and the lower one is turned ON, thus maintaining the current within the hysteresis band limits. Therefore, the hysteresis bandwidth sets the standard for the current tracking performance of the HCC.

Initially, the proportional-integral (PI) controller generates the torque-producing component (i_q), while the i_d componentis obtained as a function of i_q according to the maximum torque per ampere (MTPA) detailed in the following section. Furthermore, the hysteresis bandwidth value is fixed for better control performance. Then, the reference VV is calculated by using three hysteresis comparators for each phase with the operation principle summarized by (1) and further detailed above, in which each hysteresis comparator takes, as an input, the stator current and its respective reference obtained from the transformation of the reference current components in the rotor reference frame to the *abc* reference frame, thus generating the initial reference VV. Subsequently, the VVs neighbor near to the initial reference VV are selected according to Table 1. For instance, if HCC computes the vector V_1 (green) as the reference VV, then the neighbor vectors V_0, V_2 and V_6 (red) are also selected. Figure 1 depicts the aforementioned scenario, where the reference and near neighbor VVs selection process are shown in green and red, respectively. Moreover, a diagram and a flowchart comprising the VV selection process from the HCC can be seen in Figures 2 and 3, respectively.

Table 1. VV selection used in HCC–MPCC.

$V_{HCC}|_i$	$N_{V_{HCC}}\{x_0, x_1, x_2, x_3\}$
V_1	V_0, V_1, V_2, V_6
V_2	V_0, V_1, V_2, V_3
V_3	V_0, V_2, V_3, V_4
V_4	V_0, V_3, V_4, V_5
V_5	V_0, V_4, V_5, V_6
V_6	V_0, V_1, V_5, V_6
V_0 or V_7	V_0, V_0, V_0, V_0

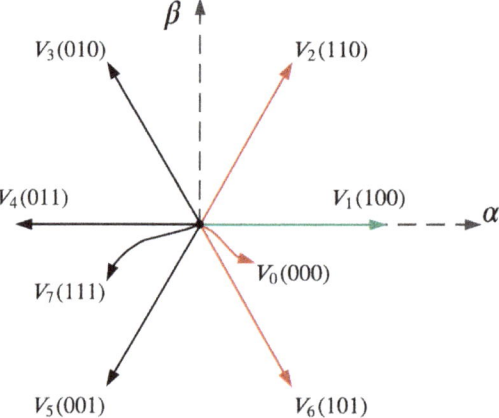

Figure 1. Hexagon VVs in the α–β frame and the corresponding switching states. HCC computed reference VV (green) and selected near neighbor VVs (red).

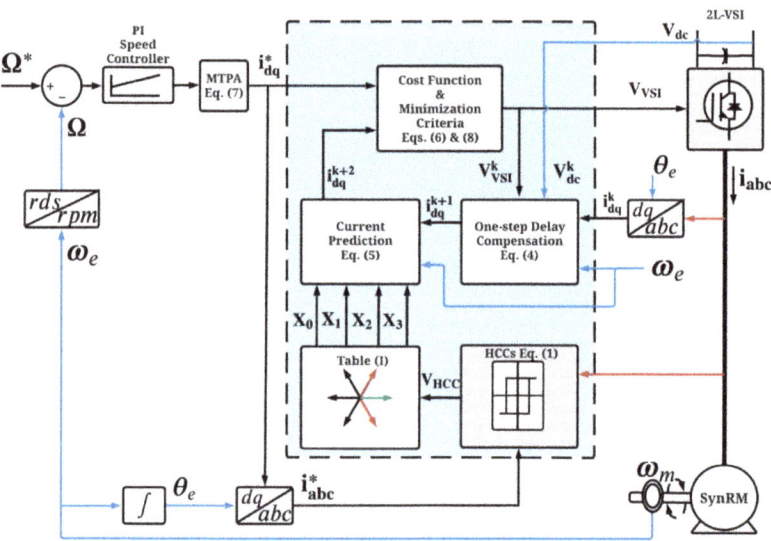

Figure 2. Block diagram of the HCC–MPCC.

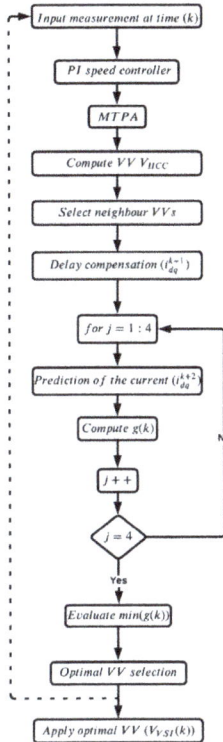

Figure 3. Flowchart of the proposed HCC–MPCC.

It is important to emphasize that the inverter allows only eight switching states to exist, resulting in six active VVs and two identical zero VVs at the origin of the coordinates, namely, V_0 or V_7. However, given the difficulty of differentiating between the two output voltages for the zeroVVs, choosing either switching states can significantly reduce the difficulty in implementation [36]. In terms of the scope of this work, only V_0 is defined as the zero VV for the sake of simplicity and further reduction in the employed VV, to be used in conjunction with the active VVs, thus ensuring more ripple reduction [30]. Table 1 presents the relation of the near neighbor VV ($N_{V_{HCC}}$) selection based on the HCC reference VV (V_{HCC}) calculation, where $V_{HCC}|_i (i = 0, \ldots, 7)$.

The 4selected 4 VVs are then used in the proposed HCC–MPCC to predict the stator currents and determine the cost function. Subsequently, the optimal VV is chosen by minimizing the cost function presented in the next section.

2.2. HCC–MPCC

Since the main focus of this paper is to reduce the number of VVs for MPC, thereby reducing the computational burden, the saturation effect of the SynRM is neglected for the sake of simplicity. Therefore, the stator voltage and current equations of the SynRM in a synchronous rotating frame can be expressed as follows:

$$\begin{cases} v_d = R_s i_d - \omega_e L_q i_{qm} + L_d \frac{di_{dm}}{dt} \\ v_q = R_s i_q + \omega_e L_d i_{dm} + L_q \frac{di_{qm}}{dt} \\ i_d = i_{dm} - \frac{1}{R_c}(\omega_e L_q i_{qm}) \\ i_q = i_{qm} - \frac{1}{R_c}(\omega_e L_d i_{dm}) \end{cases} \quad (2)$$

where L_d and L_q are the direct and quadrature inductances, v_d and v_q are the direct and quadrature axis terminal voltages, i_d and i_q are the direct and quadrature axis terminal currents, i_{dm} and i_{qm} are the direct and quadrature axis torque-producing currents, R_s and R_c are the stator resistance and iron loss resistance per phase and ω_e is the rotor's electrical angular speed. This is defined as a model without saturation. Since this model does not consider magnetic saturation, the inductances are assumed to be constant [37,38].

Given that the resistance R_c typically approaches very high values [39,40] and the motor used in this analysis is of high efficiency, the iron losses are dismissed [41]. Consequently, the torque producing currents i_{dm} and i_{qm} are made equal to the stator currents i_d and i_q, respectively. Therefore, given (2), the equivalent stator voltage equations can be expressed as

$$\begin{cases} v_d = R_s i_d - \omega_e L_q i_q + L_d \frac{di_d}{dt} \\ v_q = R_s i_q + \omega_e L_d i_d + L_q \frac{di_q}{dt} \end{cases} \quad (3)$$

Considering the discrete-time version equations corresponding to (3), the predicted stator currents in the $(k+1)th$ sampling period can be stated as

$$\begin{cases} i_d^{k+1} = \left(1 - \frac{R_s T_s}{L_d}\right) i_d^k + \omega_e T_s \frac{L_q}{L_d} i_q^k + \frac{T_s}{L_d} v_d^k \\ i_q^{k+1} = \left(1 - \frac{R_s T_s}{L_q}\right) i_q^k - \omega_e T_s \frac{L_d}{L_q} i_d^k + \frac{T_s}{L_q} v_q^k \end{cases} \quad (4)$$

where T_s is the sampling interval, i_d^k and i_q^k are the direct and quadrature axis terminal measured currents at the $(k)th$ instant and v_d^k and v_q^k are the direct and quadrature axis voltages obtained from the optimal VV applied to the VSI at the instant $(k)th$. Using the MPCC with delay compensation from [42] and according to (4), the predicted currents in the $(k+2)th$ sampling period can be written as

$$\begin{cases} i_d^{k+2} = \left(1 - \frac{R_s T_s}{L_d}\right) i_d^{k+1} + \omega_e T_s \frac{L_q}{L_d} i_q^{k+1} + \frac{T_s}{L_d} v_d^{k+1} \\ i_q^{k+2} = \left(1 - \frac{R_s T_s}{L_q}\right) i_q^{k+1} - \omega_e T_s \frac{L_d}{L_q} i_d^{k+1} + \frac{T_s}{L_q} v_q^{k+1} \end{cases} \quad (5)$$

In the proposed HCC–MPCC, v_d^{k+1} and v_q^{k+1} are the direct and quadrature axis voltages computed from four VVs obtained from HCC according to Table 1. However, in classic MPCC, v_d^{k+1} and v_q^{k+1} are reconstructed from the 8 VVs of the hexagon voltage that the converter can synthesize, turning (5) into a computationally demanding task.

Then, the cost function is defined with an emphasis on the desired behavior of the SynRM. Therefore, considering that the implemented algorithm focuses on predictive currents, the cost function is then defined to evaluate the error between the predicted currents and their respective references. Hence, the cost function is given by

$$g(k)|_{x_l} = \left[i_d^* - i_d^{k+2}\right]^2 + \left[i_q^* - i_q^{k+2}\right]^2; \ l = 0,\ldots,3 \quad (6)$$

In the SynRM control, the reference current i_q^* is generated by the speed controller, while i_d^* is derived from considering the MTPA strategy in [39], given by

$$i_d^* = -0.0589 i_q^{*2} + 1.0515 i_q^* - 0.2374 \quad (7)$$

Regarding Table 1, it can be further observed that each reference VV previously computed by the HCC V_{HCC} corresponds to a combination of 4 selected VVs $N_{V_{HCC}}$, thus yielding predicted current values through (5). Therefore, by optimizing (6), the optimal VV can be determined as follows:

$$V_{VSI}(k) = \arg \min_{\{x_0, x_1, x_2, x_3\}} g(k)|_{x_l}; \ l = 0,\ldots,3 \quad (8)$$

where the optimal VV satisfying the criteria defined by (8) by which the chosen (minimal) value of the defined cost function $g(k)$, which is dependent on the 4-element VV, is then adopted to control the six insulated gate bipolar transistors (IGBTs) of the VSI in the $(k+2)th$ sampling period, according to Table 2, where the relationship between the output voltages V_{VSI} and the conducing modes of the VSI is presented, with $V_{VSI}|_j (j = 0, \ldots, 7)$.

Table 2. Converter VVs.

$V_{VSI}|_j(s_a, s_b, s_c)$	v_a	v_b	v_c
V_1	$2/3V_{dc}$	$-1/3V_{dc}$	$-1/3V_{dc}$
V_2	$1/3V_{dc}$	$1/3V_{dc}$	$-2/3V_{dc}$
V_3	$-1/3V_{dc}$	$2/3V_{dc}$	$-1/3V_{dc}$
V_4	$-2/3V_{dc}$	$1/3V_{dc}$	$1/3V_{dc}$
V_5	$-1/3V_{dc}$	$-1/3V_{dc}$	$2/3V_{dc}$
V_6	$1/3V_{dc}$	$-2/3V_{dc}$	$1/3V_{dc}$
V_0 or V_7	0	0	0

In (5)–(8) of the proposed HCC–MPCC control scheme, only 4 out of the 8 available VVs of the VSI, previously calculated by HCC, are used to perform the prediction of the current and evaluation of the cost function within every sampling interval Ts, thus, computing the optimal VV, which is then applied to the converter. However, it is essential to distinguish that, in classical MPCC, all 8 VVs are used to predict the current and to evaluate the cost function.

3. Results and Discussion

The considered configuration of the drive system consists of a three-phase 2L-VSI linked to the SynRM, where the control system outputs the optimal VV through a combination of the switching signals s_a, s_b and s_c. In addition, a closed-loop scheme with feedback sensors, where rotor location, stator currents and dc-link voltage are measured, is considered for high drive efficiency. Figure 2 shows the block diagram configuration for the proposed HCC–MPCC strategy in detail. Furthermore, the flowchart for the proposed algorithm can be seen in Figure 3. In addition, the algorithm for the proposed control strategy comprises the following steps:

1. Measurement of speed ω_e, stator currents $i_{abc}{}^k$ and reconstruction of voltages $v_{dq}{}^k$ and currents $i_{dq}{}^*$.
2. Apply the optimal VV $V_{VSI}(k)$.
3. Computation of the initial reference VV V_{HCC} by the HCC through (1) and the neighbor VVs according to Table 1.
4. First-step prediction of the currents $i_{dq}{}^{k+1}$ given the optimal VV $V_{VSI}(k)$ by using (4).
5. Second-step prediction of the currents $i_{dq}{}^{k+2}$ given the selected VV in Table 1 by using (5).
6. Evaluation of the predicted currents in the cost function through (6) and selecting the optimal VV using (8).

The experimental test rig comprised a 2.2 kW SynRM coupled to an AC electric machine used as a load due to its similar power characteristics and speed range as the SynRM used for the proposed method. The AC electric machine in question was a 2.2 kW PMSG with a nominal speed of 1750 rpm. A Powerex POW-R-PAK VSI, a diode bridge rectifier and a dSPACE DS1103 digital controller were also part of the experimental configuration, as shown in Figure 4. The SynRM parameters are given in Table 3.

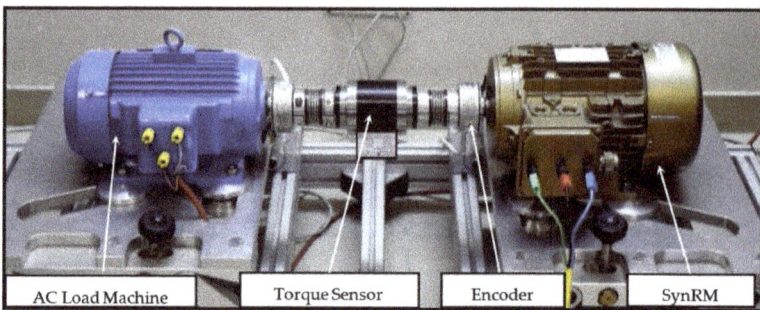
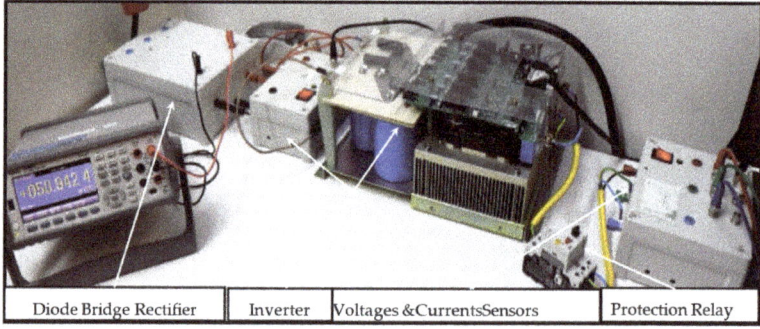

Figure 4. Experimental configuration of the SynRM drive.

Table 3. Parameters of the used SynRM.

Power	P = 2.2 kW	Voltage	V = 366 V
Speed	N = 1500 rpm	Current	I = 5.7 A
No. of pole pairs	p = 2	Torque	T_L = 14 N.m
d-axis inductance	L_d = 0.24 H	q-axis inductance	L_q = 0.057 H

The classical MPCC and the proposed HCC–MPCC algorithms were applied to the VSI. The same PI speed controller for closed-loop speed control was used for both control schemes. For the proposed HCC–MPCC, the hysteresis band was imposed at 0.2 A, approximately 3.5% of the rated current, for better control performance.

3.1. Computational Effort

The classical MPCC and the proposed HCC–MPCC algorithms were separately implemented, under the MATLAB/Simulink environment, into the dSPACE digital controller board. The computational prerequisites of a given algorithm are determined by the complexity and demands of the applied programming language. One way to estimate such prerequisites is to calculate the computational effort placed on the controller in order to execute all the algorithmic calculations. Considering the procedure described in [43], Table 4 presents the average execution times taken by each algorithm in the dSPACE DS1103 controller and the real-time implementation details. The computation effort of the proposed HCC–MPCC algorithm took only 18.82 µs to complete the code, which is significantly lower than the classical MPCC's execution time of 24.26 µs. Therefore, given that the sampling time Ts must be greater than the execution time and that the control variable ripples are heavily dependent on the Ts, the Ts for the classical MPCC cannot be considerably less than 35 µs due to the high algorithmic computation time. However, by using four VVs in the proposed HCC–MPCC, the Ts could be effectively reduced to 28 µs, thereby improving the overall performance of the control process.

Table 4. VV number and execution time of HCC–MPCC and classical MPCC.

Control Algorithm	Number of VVs	Execution Time (μs)	Sampling Time (μs)
MPCC	8	24.26	35
HCC–MPCC	4	18.82	28

3.2. Control Performance

For an adequate assessment of the proposed algorithm's control efficiency and performance analysis, the total harmonic distortion (*THD*) expression was employed to quantify the distortion of the currents [30], further in compliance with the IEEE guidelines specified in [44]. Similarly, the total waveform oscillation (*TWO*) factor was employed to quantify the ripple/oscillation content of said quantity, where a high ripple content is undesirable [30,45]. The *THD* can be expressed as

$$THD = \sqrt{\frac{THD_A^2 + THD_B^2 + THD_C^2}{3}} \times 100\% \qquad (9)$$

Furthermore, the *TWO* can be given by

$$TWO = \frac{\sqrt{X_{eRMS}^2 - X_{eDC}^2}}{|X_{eDC}|} \times 100\% \qquad (10)$$

where X_{eRMS} and X_{eDC} stand for the RMS values and average values of a given quantity, respectively.

Extensive experimental tests were conducted to validate the proposed HCC–MPCC strategy, feasibility and control performance. Furthermore, the classic MPCC was applied alongside the proposed algorithm for comparative purposes, but with different sampling times. Both control schemes were tuned in order to give the best possible performance and they were tested under the same conditions. The performance evaluation considered the analysis of the system's dynamic response to a set of operating conditions as well as the *THD* of the phase stator currents and the *TWO* values of the d-q axis currents.

Figure 5 shows a comparison between the classical MPCC at 35 us (Figure 5a), the proposed HCC–MPCC at 35 us (Figure 5b) and the proposed HCC–MPCC at 28 μs (Figure 5c) under a step-torque torque. The speed reference was set to 1000 rpm, whereas the load step-torque was applied at t = 0.5 s, ranging from 0 to 5 Nm. It can be observed that all control strategies exhibited a similar rapid dynamic response for the considered operation conditions, showcasing good and precise speed tracking capability, thus exhibiting their strength in withstanding rapid and load torque variations. Consequently, the d–q-axis currents presented an expected behavior as they varied according to the demanded load torque, displaying a good torque response. Moreover, it can also be observed that the stator current waveforms were effectively sinusoidal.

Nonetheless, unlike classical MPCC, the proposed HCC–MPCC did not test all the eight possible VVs of the VSI for evaluation and prediction; therefore, classical MPCC displayed a slightly better performance than the proposed HCC–MPCC for the same sampling time of T_s = 35 μs, evidenced by the fact that, for the same sampling time of T_s = 35 μs, classical MPCC (Figure 5a) had an overall slightly better performance indicated by the lower *TWO* values and *THD* in d–q-axis currents and the stator current waveform, respectively, in comparison with HCC–MPCC (Figure 5b), given the slightly higher *TWO* values and *THD* of the latter. However, in contrast with classical MPCC, as previously mentioned, the proposed HCC–MPCC reduced the VVs used for prediction and evaluation of the cost function, thus inherently requiring a shorter execution time, which translates itself to a shorter sampling time. Therefore, as indicated in Table 4, the sampling time of the proposed HCC–MPCC (Figure 5c) was set to T_s = 28 μs, consequently displaying superior control performance evidenced by the decrease in the overall *TWO* values in the d–q-axis currents and, subsequently, a lower ripple content in the stator current waveforms in comparison with the previously mentioned control configurations, evidenced in the zoomed stator currents. Furthermore, it is important to highlight that a smaller sampling time of T_s = 28 μs was not available for classical MPCC, thus this was set to T_s = 35 μs. In addition, it is also necessary to emphasize that, given the MPCC's high parameter dependency on the SynRM model, slight deviations between the q-axis current and its respective reference can be observed in Figure 5 for the employed control strategies. Moreover, the nonlinear nature of the operation conditions inherent to the experimental procedure and several other reasons are also contributing factors for the SynRM modeling accuracy.

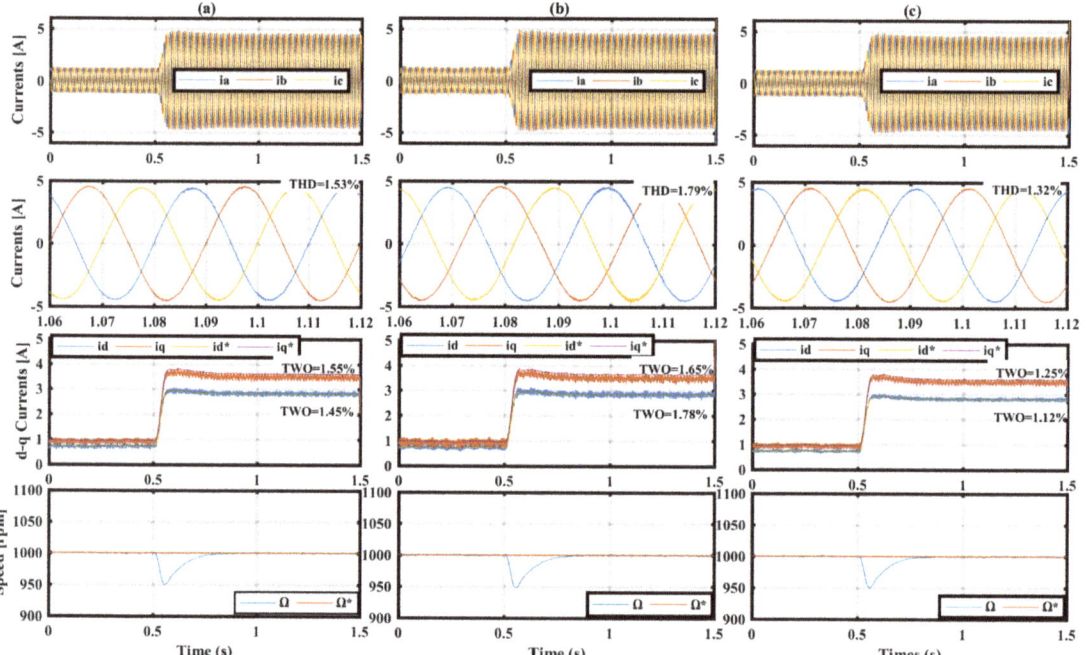

Figure 5. Experimental results: (**a**) MPCC (T_s = 35 μs), (**b**) HCC–MPCC (T_s = 35 μs) and (**c**) HCC–MPCC (T_s = 28 μs), under a step-torque load.

Figure 6 shows the control scheme performance under a speed progression from 500 to 1000 rpm, with a load torque of 2 Nm imposed to the SynRM. The change in the speed reference was given at t = 0.5 s with an acceleration rate of 1000 rpm/s. It can be observed that, for both MPCC and HCC–MPCC control strategies, the new speed reference value was tracked accurately and without any noticeable overshoot, evidenced by the waveform smoothness under the employed speed progression (see Figure 6a–c). Similarly, the d–q-axis currents tracked their reference well, changing along with the speed progression, displaying a great dynamic response in the transient state. However, similarly to the previous operating condition, for the same sampling time of T_s = 35 μs, given its higher resolution, classical MPCC (Figure 6a) exhibited lower *TWO* values and ripple content in the d–q-axis currents and the stator current waveforms, respectively, in contrast with the proposed HCC–MPCC (Figure 6b). Nonetheless, for the employed control strategy in Figure 6c with a lower sampling time of T_s = 28 μs, it can be observed that the d–q-axis currents presented lower *TWO* values than the other control scheme configurations with a higher sampling time, consequently leading to sinusoidal stator currents with less harmonic distortion, showcasing the proposed HCC–MPCC's superior control performance.

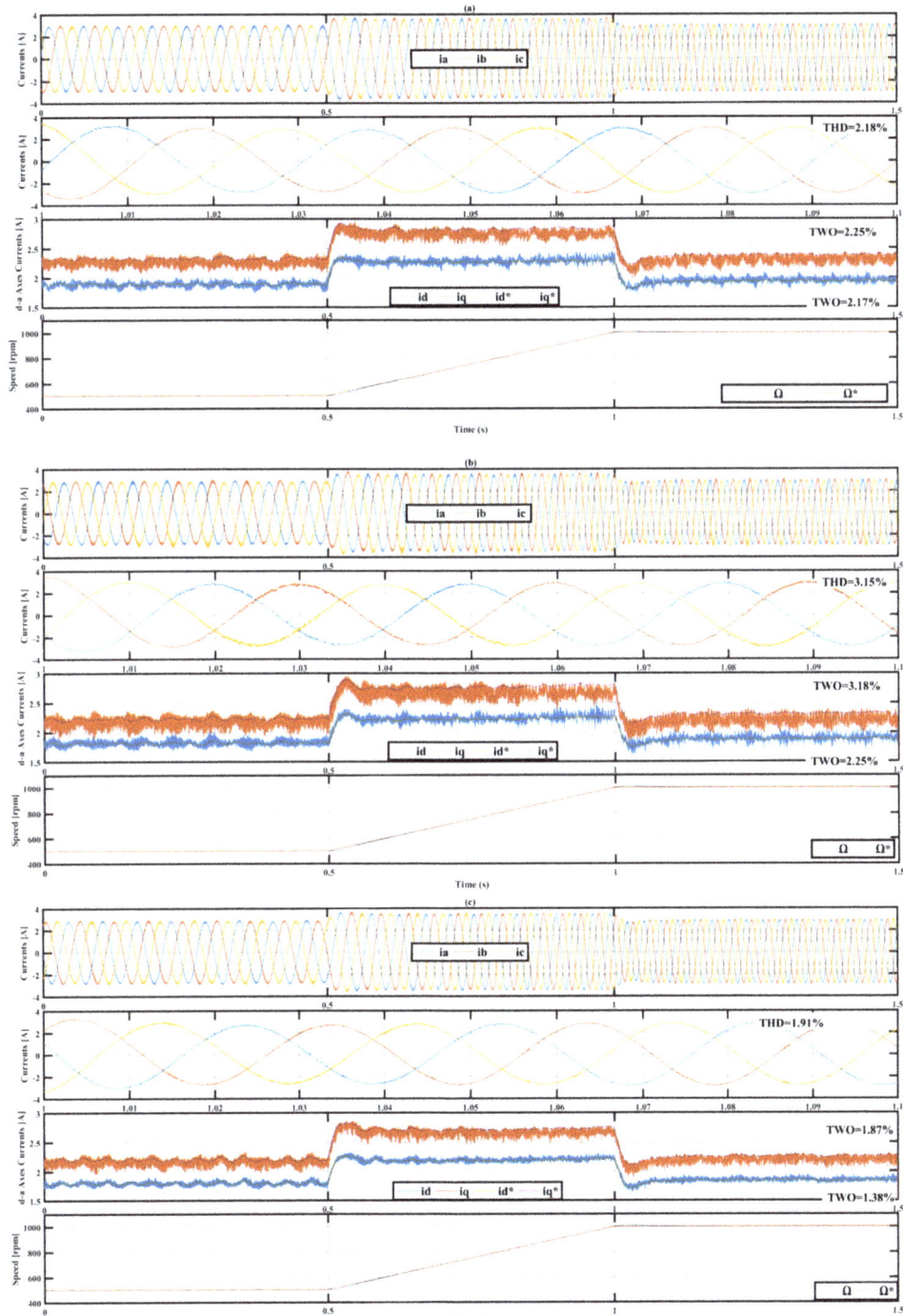

Figure 6. Experimental results of (**a**) MPCC ($T_s = 35 \mu s$), (**b**) HCC–MPCC ($T_s = 35 \mu s$) and (**c**) HCC–MPCC ($T_s = 28 \mu s$), under speed variations.

In summary, it deserves restating that, for the same sampling time of T_s = 35 us, Figures 5b and 6b showcase slightly higher *TWO* values and *THD* in the d–q-axis currents and the stator current waveform, respectively, under both step-load torque and speed variations, in comparison with the classical MPCC's results in Figures 5a and 6a, that is, due to a lower resolution of the proposed control scheme at a sampling time of T_s = 35 us, with such occurrence lying in two main reasons. Firstly, the predicted vectors were selected based on the hysteresis current controller (HCC) reference VV, which is solely dependent on the HCC bandwidth. Secondly, not all feasible voltage vectors (VV) were used for prediction and evaluation of the cost function. Nonetheless, it is essential to note that the computational running time for each algorithm's execution varied. Table 4 presents and compares the average execution times of the algorithms. In comparison to conventional MPCC, the proposed HCC–MPCC eliminates the need for excessive calculations. As a result, the execution time was significantly reduced. In particular, the proposed HCC–MPCC dispensed with evaluating all feasible VVs of the VSI, reducing the number of candidate voltage vectors (VV) for prediction and evaluation in the cost function from eight to four VVs. This ultimately reduced the algorithm's execution time.

Therefore, to reap the benefits of the related decrease in execution time, the sampling time could also be reduced. Thus, the sampling time could be set to 28 μs for the proposed HCC–MPCC, given that only four VV were evaluated, where a sampling time lower than 35 μs is not available for classical MPCC. The implementation details in Table 4 reveal a 20% reduction in the excessive computational burden inherent to classical MPCC, further conceiving additional benefits to the proposed HCC–MPCC, thereby excelling and showcasing the best control performance by exhibiting lower *TWO* values and *THD* in the d–q-axis currents and the stator current waveforms, respectively, as shown in Figures 5c and 6c compared to the classical strategy and further widening its applicability to cheap and less power-demanding microprocessors.

4. Conclusions

This paper presents a computationally efficient HCC–MPCC control scheme of SynRM drives. The reduction in the computational cost was achieved by a merger between MPCC and HCC, thus defining only four VVs used to predict the current and evaluate the cost function. Compared with classical MPCC, the adoption of the proposed HCC–MPCC represents a reduction of 20% in the computational effort while simultaneously maintaining and exhibiting the best control performance, making it an attractive, cost-effective solution.

Moreover, the proposed HCC–MPCC scheme further proved to improve on the inherent drawbacks of both HCC and MPCC, with the conducted experimental results also showing an overall reduction in the *TWO* values and harmonic distortion content as well as the ability to withstand parameters variability, yielding overall excellent results compared with HCC and MPCC alone.

Author Contributions: Conceptualization, W.B. and I.J.; methodology, A.J.M.C., I.J. and W.B.; formal analysis, W.B., I.J. and A.J.M.C.; investigation, W.B. and I.J.; resources, A.J.M.C.; data curation, W.B.; writing—original draft preparation, W.B.; writing—review and editing, W.B., I.J. and A.J.M.C.; visualization, W.B., I.J. and A.J.M.C.; supervision, I.J., A.J.M.C.; project administration, A.J.M.C.; funding acquisition, A.J.M.C. All authors have read and agreed to the published version of the manuscript.

Funding: This work was supported by the European Regional Development Fund (ERDF) through the Operational Programme for Competitiveness and Internationalization (COMPETE 2020), under Project POCI-01-0145-FEDER-029494 and by National Funds through the FCT—Portuguese Foundation for Science and Technology—under Projects PTDC/EEI-EEE/29494/2017, UIDB/04131/2020 and UIDP/04131/2020.

Conflicts of Interest: The authors declare no conflict of interest.

References

1. Taghavi, S.M.; Pillay, P. A Sizing Methodology of the Synchronous Reluctance Motor for Traction Applications. *IEEE J. Emerg. Sel. Top. Power Electron.* **2014**, *2*, 329–340. [CrossRef]
2. Matsuo, T.; Lipo, T.A. Rotor design optimization of synchronous reluctance machine. *IEEE Trans. Energy Convers.* **1994**, *9*, 359–365. [CrossRef]
3. Betz, R.; Lagerquist, R.; Jownovic, M.; Miller, T.J.E.; Middleton, R. Control of Synchronous Reluctance Machines. *IEEE Trans. Ind. Appl.* **1993**, *29*, 1–6. [CrossRef]
4. Fratta, A.; Vagati, A. A reluctance motor drive for high dynamic performance application. *IEEE Trans. Ind. Appl.* **1992**, *28*, 873–879. [CrossRef]
5. De Martin, I.D.; Pasqualotto, D.; Tinazzi, F.; Zigliotto, M. Model-Free Predictive Current Control of Synchronous Reluctance Motor Drives for Pump Applications. *Machines* **2021**, *9*, 217. [CrossRef]
6. Gonzalez-Prieto, A.; Gonzalez-Prieto, I.; Duran, M.J.; Aciego, J.J.; Salas-Biedma, P. Current Harmonic Mitigation Using a Multi-Vector Solution for MPC in Six-Phase Electric Drives. *IEEE Access* **2021**, *9*, 117761–117771. [CrossRef]
7. Galuppini, G.; Magni, L.; Raimondo, D.M. Model predictive control of systems with deadzone and saturation. *Control Eng. Pract.* **2018**, *78*, 56–64. [CrossRef]
8. Guechi, E.-H.; Bouzoualegh, S.; Zennir, Y.; Blažič, S. MPC Control and LQ Optimal Control of A Two-Link Robot Arm: A Comparative Study. *Machines* **2018**, *6*, 37. [CrossRef]
9. Chai, M.; Gorla, N.B.Y.; Panda, S.K. Fault Detection and Localization for Cascaded H-Bridge Multilevel Converter with Model Predictive Control. *IEEE Trans. Power Electron.* **2020**, *35*, 10109–10120. [CrossRef]
10. Zhou, D.; Yang, S.; Tang, Y. A Voltage-Based Open-Circuit Fault Detection and Isolation Approach for Modular Multilevel Converters with Model-Predictive Control. *IEEE Trans. Power Electron.* **2018**, *33*, 9866–9874. [CrossRef]
11. Mesai-Ahmed, H.; Jlassi, I.; Cardoso, A.J.M.; Bentaallah, A. Model-Free Predictive Current Control of Synchronous Reluctance Motors Based on a Recurrent Neural Network. *IEEE Trans. Ind. Electron.* **2021**, *9*, 217. [CrossRef]
12. Bento, F.; Jlassi, I.; Cardoso, A.J.M. Model-Free Predictive Control of Interleaved DC-DC Converters, Based on Ultra-Local Model, with Constant Switching Frequency. In Proceedings of the 2021 IEEE Energy Conversion Congress and Exposition (ECCE), Vancouver, BC, Canada, 10–14 October 2021; pp. 2022–2028. [CrossRef]
13. Laadjal, K.; Bento, F.; Jlassi, I.; Cardoso, A.J.M. Online Condition Monitoring of Electrolytic Capacitors in DC-DC Interleaved Boost Converters, Adopting a Model-Free Predictive Controller. In Proceedings of the 2021 IEEE 15th International Conference on Compatibility, Power Electronics and Power Engineering (CPE-POWERENG), Florence, Italy, 14–16 July 2021; pp. 1–6.
14. Cortes, P.; Kazmierkowski, M.P.; Kennel, R.M.; Quevedo, D.E.; Rodriguez, J. Predictive Control in Power Electronics and Drives. *IEEE Trans. Ind. Electron.* **2008**, *55*, 4312–4324. [CrossRef]
15. Vazquez, S.; Rodriguez, J.; Rivera, M.; Franquelo, L.G.; Norambuena, M. Model predictive control for power converters and drives: Advances and trends. *IEEE Trans. Ind. Electron.* **2017**, *64*, 935–947. [CrossRef]
16. Kouro, S.; Cortes, P.; Vargas, R.; Ammann, U.; Rodriguez, J. Model predictive control—A simple and powerful method to control power converters. *IEEE Trans. Ind. Electron.* **2009**, *56*, 1826–1838. [CrossRef]
17. Jlassi, I.; Cardoso, A.J.M. Open-circuit fault-tolerant operation of permanent magnet synchronous generator drives for wind turbine systems using a computationally efficient model predictive current control. *IET Electr. Power Appl.* **2021**, *15*, 837–846. [CrossRef]
18. Gmati, B.; Jlassi, I.; EL Khil, S.K.; Cardoso, A.J.M. Open-switch fault diagnosis in voltage source inverters of PMSM drives using predictive current errors and fuzzy logic approach. *IET Power Electron.* **2021**, *14*, 1059–1072. [CrossRef]
19. Siami, M.; Khaburi, D.A.; Rivera, M.; Rodríguez, J. A computationally efficient lookup table based FCS-MPC for PMSM drives fed by matrix converters. *IEEE Trans. Ind. Electron.* **2017**, *64*, 7645–7654. [CrossRef]
20. Yaramasu, V. Predictive Control of Multilevel Converters for Megawattwind Energy Conversion Systems. Ph.D. Thesis, Ryerson University, Toronto, ON, Canada, 2014.
21. Hu, J.; Zhu, J.; Lei, G.; Platt, G.; Dorrell, D.G. Multi-objective model-predictive control for high-power converters. *IEEE Trans. Energy Convers.* **2013**, *28*, 652–663.
22. Zhang, Y.; Xie, W. Low complexity model predictive control single vector-based approach. *IEEE Trans. Power Electron.* **2014**, *29*, 5532–5541. [CrossRef]
23. Xie, W.; Wang, W.X.; Wang, F.; Xu, W.; Kennel, R.M.; Gerling, D.; Lorenz, R.D. Finite-control-set model predictive torque control with a deadbeat solution for PMSM drives. *IEEE Trans. Ind. Electron.* **2015**, *62*, 5402–5410. [CrossRef]
24. Zhang, J.; Sun, T.; Wang, F.; Rodríguez, J.; Kennel, R. A computationally efficient quasi-centralized DMPC for back-to-back converter pmsg wind turbine systems without dc-link tracking errors. *IEEE Trans. Ind. Electron.* **2016**, *63*, 6160–6171. [CrossRef]
25. Serra, J.; Jlassi, I.; Cardoso, A.J.M. A Computationally Efficient Model Predictive Control of Six-Phase Induction Machines Based on Deadbeat Control. *Machines* **2021**, *9*, 306. [CrossRef]
26. Jlassi, I.; Cardoso, A.J.M. Fault-tolerant back-to-back converter for direct-drive PMSG wind turbines using direct torque and power control techniques. *IEEE Trans. Power Electron.* **2019**, *34*, 11215–11227. [CrossRef]
27. Wu, X.; Song, W.; Xue, C. Low-complexity model predictive torque control method without weighting factor for five-phase PMSM based on hysteresis comparators. *IEEE J. Emerg. Sel. Top. Power Electron.* **2018**, *6*, 1650–1661. [CrossRef]

28. Jlassi, I.; Cardoso, A.J.M. Lookup-Table-Based Model Predictive Torque Control without Weighting Factors for PMSM Drives. In Proceedings of the IECON 2019-45th Annual Conference of the IEEE Industrial Electronics Society, Lisbon, Portugal, 14–17 October 2019; pp. 1165–1170.
29. Habibullah, M.; Lu, D.D.C.; Xiao, D.; Rahman, M.F. A simplified finite-state predictive direct torque control for induction motor drive. *IEEE Trans. Ind. Electron.* **2016**, *63*, 3964–3975.
30. Jlassi, I.; Cardoso, A.J.M. Enhanced and computationally efficient model predictive flux and power control of PMSG drives for wind turbine applications. *IEEE Trans. Ind. Electron.* **2021**, *68*, 6574–6583. [CrossRef]
31. Siami, M.; Khaburi, D.A.; Rodriguez, J. Simplified finite control set-model predictive control for matrix converter-fed PMSM drives. *IEEE Trans. Power Electron.* **2018**, *33*, 2438–2446. [CrossRef]
32. Habibullah, M.; Lu, D.D.C.; Xiao, D.; Osman, I.; Rahman, M.F. Selected prediction vectors based FS-PTC for 3L-NPC inverter fed motor drives. *IEEE Trans. Ind. Appl.* **2017**, *53*, 3588–3597. [CrossRef]
33. Yang, Y.; Wen, H.; Fan, M.; Xie, M.; Chen, R. Fast finite-switching-state model predictive control method without weighting factors for T-type three-level three-phase inverters. *IEEE Trans. Ind. Inf.* **2019**, *15*, 1298–1310. [CrossRef]
34. Geyer, T.; Quevedo, D.E. Multistep finite control set model predictive control for power electronics. *IEEE Trans. Power Electron.* **2014**, *29*, 6836–6846. [CrossRef]
35. Zhang, Z.; Hackl, C.; Kennel, R. Computationally efficient DMPC for three-level NPC back-to-back converters in wind turbine systems with PMSG. *IEEE Trans. Power Electron.* **2017**, *32*, 8018–8034. [CrossRef]
36. Rodriguez, J.; Pontt, J.; Silva, C.A.; Correa, P.; Lezana, P.; Cortés, P.; Ammann, U. Predictive Current Control of a Voltage Source Inverter. *IEEE Trans. Ind. Electron.* **2007**, *54*, 495–503. [CrossRef]
37. Chiang, H.K.; Tseng, C.H. Design and implementation of a grey sliding mode controller for synchronous reluctance motor drive. *Control Eng. Pract.* **2004**, *12*, 155–163. [CrossRef]
38. Lee, H.-D.; Kang, S.-J.; Sul, S.-K. Efficiency-optimized direct torque control of synchronous reluctance motor using feedback linearization. *IEEE Trans. Ind. Electron.* **1999**, *46*, 192–198.
39. Jlassi, I.; Cardoso, A.J.M. Model predictive current control of synchronous reluctance motors, including saturation and iron losses. In Proceedings of the 2018 23rd International Conference on Electrical Machines, ICEM, Alexandroupoli, Greece, 3–6 September 2018; Volume 2018, pp. 1598–1603.
40. Matos, D.; Estima, J.; Khaled, Y.; Cardoso, A.J.M. Modeling and implementation of MTPA control strategy for synrm variable speed drives. *Int. J. Elec. Eng.* **2014**, *9*, 6. [CrossRef]
41. Hadla, H.; Cruz, S. Predictive Stator Flux and Load Angle Control of Synchronous Reluctance Motor Drives Operating in a Wide Speed Range. *IEEE Trans. Ind. Electron.* **2017**, *64*, 6950–6959. [CrossRef]
42. Cortes, P.; Rodriguez, J.; Silva, C.; Flores, A. Delay compensation in model predictive current control of a three-phase inverter. *IEEE Trans. Ind. Electron.* **2012**, *59*, 1323–1325. [CrossRef]
43. *dSPACE FAQ 23, Measuring Execution Times of Block and Subsystems*; dSPACE GmbH: Paderborne, Germany, 2011; p. 4.
44. IEEE Recommended Practices and Requirements for Harmonic Control in Electrical Power Systems. In *IEEE Std 519-1992*; IEEE: Piscataway, NJ, USA, 1993; pp. 1–112. [CrossRef]
45. Luis, C.-M. Technological Innovation for Sustainability. In Proceedings of the Second IFIP WG 5.5/SOCOLNET Doctoral Conference on Computing, Electrical and Industrial Systems, DoCEIS 2011, Costa de Caparica, Portugal, 21–23 February 2011. [CrossRef]

Article

A Modified Dynamic Model of Single-Sided Linear Induction Motors Considering Longitudinal and Transversal Effects

Hamidreza Heidari [1,*], Anton Rassõlkin [1], Arash Razzaghi [2], Toomas Vaimann [1], Ants Kallaste [1], Ekaterina Andriushchenko [1], Anouar Belahcen [1,3] and Dmitry V. Lukichev [4]

1. Department of Electrical Power Engineering and Mechatronics, Tallinn University of Technology, 19086 Tallinn, Estonia; anton.rassolkin@taltech.ee (A.R.); toomas.vaimann@taltech.ee (T.V.); ants.kallaste@taltech.ee (A.K.); ekandr@taltech.ee (E.A.); anouar.belahcen@aalto.fi (A.B)
2. Department of Electrical Engineering, University of IAU, Mianeh 5315836511, Iran; razzaghi.ieee@gmail.com
3. Department of Electrical Engineering, Aalto University, 11000 Aalto, Finland
4. Faculty of Control Systems and Robotics, ITMO University, 197101 Saint Petersburg, Russia; lukichev@itmo.ru or dmitry.v.lukichev@gmail.com
* Correspondence: haheid@taltech.ee; Tel.: +372-56139797

Abstract: This paper proposes a modified dynamic equivalent circuit model for a linear induction motor considering both longitudinal end effect and transverse edge effect. The dynamic end effect (speed-dependent end effect) is based on conventional Duncan's approach. The transverse edge effect is investigated by using three correction factors applied to the secondary resistance and magnetizing inductance. Moreover, the iron saturation effect, the skin effect, and the air-gap leakage effect are incorporated into the proposed model by using the field-analysis method. A new topology of the steady-state and space-vector model of linear induction, regarding all mentioned phenomena, is presented. The parameters of this model are calculated using both field analysis and the finite-element method. The steady-state performance of the model is first validated using the finite-element method. Additionally, the dynamic performance of the proposed model is studied. The results prove that the proposed equivalent circuit model can precisely predict the dynamic and steady-state performances of the linear induction.

Keywords: dynamic performance; equivalent circuit model; finite-element method; linear induction motor; longitudinal end effect; transverse edge effect

1. Introduction

Nowadays, linear induction motors (LIMs) are widely used in industrial applications such as transportation systems, production lines of factories, electromagnetic launchers, etc. Comparing LIMs with the conventional structures to produce linear motion (including rotary electric motor and gearbox), there is no need for the mechanical interface for these types of motors, which reduces the mechanical losses and stresses. Moreover, the range of velocity and acceleration of LIMs is more extensive. However, the asymmetrical structures of LIMs in both the longitudinal and transversal directions are two main disadvantages of LIMs, which yield the longitudinal end effect and the transversal edge effect, respectively. Such phenomena lead to an increment in the complexity of the LIM modeling and control [1–3].

Dynamic and steady-state modeling of the LIM has been widely addressed in the literature. In this regard, the literature can be divided into four categories, including modified mechanical equation-based models (MMEMs) [4–6], winding function-based models (WFMs) [7–9], field theory-based models (FTMs) [10–14], and Duncan's approach based models (DAMs) [15–20].

The MMEMs are based on the fact that the final effect of the longitudinal asymmetry is producing a braking force in the opposite direction of the LIM motion. Hence, the longitudinal end effect can be considered as a braking force in the mechanical equation of the LIM and the electrical equations of LIMs are considered as rotary induction motor (RIM) ones. The braking force due to the end effect has been modeled by using the Taylor series, which is a function of linear velocity [4,5]. In [6], the resultant propulsive force was calculated using the air-gap flux density with consideration of the longitudinal end effect. The MMEMs are simple and can also predict the dynamic performance of LIMs. However, consideration of the transverse edge effect in these models is still a challenging task.

In the WFMs, some suitable winding functions are defined for both primary and secondary parts of the LIM, and then the matrix of the LIM inductances and subsequently the terminal voltages and flux linkages are calculated. A WFM has been first introduced in [7] for a high-speed double-sided LIM (DLIM) and implemented on a single-sided LIM (SLIM) with different sets of winding functions [8,9]. The application of WFMs has received attention from researchers due to its high accuracy. The counterpart of this advantage is the complexity of WFMs because of high computation, which makes these models unsuitable for analyzing the dynamic performance of LIMs, especially in variable-speed drive systems with consideration of the transverse edge effect.

The FTMs employ N-dimensional (N = 1,2,3) field theory to obtain an accurate equivalent circuit model for the LIM while deriving its parameters. It is worth mentioning here that the majority of equivalent circuit models use field analysis because of its accuracy. However, these models usually describe the steady-state behavior of the LIM and do not give any information about the dynamic operation of the LIM. In [10], most undesirable phenomena, such as longitudinal end effects, transverse edge effect, and back-iron saturation, are considered using field analysis. In [11,12], the air-gap electromotive force (EMF) has been modified by a longitudinal end effect factor. An improved series equivalent circuit model based on field theory was presented in [13]. The secondary resistance and the magnetic inductance were modified by some coefficients to consider the longitudinal end effect and the transverse edge effect in [14].

In the DAMs, the longitudinal end effect is considered by a correction factor, as a function of linear speed, applied to the magnetizing branch of the LIM's equivalent circuit model [15]. Duncan's model is widely used for the design of variable-speed drive systems because it considers both the dynamic and steady-state performance of LIMs. In this regard, the d-q equivalent circuit model and space-vector model were presented in [16,17], respectively. A modified steady-state Duncan's model was developed in [18] to cover special phenomena such as the transverse edge effect. All aforementioned DAMs only take into account the dynamic end effect, which is related to linear speed. The dynamic d-q and steady-state equivalent circuit models with consideration of both dynamic and static end effect (or speed-independent end effect) have been investigated in [19,20], respectively.

Modeling of motors is crucial for many objectives, including life-cycle analysis, performance analysis, and more importantly, control purposes [21–23]. In this paper, a modified dynamic equivalent circuit model of LIMs is proposed. The model considers most special phenomena of LIMs, including (1) the dynamic longitudinal end effect using the conventional Duncan's approach, (2) the transverse edge effect using three correction factors for modifying secondary resistance and magnetizing inductance, (3) the iron saturation effect, (4) the skin effect and (5) the air-gap leakage effect. A new topology of the steady-state and space-vector model of LIMs is presented. The proposed model can analyze both the steady-state and dynamic performance of LIMs, and hence it is useful for obtaining an accurate variable-speed drive system. To validate the proposed model, finite-element method (FEM) is employed. The rest of the paper is organized as follows. Section 1 briefly reviews Duncan's equivalent circuit model. Section 2 describes the proposed equivalent circuit model, which includes preliminary remarks, the transverse edge effect, iron saturation, the skin effect and the air-gap leakage effect, the proposed dynamic model, and parameters' calculation of the proposed model. The results and discussion are presented in Section 3. Finally, the conclusions of the paper are synthesized in Section 4.

2. A Review of Duncan's Equivalent Circuit Model of LIM

The structure of a LIM is shown in Figure 1. In the LIM, when the primary part moves along with the secondary part, it continuously encounters a new material of the secondary part. Because of the appearance of this new material, the air-gap flux density is gradually increased at the entry of the primary part with a total secondary time constant that is described by $T_r = (L_m + L_{lr})/R_r$, where L_m, L_{lr}, and R_r are magnetizing inductance, secondary leakage inductance, and secondary resistance, respectively. The flux density is decreased at the exit of the primary part with the secondary leakage time constant in the following way: $T_{r0} = L_{lr}/R_r$.

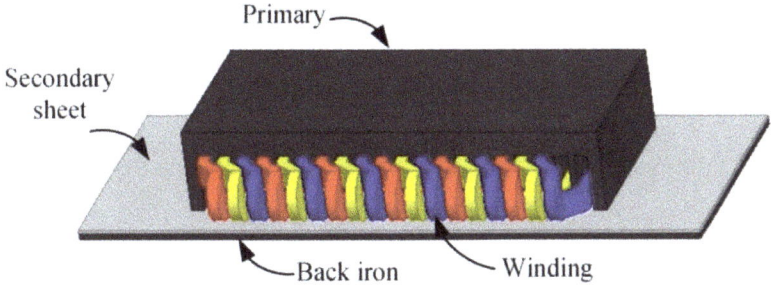

Figure 1. The structure of a single-sided linear induction motor (SLIM) 2. Materials and Methods.

Figure 2 shows the gradual increase and sudden decrease of the normalized air-gap flux density versus time.

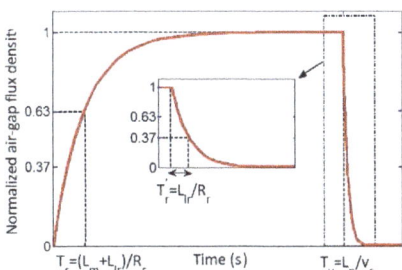

Figure 2. Normalized air-gap flux density versus time.

In this figure, the term $T_v = L_p/v_l$ is the time of traverse of an imaginary point by the primary core, where L_p and v_l are the primary lengths and linear speed, respectively. Increasing and decreasing the air-gap flux density causes an eddy current in the secondary sheet. The eddy current deteriorates the air-gap flux density in the longitudinal direction as well as increasing the ohmic losses. Such phenomena are the so-called longitudinal end effect, which can be described by the end effect factor as follows [15]:

$$Q = \frac{T_v}{T_r} = \frac{L_p/v_1}{(L_m + L_{lr})/R_r} \tag{1}$$

This factor amends the magnetizing inductance in the following way:

$$M = L_m(1 - f(Q)) \tag{2}$$

where:

$$f(Q) = \frac{1 - e^{-Q}}{Q} \tag{3}$$

3. Proposed Dynamic Equivalent Circuit Model of LIM

3.1. Preliminary Remarks

A LIM is usually made so that the widths of the primary and the secondary parts are not equal. This difference between them may lead to non-uniform distribution of the transversal flux density [24]. With the assumption that the movement direction is along the x-axis, the quadrature axis of that is called the y-axis and the transversal direction is along the z-axis, there is a depression in the middle area of the air-gap flux density, which has a smaller amplitude than the terminals. This phenomenon is well-known as the "transversal edge effect," which leads to an increase in the equivalent resistance of the secondary sheet. Similar to the end effect, the final influence of this phenomenon produces a braking thrust that is opposite to the developed thrust in the air-gap.

Although Duncan's model is simple and can also predict the dynamic performance of the LIM, some unwanted phenomena, particularly the transversal edge effect, are not considered in this model. This paper considers both the longitudinal end effect and the transversal edge effect. For this purpose, a dimensional structure of a LIM is illustrated in Figure 3, where W_p is the primary width, W_s is the secondary width, g is the mechanical air-gap distance, d_s is the thickness of the secondary sheet, d_b is the thickness of the back iron, h_1 is the depth of the slot, h_2 is the height of the yoke, w_1 is the width of the primary teeth, and w_2 is the width of the secondary teeth. In the next sections, the modification procedure of Duncan's model will be explained.

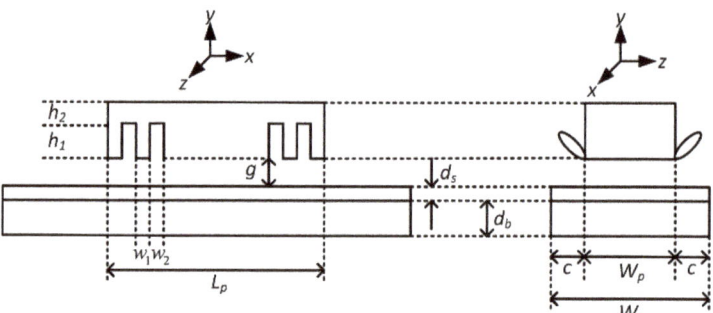

Figure 3. The dimensional structure of a linear induction motor (LIM).

3.2. Transverse Edge Effect

As mentioned earlier, the transversal edge effect results from unequal widths of the primary and the secondary parts. This effect causes an increase in the secondary resistance and a decrease in the magnetizing inductance. This paper utilizes a complex power method to consider the transversal edge effect to modify the secondary resistance and magnetizing inductance [10]. In this approach, the air-gap flux linkage is analytically calculated by Maxwell's field equations. The complex power equation is then derived by using the air-gap flux linkage. This equation is based on the structural parameters and linear velocity of the LIM. On the other hand, the complex power equation can also be achieved from an electric equivalent circuit. Thus, the coefficients of the transversal edge effect as well as the parameters of the equivalent circuit can be obtained from the equality of the analytical expressions for the complex power, which are derived from the magnetic and the electric circuits.

The transversal edge effect on the secondary sheet can be modeled using the K_1 and K_2 coefficients, which are expressed in terms of Bolton's coefficients as follows [25]:

$$K_1 = K_x \frac{1 + s^2 G^2 K_r^2 / K_x^2}{1 + s^2 G^2} \qquad (4)$$

$$K_2 = \frac{K_x^2}{K_r}\frac{1+s^2G^2K_r^2/K_x^2}{1+s^2G^2} \tag{5}$$

where K_r and K_x are defined as:

$$K_r = 1 - Re\left\{(1-jsG)\frac{2\lambda}{a\alpha}tanh(0.5a\alpha)\right\} \tag{6}$$

$$K_x = 1 - Re\left\{(Gs+j)Gs\frac{2\lambda}{a\alpha}tanh(0.5a\alpha)\right\} \tag{7}$$

The parameters that are used in the above equations are given by:

$$\lambda = \left[1 + \sqrt{1+jsG}tanh(0.5a\alpha)tanh(0.5\beta(W_s - \alpha))\right]^{-1} \tag{8}$$

$$\alpha = \beta\sqrt{1+jG} \tag{9}$$

$$a = W_p + g_0 \tag{10}$$

$$g_0 = d_s + g \tag{11}$$

The goodness factor G is computed as:

$$G = \frac{\omega_s\mu_0 d_s\sigma_e}{\beta^2 g_e} \tag{12}$$

In these equations, s is slip, $\beta = \pi/\tau$ is the wave number, ω_s is the input frequency, σ_e is the equivalent conductivity of the secondary part, and g_e is the equivalent air-gap length. The transversal edge effect on the back iron can be expressed by inserting $\omega_s = a$ into the term of K_2, which is named K_3. As a result, the transversal edge effect on the secondary sheet and the back iron can be considered by using modification coefficients K_1, K_2, and K_3, which modify the magnetic inductance, secondary sheet resistance, and back iron resistance, respectively. Assume that $sG \ll 1$; these coefficients will be simplified as follows:

$$K_1 = 1 \tag{13}$$

$$K_2 = \left[1 - \frac{2tanh(0.5\alpha\beta)}{\alpha\beta[1+tanh(0.5\alpha\beta)tanh(0.5\beta(W_s-\alpha))]}\right]^{-1} \tag{14}$$

$$K_3 = \left[1 - \frac{2tanh(0.5\alpha\beta)}{\alpha\beta}\right]^{-1} \tag{15}$$

3.3. Iron Saturation Effect, Skin Effect, and the Air-Gap Leakage Effect

The air-gap leakage and the iron saturation effects lead to a change in the equivalent air-gap length, which can be expressed by [10]:

$$g_e = g_0 K_l K_c(1+K_s) \tag{16}$$

in which:

$$K_l = \frac{sin(\beta g_0 K_c)}{\beta g_0 K_c} \tag{17}$$

$$K_s = \frac{\mu_0}{\mu_{fe}\delta_b g_0 K_c\beta^2} \tag{18}$$

where K_c is Carter's coefficient, K_l is the air-gap leakage coefficient, and K_s is the iron saturation coefficient. δ_b is the depth of the flux density into the back iron, which is obtained as:

$$\delta_b = Re\left\{\frac{1}{(\beta^2+j\omega_s\mu_{fe}s\sigma_b)^{0.5}}\right\} \tag{19}$$

where σ_b is the conductivity of the back iron. The skin effect can be considered by a coefficient that modifies the equivalent conductivity of the secondary sheet as:

$$K_{sk} = \frac{d_s}{2\delta_s} \frac{\sinh\left(\frac{d_s}{\delta_s}\right) + \sin\left(\frac{d_s}{\delta_s}\right)}{\cosh\left(\frac{d_s}{\delta_s}\right) - \cos\left(\frac{d_s}{\delta_s}\right)} \qquad (20)$$

where σ_s is the conductivity of the secondary sheet. The skin effect coefficient K_{sk} modifies the equivalent conductivity of the secondary sheet as follows:

$$\sigma_{es} = \frac{\sigma_s}{K_{sk}} \qquad (21)$$

Finally, the saturation effect, the skin effect, and the air-gap leakage effect lead to modification of the goodness factor G (Equation (12)), in which σ_e is equal to:

$$\sigma_e = \sigma_{es} + \frac{\delta_b}{d_s}\sigma_b \qquad (22)$$

3.4. Proposed Dynamic Model

In the proposed equivalent circuit model of the LIM, the transversal edge effect is considered by the K_1, K_2, and K_3 coefficients, which modify the magnetic inductance, the resistance of the secondary sheet, and the resistance of the back iron, respectively. The longitudinal end effect is expressed using Duncan's approach. The saturation effect, the skin effect, and the air-gap leakage effect are also included by the equations that are described in Section 3.3. The proposed steady-state and dynamic equivalent circuit models are shown in Figure 4a,b, respectively.

The total secondary resistance is calculated as:

$$R_r = \frac{K_2 K_3 R_{sheet} R_{iron}}{K_2 R_{sheet} + K_3 R_{iron}} \qquad (23)$$

It should be remarked that with the proposed model, both the dynamic and steady-state performances of the LIM can be analyzed. Hence, it can be used to provide an efficient variable-speed drive system for LIMs. In comparison to most WFMs or FTMs, dynamic performance prediction is the advantage of the proposed model. In comparison to DAMs, the parameters R_r and L_m vary with the linear velocity to consider the transverse edge effect.

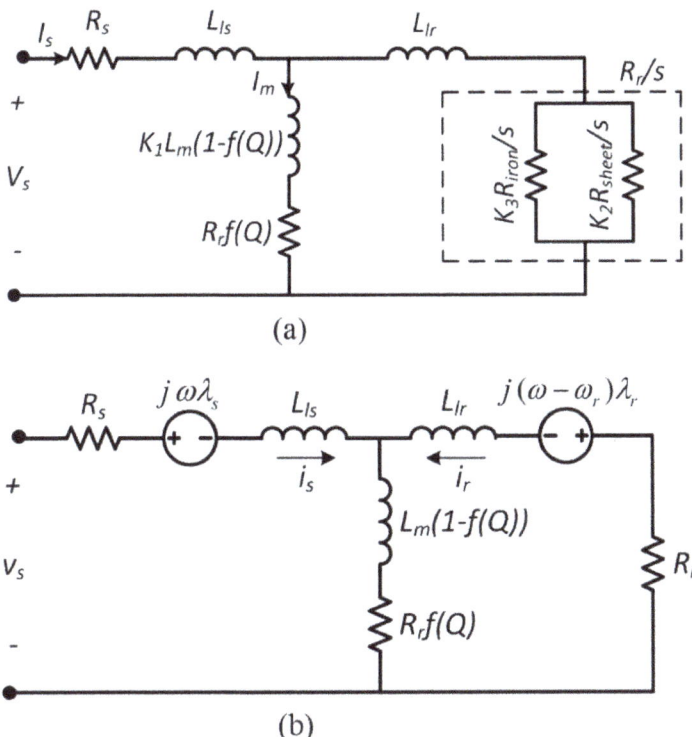

Figure 4. Proposed (**a**) steady-state and (**b**) dynamic equivalent circuit model of a LIM.

3.5. Parameters Calculation of the Proposed Model

In this paper, analytical methods based on field analysis are used for the calculation of the proposed equivalent circuit parameters, because the identification process of the equivalent circuit parameters by using practical methods, i.e., open circuit and short circuit tests, suffer from several problems so that applying these tests is impossible in some cases [26]. The resistance of the secondary sheet and the resistance of the back iron can be obtained as follows:

$$R_{sheet} = \frac{4m}{\sigma_s} \frac{(NK_\omega)^2}{p} \frac{W_p}{d_s \tau} \qquad (24)$$

$$R_{iron} = \frac{4m}{\sigma_b} \frac{(NK_\omega)^2}{p} \frac{W_p}{\delta_b \tau} \qquad (25)$$

where m is the number of phases, N is winding turns per phase, and K_ω is the winding coefficient. The magnetic inductance is calculated as [1,27]:

$$L_m = \frac{4m\mu_0(K_\omega N)^2(W_p + g_0)\tau}{\pi^2 p g_e} \qquad (26)$$

R_1 is the primary resistance per phase, which is [1,27]:

$$R_1 = \frac{2(W_p + l_{ec})N}{\sigma_\omega A_\omega} \qquad (27)$$

where l_{ec} is the length of the end connection, and σ_ω and A_ω are conductivity and cross-sectional area of the primary winding conductor, respectively. The primary leakage inductance is equal to [1,27]:

$$L_{ls} = \frac{4\mu_0 N^2}{p}\left\{\left(\lambda_s\left(1+\frac{3}{p}\right)+\lambda_d\right)\frac{W_p}{q}+\lambda_e l_{ec}\right\} \tag{28}$$

where q is the number of slots per pole, and λ_s, λ_d, and λ_e are permeances of slot, end connection, and air-gap leakage, respectively, which are computed as follows:

$$\lambda_s = \frac{h_1(1+3K_p)}{12\omega_2} \tag{29}$$

$$\lambda_d = \frac{5g_e/\omega_2}{5+4g_e/\omega_2} \tag{30}$$

$$\lambda_e = 0.3(3K_p - 1) \tag{31}$$

where K_p is the pitch factor.

4. Results and Discussion

4.1. Verification of Proposed Model Using FEM

To validate the proposed model, the results were compared using 3-D FEM. In this method, all undesirable phenomena that can happen in the LIM, such as a longitudinal end and transversal edge effects, are considered with acceptable accuracy. For this purpose, Ansoft/Maxwell 14.0 software was employed. The structure parameters of the LIM are tabulated in Table 1. The 3-D view of the LIM in Maxwell software is illustrated in Figure 1.

Table 1. Structure parameters of the LIM.

Parameter Description	Symbol	Unit	Value
Primary frequency	f	Hz	60
No. of poles	p	–	6
No. of phases	m	–	3
No. of slots	z	–	20
No. of slots per phase per pole	q	–	1
Pole pitch	τ	mm	66.67
Mechanical air-gap	g	mm	3.2
Primary length	L_p	mm	400
Primary width	W_p	mm	177.8
Secondary sheet thickness	d_s	mm	3.2
Back iron thickness	d_b	mm	6.4
Secondary width	W_s	mm	247.8
Slot depth	h_1	mm	52.5
Yoke height	h_2	mm	26.3
Opening slot	b_{s0}	mm	12.7
Slot pitch	τ_s	mm	19
Secondary sheet conductivity	σ_s	Ms/m	24.59
Back iron sheet conductivity	σ_b	Ms/m	5.8

Figure 5a–d show changes of saturation coefficient, goodness factor, the ratio of the equivalent conductivity to the nominal conductivity, and the ratio of the equivalent air-gap length to the nominal air-gap length with velocity, respectively. It should be mentioned that all of these figures were obtained at 60 Hz frequency. As can be seen, the fundamental parameters of the LIM were varied with a velocity that yields the changes in the electric parameters of the equivalent circuit including the secondary resistance and the magnetic inductance, while these are considered constant in conventional models.

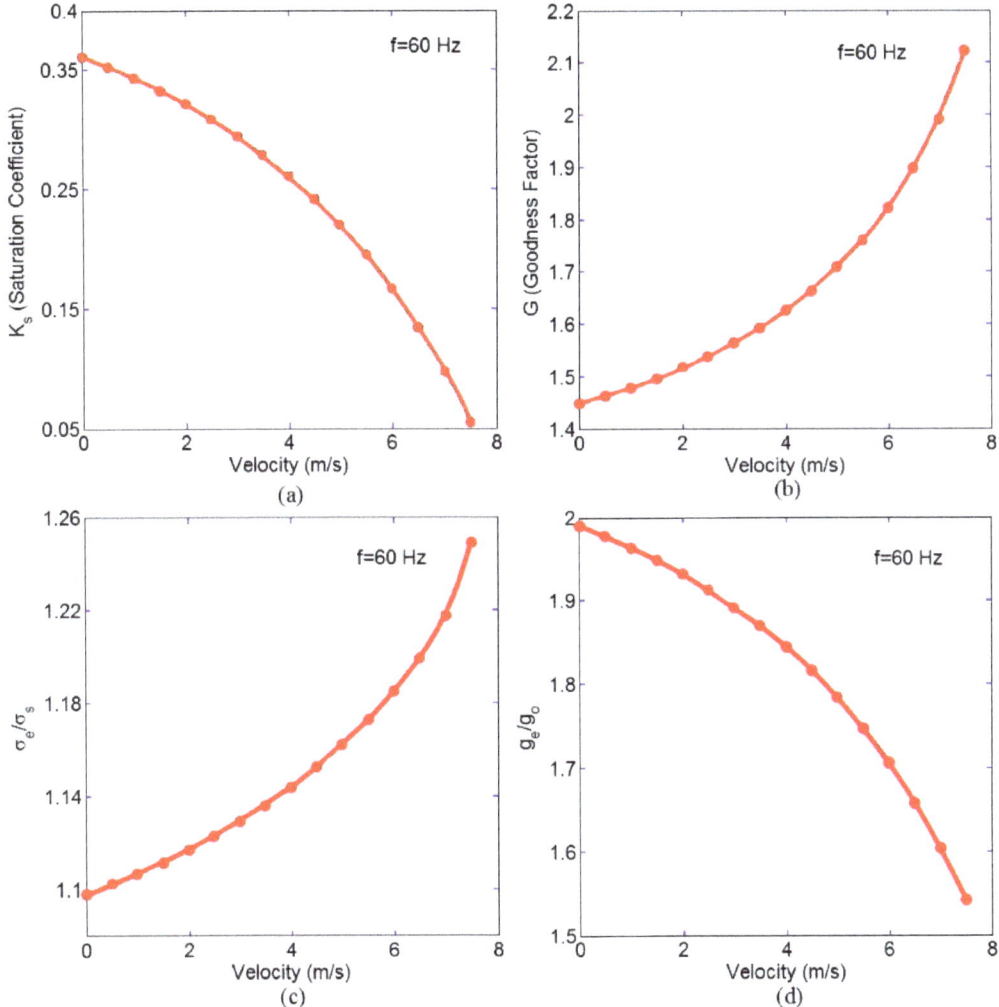

Figure 5. Field analysis results versus the velocity: (**a**) saturation coefficient (**b**) goodness factor (**c**) ratio of the secondary equivalent conductivity to the nominal conductivity, and (**d**) ratio of the equivalent air-gap length to the nominal air-gap length.

In this paper, the parameters of the LIM equivalent circuit are evaluated by two methods. The first one is the field analysis, which is described in Section 3.4 in detail, and the second one is FEM, which validates the results of the field analysis. Figures 6 and 7 present the magnetic inductance and the secondary resistance curves with velocity, respectively. As can be seen, the analytical method accurately provides the equivalent circuit parameters. The magnetic inductance is increased and the secondary resistance is reduced by increasing the velocity from zero to rated speed. It should be mentioned here that the longitudinal end effect is not considered in Figures 6 and 7, because it is first indicated that the changes of magnetic inductance and the secondary resistance with the velocity due to transversal edge effect, the iron effect, the skin effect, and the air-gap leakage effect. Hence, the end effect factor (Equation (1)) modifies the parallel branch of an equivalent circuit for considering the longitudinal end effect. The values of the leakage inductance and the primary resistance from the analytical method and FEM are listed in Table 2. Figure 8 shows the thrust versus velocity characteristic of LIMs using Duncan's model, the proposed model, and FEM. As can be seen, the proposed method agrees better with the 3-D FEM. The figure shows the superiority of the proposed method against the Duncan model in all speed regions. This improvement reaches up to 10 percent in the thrust estimation at the velocity of 3.5 m/s.

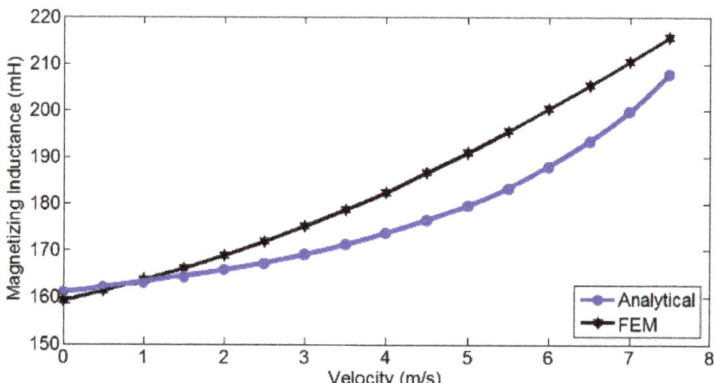

Figure 6. Magnetic inductance variations versus the velocity.

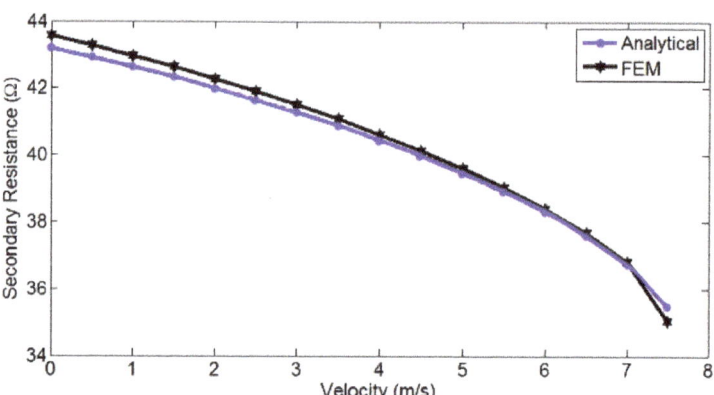

Figure 7. Secondary equivalent resistance variations versus the velocity.

Table 2. Equivalent circuit parameters of the LIM.

Parameter	Field Analysis Method	Finite Element Method
L_{ls}	61.2 mH	63.9 mH
R_s	10.62 Ω	10.3 Ω

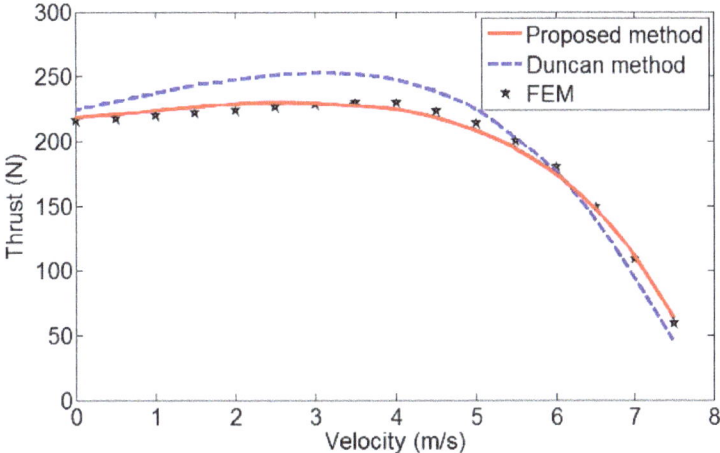

Figure 8. Thrust versus velocity curve.

4.2. Dynamic Characteristics of LIMs Based on the Proposed Model

The dynamic equivalent circuit of the LIM, in the form of the space-vector model, was shown in Figure 4b. The secondary resistance R_r can be computed by Equation (23). The LIM voltage equations in the arbitrary reference frame are as follows [28]:

$$v_s = R_s i_s + j\omega\lambda_s + p\lambda_s + R_{sh}(i_s + i_r) \tag{32}$$

$$v_r = 0 = R_r i_r + j(\omega - \omega_r)\lambda_r + p\lambda_r + R_{sh}(i_s + i_r) \tag{33}$$

The flux linkages are:

$$\lambda_s = L_s i_s + M i_r \tag{34}$$

$$\lambda_r = L_r i_r + M i_s \tag{35}$$

$$L_s = L_{ls} + M \tag{36}$$

$$L_r = L_{lr} + M \tag{37}$$

$$R_{sh} = R_r f(Q) \tag{38}$$

The mechanical equation of LIMs is given as follows:

$$F_e - F_l = m_p \frac{dv_r}{dt} \tag{39}$$

where F_e is the electromagnetic thrust, F_l is the load force and m_p is the mass of the mover. The electromagnetic thrust is calculated as:

$$F_e = \frac{3}{2}\frac{p}{2}\frac{\pi}{\tau} Re\{j\lambda_s i_s^*\} \tag{40}$$

Equations (32)–(40) are employed for dynamic performance simulation of LIMs. The values of R_r and L_m are acquired using look-up tables according to Figures 6 and 7. It means that the appropriate values of these parameters are determined based on LIM velocity to consider the transversal edge effect, the iron effect, the skin effect, and the air-gap leakage effect. A block diagram of the look-up tables is shown in Figure 9.

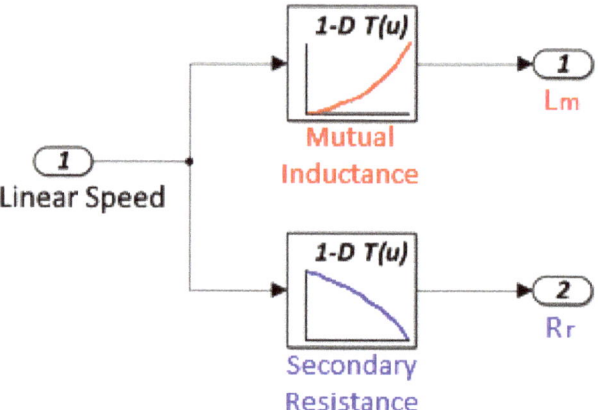

Figure 9. Look-up table structure for calculation of the secondary resistance and the magnetic inductance.

In the conventional Duncan's equivalent circuit (EC), the secondary resistance and the magnetic inductance are considered constant as values while they may vary with linear speed. In the proposed method, the characteristics of the secondary resistance and the magnetic inductance versus linear speed are determined using analytical methods. Then, it is used to predict the characteristic of LIMs both in transient and steady-state operation conditions. FEM is used to validate the proposed characteristic.

It is assumed that the load force Fl is equal to 50 N and the LIM is supplied by three-phase nominal voltage. Figure 10 shows the linear velocity of the LIM versus time using the proposed and Duncan's models. It is clear that the time constant of the proposed model is larger than Duncan's model, which was predictable because of greater secondary equivalent resistance at low linear velocities. Additionally, the electromagnetic thrust characteristics using the proposed model and Duncan's one are shown in Figure 11. The free acceleration characteristic of electromagnetic thrust in a LIM is similar to the free acceleration characteristic of the electromagnetic torque in a RIM. The machine accelerates to the near synchronous speed, where for running the machine, the starting thrust should be higher than the load thrust.

Firstly, this figure verifies the results obtained from Figure 8, and secondly, it demonstrates the impact of the transversal edge effect on the dynamic behavior of LIMs in comparison with Duncan's model, which only considers the longitudinal end effect.

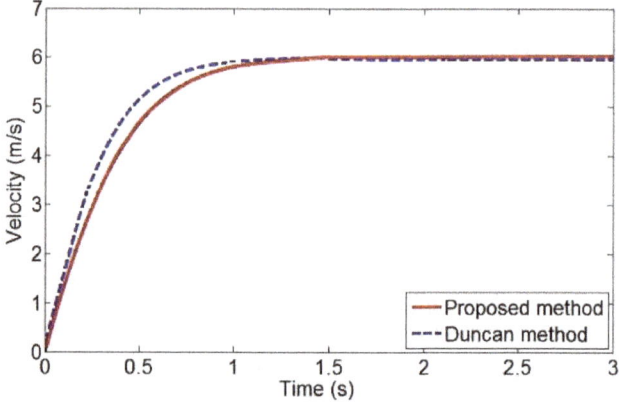

Figure 10. Linear velocity versus time characteristic using the proposed and Duncan's approaches.

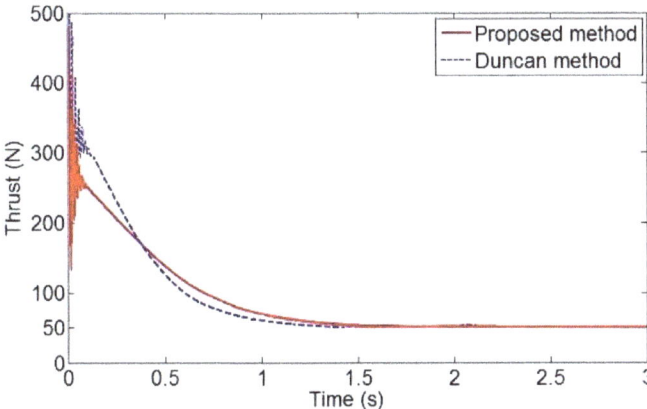

Figure 11. Thrust versus time characteristics using the proposed and Duncan's approaches.

5. Conclusions

In this paper, a new steady-state and space-vector equivalent circuit model of LIMs was proposed. For this, Duncan's model was modified so that the transversal edge effect, the iron saturation effect, the skin effect, and the air-gap leakage effect are also included alongside the longitudinal end effect. The transversal edge effect is expressed in terms of Bolton's coefficients and the other mentioned effects are incorporated in the electric parameters of the proposed equivalent circuit. The electric parameters of LIMs have been computed using both field analysis and FEM. The results show good agreement between these two approaches. To validate the proposed method, 3-D FEM was employed. Using the thrust versus velocity characteristic of LIMs, it can be derived that the proposed method provides more precision as compared to Duncan's model. In this paper, the dynamic performance of LIMs was also investigated. For this purpose, the dynamic equivalent circuit based on the proposed model was first described and then the voltage equations were provided. Values of the secondary resistance and the magnetic inductance were computed according to the linear velocity by using the look-up tables. Comparing the dynamic performance of the proposed model with Duncan's approach, it is concluded that the dynamic performance of the proposed model is slower because of consideration of the transversal edge effect and other undesirable phenomena.

Author Contributions: Conceptualization, methodology, validation, formal analysis, writing—original draft preparation, H.H. and A.R. (Anton Rassõlkin); writing—review and editing, resources, funding acquisition, A.R. (Arash Razzaghi); project administration, T.V.; investigation, A.K., E.A. and D.V.L.; supervision, A.B. The literature review was carried out by H.H. towards Ph.D. study under the supervision of A.R. (Anton Rassõlkin) and A.B. The study was managed by A.K., T.V., D.V.L. and E.A. collaborated in the survey for revision and collecting the database. All authors have read and agreed to the published version of the manuscript.

Funding: The research has been supported by the Estonian Research Council under grant PSG453 "Digital twin for propulsion drive of an autonomous electric vehicle".

Data Availability Statement: Data are contained within the article.

Conflicts of Interest: The authors declare no conflict of interest.

References

1. Boldea, I.; Nasar, S. *Linear Electric Actuators and Generators*; Cambridge University Press: New York, NY, USA, 1997.
2. Gerra, D.D.; Iakovleva, E.V. Sun Tracking System for Photovoltaic Batteries in Climatic Conditions of the Republic of Cuba. In Proceedings of the International Scientific Electric Power Conference, Saint Petersburg, Russia, 23–24 May 2019.
3. Gieras, J.F. *Linear Induction Drives*; Clarendon Press: Oxford, UK, 1994.

4. Liu, P.; Hung, C.Y.; Chiu, C.S.; Lian, K.Y. Sensorless linear induction motor speed tracking using fuzzy observers. *Electr. Power Appl. IET* **2011**, *5*, 325–334. [CrossRef]
5. Huang, C.I.; Fu, L.C. Adaptive Approach to Motion Controller of Linear Induction Motor with Friction Compensation. *IEEE ASME Trans. Mechatron.* **2007**, *12*, 480–490. [CrossRef]
6. Creppe, R.; De Souza, C.; Simone, G.; Serni, P. Dynamic behaviour of a linear induction motor. In Proceedings of the MELECON '98. 9th Mediterranean Electrotechnical Conference, Tel-Aviv, Israel, 18–20 May 1998; Volume 2, pp. 1047–1051.
7. Nondahl, T.; Novotny, D. Three-phase pole-by-pole model of a linear induction machine. *IEE Proc. B Electr. Power Appl.* **1980**, *127*, 68–82. [CrossRef]
8. Lu, C.; Eastham, T.; Dawson, G.E. Transient and dynamic performance of a linear induction motor. In Proceedings of the Conference Record of the 1993 IEEE Industry Applications Conference Twenty-Eighth IAS Annual Meeting, Toronto, ON, Canada, 2–8 October 1993; pp. 266–273.
9. Xu, W.; Sun, G.; Wen, G.; Wu, Z.; Chu, P. Equivalent Circuit Derivation and Performance Analysis of a Single-Sided Linear Induction Motor Based on the Winding Function Theory. *IEEE Trans. Veh. Technol.* **2012**, *61*, 1515–1525. [CrossRef]
10. Pai, R.; Boldea, I.; Nasar, S. A complete equivalent circuit of a linear induction motor with sheet secondary. *IEEE Trans. Magn.* **1988**, *24*, 639–654. [CrossRef]
11. Gieras, J.; Dawson, G.; Eastham, A. A New Longitudinal End Effect Factor for Linear Induction Motors. *IEEE Trans. Energy Convers.* **1987**, *EC-2*, 152–159. [CrossRef]
12. Faiz, J.; Jagari, H. Accurate modeling of single-sided linear induction motor considers end effect and equivalent thickness. *IEEE Trans. Magn.* **2000**, *36*, 3785–3790. [CrossRef]
13. Xu, W.; Zhu, J.G.; Zhang, Y.; Li, Y.; Wang, Y.; Guo, Y. An Improved Equivalent Circuit Model of a Single-Sided Linear Induction Motor. *IEEE Trans. Veh. Technol.* **2010**, *59*, 2277–2289. [CrossRef]
14. Xu, W.; Zhu, J.G.; Zhang, Y.; Li, Z.; Li, Y.; Wang, Y.; Guo, Y.; Li, Y. Equivalent Circuits for Single-Sided Linear Induction Motors. *IEEE Trans. Ind. Appl.* **2010**, *46*, 2410–2423. [CrossRef]
15. Duncan, J. Linear induction motor-equivalent-circuit model. *IEE Proc. B Electr. Power Appl.* **1983**, *130*, 51–57. [CrossRef]
16. Kang, G.; Nam, K. Field-oriented control scheme for linear induction motor with the end effect. *IEE Proc. Electr. Power Appl.* **2005**, *152*, 1565–1572. [CrossRef]
17. Pucci, M. State Space-Vector Model of Linear Induction Motors. *IEEE Trans. Ind. Appl.* **2014**, *50*, 195–207. [CrossRef]
18. Mirsalim, M.; Doroudi, A.; Moghani, J. Obtaining the operating characteristics of linear induction motors: A new approach. *IEEE Trans. Magn.* **2002**, *38*, 1365–1370. [CrossRef]
19. Kim, D.K.; Kwon, B.I. A Novel Equivalent Circuit Model of Linear Induction Motor Based on Finite Element Analysis and Its Coupling with External Circuits. *IEEE Trans. Magn.* **2006**, *42*, 3407–3409. [CrossRef]
20. Amiri, E.; Mendrela, E. A Novel Equivalent Circuit Model of Linear Induction Motors Considering Static and Dynamic End Effects. *IEEE Trans. Magn.* **2014**, *50*, 120–128. [CrossRef]
21. Heidari, H.; Rassõlkin, A.; Kallaste, A.; Vaimann, T.; Andriushchenko, E.; Belahcen, A.; Lukichev, D.V. A review of synchronous reluctance motor-drive advancements. *Sustainability* **2021**, *13*, 729. [CrossRef]
22. Heidari, H.; Rassõlkin, A.; Vaimann, T.; Kallaste, A.; Taheri, A.; Holakooie, M.H.; Belahcen, A. A novel vector control strategy for a six-phase induction motor with low torque ripples and harmonic currents. *Energies* **2019**, *12*, 1102. [CrossRef]
23. Heidari, H.; Andriushchenko, E.; Rassolkin, A.; Kallaste, A.; Vaimann, T.; Demidova, G.L. Comparison of synchronous reluctance machine and permanent magnet-assisted synchronous reluctance machine performance characteristics. In Proceedings of the 2020 27th International Workshop on Electric Drives: MPEI Department of Electric Drives 90th Anniversary (IWED), Moscow, Russia, 27–30 January 2020; Institute of Electrical and Electronics Engineers Inc.: Piscataway, NJ, USA, 2020. [CrossRef]
24. Preston, T.W.; Reece, A.B.J. Transverse edge effects in linear induction motors. *Proc. Inst. Electr. Eng.* **1969**, *116*, 973–979. [CrossRef]
25. Bolton, H. Transverse edge effect in sheet-rotor induction motors. *Proc. Inst. Electr. Eng.* **1969**, *116*, 725–731. [CrossRef]
26. Pucci, M. Direct field oriented control of linear induction motors. *Electr. Power Syst. Res.* **2012**, *89*, 11–22. [CrossRef]
27. Shiri, A.; Shoulaie, A. Design Optimization and Analysis of Single-Sided Linear Induction Motor, Considering All Phenomena. *IEEE Trans. Energy Convers.* **2012**, *27*, 516–525. [CrossRef]
28. Holakooie, M.H.; Ojaghi, M.; Taheri, A. Full-order Luenberger observer based on fuzzy logic control for sensorless field-oriented control of a single-sided linear induction motor. *ISA Trans.* **2016**, *60*, 96–108. [CrossRef] [PubMed]

Article

A Novel, Improved Equivalent Circuit Model for Double-Sided Linear Induction Motor

Qian Zhang, Huijuan Liu *, Tengfei Song and Zhenyang Zhang

School of Electrical Engineering, Beijing Jiaotong University, Beijing 100044, China; qianzh@bjtu.edu.cn (Q.Z.); 18117020@bjtu.edu.cn (T.S.); 16117375@bjtu.edu.cn (Z.Z.)
* Correspondence: hjliu@bjtu.edu.cn; Tel.: +86-10-5168-4831

Abstract: A novel, improved equivalent circuit model of double-sided linear induction motors (DLIMs) is proposed, which takes the skin effect and the nonzero leakage reactance of the secondary, longitudinal, and transverse end effects into consideration. Firstly, the traditional equivalent circuit with longitudinal and transverse end effects are briefly reviewed. Additionally, the correction coefficients for longitudinal and transverse end effects derived by one-dimensional analysis models are given. Secondly, correction factors for skin effect, which reflects the inhomogeneous air gap magnetic field vertically, and the secondary leakage reactance are derived by the quasi-two-dimensional analysis model. Then, the proposed equivalent circuit is presented, and the excitation reactance and secondary resistance are modified by the correction coefficients derived from the three analytical models. Finally, a three-dimensional (3D) finite element model is used to verify the proposed equivalent circuit model under varying air gap width and frequency, and the results are also compared with that of the traditional equivalent circuit models. The calculated thrust characteristics by the proposed equivalent circuit and 3D finite element model are experimentally validated under a constant voltage–frequency drive.

Keywords: DLIM; equivalent circuit; end effect; thrust; finite element

1. Introduction

The wide range of velocity and acceleration of the linear induction motor (LIM) avoids the intermediate transmission mechanism of linear motion, which reduces the mechanical losses and stresses and improves the system's reliability [1]. The LIMs have been utilized widely in industrial applications such as aircraft electromagnetic launch or accelerator systems [2,3], transportation systems [4–6], handling systems [7], new microgravity drop tower systems [8], etc.

A typical feature of LIM is that it has an entry end and an exit end in the traveling direction (longitudinal) for the primary or secondary cutoff of the LIM, which produces the longitudinal end effect, which the rotary machine does not have. Another feature of LIMs is that the secondary is invariably wider than the primary core in the transverse direction, resulting in the transverse end effect. In addition, the relatively larger air gap between primary and secondary is often inherent in the construction of a LIM [1]. The unique feature of LIM makes its performance different from that of a rotary induction motor. The finite element method (FEM) [9], numerical analysis method [4], equivalent circuit, and magnetic equivalent circuit [10,11] are the main methods used to analyze and calculate the characteristics of LIMs.

The finite element simulation software is convenient for the optimization design of LIMs [12,13]. The FEM is also convenient for the performance calculation of some special cases of linear motors, such as special primary or secondary structure [14], and primary and secondary relative position, e.g., the secondary sheet is displaced sideways from a symmetrical position [15], etc. For a large size linear induction motor, it is not possible to establish a FEM model of partial pole pairs such as rotary motor and a complete pole pairs model of LIM means that it takes longer calculation time and computer resources [16].

The analytical method is another method to solve the performance of a LIM. The one-dimensional (1D) analytical method is the most used. In order to consider the performance and parameters of a LIM more comprehensively, two-dimensional (2D) and three-dimensional (3D) fields are also used to solve the magnetic field and thrust [17–19]. It shows that the theoretical results agree very well with the experimental ones, and the 2D solution agrees very well with the rigid 3D solution. The analytical solution of the LIM is helpful to clearly understand the spatial distribution of the electromagnetic field, but it cannot directly reflect the impedance parameters of the motor.

The analysis of electromagnetic fields in the air gap shows that the end effect has a great influence on the operating characteristics of the LIM. The end effect is usually determined by boundary conditions in analytical solution, while the end effect is reflected by modifying the motor impedance parameters in the equivalent circuit of a LIM. In [20], a fast and accurate d–q axis-equivalent circuit model of LIM for drive system simulations was developed based on nonlinear transient finite element analysis. Duncan's equivalent circuit model is widely utilized in the analysis of characteristics of single-sided linear induction motors (SLIMs) [21–23], which provided a practical way to estimate the characteristics of SLIMs. The field-theory-based T-type equivalent circuit is another commonly used model [11,24–27]. In [24,25], a novel equivalent circuit is presented, and an equivalent circuit considering the asymmetric secondary sheet is developed in [11]. Although the equivalent circuit of SLIM has been widely studied, the equivalent circuit of two kinds of motors is different due to the different structures between SLIM and DLIM—the secondary of SLIM has back iron, while the secondary of DLIM is usually a metal conductive plate. The research on the equivalent circuit of DLIM is not as extensive as that of SLIM because of its limited application. In the traditional equivalent circuit of DLIM, the secondary leakage reactance is usually considered to be negligible, the longitudinal and transverse end effect on the performance of DLIM is demonstrated by coefficients corrected secondary resistance and excitation reactance [26,28]. In the high-speed applications of DLIM, the equivalent circuit only with the longitudinal end effect may be enough to analyze the operating characteristics accurately, while the transverse end effect is neglected [26,27]. Nevertheless, for the large air gap DLIM with low speed, the secondary leakage reactance may not be negligible as high-speed DLIM, and it has a large ratio to the secondary resistance. The inhomogeneous distribution of the air gap magnetic field in the vertical direction will significantly affect the excitation reactance and secondary resistance parameters in the equivalent circuit. In the equivalent circuit model above, few papers take the vertical distribution of the air gap magnetic field into the impedance parameters of the equivalent circuit.

In this paper, an improved equivalent circuit model of DLIMs is developed, which takes the skin effect, the nonzero leakage reactance of the secondary, longitudinal, and transverse end effects into consideration independently, based on the three independent directions model of DLIMs, i.e., longitudinal, transverse and vertical. The paper is organized as follows. In Section 2, the traditional equivalent circuit with longitudinal end effect and the transverse end effect is briefly reviewed. Additionally, correction factors for longitudinal and transverse end effects derived by the 1D analysis models are presented, i.e., longitudinal and transversal models. Then, the new correction factors of the transverse end effect are given [29]. In Section 3, the quasi-two-dimensional (quasi-2D) analysis model is established, and the correction coefficients for skin effect, which considers the inhomogeneous air gap magnetic field vertically, and the secondary leakage reactance are derived. The improved equivalent circuit is proposed, in which skin effect, secondary leakage reactance, longitudinal end effect, and transverse end effect are considered. In Section 4, FEM 3D is used to compare the calculation results in order to verify the proposed equivalent circuit model under different mechanical air gap widths and power frequencies. The FEM results are also compared with the traditional equivalent circuit models. Additionally, variations of forces under negative sequence braking and motoring operations are presented under a constant voltage–frequency inverter; the calculated forces by the proposed equivalent circuit and FEM 3D are experimentally validated. The conclusions of the paper are summarized in Section 5.

2. Traditional Equivalent Circuit Model of DLIM

A model was developed in 3D of the linear induction motor and is presented in Figure 1. The direction of the X-axis is longitudinal and is the direction of the secondary (or primary) moving and magnetic-field-traveling wave; vertical moves along the normal line of the secondary surface (Y-axis), and transverse moves along the primary slots (Z-axis). In the field of analytical theories, the 1D method is a practical way to solve the characteristics of DLIMs. The longitudinal and transverse end effects can be considered to act independently or be neglected. The longitudinal and transversal 1D analysis models are shown in Figure 2, where L_1 is the length of primary, $2d$ is the thickness of secondary, g is the mechanical air gap width, τ is the pole pitch, $2a$ is the width of the primary core, and $2c$ is the width of secondary.

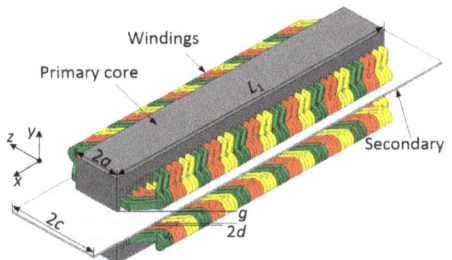

Figure 1. Structure of DLIM.

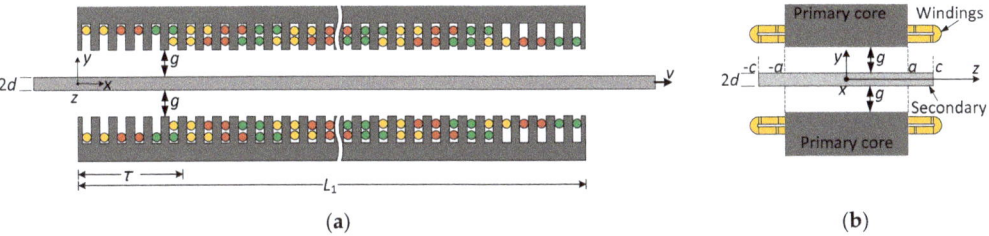

Figure 2. Analytical model of DLIM: (**a**) longitudinal model in the *XOY* plane; (**b**) transverse model in the *YOZ* plane.

2.1. Longitudinal Analytical Model of DLIMs

In order to simplify the derivation of the equivalent circuit considering the longitudinal end effect, the assumptions are presented as [26]. As shown in the longitudinal 1D model in Figure 2a, due to the limit length of the primary core, slots containing only one layer of coils at both ends of the primary are called half-filled slots. Numbers of half-filled slots at two ends of the primary both are $\beta_\tau \cdot m_1 \cdot q_1$, which decided by the primary winding short pitch ε. The length of primary can be obtained by

$$L_1 = (2p - 1 + \beta_\tau)\tau, \ \beta_\tau = 1 - \varepsilon/m_1 q_1 \tag{1}$$

These half-filled slots at two ends of the primary extend about lengths of $\beta_\tau \cdot \tau$, and lengths of filled slots are $(2p-1-\beta_\tau)\cdot\tau$. The magnetomotive force (MMF) of the primary is presented in Figure 3. Due to only one-layer coil in the half-filled slots, MMF of regions II and III are half of region I, which contains a two-layer coil.

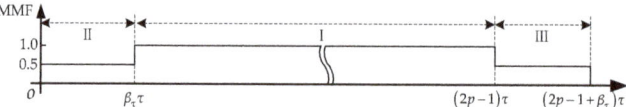

Figure 3. Longitudinal distribution of MMF.

The current of the primary winding is transformed into an infinitely thin equivalent current density, according to the principle of equal MMF. The expression of primary equivalent current density can be divided into three regions, i.e., the half-filled slots at both ends and full-filled slots, for the existence of half-filled slots at the two ends of the primary core. Additionally, the air gap flux density can then be obtained using Maxwell's equations. The equivalent circuit parameters, such as secondary resistance and magnetizing reactance, can be obtained using the equal complex power relationship between the magnetic field and the electrical circuit.

The longitudinal end effect coefficients K_r and K_x are denoted as Equations (2) and (3), where K_r is the correction factor of the secondary resistance, and K_x is the correction factor of the magnetizing reactance.

$$K_r = \frac{sG}{2p_e\tau\sqrt{1+s^2G^2}} \frac{K_1^2 + K_2^2}{K_1} \tag{2}$$

$$K_x = \frac{1}{2p_e\tau\sqrt{1+s^2G^2}} \frac{K_1^2 + K_2^2}{K_2} \tag{3}$$

where K_1 and K_2 are the functions of slip s and goodness factor G. The number of equivalent pole pairs p_e is corrected in [11], due to the half-filled slots may affect the precise of the calculation, where p is the actual number of the pole pairs, m_1 is the number of primary phases, and q_1 is the number of coil sides per phase per pole.

$$p_e = \frac{(2p-1)^2}{4p - 3 + \varepsilon/(m_1 q_1)} = \frac{(2p-1)^2}{4p - 2 - \beta_\tau} \tag{4}$$

2.2. Transverse Analytical Model of DLIMs

The motor is divided into two independent models—longitudinal and transverse. The longitudinal end effect is neglected when solving the transverse end effect [28]. The correction factors considering the transverse edge effect C_r and C_x are given by

$$C_r = sG \cdot \frac{\mathrm{Re}^2[T] + \mathrm{Im}^2[T]}{\mathrm{Re}[T]} \tag{5}$$

$$C_x = \frac{\mathrm{Re}^2[T] + \mathrm{Im}^2[T]}{\mathrm{Im}[T]} \tag{6}$$

These two coefficients are used to correct the secondary resistance and excitation reactance, respectively. The T in Equations (5) and (6) is obtained by (7) as follows:

$$T = j\left(r^2 + (1-r^2)\frac{\lambda}{\alpha a}\tanh(\alpha a)\right) \tag{7}$$

where r, λ, α are given as Equations (8)–(10), T is the function of the slip s, goodness factor G, and motor parameters, such as the width of primary core $2a$ and pole pitch τ, and $k = \pi/\tau$.

$$r^2 = (1 + jsG)^{-1} \tag{8}$$

$$\lambda = \left((r)^{-1} \cdot \tanh(\alpha a)\tanh(kc - ka) + 1\right)^{-1} \tag{9}$$

$$\alpha = k\sqrt{1+jsG} \tag{10}$$

The transverse end effect may be accounted for by introducing a larger (equivalent) primary stack width $2a_e$ instead of $2a$, and $2a_e = 2a + k_g \cdot (2d + 2g)$, and range of correction coefficient k_g is 1.2 to 2 [29]. By introducing the new equivalent stack thickness into Equations (5)–(9), new correction coefficients C_{er} and C_{ex} of transverse end effect can be obtained.

2.3. Equivalent Circuit of DLIM with Longitudinal and Transverse End Effects

The conventional T-type equivalent circuit with longitudinal and transverse end effects is represented in Figure 4. The parameters in the T-circuit, namely, the primary resistance r_1, primary leakage reactance x_1, secondary resistance reduced to the primary r_2, exciting inductance x_m, and secondary leakage reactance x_2 are usually considered to be 0 for plate DLIM [26].

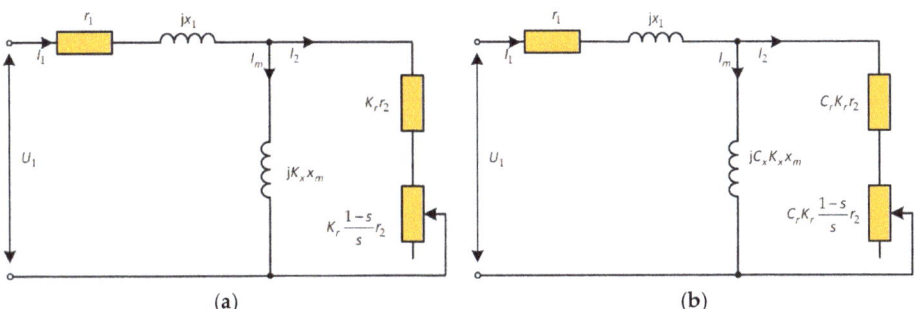

Figure 4. Equivalent circuit of DLIM: (**a**) only longitudinal end effect considered (EC-L); (**b**) both longitudinal and transverse end effect considered (EC-LT).

When coefficients C_{er} and C_{ex} are used to replace the traditional transverse end effect correction factors C_r and C_x in Figure 4b, a new equivalent circuit (EC-LTe) can be used to calculate the characteristics of a DLIM. When the coefficients K_r, K_x, C_r (C_{er}), and C_x (C_{ex}) are 1, the longitudinal and transversal end effects are neglected. The equivalent circuit of DLIM is similar to that of rotary induction motor (RIM); therefore, it is convenient to analyze the performance of DLIM as that of RIM based on the equivalent circuit.

3. Proposed Novel Equivalent Circuit Model of DLIMs

Based on the traditional equivalent circuit, the proposed model for the large air gap DLIM in this paper also considers the secondary leakage reactance and skin effect and derives correction coefficients for the equivalent circuit impedance by quasi-2D field model, that is, in the quasi-2D field, the influence of the air gap magnetic field variation in the vertical direction on the performance of DLIM is further considered, while the previous longitudinal and transverse analysis models consider that the air gap magnetic field remains unchanged in the vertical direction, as discussed in Section 2.

Since the longitudinal and transverse end effects were taken into account independently in the previous equivalent circuit, they are not considered in the quasi-2D field analysis in this section.

3.1. Vertical Quasi-Two-Dimensional Analytical Model of DLIMs

To simplify the analytical model, the assumptions are as follows [4,11,17]:
(1) The primary core will not be saturated, and the conductivity of the cores is equal to zero;
(2) The primary and secondary are infinitely long in the longitudinal direction and wide enough in the transverse direction;

(3) Primary and secondary currents flow in the z-direction, and primary currents flow in infinitesimally thin sheets.

The quasi-2D representation of the DLIM is shown in Figure 5.

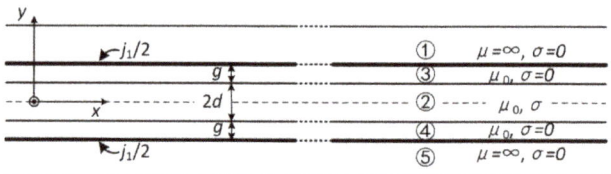

Figure 5. Quasi-2D analytical model of DLIM.

On the basis of the theory of the linear induction motor and Maxwell's equations, the magnetic flux density and electric field intensity can be calculated by

$$\nabla^2 A = \mu_0 \sigma \left[\frac{\partial A}{\partial t} - v(\nabla \times A) \right] \quad (11)$$

For the reason that the current of primary and secondary flow in the z-direction, the vector magnetic potential A can be simplified as

$$A_z = A_m(y) \cdot e^{j(\omega t - kx)} \quad (12)$$

In region 2 (secondary), the following Equation (13) is obtained:

$$\frac{\partial^2 A_2(y)}{\partial y^2} - \left(k^2 + j\mu_0 \sigma s \omega \right) A_2(y) = 0 \quad (13)$$

where μ_0 is the air magnetic permeability, σ is the conductivity of the secondary, and ω is the angular supply frequency of primary. In regions 3 and 4, the conductivity σ in these regions are 0 for no conductor in this region, and Equation (13) can be simplified as follows:

$$\frac{\partial^2 A_3(y)}{\partial y^2} - k^2 A_3(y) = 0, \quad \frac{\partial^2 A_4(y)}{\partial y^2} - k^2 A_4(y) = 0 \quad (14)$$

Solutions of A_{zi} in domains 2 to 4 are given by

$$\begin{aligned} A_{z2} &= [c_1 \cosh(\beta y) + c_2 \sinh(\beta y)] \cdot e^{j(\omega t - kx)} \\ A_{z3} &= [c_3 \cosh(ky) + c_4 \sinh(ky)] \cdot e^{j(\omega t - kx)} \\ A_{z4} &= [c_5 \cosh(ky) + c_6 \sinh(ky)] \cdot e^{j(\omega t - kx)} \end{aligned} \quad (15)$$

where $\beta = \sqrt{k^2 + j s \omega \mu_0 \sigma}$, $\beta = \beta_1 + j\beta_2$.

Undetermined constants c_1 to c_6 in Equation (15) are solved by the satisfactions of the following boundary conditions:

(1) Primary surface (domains 1 and 3; 4 and 5): $y = \pm g_e = \pm(d+g)$;

$$\frac{1}{\mu_0} \frac{\partial A_{z3}}{\partial y} \bigg|_{y=d+g} = \frac{j_1}{2}, \quad \frac{1}{\mu_0} \frac{\partial A_{z4}}{\partial y} \bigg|_{y=-(d+g)} = -\frac{j_1}{2} \quad (16)$$

(2) Secondary surface (domains 2 and 3; 2 and 4): $y = \pm d$;

$$-\frac{\partial A_{z2}}{\partial x} \bigg|_{y=d} = -\frac{\partial A_{z3}}{\partial x} \bigg|_{y=d}, \quad \frac{\partial A_{z2}}{\partial y} \bigg|_{y=d} = \frac{\partial A_{z3}}{\partial y} \bigg|_{y=d} \quad (17)$$

(3) According to the symmetry distribution of the magnetic field in the air gap,

$$-\frac{\partial A_{z3}}{\partial x}\bigg|_{y=d} = -\frac{\partial A_{z4}}{\partial x}\bigg|_{y=-d}, \frac{\partial A_{z3}}{\partial y}\bigg|_{y=d} = -\frac{\partial A_{z4}}{\partial y}\bigg|_{y=-d} \quad (18)$$

The electric field intensity in the air gap and the secondary is denoted by the following:

$$E_{zi} = -\frac{\partial A_{zi}}{\partial t}, i = 2, 3, 4 \quad (19)$$

3.2. Parameters Calculation for the Proposed Equivalent Circuit Model

The electromagnetic power transferred from the primary to the air gap and secondary can be calculated by the following equation:

$$S_{23} = 2 \times \int_{-a}^{a}\int_{0}^{L_1} \frac{1}{2}\left(-\frac{\overline{j_1}}{2}\right)\left(E_{z3}|_{y=g_e}\right) dxdz = P_{23} + jQ_{23} \quad (20)$$

where the E_{z3} is the electric field intensity in the air gap, and $P_{23} = P_2 + P_3$, P_3 is the active power in the air gap, which is usually considered as 0.

When the slip is 0, the complex power calculated by Equation (20) only has the reactive power Q_{30} on the exciting reactance. There is no active power and reactive power in the secondary, i.e., $P_{23} = 0$ and $Q_{20} = 0$, where $Q_{23} = Q_{20} + Q_{30}$.

$$jQ_{30} = j \cdot aL_1\omega \frac{\mu_0 J_1^2}{2 \cdot k\sinh(kg_e)} \cosh(kg_e) \quad (21)$$

The current of the secondary branch reduced to the primary is 0. Therefore, the excitation reactance with secondary leakage reactance and skin effect considered can be obtained by the following expression:

$$x_{ms} = \frac{Q_{30}}{m_1 I_1^2} = \frac{8a\mu_0 m_1 f \tau (W_1 k_w)^2}{\pi p \delta} \frac{k\delta \cosh(kg_e)}{2 \cdot \sinh(kg_e)} = x_m \cdot K_m \quad (22)$$

where K_m is the correction coefficient of excitation reactance without end effect.

When the slip is not 0, the power in the air gap and secondary is the power on the excitation reactance, secondary leakage reactance, and secondary resistance and is given by

$$S_{23} = \frac{4a(m_1 W_1 k_w I_1)^2 \mu_0 f}{p} \frac{(C_2 D_1 - C_1 D_2) + j(C_1 D_1 + C_2 D_2)}{(C_1^2 + C_2^2)} \quad (23)$$

The constants C_1, C_2, D_1, and D_2 in Equation (23) can be seen in Appendix B.
The primary induced electromotive force (emf) E_1 can be calculated by

$$-\dot{E}_1 = \frac{S_{23}}{m_1 I_1} = \frac{4am_1(W_1 k_w)^2 I_1 \mu_0 f}{p} \frac{(C_2 D_1 - C_1 D_2) + j(C_1 D_1 + C_2 D_2)}{C_1^2 + C_2^2} \quad (24)$$

The reactive power in the air gap is as follows:

$$Q_3 = \frac{m_1\left|-\dot{E}_1\right|^2}{x_{ms}} = \frac{4a(m_1 W_1 k_w I_1)^2 \mu_0 f}{p} \frac{\sinh(kg_e)}{\cosh(kg_e)} \frac{(D_1^2 + D_2^2)}{(C_1^2 + C_2^2)} \quad (25)$$

The complex power in the secondary can be obtained by the following equation:

$$S_2 = S_{23} - jQ_3 = P_2 + jQ_2 \quad (26)$$

The active power P_2 and reactive power Q_2 in the secondary are

$$P_2 = \omega \cdot (m_1 W_1 k_w I_1)^2 \frac{2a\mu_0}{p\pi} \frac{C_2 D_1 - C_1 D_2}{C_1^2 + C_2^2} \tag{27}$$

$$Q_2 = \omega \cdot (m_1 W_1 k_w I_1)^2 \frac{2a\mu_0}{p\pi} \frac{1}{C_1^2 + C_2^2} \left[(C_1 D_1 + C_2 D_2) - \frac{\sinh(kg_e)}{\cosh(kg_e)} \left(D_1^2 + D_2^2 \right) \right] \tag{28}$$

The conjugate current of the secondary branch reduced to the primary is

$$\dot{I}_2^* = \frac{S_2}{m_1 \left(-\dot{E}_1 \right)} = \left[1 - j \cdot \frac{\sinh(kg_e)}{\cosh(kg_e)} \frac{(C_2 D_1 - C_1 D_2) - j(C_1 D_1 + C_2 D_2)}{C_1^2 + C_2^2} \right] I_1 \tag{29}$$

The active power P_2 and reactive power Q_2 are the power of secondary resistance and leakage reactance, respectively. Hence, the resistance and the leakage reactance of the secondary sheet can be obtained according to the following Equations (30) and (31). Both the resistance considering skin effect and the leakage reactance of the secondary can be expressed by the secondary resistance without end effect.

$$R_2 = \frac{P_2}{m_1 \left| \dot{I}_2^* \right|^2} = \frac{r_2'}{s} \frac{sG \cdot \frac{1}{2} k\delta (C_2 D_1 - C_1 D_2)}{[C_1 - D_1 \tanh(kg_e)]^2 + [C_2 - D_2 \tanh(kg_e)]^2} = \frac{r_2'}{s} \cdot K_f \tag{30}$$

$$x_2 = \frac{Q_2}{m_1 \left| \dot{I}_2^* \right|^2} = \frac{r_2'}{s} \cdot \frac{1}{2} sG k\delta \frac{D_1 [C_1 - D_1 \tanh(kg_e)] + D_2 [C_2 - D_2 \tanh(kg_e)]}{[C_1 - D_1 \tanh(kg_e)]^2 + [C_2 - D_2 \tanh(kg_e)]^2} \tag{31}$$

From Equations (22) and (30), the correction coefficients of secondary resistance and excitation reactance considering skin effect and secondary leakage reactance are calculated as Equations (32) and (33).

$$K_f = \frac{sG \cdot \frac{1}{2} k\delta (C_2 D_1 - C_1 D_2)}{[C_1 - D_1 \tanh(kg_e)]^2 + [C_2 - D_2 \tanh(kg_e)]^2} \tag{32}$$

$$K_m = \frac{k\delta \cosh(kg_e)}{2 \cdot \sinh(kg_e)} \tag{33}$$

The equations show that these two correction coefficients are closely related to the parameters of the DLIM, e.g., the secondary thickness and the mechanical air gap.

3.3. Proposed Equivalent Circuit Models

Let the coefficients of transverse end effect be 1, that is, ignore the influence of transverse end effect, add secondary leakage reactance on the secondary branch, and use the correction coefficients of Equations (32) and (33) to modify the secondary resistance and excitation reactance; then, a new T-type equivalent circuit without considering transverse end effect can be obtained, as shown in Figure 6a.

In the traditional equivalent circuit shown in Figure 4b, the excitation reactance and secondary resistance are modified, respectively, by using the correction coefficients derived in this section, and secondary leakage reactance is added to the secondary branch. An improved equivalent circuit proposed in this paper can be obtained, as shown in Figure 6b. Similarly, if the transverse end effect coefficients C_{er} and C_{ex} are used to replace the traditional C_r and C_x in Figure 6b, respectively, another new T-type equivalent circuit (EC-LTeS) for solving the motor characteristics is obtained.

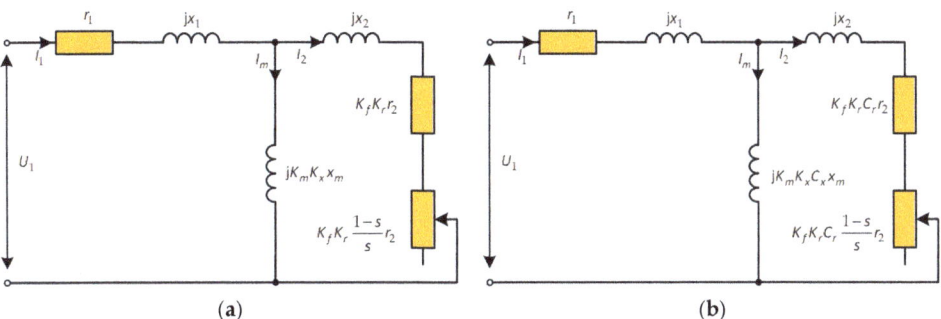

Figure 6. Novel equivalent circuits of DLIM: (**a**) with skin effect, secondary leakage reactance, and longitudinal end effect considered (EC-LS); (**b**) with longitudinal end effect, transverse end effect, and skin effect and secondary leakage reactance considered (EC-LTS).

In the equivalent circuit of Figure 6b, the correction coefficients of three directions and secondary leakage reactance of the DLIM model are considered. The mechanical power considering all effects is as follows:

$$P_M = (1-s) \cdot \text{Re}\left[m_1 \dot{I}_1^2 \frac{\left(K_f K_r C_r \frac{r_2'}{s} + jx_2\right) \cdot K_m K_x C_x \cdot jx_m}{K_f K_r C_r \frac{r_2'}{s} + jx_2 + K_m K_x C_x \cdot jx_m}\right] \quad (34)$$

The mechanical power of the equivalent circuit shown in Figure 6a can be obtained by setting the correction coefficients of the transverse end effect to 1. After the same method, the calculated mechanical power of the equivalent circuit in Figure 4 can be obtained.

4. Experiments and Discussion

4.1. Calculation of Operating Characteristics by Traditional and Improved Models

The results of the 3D finite element model were compared with those of the improved equivalent circuit in order to verify the proposed equivalent circuit model. The results were also compared with the 2D FEM, the traditional equivalent circuit model, which only considers the longitudinal end effect, and the equivalent circuit, which includes the longitudinal and transverse end effects.

The thrust slip characteristics of different mechanical air gap widths calculated by the equivalent circuits were compared with the results calculated by the FEM 3D and 2D models, as shown in Figures 7–9. In the simulations and calculations, the secondary thickness is 3 mm, the current is 6.85 A, and the thickness of the mechanical air gap is 0.0075, 0.0105, 0.0135 m, respectively. The specifications of the DLIM are shown in Table A1.

The 2D simulation results are close to the 3D results only in a small slip range, and the difference becomes larger with the increase of slip. In the negative braking region (s > 1), the maximum errors between 3D and 2D calculation results are 24.3%, 20.5%, and 14.8%, respectively, when the mechanical air gap is 0.0075, 0.0105, 0.0135 m.

The thrust calculated by the equivalent circuit, which considers only the longitudinal end effect, the equivalent circuit, which considers longitudinal end effect, the skin effect, and secondary leakage reactance are larger than the 2D simulation results in the slip range, which also cannot accurately reflect the trend of the 3D calculation results with different mechanical air gap widths.

For the DLIM with a large air-gap-to-pole-pitch ratio, the calculated thrust of equivalent circuit considering longitudinal and transverse end effect (EC-LT and EC-LTe) is consistent with 3D simulation values within a certain slip range. In the range of slip, with the increase of air gap width, this kind of equivalent circuit cannot reflect the motor performance well, and the average errors of the motor with the three mechanical air gap widths are 10.7%, 13.63%, and 17.33%, respectively. Even if the new transverse end effect coefficients are used in the equivalent circuit (EC-LTe), the average errors of the thrust are reduced by about 3%.

The results of the proposed equivalent circuit (EC-LTS or EC-LTeS) in the slip range are basically consistent with the results of the FEM 3D. The proposed equivalent circuit can more accurately reflect the thrust characteristics of the large air gap DLIM, compared with other equivalent circuits, as shown in Figures 7–9. With the three mechanical air gaps, the average error between the calculated results and the 3D simulation ones are 1.95%, 3.11%, and 5.17%, respectively.

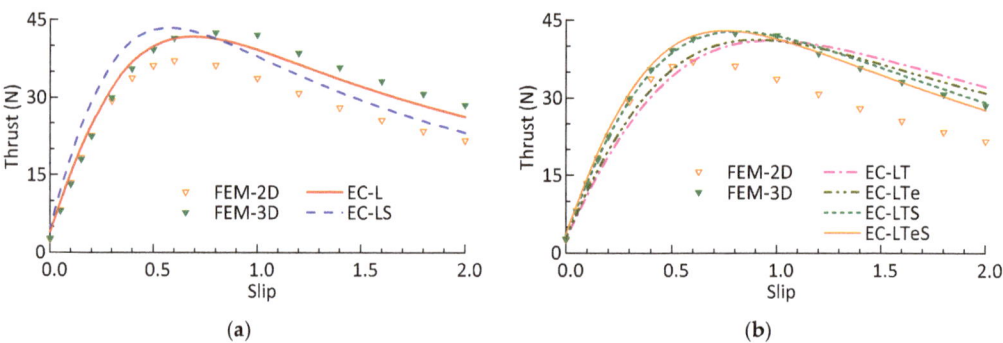

Figure 7. Thrust versus slip characteristics with a mechanical gap of 0.0075 m: (**a**) is calculated by equivalent circuit with longitudinal end effect (EC-L), skin effect, the air gap leakage, and longitudinal end effect considered (EC-LS), FEM 2D, and FEM 3D model; (**b**) is calculated by longitudinal end effect, transverse end effect (EC-LT, EC-LTe), in addition to skin effect and secondary leakage reactance considered (EC-LTS, EC-LTeS), FEM 2D and 3D model.

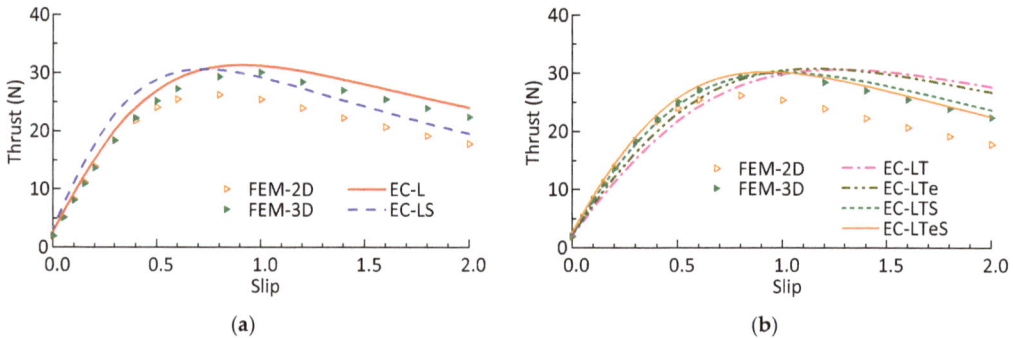

Figure 8. Thrust versus slip characteristics with a mechanical gap of 0.0105 m: (**a**) is calculated by equivalent circuit EC-L, EC-LS, FEM 2D, and FEM 3D model; (**b**) is calculated by equivalent circuit EC-LT, EC-LTe, EC-LTS, EC-LTeS, FEM 2D, and 3D model.

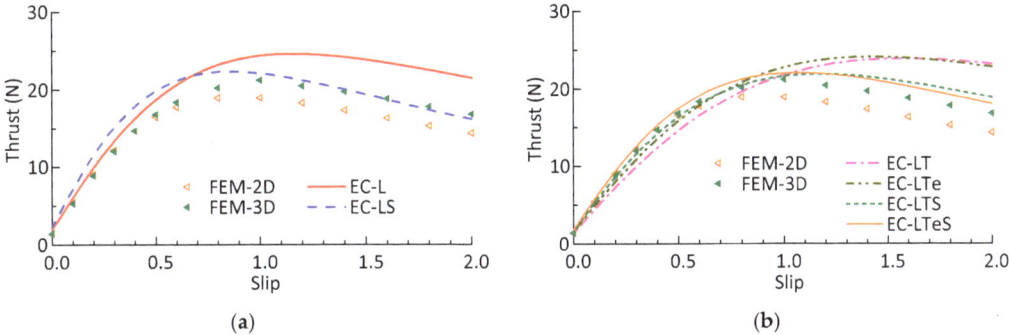

Figure 9. Thrust versus slip characteristics with a mechanical gap of 0.0135 m: (**a**) is calculated by equivalent circuit EC-L, EC-LS, FEM 2D, and FEM 3D model; (**b**) is calculated by equivalent circuit EC-LT, EC-LTe, EC-LTS, EC-LTeS, FEM 2D, and 3D model.

The thrust characteristic curve calculated by the equivalent circuit with new transverse end effect correction coefficients (C_{er} and C_{ex}) is slightly different from that calculated by the traditional ones (C_r and C_x), whether the traditional equivalent circuit only considers longitudinal and transverse, or the improved equivalent circuit proposed in this paper. The proposed equivalent circuit with the new transverse end effect coefficient has smaller errors in the negative braking region, which are 1.12%, 2.17%, and 7.5%, respectively, compared with the corresponding errors of 3.4%, 5.82%, and 10.37% with traditional ones.

In Figure 10, the calculated thrust obtained by the equivalent circuits are compared with the results of the FEM 3D model. In the simulations and calculations, all the results are a function of the velocity when the mechanical air gap length is 0.0135 m, the current is 6.85 A, frequency is 40, 60, 80, 100, and 120 Hz.

The calculated thrust of the equivalent circuit considering only the longitudinal end effect (EC-L) is larger than that of FEM 3D because the transverse end effect, the vertical variation of air gap magnetic field, and the secondary leakage reactance are neglected. In the negative braking region, the calculated results by the equivalent circuit with skin effect and longitudinal end effect (EC-LS) are closer to the 3D simulation ones, compared with EC-L in Figure 10a. However, the minimum average error between the calculated (EC-LS) and the simulated thrust in the slip region is still more than 11%.

In Figure 10b, the thrust characteristics of simulation and calculated by two equivalent circuits considering longitudinal and transverse end effects (EC-LT and EC-LTe) are compared. In the motoring region of the synchronous speed side before the maximum FEM 3D value, and the thrust calculated by the equivalent circuit EC-LTe is closer to that of 3D simulation. However, the calculation errors of the two equivalent circuits are more than 12% in the slip range. In the negative braking region, the average errors between the calculation results of these two equivalent circuits and the simulation results are even more than 40%, 35%, respectively; hence, these equivalent circuits cannot accurately reflect the force characteristics of the motor.

Compared with the previous four equivalent circuits, the improved equivalent circuit proposed in this paper can be in good agreement with the FEM 3D calculation values in both the motoring and negative braking region, although there is a slight difference in the thrust velocity characteristic curve by using two different transverse end effect coefficients, as shown in Figure 10c. At low frequency, e.g., 40 Hz, the results calculated by using traditional transverse end effect coefficients are closer to that of simulation, and the average error between the calculated and simulation results is 4.24%, while at higher frequencies, the results calculated by using the new transverse end effect coefficients may be better consistent with the simulation ones, and the average error between the calculated thrust and FEM results is less than 3%.

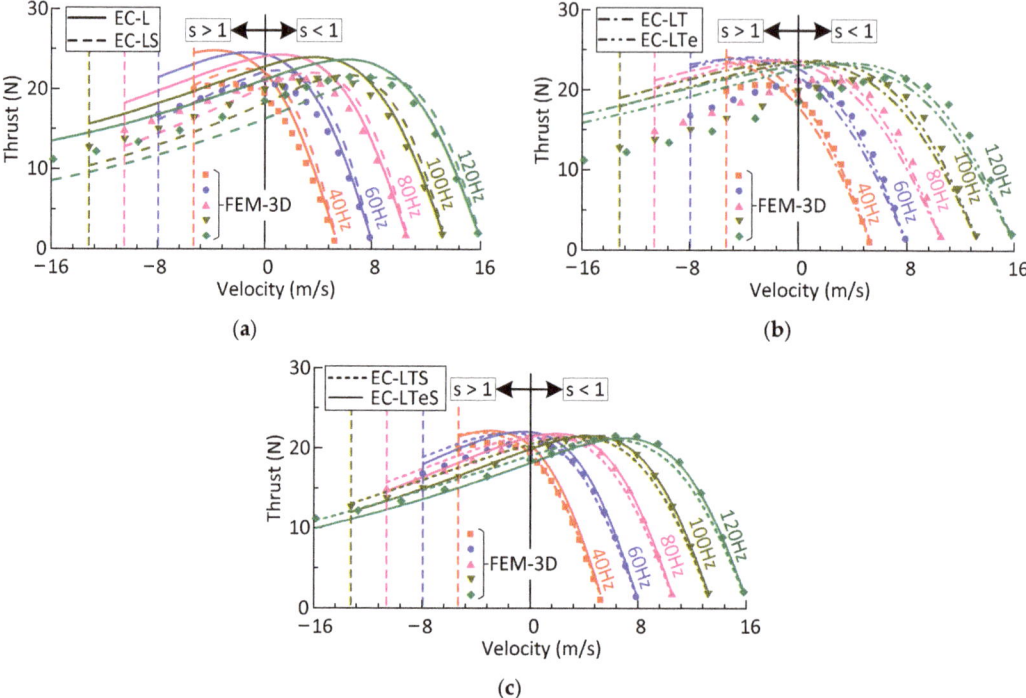

Figure 10. Thrust versus velocity characteristics at constant current calculated by FEM 3D model: (**a**) equivalent circuit EC-L and EC-LS model; (**b**) equivalent circuit EC-LT and EC-LTe model; (**c**) equivalent circuit EC-LTS and EC-LTeS model.

4.2. Experimental Validation

In Figure 11, the analytically calculated thrust versus slip characteristics under a constant voltage–frequency drive is compared with the FEM results and measurements at 60 Hz and 110 Hz, and the mechanical air gap is 0.0135 m. The trend of analyzed results by the proposed equivalent circuit (EC-LTS and EC-LTeS) over the whole slip range is basically in accordance with the measurements and FEM results. Additionally, it presents slight differences in variation of the transverse end effect coefficients.

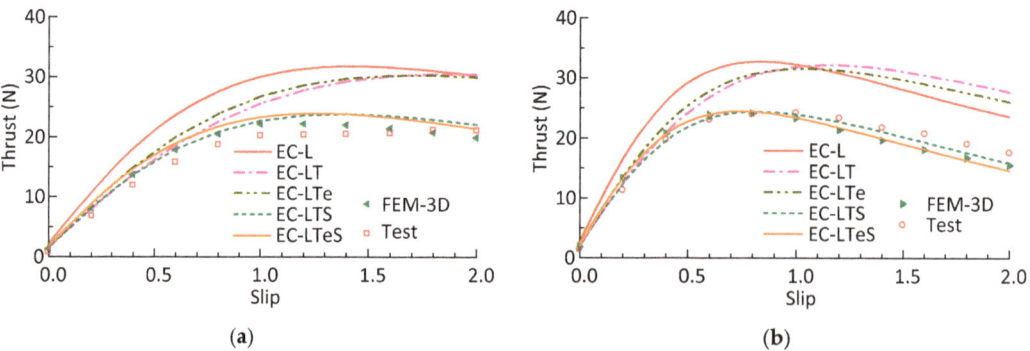

Figure 11. Calculation, simulation, and test results of thrust: (**a**) at 60 Hz; (**b**) at 110 Hz.

When the motor is driven by a constant voltage–frequency inverter, the equivalent circuit with longitudinal end effect (EC-L) has the largest error in the motoring region, compared with other equivalent circuit models. With the increase of slip, the difference between the calculated and the measured value becomes larger, the maximum errors between them are more than 50%, and the average error between them is 52.41% and 34.51% at 60 Hz and 110 Hz, respectively.

The calculation results of the equivalent circuits considering the longitudinal and transverse end effects (EC-LT), including the equivalent circuit with new transverse end effect correction coefficients (EC-LTe), have less error with the simulation and measurement values only when the speed is close to the synchronous speed. The average error of the slip range between the calculated thrust and measured ones is more than 30% at both 60 Hz and 110 Hz. In the motoring region with high slip and the negative braking region, the equivalent circuit cannot meet the calculation accuracy for the motor with a large air-gap-to-pole-pitch ratio due to the large error.

The equivalent circuit considering longitudinal and transverse end effects, skin effect, and secondary leakage reactance can reflect the thrust slip characteristics more accurately. In general, the average errors between the measured and the calculated value of EC-LTS under the two frequencies are 11.68% and 5.85%, respectively, which is smaller than that between the measured and the calculated value of EC-LTeS. The error between the 3D simulation and the measured results is less than 10%. In order to simplify the model and facilitate the calculation, some assumptions are made in the longitudinal, transverse and vertical models, and therefore, there are some errors between the calculated values and the simulation and test values.

5. Conclusions

A novel, improved equivalent circuit model is proposed as a quasi-2D vertical model that considers the vertical distribution of air gap magnetic field and secondary leakage reactance on the basis of traditional equivalent circuits, and the influences on operating characteristics of a DLIM with different equivalent circuit models are fully investigated. Three-dimensional (3D) FEM is used to compare the calculation results in order to verify the proposed equivalent circuit model. The analytical calculations are validated by the measurements on a prototype low-speed DLIM under a constant voltage–frequency drive [30]. Based on the comprehensive comparison in the four equivalent circuit models, conclusions include the following:

(1) Considering the vertical distribution of the magnetic field in the equivalent circuit, two coefficients can be used to modify the secondary resistance and excitation reactance, respectively.

(2) The average errors between FEM calculation and the proposed equivalent circuit results, which considers longitudinal, transverse end effects, and skin effect, are 1.95%, 3.11%, and 5.17% with the mechanical air gap width of 0.0075, 0.0105, and 0.0135 m, respectively, while that of the traditional equivalent circuit (EC-LT) are 10.7%, 13.63%, and 17.33%, respectively; when a new transverse end effect coefficient is used in the equivalent circuit (EC-LTe), the average errors of the thrust are reduced by about 3%.

(3) When the large air gap DLIM is driven by a constant current source with different frequencies, the thrust calculation results of the equivalent circuit, which do not fully consider the correction coefficients of the three direction models, i.e., equivalent circuit model EC-L, EC-LS, and EC-LT(e), have more than 11% errors with the FEM simulation results in the slip range, while the errors between the value of proposed equivalent circuit and simulation are less than 5%. When the DLIM is driven by a constant voltage–frequency inverter, the calculated results of the proposed equivalent circuit are in good agreement with the measured and simulated ones.

(4) The improved equivalent circuit proposed in this paper takes into account the correction coefficients of the longitudinal, transverse, and vertical model of DLIM, which can

reflect the thrust characteristics of the motor more accurately, compared with the traditional equivalent circuits, especially for the large air-gap-to-pole-pitch ratio DLIMs.

Author Contributions: Conceptualization, Q.Z. and Z.Z.; methodology, T.S.; validation, Q.Z., T.S. and Z.Z.; formal analysis, investigation, writing—original draft preparation, Q.Z.; data curation, T.S.; writing—review and editing, Q.Z. and H.L.; visualization, T.S.; resources, supervision, project administration, H.L. All authors have read and agreed to the published version of the manuscript.

Funding: This research was funded by the Fundamental Research Funds for the Central Universities, Grant Number 2021YJS159.

Data Availability Statement: Data are contained within the article.

Acknowledgments: Some simulation results are completed by Yu Wang; School of Electrical Engineering, Beijing Jiaotong University.

Conflicts of Interest: The authors declare no conflict of interest.

Appendix A

Table A1. Specifications of DLIM.

Quantity	Symbol	Valve	Unit
Number of phases	m	3	
Number of poles	p	6	
Number of slots per phase per pole	q_1	2	
Coil pitch	β_τ	5/6	
Number of slots	Q_1	41	
pole pitch	τ	0.066	m
Primary length	L_1	0.451	m
Primary width	$2a$	0.07	m
Opening slot	b_s	0.006	m
Slot depth	h_s	0.03	m
Mechanical air gap length	g	0.0075 to 0.0135	m
Secondary thickness	$2d$	0.003	m
Secondary sheet conductivity	σ	4.8×10^7	S/m

Appendix B

The expressions of constants $C_1, C_2, D_1,$ and D_2 in Equations (19)–(27) are as follows:

$$\left.\begin{aligned}
C_1 &= k\cosh(\beta_1 d)\cos(\beta_2 d)\sinh(kg_e - kd) + [\beta_1 \sinh(\beta_1 d)\cos(\beta_2 d) - \beta_2 \cosh(\beta_1 d)\sin(\beta_2 d)]\cosh(kg_e - kd) \\
C_2 &= k\sinh(\beta_1 d)\sin(\beta_2 d)\sinh(kg_e - kd) + [\beta_1 \cosh(\beta_1 d)\sin(\beta_2 d) + \beta_2 \sinh(\beta_1 d)\cos(\beta_2 d)]\cosh(kg_e - kd) \\
D_1 &= k\cosh(\beta_1 d)\cos(\beta_2 d)\cosh(kg_e - kd) + [\beta_1 \sinh(\beta_1 d)\cos(\beta_2 d) - \beta_2 \cosh(\beta_1 d)\sin(\beta_2 d)]\sinh(kg_e - kd) \\
D_2 &= k\sinh(\beta_1 d)\sin(\beta_2 d)\cosh(kg_e - kd) + [\beta_1 \cosh(\beta_1 d)\sin(\beta_2 d) + \beta_2 \sinh(\beta_1 d)\cos(\beta_2 d)]\sinh(kg_e - kd)
\end{aligned}\right\}$$

References

1. Boldea, I.; Nasar, S. Linear electric actuators and generators. *IEEE Trans. Energy Convers.* **1999**, *14*, 712–717. [CrossRef]
2. Meeker, D.; Newman, M. Indirect Vector Control of a Redundant Linear Induction Motor for Aircraft Launch. *Proc. IEEE* **2009**, *97*, 1768–1776. [CrossRef]
3. Bertola, L.; Cox, T.; Wheeler, P.; Garvey, S.; Morvan, H. Thermal Design of Linear Induction and Synchronous Motors for Electromagnetic Launch of Civil Aircraft. *IEEE Trans. Plasma Sci.* **2017**, *45*, 1146–1153. [CrossRef]
4. Lv, G.; Zeng, D.; Zhou, T. A Novel MMF Distribution Model for 3-D Analysis of Linear Induction Motor with Asymmetric Cap-Secondary for Metro. *IEEE Trans. Magn.* **2017**, *53*, 8107907. [CrossRef]
5. Lv, G.; Zhou, T.; Zeng, D.; Liu, Z. Influence of Secondary Constructions on Transverse Forces of Linear Induction Motors in Curve Rails for Urban Rail Transit. *IEEE Trans. Ind. Electron.* **2018**, *66*, 4231–4239. [CrossRef]
6. Abdollahi, S.E.; Mirzayee, M.; Mirsalim, M. Design and Analysis of a Double-Sided Linear Induction Motor for Transportation. *IEEE Trans. Magn.* **2015**, *51*, 1–7. [CrossRef]
7. Mihalachi, M.; Leidhold, R.; Mutschler, P. Long primary linear drive for material handling. In Proceedings of the 2009 International Conference on Electrical Machines and Systems, Tokyo, Japan, 15–18 November 2009; pp. 1–6.

8. Liu, H.; Zhang, Q.; Ma, J. Thrust Characteristics Analysis of Long Primary Double Sided Linear Induction Machine with Plate and Novel Shuttle Secondary Structure. *Trans. Nanjing Univ. Aeronaut. Astronaut.* **2019**, *36*, 693–702. [CrossRef]
9. De Oliveira, R.A.H.; Berger, D.; Schultz, L.; Stephan, R.M.; Ferreira, A.C. Finite element analysis of the forces developed on linear induction motors. In Proceedings of the 2015 IEEE 13th Brazilian Power Electronics Conference and 1st Southern Power Electronics Conference (COBEP/SPEC, Fortaleza, Brazil, 29 November–2 December 2015; pp. 1–6.
10. Naderi, P.; Shiri, A. Modeling of Ladder-Secondary-Linear Induction Machine Using Magnetic Equivalent Circuit. *IEEE Trans. Veh. Technol.* **2018**, *67*, 11411–11419. [CrossRef]
11. Zeng, D.; Lv, G.; Zhou, T. Equivalent Circuits for Single-Sided Linear Induction Motors with Asymmetric Cap Secondary for Linear Transit. *IEEE Trans. Energy Convers.* **2018**, *33*, 1729–1738. [CrossRef]
12. Isfahani, A.; Ebrahimi, B.; Lesani, H. Design Optimization of a Low-Speed Single-Sided Linear Induction Motor for Improved Efficiency and Power Factor. *IEEE Trans. Magn.* **2008**, *44*, 266–272. [CrossRef]
13. Ravanji, M.H.; Nasiri-Gheidari, Z. Design Optimization of a Ladder Secondary Single-Sided Linear Induction Motor for Improved Performance. *IEEE Trans. Energy Convers.* **2015**, *30*, 1595–1603. [CrossRef]
14. Lee, B.-J.; Koo, D.-H.; Cho, Y.-H. Investigation of Linear Induction Motor According to Secondary Conductor Structure. *IEEE Trans. Magn.* **2009**, *45*, 2839–2842. [CrossRef]
15. Bolton, H. Forces in induction motors with laterally asymmetric sheet secondaries. *Proc. Inst. Electr. Eng.* **1970**, *117*, 2241–2248. [CrossRef]
16. Lv, G.; Zhou, T.; Zeng, D.; Liu, Z. Design of Ladder-Slit Secondaries and Performance Improvement of Linear Induction Motors for Urban Rail Transit. *IEEE Trans. Ind. Electron.* **2018**, *65*, 1187–1195. [CrossRef]
17. Yoshida, K.; Kawamura, I. A method of two-dimensional analysis for short primary linear induction motors. *Electr. Eng. Jpn.* **1980**, *100*, 51–59. [CrossRef]
18. Nonaka, S.; Fujii, N. Simplified two-dimensional analysis of linear induction motors. *IEEE Trans. Magn.* **1987**, *23*, 2832–2834. [CrossRef]
19. Yamamura, S.; Ito, H. Three-dimensional analysis of linear induction motors. *Electr. Eng. Jpn.* **1976**, *96*, 55–61. [CrossRef]
20. Kim, D.-K.; Kwon, B.-I. A Novel Equivalent Circuit Model of Linear Induction Motor Based on Finite Element Analysis and Its Coupling with External Circuits. *IEEE Trans. Magn.* **2006**, *42*, 3407–3409. [CrossRef]
21. Heidari, H.; Rassõlkin, A.; Razzaghi, A.; Vaimann, T.; Kallaste, A.; Andriushchenko, E.; Belahcen, A.; Lukichev, D. A Modified Dynamic Model of Single-Sided Linear Induction Motors Considering Longitudinal and Transversal Effects. *Electron.* **2021**, *10*, 933. [CrossRef]
22. Woronowicz, K.; Safaee, A. A novel linear induction motor equivalent-circuit with optimized end effect model. *Can. J. Electr. Comput. Eng.* **2014**, *37*, 34–41. [CrossRef]
23. Lv, G.; Zeng, D.; Zhou, T. An Advanced Equivalent Circuit Model for Linear Induction Motors. *IEEE Trans. Ind. Electron.* **2018**, *65*, 7495–7503. [CrossRef]
24. Xu, W.; Zhu, J.; Zhang, Y.; Li, Y.; Wang, Y.; Guo, Y. An Improved Equivalent Circuit Model of a Single-Sided Linear Induction Motor. *IEEE Trans. Veh. Technol.* **2010**, *59*, 2277–2289. [CrossRef]
25. Xu, W.; Zhu, J.; Zhang, Y.; Li, Z.; Li, Y.; Wang, Y.; Guo, Y.; Li, Y. Equivalent Circuits for Single-Sided Linear Induction Motors. *IEEE Trans. Ind. Appl.* **2010**, *46*, 2410–2423. [CrossRef]
26. Lu, J.; Ma, W. Research on End Effect of Linear Induction Machine for High-Speed Industrial Transportation. *IEEE Trans. Plasma Sci.* **2010**, *39*, 116–120. [CrossRef]
27. Hirasa, T.; Ishikawa, S.; Yamamuro, T. Equivalent circuit of linear induction motors with end effect taken into account. *Electr. Eng. Jpn.* **1980**, *100*, 65–71. [CrossRef]
28. Bolton, H. Transverse edge effect in sheet-rotor induction motors. *Proc. Inst. Electr. Eng.* **1969**, *116*, 725. [CrossRef]
29. Boldea, I.; Nasar, S.A. *The Induction Machine Handbook*; CRC Press LLC: Boca Raton, FL, USA, 2002.
30. Umezu, N.; Nonaka, S. Characteristics of Low-Speed Linear Induction Machines. *Electr. Eng. Jpn.* **1977**, *97*, 50–60. [CrossRef]

Article

Performance Comparison of Quantized Control Synthesis Methods of Antenna Arrays

David Pánek [1,*], Tamás Orosz [2], Pavel Karban [1], Deubauh Cedrick D. Gnawa [1] and Hamid Keshmiri Neghab [1]

1. Department of Theory of Electrical Engineering, University of West Bohemia, 306 14 Plzeň, Czech Republic; karban@kte.zcu.cz (P.K.); gnawa@fel.zcu.cz (D.C.D.G.); neghab@fel.zcu.cz (H.K.N.)
2. Faculty of Engineering Sciences, Department of Automation, Széchenyi István University of Győr, Egyetem tér 1, H-9026 Győr, Hungary; orosz.tamas@sze.hu
* Correspondence: panek50@fel.zcu.cz; Tel.: +420-377-634-657

Abstract: There is a great potential in small satellite technology for testing new sensors, processes, and technologies for space applications. Antennas need careful design when developing a small satellite to establish stable communication between the ground station and the satellite. This work is motivated by the design of an antenna array for a future rotatorless base station for the VZLUSAT group of Czech nano-satellites. The realized antenna array must cover a relatively broad range of elevation and azimuth angles, and the control must be fast enough to track the satellite in low Earth orbits. The paper deals with possibilities of synthesis of quantized control of the antenna array. It compares quantization influence for well-known deterministic synthesis methods. It shows the method for decreasing computational cost of synthesis using optimization approach and presents the multi-criteria optimization as a tool for reaching required radiation pattern shape and low sensitivity to quantization at the same time.

Keywords: antenna array; synthesis control; quantized control; array factor

1. Introduction

The CubeSat Launch Initiative provided an attractive opportunity for universities, high schools, and non-profit organizations to build small satellites, which can fit an N-Unit cubic structure [1–3]. Here, each unit of the CubeSat should fit an $N \times 1$ dm^3 cube (=1U size), which can contain one or more systems of the satellite. The common CubeSats has a very small 1U, 2U, or 3U size [4–7]; due to the recent upgrade of the standard, the largest satellites can reach a 27U size. These satellites are launched to Low-Earth-Orbit (LEO) with 250–900 km altitude above the ground. Most of the CubeSats use Radioamateur frequency band for the main communication [8], but licensed bands are now often used due to the commercial nature of some missions. Due to the reduced launch costs and the inspiring increase in complex applications, this platform started to attract many commercial, military, and governmental organizations [6,9]. These applications increased the need for larger transfer rates. The Ka-band started to be explored as a possible solution besides the S and X bands.

An interesting solution to this problem can be achieved by antenna array technology, which can have many advantages over parabolic antennas. From a mechanical point of view, it does not require design and maintains a drive system, which sets the azimuth and the elevation angles. Such systems have a simpler feeding network that cannot be disconnected during the connection time. These tools are insensitive to the moisture and weather conditions during the mission. Moreover, with a pattern reconfigurability algorithm, they can support multi-task missions [6,10].

Although the field of antenna array design and control synthesis have broadly been studied for many decades, there are still many sub-domains that have received less attention so far. One of such sub-domains is their robust design, which takes into account various uncertainties in their design and suppresses their influence. The robust design is becoming more and more important together with the development of new technologies which allow creating antennas on flexible and stretchable materials such as Aerosol Jet Print [11–13]. In specific applications, such as printing antennas on flexible materials which can be bent and placed into the capsule of in-body antenna, printing patterns on curved surfaces of in-body antennas, or incorporating antennas into wearable electronics, it is important to study the influence of the change in geometry on the system properties [14–16].

The second area that has received little attention is the design of quantized control of the antenna array [17]. The recent review dedicated to the control synthesis methods was published in [18]. This paper offers a detailed analysis of methods, especially in connection with the 5G communication systems. The advantage of quantized control of antenna array consists mainly in the potential for fast and precise reconfiguration of the antenna array beam direction, which is important for tracking satellite position. Within the field of antenna array synthesis, a number of numerical techniques are commonly used, which can be divided into three groups:

- deterministic methods,
- optimization techniques,
- machine-learning tools.

Deterministic methods mean the two main classes of the array control synthesis methods [19–21]. The first class uses electromagnetic field simulation. The simulation takes into account a complex model of the antenna array including mutual coupling and also feeding circuits. The second class starts from the analysis of the array factor that is based on the assumption that all elements of the antenna array are identical and mutual couplings between particular elements are negligible.

Many papers aimed at the optimization methods for the control synthesis [22–26] have already been published. It is possible to say that most of the published approaches are based on evolutionary methods such as Genetic Algorithms (GA), Particle Swarm Optimization (PSO), Simulated Annealing (SA), and Ant Colony Optimization (ACO) [27]. Due to the high computational cost of the proposed methodologies, great efforts were also devoted to reducing the computational complexity. For example, paper [28] takes advantage of the Taguchi's method for control linear array control synthesis. Ref. [19] proposed the use of SMPSO for sparse antenna array synthesis. In the paper, the performance is compared with differential evolution and genetic algorithm. The main drawback of these techniques is that they usually consider only the array factor with the aid of deterministic methods, but neglect the mutual coupling between particular between array elements. The machine learning-based tools play an increasingly important role to resolve this problem and design smart antennas (antenna arrays with dynamic control) [29].

Like most of the CubeSat projects [8], VZLUSAT uses a radio-amateur frequency band 435–438 MHz (70 cm) for communication [6] and the satellites are deployed on a Low Earth Orbit (LEO), commonly ranging from 350 km to 900 km from the Earth surface. This particular application require specific demands to be satisfied to ensure the maximal contact time with the satellite. For one ground station, two or up to four long contacts with good communication conditions are possible in a day. These long contacts usually take no more than 15 min. From these data, the maximum communication distance between the ground station and the satellite can be calculated. It varies from 2000 to 3500 km, while the orbit revolution time is 91 to 103 min. The transmission to the satellite generally starts above 5° elevation to avoid interference with terrestrial systems. The Doppler shift and relative position of LEO satellites to the ground station are changing rapidly during contacts in high elevation angles, which increases the demand on the antenna positioning system [4,6].

The current VZLUSAT-1 and VZLUSAT-2 nanosatellite projects inspired the proposed application [4,5] to design an antenna array for communication with the future small satellites. The main goal of the work is to find a methodology for the synthesis of control for the antenna arrays, which is robust in the sense that the effect of perturbations in the excitation is minimized. The proposed methodology will be compared with a small theoretical example. The goal of the comparison is to select the most appropriate methodology, which can be used together with the more complex, 3D FEM-based calculations for the more detailed antenna analysis. The proposed methodologies and the source code of the model can be accessed from the homepage of the project (https://github.com/panek50/pyntenna, accessed on 20 March 2022).

2. Control Synthesis

The problem of control synthesis is closely related to the design of the antenna array itself, and it was divided into three steps:

- Preliminary design—the control is designed according to application requirements, usually using well-known deterministic methods. In this step, implementation details, such as connecting circuits and electronic parts, are not considered in the field models. Therefore, the results obtained using simplified methods (such as the array factor approach described below) are relatively good with the field models.
- Design—the field models contain all important details. The results of full-field simulations differ from simplified methods. In this step, optimization methods and methods based on matrix inversions are usually used.
- Implementation and calibration the results obtained by measuring manufactured hardware differ from results obtained using full-field simulation.

2.1. Model Example

As a model example, the control synthesis for the application of the base station for nanosatellites was chosen. This application brings certain requirements for the antenna array:

- As a compromise between the complexity of control and the required gain of the antenna array, the size of the array was chosen to be 11×11.
- The antenna array is designed for the S band and particular frequency $f = 2.405\,\text{MHz}$. The required bandwidth is 50 GHz.
- The required elevation steering angle is $\Delta\theta = 30°$ and the required steering azimuth angle is $\Delta\phi = 30°$.
- The maximal radiated power is 0.5 W per patch; the overall radiated power is $P = 60.5\,\text{W}$, which corresponds to the power radiated from currently used parabolic antenna with the diameter 2 m.
- The minimal beam-width is $6°$.

The synthesis will be based on the candidate design of the antenna element. The element was designed using Antenna Magus 2020 software [30]. The shape of the element is shown in Figure 1 and the specific dimensions are summarized in Table 1.

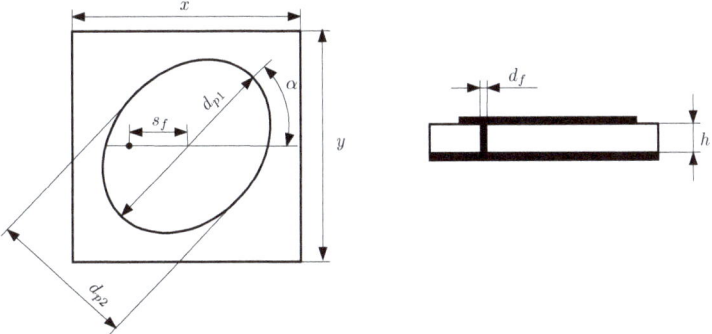

Figure 1. Shape of the antenna array element.

Table 1. Dimensions of designed patch (distances are in millimeters).

f [MHz]	Z_{in} [Ω]	x	y	α	d_f	d_{p1}	d_{p2}	s_f
2.405	50	48.2	48.2	45°	0.91	49.2	47.16	8.4

The directivity of one patch defined as

$$D(\theta, \varphi) = 4\pi \frac{P_U}{P_T}, \qquad (1)$$

where P_U stands for the power radiated per unit of the solid angle and P_T means the total radiated power, is depicted in Figure 2. As mentioned above, the considered array consists of 11 × 11 elements. The distance of centers of two elements in x-direction and y-direction is

$$d_x = d_y = \frac{\lambda}{2} = \frac{c}{2f} = \frac{3 \cdot 10^8}{2 \cdot 2.405 \cdot 10^9} \approx 0.062 \text{ mm}. \qquad (2)$$

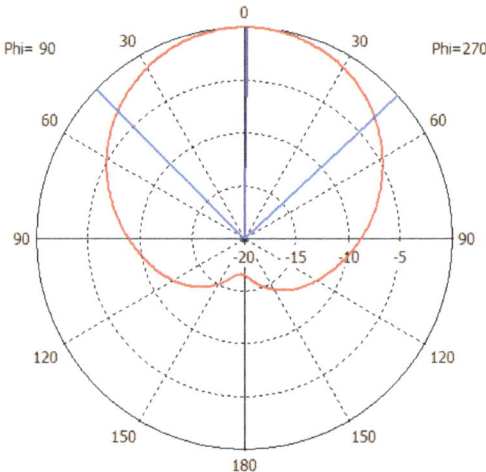

Figure 2. The diagram shows the directivity of one antenna array element.

The model of the antenna array is depicted in Figure 3a, and the corresponding directivity pattern for uniform excitation is depicted in Figure 3b.

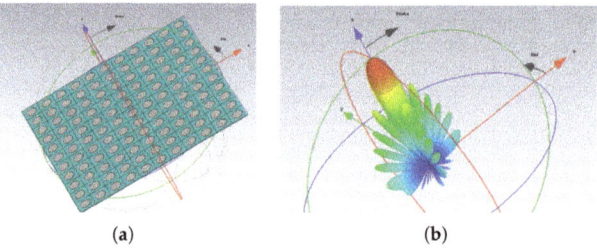

Figure 3. Figure (a) shows the model of the antenna array in CST Studio, while picture (b) plots the directivity pattern of the proposed antenna array.

2.2. Array Factor

As the full field solution for larger antenna arrays is often too computationally complex, it is often used simplified using the array factor. The electromagnetic field produced by the antenna array can be described using electric field strength E and magnetic field strength H, which for a harmonic source, satisfies the equations

$$\Delta \underline{H} + \underline{k}^2 \underline{H} = \underline{0}, \qquad \Delta \underline{E} + \underline{k}^2 \underline{E} = \underline{0}, \qquad (3)$$

where $\underline{k} = -\mathrm{j} \cdot \omega \mu (\gamma + \mathrm{j} \cdot \omega \varepsilon)$.

The vector of electric field strength produced by antenna array $\underline{E}(\vartheta, \varphi)$ can be, at a particular point, expressed as [31]

$$\underline{E}(\vartheta, \varphi) = \underline{f}_e(\vartheta, \varphi) \cdot S_a(\vartheta, \varphi), \qquad (4)$$

where ϑ stands for the elevation, φ for azimuth, $\underline{f}_e$ is the electric field produced by one element, and S_a is the array factor in the form

$$S_a(\varphi, \vartheta) = \sum_{n=1}^{N} \sum_{m=1}^{M} I_{nm} \exp\left[\mathrm{j} \cdot k_0 \cdot n \cdot d_x \sin(\theta) \cos(\varphi) + k_0 \cdot m \cdot d_y \sin(\vartheta) \sin(\varphi)\right], \qquad (5)$$

where N is the number of elements in the x direction, M is the number of elements in the y direction, d_x and d_y are the distances between the patches, and $k_0 = 2\pi/\lambda$ is the wave number. The dimensions are depicted in Figure 4. For other derived quantities, as directivity defined in Equation (1), the decomposition into the patch pattern and array factor works in the same way.

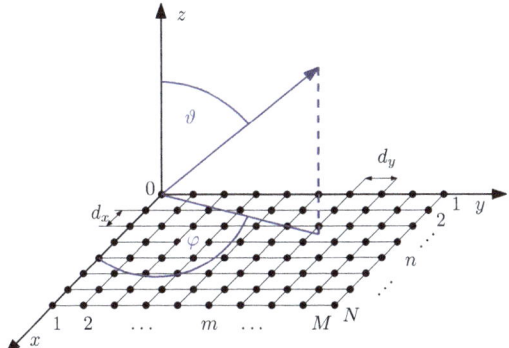

Figure 4. Planar antenna array with $N \times M$ elements.

The control synthesis based on array factor obviously cannot bring the optimal results, but it represents a suitable first step to obtain the point from which the optimization can start. It also can bring an idea about the physical limits which can be (at least theoretically) reached.

2.3. Matrix Formulation of Array factor

The computational complexity of the array factor calculation can be reduced using a matrix formulation in the form

$$S_a = LI = \begin{bmatrix} \alpha_{11} & \alpha_{12} & \cdots & \alpha_{1k} \\ \alpha_{21} & \alpha_{22} & \cdots & \alpha_{2k} \\ \vdots & \vdots & \ddots & \vdots \\ \alpha_{l1} & \alpha_{l2} & \cdots & \alpha_{lk} \end{bmatrix} \cdot \begin{bmatrix} I_{11} \\ I_{12} \\ \vdots \\ I_{lk} \end{bmatrix}, \qquad (6)$$

where
$$\alpha_{mn} = \exp\left[j \cdot k_0\, m\, d_x \sin(\theta)\cos(\phi) + k_0\, n\, d_y \sin(\theta)\sin(\phi)\right] \tag{7}$$
and I is the vector of excitation of particular patches.

This formulation is advantageous for repeated calculations, while the computational complexity is removed in the assembling process. The complexity can consequently be reduced using the Principal Component Analysis (PCA) [32]. The correlation matrix C of the transformation matrix L can be calculated as
$$C = L \cdot L^T. \tag{8}$$

Only a limited number of eigenvalues play the important role, as can be seen in Figure 5a. Figure 5b shows the comparison of array factor calculated from excitation obtained by direct usage of Dolph–Chebychev method and reconstructed by pseudo-inverse with PCA reduction.

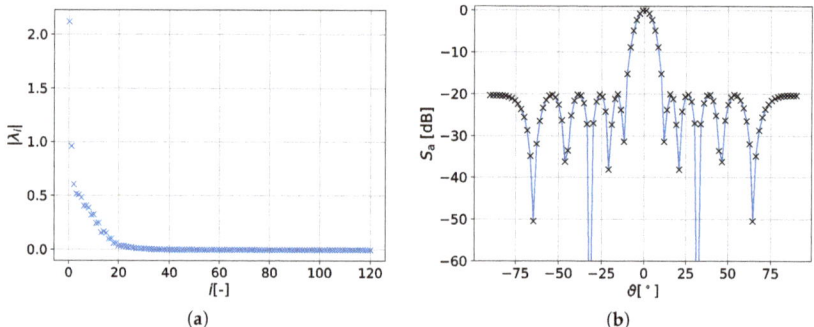

Figure 5. Order reduction and pseudo-inverse. (**a**) Eigenvalues of transformation matrix; (**b**) Comparison of array factor calculated from excitation obtained by direct usage of Dolph–Chebychev method and reconstructed by pseudo-inverse.

The reduced matrix can be also used within the Penrose–Moore pseudo-inverse for the control synthesis. The transformation matrix can be decomposed using Singular Value Decomposition (SVD) as
$$L = U \cdot \Sigma \cdot V^T, \tag{9}$$
where Σ is a diagonal matrix with singular values in the main diagonal and U, V are orthogonal matrices containing singular vectors. The pseudo-inverse of this matrix Σ^* contains inverse singular values on the diagonal. The pseudo-inverse of the transformation matrix can be then written as
$$L^* = V\Sigma^* U^T. \tag{10}$$

The usage of matrix pseudo-inverse can be useful for large arrays, however it tends to become weakly-conditioned for low resolution in ϑ and φ.

2.4. Deterministic Control Synthesis Methods

The deterministic methods use the tools common in the area of *digital signal processing*. These methods can be divided into three main sub-classes [28]:

- synthesis based on possessing nulls of the characteristic polynomial, commonly used for suppressing particular noise from the given direction, represented by Schelkunoff zero-placement method;
- methods based on so called beam shaping, i.e. specifying beam sector pattern and inverse transformation to obtain excitation, represented by Woodward–Lawson method;
- methods for synthesis narrow beams and low side lobes, represented by the Dolph–Chebychev method.

2.4.1. Woodward–Lawson Method

This design method is based on inverse Discrete Fourier Transform. The excitation of particular elements of the antenna array given by [33] was modified (for reaching a better efficiency) to the form

$$I(n,m) = \sum_{k=1}^{K} \sum_{l=1}^{L} S_A \cdot \exp(jk_0 \cdot (\mathbf{N} \cdot \Delta_x[k,l] + \mathbf{M} \cdot \Delta_y[k,l])), \tag{11}$$

where I is a matrix with complex numbers representing excitation, k_0 is the wave number, $\mathbf{N}$ and $\mathbf{M}$ are pre-assembled matrices containing numbers $1\ldots N$ and $1\ldots M$, respectively, in rows, and symbols Δ_x, and Δ_y stand for preassembled matrices where

$$\Delta_x = \begin{bmatrix} d_x \sin(\vartheta_0)\cos(\varphi_0) & d_x \sin(\vartheta_0)\cos(\varphi_1) & \cdots & d_x \sin(\vartheta_0)\cos(\varphi_K) \\ d_x \sin(\vartheta_1)\cos(\varphi_0) & d_x \sin(\vartheta_1)\cos(\varphi_1) & \cdots & d_x \sin(\vartheta_1)\cos(\varphi_L) \\ \vdots & \vdots & \ddots & \vdots \\ d_x \sin(\vartheta_K)\cos(\varphi_0) & d_x \sin(\vartheta_K)\cos(\varphi_1) & \cdots & d_x \sin(\vartheta_K)\cos(\varphi_L) \end{bmatrix}. \tag{12}$$

and matrix Δ_y is built in a similar way.

2.4.2. Schelkunoff's Zero-Placement Method

The array factor (expressed in the Z-transformation) produced by $N \times M$ elements antenna array can be expressed as a product of $N-1$ and $M-1$ degree polynomials using its roots (zeros) in the form (extended from the 1D version published in [33])

$$S_a(z) = \sum_{n=0}^{N-1} \sum_{m=0}^{M-1} a_n b_m z^m z^n = \tag{13}$$

$$(z-z_1)(z-z_2)\ldots(z-z_{N-1})a_{N-1} \cdot (y-z_1)(y-y_2)\ldots(y-y_{M-1})b_{M-1}.$$

The magnitudes and phases on the antenna array can be expressed as a dyadic product of two complex vectors

$$\mathbf{I} = \mathbf{a} \otimes \mathbf{b}, \tag{14}$$

where $\mathbf{a} = (a_0, a_1, \ldots, a_{N-1})$ and $\mathbf{b} = (b_0, a_1, \ldots, b_{M-1})$ are coefficients of polynomials from equation (13). The first step of the method is proper placing of zeros z_n and y_n in the ϑ direction or φ direction, respectively. Consequently, the coefficient of polynomials a_n and b_m are calculated. The excitation matrix is then obtained directly using the dyadic product from equation (14).

2.4.3. Dolph–Chebychev Method

It can be proven that the lowest main-lobe width and highest ratio of suppression of side lobes at the same time can be achieved if all side lobes have the same level. This can be achieved using the Dolph–Chebychev window which is based on the Chebychev polynomials. The Chebychev polynomial of degree n is given by expression

$$P_n(x) = \cos(n \arccos(x)). \tag{15}$$

The procedure itself is similar to the zero-placement method, but the position of zeros in the z-plane is given by zeros of the Chebychev polynomials as

$$z_i = \exp(j \cdot \psi), \qquad y_i = \exp(j \cdot \zeta), \tag{16}$$

where

$$\psi = 2 \cdot \arccos\left(\frac{\alpha_n}{\alpha_0}\right), \tag{17}$$

$$\zeta = 2 \cdot \arccos\left(\frac{\beta}{\beta_0}\right). \tag{18}$$

There holds

$$\alpha_0 = \cosh\left(\frac{\operatorname{arccosh}(R_a)}{N-1}\right), \qquad \beta_0 = \cosh\left(\frac{\operatorname{arccosh}(R_a)}{M-1}\right), \tag{19}$$

where R_a is the required suppression of side lobes level,

$$\alpha_n = \cos\left(\pi \cdot \frac{n-0.5}{N-1}\right), \qquad \beta_n = \cos\left(\pi \cdot \frac{m-0.5}{M-1}\right). \tag{20}$$

2.5. Optimization Methods

Computational complexity of control synthesis can be divided into two main groups: computational complexity during the synthesis itself and computational complexity during the real deployment. Regardless of the numerical techniques used, the measure of complexity is the required number of array factor calculations or electromagnetic field simulations. It seems that the pure usage of optimization tools for array factor synthesis does not bring any significant advantage. Although the optimization tools seem to provide more freedom in choosing the target, there is a certain equivalence between the optimization with a particular goal function and some deterministic approach. For example, the optimization where the goal is to maximize the magnitude of main lobe gives the same result as the Woodward–Lawson method with a rectangular window (see Figure 6).

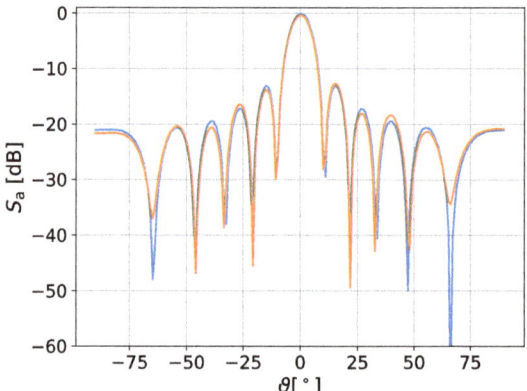

Figure 6. Comparison of Woodward–Lawson method (orange line) and optimization (blue line).

The most computationally expensive part of the control synthesis is an optimization procedure, provided it is used. Although the results from the array factor analysis are presented in the paper, the goal is to find an approach that will work together with electromagnetic field simulation. This fact limits the number of calculating goal functions to hundreds or lower thousands. The paper deals with testing three different sets of optimization parameters:

- Magnitude and phase of each particular element represent the optimization parameters.
- Coefficients of polynomials a, b from Equations (13) and (14) are parameters of optimization.
- Positions of zeros y_i and z_i from Equation (13) are subject of optimization.

In preliminary tests, it appeared that gradient-based methods and methods following from convex optimization such as Nelder–Mead, COBYLA, BOBYQA showed poor convergence. Surprisingly, bad convergence also appeared by methods commonly used in machine learning such as Covariance Matrix Adaptation Evolution Strategy (CMA-ES). Together with the requirement on the possibility of multi-criteria optimization as promising candidates appeared methods based on genetic algorithms NSGA-II, EPS-MOEA, and swarm optimisation algorithm SMPSO. The aim was to assess the speed of convergence, especially at the end of the optimization process. This is based on the idea of a hybrid algorithm, where the starting point (population) of optimization is constructed on the basis of deterministic methods or methods based on electromagnetic field simulation.

2.6. Quantization

There are several approaches to quantization in the microwave technology. The particular approach depends on practical realization. In this paper, the quantization is performed on the level of array factor, which corresponds with the aimed realization using digitally controlled Variable Gain Amplifiers (VGA). The quantized magnitude $\hat{I}_{nm}$ of the coefficient $\underline{I}_{nm}$ represents the control of the gain of amplifier, the quantized phase $\hat{\varphi}$ represents the digital control of phase shifters. The quantization is performed using formula

$$\hat{I}_m = \lfloor I_m \cdot 2^n \rfloor / 2^n, \tag{21}$$

where $\hat{I}_m$ is the quantized weight, I_{mn} is the normalized weight and symbols $\lfloor \rfloor$ are used for rounding.

$$\hat{\varphi} = \lfloor \varphi/\pi \cdot 2^n \rfloor / 2^n \cdot \pi. \tag{22}$$

The quantized magnitude and the quantized phase are directly used in simulations as weights for control excitation, and in practical realization they are interpreted as *n*-bits words used for control of VGA or phase sifters, respectively.

3. Results and Discussion

The first part of the study is dedicated to the comparison of effect of quantization for selected well-known methods. The influence of quantization on the array factor obtained by deterministic methods is depicted in Figure 7.

It is evident that the sensitivity strongly depends on the selected way of synthesis (All results presented in this section were obtained using software packages Pyntenna [34] and Artap [35,36], which are available at GitHub https://github.com/artap-framework/artap, accessed on 20 March 2022). It seems that the most robust method from the deterministic ones is the Woodward–Lawson method with a rectangular window (Figure 7a). The suppression of side lobes can be reached using windowing (Figure 7b), but application of a window increases the sensitivity to quantization. In the case of the Dolph–Chebychev method (Figure 7c), the sensitivity to quantization depends on the chosen level of suppressing the side lobes, the effect of quantization is greater with the greater required suppression of side lobes. The design using Schelkunoff's zero-placement method (Figure 7d) is an example of the design which could be acceptable for a continuous control but which is extremely sensitive to quantization (The position of zeros was chosen on purpose to demonstrate effect of quantization; we do not state that this is property of Schelkunoff's zero-placement method).

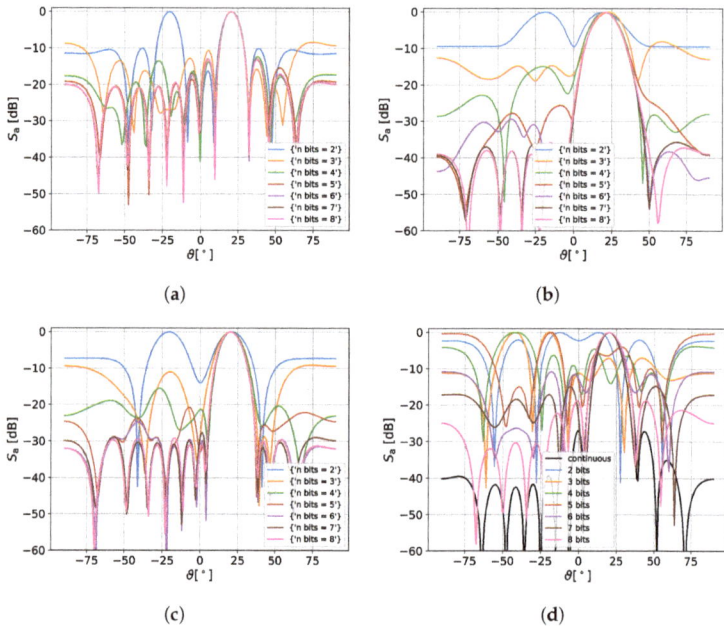

Figure 7. The influence of quantization of coefficients. (**a**) Fourier method with rectangular window; (**b**) Fourier method with Hamming window; (**c**) Dolph–Chebychev method with required side lobe level −30 dB; and (**d**) Schelkunoff's zero-placement method.

The dependence of the array factor on the scanning angle together with the effect of quantization is depicted in Figure 8. In all graphs in the figure, there is elevation angle ϑ on the x-axis, and on the y-axis is

$$\Delta = S_{a1} - S_{a2}, \quad (23)$$

where S_{a1} stands for level of the main lobe and S_{a2} represents the level of biggest side lobe. Figure 7 demonstrates that there is a connection between side lobe suppression and robustness against quantization error. Within the antenna array design process, it is necessary to carefully consider which criteria are more relevant for a given application. In the case of ground stations for nanosatellites, requirements on side lobes are relatively weak (compared to radar applications) but the robustness plays an important role. If steering angle is considered in a certain range, the effect of quantization is more noticeable than for a single elevation angle. The less sensitive design is reached using the Fourier method with a rectangular window (Figure 8a), where quantization using with more than four bits is acceptable. For the Fourier method with the Hamming window (Figure 8b) and the Dolph–Chebychev method (Figure 8c), the effect of quantization appears for all levels of quantization. The design using the zero placement method (Figure 8d) (and particular positions of zeros) seems to be practically inapplicable.

Besides the quantization effect, we can see the influence of the method on the range of possible scanning angle in Figure 8. Note that the sensitivity to quantization of the excitation magnitudes and phases also points to sensitivity in general.

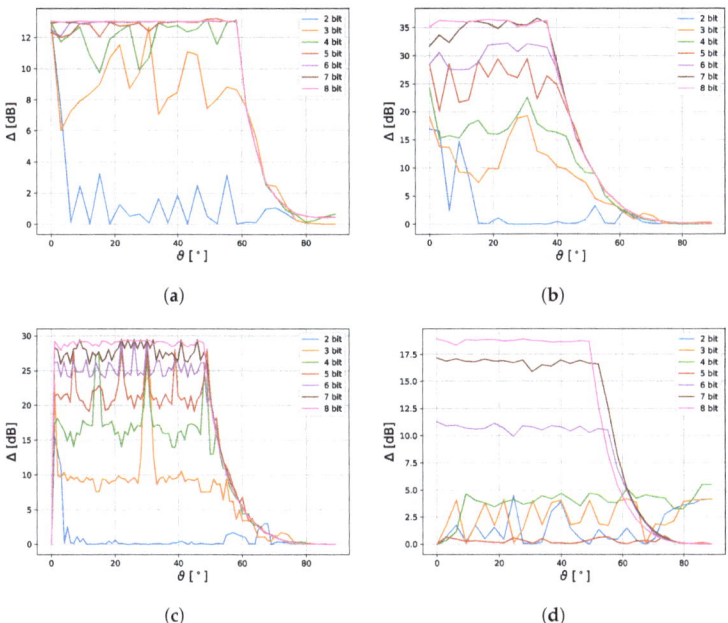

Figure 8. The influence of quantization of coefficients. (**a**) Fourier method with rectangular window; (**b**) Fourier method with Hamming window; (**c**) Dolph–Chebychev with required side lobe level −30 dB; and (**d**) Zero placement method.

Figure 9a,b show the influence of the required suppression level on zero positions. Depending on the specific application, a trade-off must be made between the required radiation pattern and sensitivity. For a rough quantization and high requirements on suppression of side lobes, the position of zeros is significantly influenced. On the other hand, the tuning of positions of zeros can be a way to decrease sensitivity to quantization.

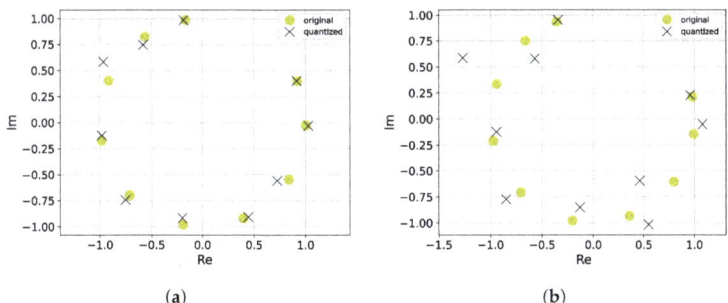

Figure 9. Influence of 3-bit quantization of coefficients on positions of zeros. (**a**) Dolph–Chebychev method 20 dB; (**b**) Dolph–Chebychev method 30 dB.

The synthesis of array factors based on the deterministic method certainly will not lead to an acceptable design. However, it can significantly reduce the number of evaluations of the goal function during the following optimization with the usage of field simulation.

For testing capabilities of different optimization algorithms, the problem of Array Factor synthesis where the goal function in the form

$$\mathcal{F}_1 = \max[S_a(\vartheta_r, \varphi_r)], \tag{24}$$

(ϑ_r and φ_r standing for the required elevation and azimuth, respectively) was chosen. As written above, the array factor obtained using this goal function is the same as the array factor obtained using the Fourier method with the rectangular window.

The optimization was performed for 200 individuals and 300 generations. The first generation was created purely randomly with the uniform distribution. After preliminary tests, the four evolutionary algorithms were chosen. The parameters of optimization were magnitudes and phases of all array elements independently. This can be useful during the calibration process, where symmetries can be broken due to possibilities of practical realization. The results of optimization are depicted in Figure 10. Figure 10a shows the dependence of array factor on elevation angle after optimization. The goal was to maximize the array factor on the elevation angle $\vartheta = 0$. Figure 10b shows the dependence of value of the array factor $S_a(0,0)$ on the number of generation. It can be seen that the fastest convergence was reached using the SMPSO algorithm over generations (K). However, the number of calculations of the goal function is too high for incorporating electromagnetic field simulation. The algorithm EPS MOEA does not converge to the correct solution at all.

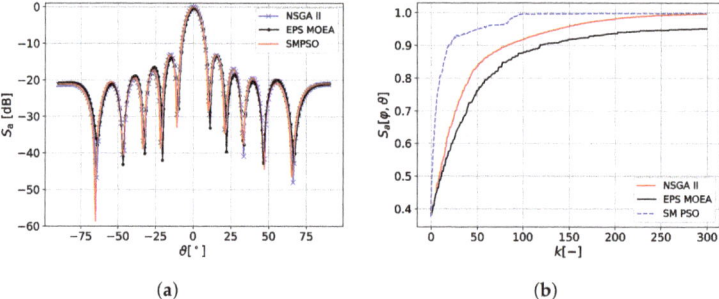

Figure 10. Comparison of algorithms NSGA II, EPS MOEA, and SMPSO. (a) Array factor; (b) Convergence.

Figure 11 shows the possibilities of speeding up the optimization process in the case of the algorithms NSGA II and SMPSO. Figure 11a shows the array factor obtained using optimization by different approaches, while Figure 11b shows the convergence of different sets of parameters. The fastest convergence seems to be reached if parameters of optimization are positions of zeros. Unfortunately, optimizing the zero positions often tends to converging to non-optimal solutions (see the red line in Figure 11b). The used objective function is not equally sensitive to the positions of all zeros. More robust convergence is observable when using polynomial coefficients as optimization parameters. The optimization using SMPSO with coefficients of polynomials as parameters is acceptably fast and seems to be applicable together with the field simulator. Although optimization of zero positions shows relatively poor convergence together with evolutionary algorithms, the change of zero position has a predictable impact on array factor (or radiation pattern). It makes the zero placing be a candidate for cooperating with machine learning for automatic tuning and calibration.

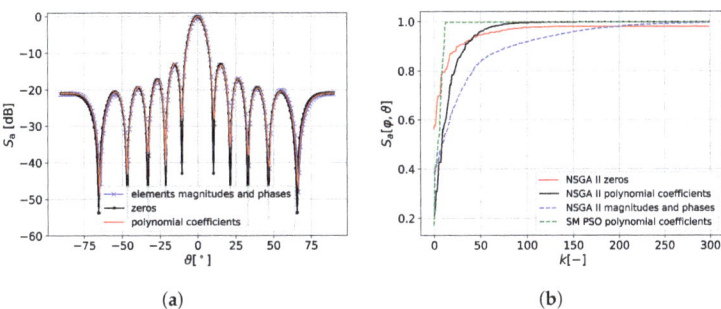

Figure 11. Convergence of algorithm with different parameter sets. (**a**) Array factor; (**b**) Convergence.

The number of enumerations of the objective function in the previous test problem would be on the edge of solvability if the field simulation is used. It is also necessary to mention that, for other objective functions, the convergence is mostly even worse. The most promising approach seems to be the set of parameters $\delta\alpha_1, \delta\alpha_2, \ldots, \delta\alpha_{n-1}$, where each parameter $\delta\alpha_i$ represents a relative angular shift of the particular zero. The optimization process therefore can start from the solution obtained using any deterministic method. In this work, the objective function was formulated as

$$\mathcal{F}_1 = \max |(S_{ari} - S_{ai})|, \tag{25}$$

where S_{ari} is the required magnitude of the i-th lobe and S_{ai} is the magnitude of the i-th lobe. The goal function described by Equation (25) leads to maximal suppression of the side lobes.

Any standard deterministic method does not take into account the sensitivity to quantization. Additionally, the single objective optimization presented above does not reduce the sensitivity.

One possible way to reach the prescribed radiation pattern and reduce the sensitivity to rounding (and sensitivity in general) at the same time, is represented by a multi-criteria optimization. First, the goal function $\mathcal{F}_1$ represents the requirements on the array factor shape, and is defined by equation (25). The second goal function represents the effect of quantization and is defined by

$$\mathcal{F}_1 = \max |(\hat{S}_{ari} - \hat{S}_{ai})|, \tag{26}$$

where ($\hat{S}_{ari}$ and $\hat{S}_{ai}$) are magnitudes of side lobes of array factor obtained using coefficients quantized by required number of bits.

Figure 12a shows all calculated solutions for multi-criteria optimization. A collection of solutions that are not dominated by other solutions (in the figure marked by red) in that set are superior to the rest of the solutions. In the search area, they are known as the Pareto front [37]. The red point at the rightmost position represents the solution in which requirement on array factor shape are best fulfilled; the red point at the leftmost position represents the solution which is less sensitive to quantization. The remaining red points represent the compromise between the required array factor shape and the sensitivity to rounding. The dependence of difference between the main lobe and the biggest side lobe for 3-bit quantization is depicted in Figure 12b. As can be seen from the Pareto front, it is possible to select a solution with an acceptable side lobe suppression and also acceptable sensitivity to quantization. Especially for quantization via a low number of bits, the proposed method offers better results than any tested deterministic method. Figure 12c,d show the comparison of the best deterministic methods and the proposed method for the array factor and required elevation angle $\vartheta = 0°$ and $\vartheta = 30°$, respectively.

Note that results were obtained using SMPSO algorithm which showed the best performance in the previous tests.

The important question is if the usage of multi-criteria optimization instead of mono-criteria optimization does not lead to significantly worse convergence. The comparison of convergence between the mono-criteria and multi-criteria processes is depicted in Figure 13a,b, respectively. The results were obtained using the SMPSO algorithm, where the whole optimization process was repeated 20 times. The figure shows the mean value and standard deviation calculated from these twenty runs for both single and multi-objective optimization. The usage of multi-criteria optimization has a certain but not critical influence on the convergence speed.

According to the results described above, the lowest number of calculations of the goal function was reached using procedure:

1. Calculating solutions using deterministic methods to reach a result close to the required radiation pattern (array factor).
2. Forming the initial population including results obtained using deterministic methods.
3. Performing the multi-criteria optimization using the SMPSO algorithm, where parameters of optimization are relative shifts of the zero positions. The first goal function describes the required shape of the array factor, while the second goal function expresses the influence of the quantization error.
4. Selecting an acceptable compromise between the array factor requirements and sensitivity to quantization from Pareto front obtained using optimization.

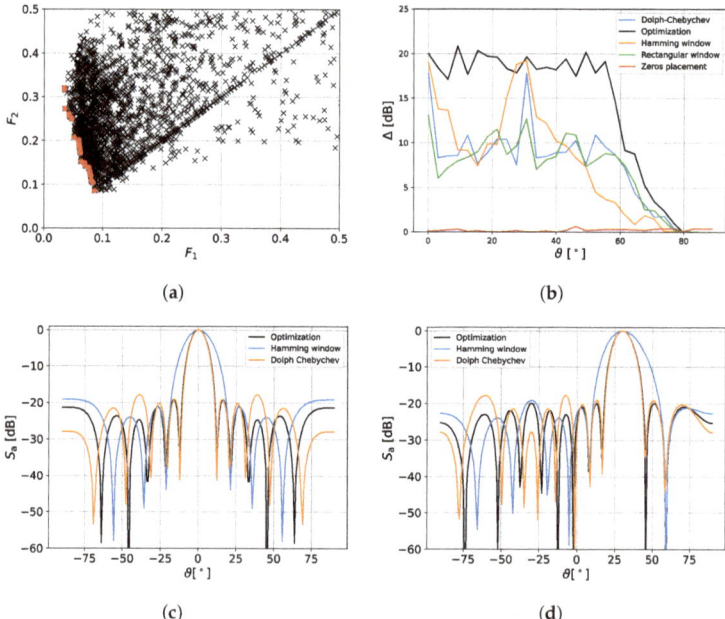

Figure 12. Results of multi-criteria optimization with 60 generations and 60 individuals in each generation. (**a**) Pareto front of the quantization error of the magnitude and the phase after the multi-criteria optimization, the points of the Pareto front is denoted by red dots; (**b**) Comparison of effect of 3-bit quantization for array factor obtained by different methods. The result of optimization—black line; (**c**) Comparison of array factors obtained by different methods with 3-bit quantized excitation for $\vartheta = 0°$; (**d**) Comparison of array factors obtained by different methods with 3-bit quantized excitation for $\vartheta = 30°$.

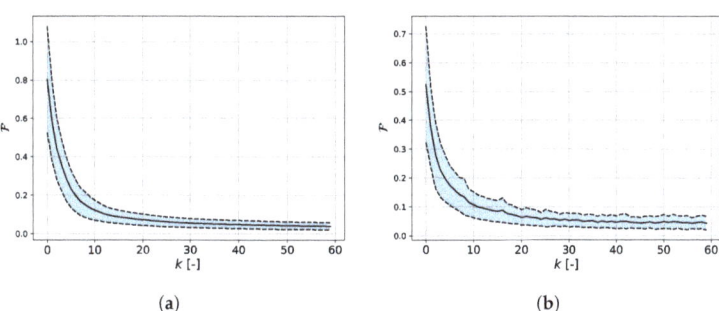

Figure 13. Mean and standard deviation calculated from 20 runs of optimization. (**a**) Single-criteria optimization; (**b**) Multi-criteria optimization.

4. Conclusions

The main goal of this research, motivated by requirements following the necessity of communication with nanosatellites, was to find the procedure of synthesis of antenna array control. This procedure should take into account the sensitivity to quantization errors, but, at the same time, the number of necessary evaluations of the goal functions (which can be based on full-field simulation) must be minimized. It was shown that the commonly used deterministic methods could lead to control, which is highly sensitive to quantization, and the following optimization step proved necessary. On the other hand, including results from the deterministic approach to the initial populations of the optimization process rapidly reduces the number of calculations of the goal functions. The fastest convergence was reached using the algorithm SMPSO when the parameters of optimization were relative angular shifts of zeros positions.

Author Contributions: Conceptualization, D.P. and T.O.; methodology, D.P.; software, T.O., D.P., H.K.N. and P.K.; validation, D.C.D.G., H.K.N. and P.K.; writing—review and editing, D.P. and T.O. All authors have read and agreed to the published version of the manuscript.

Funding: This research was funded by Czech Science Foundation (GACR) grant number 20-02046S.

Acknowledgments: This work was supported by University of West Bohemia during an internal project SGS-2021-011.

Conflicts of Interest: The authors declare no conflict of interest.

Abbreviations

The following abbreviations are used in this manuscript:

NSGA	Not-dominated sorting genetic algorithm
PSO	Partical Swarm Optimization
GA	Genetic algorithm
ACO	Anto Colony Optimization
SMPSO	Speed Constrained Partical Swarm Optimization
EPS-MOEA	Epsilon Multiobjective Evolutionary Algorithm
PCA	Principal Component Analysis
SVD	Singular Value Decomposition
SA	Simulated Annealing

References

1. Nieto-Peroy, C.; Emami, M.R. CubeSat Mission: From Design to Operation. *Appl. Sci.* **2019**, *9*, 3110. [CrossRef]
2. Poghosyan, A.; Golkar, A. CubeSat evolution: Analyzing CubeSat capabilities for conducting science missions. *Prog. Aerosp. Sci.* **2017**, *88*, 59–83. [CrossRef]

3. Crusan, J.; Galica, C. NASA's CubeSat Launch Initiative: Enabling broad access to space. *Acta Astronaut.* **2019**, *157*, 51–60. [CrossRef]
4. Veřtát, I.; Linhart, R.; Dudáček, L.; Dániel, V.; Svoboda, P. Autonomous and semi-autonomous radio commanding of VZLUSAT-1 nanosatellite from ground control station in Pilsen. In Proceedings of the 2017 International Conference on Applied Electronics (AE), Pilsen, Czech Republic, 5–6 September 2017; pp. 1–6.
5. Urban, M.; Nentvich, O.; Stehlikova, V.; Baca, T.; Daniel, V.; Hudec, R. VZLUSAT-1: Nanosatellite with miniature lobster eye X-ray telescope and qualification of the radiation shielding composite for space application. *Acta Astronaut.* **2017**, *140*, 96–104. [CrossRef]
6. Linhart, R.; Vobornik, A.; Veřtát, I. Communication Subsystem for PilsenCUBE Nanosatellite. In Proceedings of the 2018 International Conference on Applied Electronics (AE), Pilsen, Czech Republic, 11–12 September 2018; pp. 1–4.
7. Villela, T.; Costa, C.A.; Brandão, A.M.; Bueno, F.T.; Leonardi, R. Towards the thousandth CubeSat: A statistical overview. *Int. J. Aerosp. Eng.* **2019**, *2019*, 5063145. [CrossRef]
8. Saeed, N.; Elzanaty, A.; Almorad, H.; Dahrouj, H.; Al-Naffouri, T.Y.; Alouini, M.S. Cubesat communications: Recent advances and future challenges. *IEEE Commun. Surv. Tutor.* **2020**, *22*, 1839–1862. [CrossRef]
9. Lokman, A.H.; Soh, P.J.; Azemi, S.N.; Lago, H.; Podilchak, S.K.; Chalermwisutkul, S.; Jamlos, M.F.; Al-Hadi, A.A.; Akkaraekthalin, P.; Gao, S. A review of antennas for picosatellite applications. *Int. J. Antennas Propag.* **2017**, *2017*, 4940656. [CrossRef]
10. Asplund, H.; Astely, D.; von Butovitsch, P.; Chapman, T.; Frenne, M.; Ghasemzadeh, F.; Hagström, M.; Hogan, B.; Jöngren, G.; Karlsson, J.; et al. *Chapter 4—Antenna Arrays and Classical Beamforming*; Elsevier: London, UK, 2020.
11. Paulsen, J.A.; Renn, M.; Christenson, K.; Plourde, R. Printing conformal electronics on 3D structures with Aerosol Jet technology. In Proceedings of the 2012 Future of Instrumentation International Workshop (FIIW) Proceedings, Gatlinburg, TN, USA, 8–9 October 2012; pp. 1–4.
12. Arsenov, P.; Sobolev, A.; Efimov, A.; Ivanov, V. Double slot aerosol jet printed antenna for X-band applications. *J. Phys.* **2021**, *2086*, 012047. [CrossRef]
13. Orosz, T.; Rassõlkin, A.; Kallaste, A.; Arsénio, P.; Pánek, D.; Kaska, J.; Karban, P. Robust Design Optimization and Emerging Technologies for Electrical Machines: Challenges and Open Problems. *Appl. Sci.* **2020**, *10*, 6653. [CrossRef]
14. Nikolayev, D.; Zhadobov, M.; Karban, P.; Sauleau, R. Electromagnetic radiation efficiency of body-implanted devices. *Phys. Rev. Appl.* **2018**, *9*, 024033. [CrossRef]
15. Nikolayev, D. Modeling and characterization of in-body antennas. In Proceedings of the 2018 IEEE 17th international conference on Mathematical Methods in Electromagnetic Theory (MMET), Kiev, Ukraine, 2–5 July 2018; pp. 42–46.
16. Petrasova, I.; Karban, P.; Kropik, P.; Panek, D.; Dolezel, I. Optimization of selected operation characteristics of array antennas. *J. Comput. Appl. Math.* **2022**, *399*, 113726. [CrossRef]
17. Kala, D.D.; Sundari, D.T. A review on optimization of antenna array by evolutionary optimization techniques. *Int. J. Intell. Unmanned Syst.* **2021**.
18. Ogurtsov, S.; Caratelli, D.; Song, Z. A Review of Synthesis Techniques for Phased Antenna Arrays in Wireless Communications and Remote Sensing. *Int. J. Antennas Propag.* **2021**, *2021*, 5514972. [CrossRef]
19. Zhang, C.; Fu, X.; Chen, X.; Peng, S.; Min, X. Synthesis of uniformly excited sparse rectangular planar array for sidelobe suppression using multi-objective optimisation algorithm. *J. Eng.* **2019**, *2019*, 6278–6281. [CrossRef]
20. Koziel, S.; Ogurtsov, S. *Simulation-Based Optimization of Antenna Arrays*; World Scientific Europe Ltd.: London, UK, 2019. [CrossRef]
21. Wang, D.; Zhang, Y.; Wei, H.; You, X.; Gao, X.; Wang, J. An overview of transmission theory and techniques of large-scale antenna systems for 5G wireless communications. *Sci. China Inf. Sci.* **2016**, *59*, 1–18.
22. Khoshnevis, A.; Sabharwal, A. Performance of quantized power control in multiple antenna systems. In Proceedings of the 2004 IEEE International Conference on Communications (IEEE Cat. No. 04CH37577), Paris, France, 20–24 June 2004; Volume 2, pp. 803–807.
23. Darvish, A.; Ebrahimzadeh, A. Improved fruit-fly optimization algorithm and its applications in antenna arrays synthesis. *IEEE Trans. Antennas Propag.* **2018**, *66*, 1756–1766. [CrossRef]
24. Comisso, M.; Palese, G.; Babich, F.; Vatta, F.; Buttazzoni, G. 3D multi-beam and null synthesis by phase-only control for 5G antenna arrays. *Electronics* **2019**, *8*, 656. [CrossRef]
25. Marcano, D.; Durán, F. Synthesis of antenna arrays using genetic algorithms. *IEEE Antennas Propag. Mag.* **2000**, *42*, 12–20. [CrossRef]
26. Singh, U.; Salgotra, R. Synthesis of Linear Antenna Arrays Using Enhanced Firefly Algorithm. *Arab. J. Sci. Eng.* **2019**, *44*, 1961–1976. [CrossRef]
27. Banerjee, S.; Dwivedi, V.V. Linear array synthesis using Schelkunoff polynomial method and particle swarm optimization. In Proceedings of the 2015 International Conference on Advances in Computer Engineering and Applications, Ghaziabad, India, 19–20 March 2015; pp. 727–730. [CrossRef]
28. Weng, W.C.; Yang, F.; Elsherbeni, A. Electromagnetics and Antenna Optimization Using Taguchi's Method. *Synth. Lect. Comput. Electromagn.* **2007**, *2*, 1–94. [CrossRef]
29. Rawat, A.; Yadav, R.; Shrivastava, S. Neural network applications in smart antenna arrays: A review. *AEU-Int. J. Electron. Commun.* **2012**, *66*, 903–912. [CrossRef]

30. ANTENNA Magus Software: Antenna Design Software Library. 2020. Available online: https://www.3ds.com/products-services/simulia/products/antenna-magus/ (accessed on 23 January 2022).
31. Visser, H. *Array and Phased Array Antenna Basics*; Wiley: Hoboken, NJ, USA, 2005. [CrossRef]
32. Bro, R.; Smilde, A.K. Principal component analysis. *Anal. Methods* **2014**, *6*, 2812–2831. [CrossRef]
33. Orfanidis, S. Electromagnetic Waves and Antennas, Vol.1, Paperback. 2016. Available online: https://www.lulu.com/shop/sophocles-orfanidis/shop/sophocles-orfanidis/electromagnetic-waves-and-antennas-vol1-paperback/paperback/product-1r8qv2vj.html?page=1&pageSize=4 (accessed on 23 January 2022).
34. Pánek, D. Pyntenna. Available online: https://github.com/panek50/Pyntenna (accessed on 20 March 2022).
35. Karban, P.; Pánek, D.; Orosz, T.; Petrášová, I.; Doležel, I. FEM based robust design optimization with Agros and Artap. *Comput. Math. Appl.* **2021**, *81*, 618–633. [CrossRef]
36. Pánek, D.; Orosz, T.; Karban, P. Artap: Robust design optimization framework for engineering applications. In Proceedings of the 2019 Third International Conference on Intelligent Computing in Data Sciences (ICDS), Marrakech, Morocco, 28–30 October 2019; pp. 1–6.
37. Veldhuizen, D.A.V.; Lamont, G.B. Multiobjective Evolutionary Algorithms: Analyzing the State-of-the-Art. *Evol. Comput.* **2000**, *8*, 125–147. [CrossRef]

Article

Application of Particle Swarm Optimization in the Design of an ICT High-Voltage Power Supply with Dummy Primary Winding

Can Jiang [1,2], Jun Yang [1,2,*] and Mingwu Fan [1,2]

[1] State Key Laboratory of Advanced Electromagnetic Engineering and Technology, Huazhong University of Science and Technology, Wuhan 430074, China; jiangcan@hust.edu.cn (C.J.); fanmw@mail.hust.edu.cn (M.F.)
[2] School of Electrical and Electronic Engineering, Huazhong University of Science and Technology, Wuhan 430074, China
* Correspondence: jyang@hust.edu.cn

Abstract: The distribution of disk output voltage is a key factor for the design of an insulated core transformer (ICT) high-voltage power supply. The development of an ICT involves the design and optimization of many parameters, which greatly affect the uniformity of disk output voltage. A new ICT structure with dummy primary windings can compensate for the disk output voltage, which aims to improve uniformity. In this work, an optimization method based on a particle swarm optimization (PSO) algorithm was used to optimize the design parameters of an ICT with dummy primary windings. It achieved an optimal uniformity of disk output voltage and load regulation. The design parameters, including the number of secondary winding turns and the compensation capacitance, were optimized based on the finite-element method (FEM) and Simulink circuit simulation. The results show that the maximum non-uniformity of the disk output voltage is reduced from 11.1% to 4.4% from no-load to a full load for a 200 kV/20 mA HUST-ICT prototype. Moreover, the load regulation is greatly reduced from 14.3% to 9.6%. The method improves the stability and reliability of the ICT high voltage power supply and greatly reduces the design time.

Keywords: insulation core transformer; non-uniformity of disk output voltage; load regulation; voltage compensation; dummy primary winding; PSO algorithm

1. Introduction

Low-energy electron accelerators have been widely adopted in the fields of material modification, environmental protection, treatment, coating curing, etc. [1–3]. Compared with other types of electron accelerators for industrial irradiation applications, insulated core transformers (ICTs) have the outstanding advantage of high energy conversion efficiency. The performance of an electron accelerator largely depends on the high-voltage power supply.

Recently, ICT high-voltage power supply involved in attention due to high-power density. In 2009, KSI Corp. developed a novel ICT of 750 kV/100 mA [4]. In 2011, a planar ICT was designed by the Chinese Academy of Sciences, and the capacitor compensation technique is adopted [5]. Since 2012, compensation methods [6,7] and equivalent circuit models [8–10] have been developed at Huazhong University of Science and Technology.

The plane schematic diagram of a three-phase ICT is presented in Figure 1. It contains three core columns, which consist of a primary core wrapped with a primary winding and multi-secondary cores wrapped with multi-secondary windings. Insulation sheets are inserted between the cores [11]. Each core is electrically connected to the corresponding winding to achieve equipotential, and each of the three secondary windings in the same disk is connected to a DC voltage doubler. The three doubler units in the same disk are connected in series; this output DC voltage is called the disk output voltage. Each disk is surrounded by a grading ring, which is intended to distribute the electric field evenly. Finally, all disks are connected in series to obtain the high output voltage of the ICT high-voltage power supply [7]. The ICT and the high-voltage electrode on top of it are placed into a tank filled with approximately 0.6 Mpa sulfur hexafluoride gas.

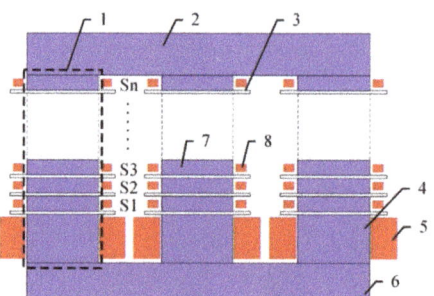

Figure 1. Plane schematic diagram of a three-phase ICT. 1—magnetic core limb; 2—top yoke; 3—insulation sheet; 4—primary core; 5—primary winding; 6—bottom yoke; 7—secondary core; 8—secondary winding. Sn represents the n-th disk.

The insulation sheets are usually made of Teflon, mica, etc., for which the magnetic permeability is much smaller than that of electrical steel. Significant magnetic flux leakage is produced by the insulation sheets of ICTs [9,12]. The leakage flux gradually increases from the bottom to the top disk [6,13]. The output voltage of disks is proportional to the working frequency, the flux amplitude, and the number of secondary winding turns. The different output voltages of the disks cause electric potential differences among the disks. On the one hand, the induced voltages of the secondary windings on different disks are different, which results in higher design and manufacturing costs. On the other hand, a permanently damaging electric breakdown tends to occur on insulating sheets between adjacent disks that have a large electric potential difference.

Increasing the number of secondary winding turns is commonly used to ensure that the disks' output voltage is as consistent as possible. To facilitate the description of the consistency of the disks' output voltage, the concept of maximum non-uniformity is introduced. The maximum non-uniformity of the disks' output voltage can be used to describe the distribution of the output voltage of all disks, indicating the possibility of high voltage breakdown. It can be defined as:

$$\sigma_0 = \frac{max(V_{sj\_NL}) - min(V_{sj\_NL})}{max(V_{sj\_NL})} \times 100\% \tag{1a}$$

$$\sigma_1 = \frac{max(V_{sj\_FL}) - min(V_{sj\_FL})}{max(V_{sj\_FL})} \times 100\% \tag{1b}$$

where σ_0 and σ_1 represent the maximum non-uniformity of disk output voltage under no-load conditions and full load conditions, respectively; V_{Sj} represents the output voltage of the j-th disk S_j, $j \leq n$; and n represents the number of disks.

Often, the upper secondary windings require an additional number of turns, which increases the output impedance. Eventually, this leads to a greater load regulation of the upper disks than the lower disks. Load regulation describes the change in the output voltage from no-load to a full load, which can be expressed by Formula (2):

$$LR = \frac{V_{no\text{-}load} - V_{fullload}}{V_{fullload}} \times 100\% \tag{2}$$

where *LR* represents the load regulation, and $V_{no\text{-}load}$ and $V_{fullload}$ represent the output high voltage under no-load conditions and full load conditions, respectively.

The differing load regulation of disks creates more challenges in selecting an appropriate number of secondary winding turns. We developed a 200 kV/20 mA HUST-ICT prototype, and Figure 2 shows the equipment during installation at Huazhong University of Science and Technology. The conversion efficiency of the HUST-ICT was up to 86%. The number of secondary winding turns (N_{S1}, N_{S2}, ... , N_{S6}) was 2736, 3080, 3400, 3671, 3863, and 3974.

Figure 2. A 200 kV/20 mA prototype HUST-ICT during installation.

The output voltage of the disk was tested in an atmospheric insulated environment with a high voltage of 20 kV under no- load. Figure 3 shows the output voltage of each disk, which was approximately 3.5 kV. The maximum error between the simulation results obtained via the finite-element method (FEM) and the experimental data was less than 5.5%. Because measurement of the output voltage of the disks was not possible under 200 kV operating conditions, the 3D FEM model and a circuit model of the HUST-ICT were built and examined with Ansys software and the MATLAB/Simulink environment, respectively. The distribution of the magnetic flux density in the 3D FEM model is shown in Figure 4. Figure 5 shows the results of the two simulation methods when the HUST-ICT was working at 200 kV with no- load and a full load. These results also match the experimental data when the accelerator was working at 200 kV/20 mA. The maximum error between the simulation results obtained via the FEM and the simulated circuit was less than 2.5%. Therefore, the FEM simulation model was considered to be reliable.

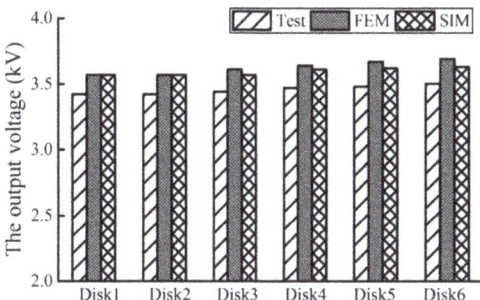

Figure 3. The output voltage distribution of disks under no-load from the experimental test, FEM, and Simulink circuit simulations.

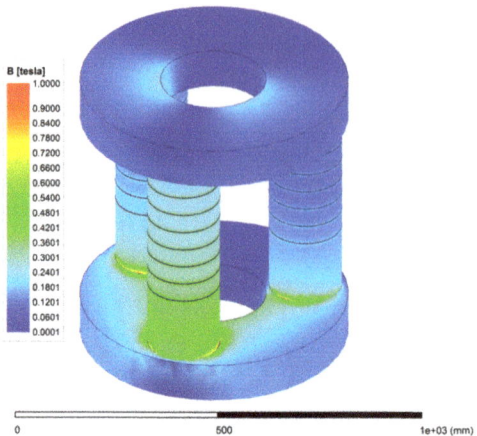

Figure 4. Distribution of the magnetic flux density in the 3D FEM model of the HUST-ICT.

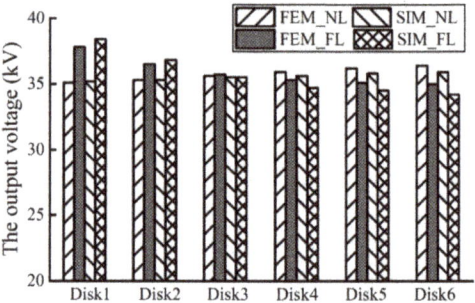

Figure 5. The output voltage distribution of disks at 200 kV under no-load and a full load obtained via FEM and Simulink circuit simulations. NL, no-load; FL, full load.

σ_0 was 3.5% and σ_1 was 11.1% based on the FEM simulation model. Although the non-uniformity of the disk output voltage was small under no-load, it was larger under a full load. Usually, both σ_0 and σ_1 are expected to be less than 10% to ensure reliable operation in industrial production systems. The *LR* of the HUST-ICT was 14.3%. The smaller the load regulation, the better the performance of the ICT high-voltage power supply. Notably, σ and *LR* did not meet expectations. Several electric breakdowns occurred on the insulation sheets.

In addition, a significant amount of time can be spent on the design of the number of secondary turns with manual iterative optimization, which mainly relies on the designer's experience. The design of an ICT contains many parameters, which interact with the transients. As a result, the manual optimization process is complex, and the result is frequently not an optimal solution for this problem.

Methods of optimizing and improving the prototype are currently being studied. On the one hand, adding a dummy primary winding is an interesting method [7]. Dummy primary winding produces a greater excitation effect on the upper secondary windings than on the lower ones. It creates a complementary effect with the primary winding and helps to improve the uniformity of the disks' output voltage. On the other hand, artificial intelligence algorithms can be used to optimize the design parameters of an ICT. The PSO algorithm is a metaheuristic algorithm, which was developed by Kennedy and Eberhart in 1995 [14]. In comparison with other algorithms (GA, ACO, ABC, GSO, SA, etc.), the major advantages of PSO include fewer control parameters, high efficiency, fast convergence, and little dependence on the initial value [15]. It has been successfully applied to both continuous and discrete optimization problems. More recently, the PSO algorithm has solved many complex scientific research and engineering application problems [16–19].

In the light of the discussion above, the design parameters of an insulated core transformer with a dummy primary winding (DICT) were optimized based on the PSO algorithm in this research. The remaining parts of this study are organized as follows. The structure of the DICT is introduced and the parameters are calculated analytically in Section 2. The optimization methods based on PSO are described in Section 3. The method is presented as an example of a 200 kV/20 mA DICT in Section 4. The results are analyzed and discussed in Section 5. Section 6 concludes this paper.

2. Design of DICT

2.1. The DICT Structure

In contrast to conventional structures, one dummy primary winding and one dummy primary core are added to the top of each phase limb of the ICT. The structural dimensions of the dummy primary windings and cores are the same as those of the primary windings and cores. The dimensional parameters of the ICT are listed in Table 1. The structure diagram of a three-phase DICT with six disks is shown in Figure 6.

Table 1. The dimensional parameters of DICT structure.

Components	Height (mm)	Radius (mm)
(Dummy) primary cores	170	89
Secondary cores	47.6	89
(Dummy) primary windings	150	94 (inner)/139 (outer)
Secondary windings	25	96 (inner)/131 (outer)
Yokes	100	130 (inner)/330 (outer)
Insulation sheets	2	100

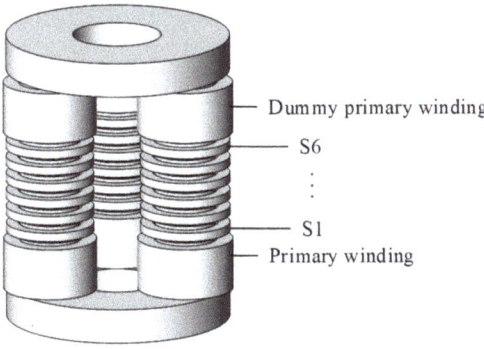

Figure 6. Structure diagram of the three-phase DICT with six disks.

The alternating magnetic flux produced by the primary winding excitation generates an induced voltage in the dummy primary winding. A suitable capacitor (calculated in the next subsection) is connected in parallel to each dummy primary winding. The current phase of the dummy primary winding is adjusted so that it is consistent with the current phase of the primary winding. This seems to increase the excitation to compensate for the magnetic flux of the secondary windings, especially the upper secondary windings. Therefore, this capacitor can be called a compensation capacitor.

2.2. Calculation of the Parameters

An ICT is a multi-winding transformer with a special structure. It is very difficult to calculate the exact value of mutual inductance using analytical expressions because the fringing flux effect around all the insulation sheets makes the calculation of the flux path complicated [20]. Numerical analysis via FEM allows for a high-precision mutual inductance matrix.

Due to the completely symmetrical structure, the magnetic circuits of each phase are equal. The equations used to calculate the number of secondary winding turns and compensation capacitance were derived and are described for a single-phase expression in the following paragraphs.

The voltage balance equations of the ideal transformer model and Ohm's Law under no-load conditions are shown below:

$$\dot{U}_p = j\omega L_p \dot{I}_p + j\omega M_{pp'} \dot{I}_{p'} + R_p \dot{I}_p \tag{3}$$

$$\dot{U}_{p'} = j\omega L_{p'} \dot{I}_{p'} + j\omega M_{pp'} \dot{I}_p + R_{p'} \dot{I}_{p'} \tag{4}$$

$$\dot{U}_{p'} = -\frac{1}{j\omega C_{com}} \dot{I}_{p'} \tag{5}$$

where p and p' represent the primary winding and the dummy primary winding, U_p and $U_{p'}$ represent the voltage of the primary winding and the dummy primary winding, I_p and $I_{p'}$ represent the current of the primary winding and the dummy primary winding, R_p and $R_{p'}$ represent the resistance of the primary winding and the dummy primary winding, L_p and $L_{p'}$ are the self-inductance of the primary winding and the dummy primary winding, $M_{pp'}$ is their mutual inductance, ω is the angular frequency of the input voltage, and C_{com} is the capacitance connected to each dummy primary winding. The resistance of the windings is much smaller than the inductive reactance and can be neglected for simplified calculations. It is necessary to generate the same excitation effect for the dummy primary windings as the primary windings. Hence, the flux of the primary winding is equal to that of the dummy primary winding, corresponding to their induced voltages. Ultimately, the compensation capacitance can be calculated by Equation (6):

$$C_{com} = \frac{L_p - M}{\omega^2 (L_p L_{p'} - M^2)} \tag{6}$$

This is related to the mutual inductance parameters and the angular frequency of the input voltage. Once the physical model has been established, the mutual inductance matrix can be obtained by FEM simulation or a formula based on experience, which can be used to calculate a preliminary value of compensation capacitance. This is optimized in Section 3.

The excitation generated by the primary windings and the dummy primary windings is cross-linked with all other windings, which satisfies the superposition theorem [21].

$$\dot{U} = j\omega(L_p + M_{pp'})\dot{I}_p + j\omega(L_{p'} + M_{pp'})\dot{I}_{p'} \tag{7}$$

$$N_{Si} = \frac{U_{Si}}{U_p} \frac{L_p^{(1)} + L_{p'}^{(1)}}{M_{pSi}^{(1)} + M_{p'Si}^{(1)}} N_p k_1 \tag{8}$$

where N_p and N_{Si} are the number of primary and secondary winding turns, respectively; $L_p^{(1)}$, $L_{p'}^{(1)}$, $M_{pSi}^{(1)}$ and $M_{p'Si}^{(1)}$ are the single-turn self- and mutual-inductance of the windings; U_p is the input RMS voltage of the primary winding; U_{Si} is the output RMS voltage of the secondary windings; and k_1 is a compensation coefficient.

3. Optimization Method for the Design Parameters of the DICT Based on PSO

The parameters of the DICT to be optimized included the number of secondary winding turns ($N_{S1}, N_{S2}, \ldots, N_{Sn}$) and the compensation capacitance (C_{com}). Obviously, this is a multi-parameter optimization problem in a typical engineering application.

The PSO algorithm mimics the foraging behavior of certain birds or other animals, which find food through their knowledge and learning from the experiences of others, there are no leaders among them. The PSO is similar to the genetic algorithm (GA) in that the system is initialized by a population of randomized solutions. Compared with the GA, each potential solution in the PSO has a random velocity, and these potential solutions are particles flying in a multi-dimensional space. They adjust their flight speed dynamically according to the individual cognitive ability and the social cognition ability (from the experience of their peers), which form positive feedback for group optimization. Each particle records its coordinates (position) associated with the best solution (the maximum or minimum value of the target function) that it has achieved so far in the search space. This value is called pbest. Meanwhile, the best solution of all particles is also recorded, this value is called gbest [22]. Next, pbest and gbest are updated through each iteration step. Specifically, at the k-th iteration, the speed and position of the i-th particle are updated through dimension d according to the following Equations [15]:

$$v_{i,d}^{k+1} = \omega v_{i,d}^k + c_1 r_1 (pbest_{i,d}^k - x_{i,d}^k) + c_2 r_2 (gbest_d^k - x_{i,d}^k) \tag{9}$$

$$x_{i,d}^{k+1} = x_{i,d}^k + v_{i,d}^k \tag{10}$$

where c_1 is the learning coefficient for individual ability and c_2 is the learning coefficient for social ability. Usually, c_1 and c_2 are taken as 2. Moreover, r_1 and r_2 are uniform random numbers between 0 and 1, d represents the dimension, and w is the inertia weight, which plays an important role in balancing the global search and the local search, since it directly affects the convergence of the objective function. It helps to reduce interactions by using a decreasing inertia weight.

The PSO algorithm is ideal for solving multi-parameter optimization problems by constructing an objective function and converting the multiple parameters to be solved into a multi-dimensional solution space. In this study, the objective function involved σ_0, σ_1, and LR.

The position of the particle is a variable vector $X = [x_1, x_2, \ldots, x_m]$ that indicates the solution of the problem to be optimized for a swarm with m particles. The merit of the position for each particle depends on the objective function.

Combined with the design processes of the DICT, the PSO-based method is summarized in the following steps:

1. Select the material of the insulating sheets, the rectifier elements, and the working magnetic flux density based on the minimum power loss and the size of the structure of the DICT, and calculate the rough value of C_{com} and $N_{S1}, N_{S2}, \ldots, N_{Sn}$ according to Equations (6) and (8);
2. Calculate the mutual inductance matrix with the FEM magnetostatic model of the DICT;
3. Generate an initial swarm with positions (x_i) and velocities (v_i). Take a range of values for each particle based on the previous calculations of $N_{S1}, N_{S2}, \ldots, N_{Sn}$, and C_{com};
4. Establish the objective function and obtain the personal best value pbest and the global best value gbest so far. $V_{S1\_NL}, V_{S2\_NL}, \ldots, V_{Sn\_NL}$ are calculated by analytical formulae. Meanwhile, $V_{S1\_FL}, V_{S2\_FL}, \ldots, V_{Sn\_FL}$ are obtained by the MATLAB codes and the Simulink circuit under full load conditions. Thus, σ_0, σ_1 and LR can be calculated by Formulas (1) and (2);
5. Update the personal best value pbest and the global best value gbest, and update the position and velocity of each particle via Equations (9) and (10) to obtain a new set of design parameters;
6. Assess the objective function and find the best fitness value so far;

7. Update the swarm, and repeat Steps 4, 5, and 6;
8. Repeat Steps 4, 5, 6, and 7 until the end condition is met;
9. Output the optimized parameters of the DICT (N_{S1}, N_{S2}, ..., N_{Sn}, C_{com}) and the output voltage of disks (V_{S1_NL}, V_{S2_NL}, ..., V_{Sn_NL}, V_{S1_FL}, V_{S2_FL}, ..., V_{Sn_FL}), and calculate σ_0, σ_1, and LR;
10. Import the optimized parameters into the FEM couple-circuit transient model of the DICT to verify the output voltage of the disks.

A flowchart of the design parameters of a DICT based on PSO is shown in Figure 7.

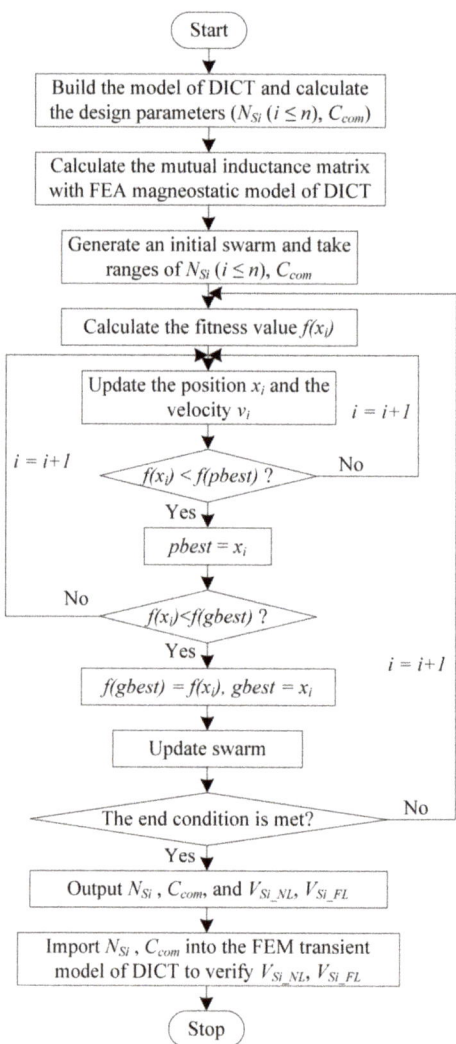

Figure 7. Flowchart of the design parameters of a DICT based on PSO.

4. An Example of a 200 kV/20 mA DICT

Based on the experience of the prototype, the fill factor of the core was about 95%, and the core material was Nippon steel of 27zh95, the BH curve for which is shown in Figure 8. The material of windings is copper and the windings are modelled using uniform multi-turn coils. At the same time, sufficient space needs to be considered for coil interleaving and interlayer insulation. The doubling rectifier circuit is the same as in [6], expect that the capacitor is set to 0.2 µF. The smaller capacitor helps to reduce stored energy and increase the reliability of the ICT. The mutual inductance matrix can be obtained with the FEM magnetostatic model. The design parameters were optimized by the method described in Section 3.

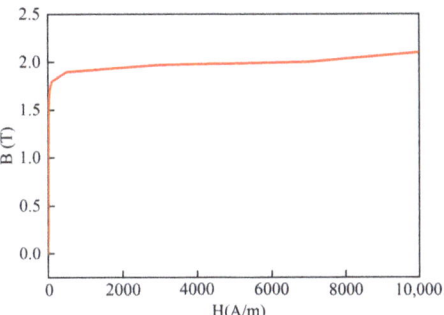

Figure 8. The BH curve of 27zh95 steel.

The working magnetic flux density was about 0.5 T, which is much lower than the saturation value, except for the corners. As a consequence, it can be described by a linear transformer model [8]. The compensation capacitance C_{com} was 213 µF, and the number of secondary winding turns (N_{S1}, N_{S2}, ..., N_{S6}) was 1997, 2097, 2146, 2146, 2097, and 1997, respectively, according to Equations (6) and (8). For simplicity, the dummy primary winding was assumed to be the same size as the primary windings. $N_{p'}$ was the same as N_p: they were both 92 turns, and N_{S1} was 2000 turns, based on the preliminary design.

4.1. Initialization

Depending on the design, the number of secondary winding turns is determined to be in the range of 1500–4000, and the compensation capacitance is taken in the range of 100–300 µF. Any phase of the ICT with a symmetric structure contains sufficient mutual inductance information. The problem has six dimensions with solution variables (N_{S2}, N_{S3}, ..., N_{S6}, C_{com}). The dynamic inertia weight w is in the range of 0.4–0.95, and a linear reduction was carried out by Equation (11) during the training. The population size was set to 100, and the maximum number of iterations was set to 60.

$$w = \frac{MaxIt - It}{MaxIt} \times (w_s - w_e) + w_e \qquad (11)$$

where w_s and w_e represent the initial value and the end value of inertia weight, respectively. *MaxIt* represents the maximum number of iterations; and *It* represents the current number of iterations.

4.2. The Objective Function

The non-uniformity of the disks' output voltage and load regulation are the main factors to be considered; hence, the objective function consists of these two factors. The objective function is established with the non-uniformity of the disks' output voltage and load regulation, which can be set as in Equation (12):

$$fitness = \omega_1 \times \max(\sigma_0, \sigma_1) + \omega_2 \times LR \qquad (12)$$

where ω_1 and ω_2 represent the weights of non-uniformity and load regulation, respectively. Because the non-uniformity is a more important indicator affecting an ICT's performance, the weight factor ω_1 was set to 1, and ω_2 was set to 0.3, based on the experience of the designer.

5. Results

The convergence curve of the PSO algorithm is shown in Figure 9, and the optimized design parameters are listed in Table 2. The results of the FEM model are in good agreement with the results of MATLAB/Simulink.

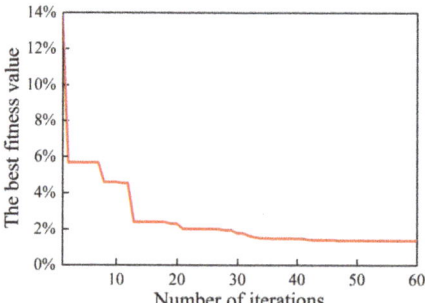

Figure 9. The best fitness value per generation calculated by PSO for the DICT.

Table 2. The optimized design parameters of the DICT.

Disk No.	S1	S2	S3	S4	S5	S6
Number of turns	2000	2122	2190	2188	2124	2024
Capacitance (C_{com}/μF)			215			

The distributions of the disks' output voltage after all the tests and optimizations with different types under no-load and a full load by FEM simulation are shown in Figure 10. The distribution of the magnetic flux density in the 3D FEM model of the DICT is shown in Figure 11. A comparison of the distribution of the magnetic flux density in the central axis of the A-phase core column between the HUST-ICT and the DICT is shown in Figure 12. Compared with Figure 4, the uniformity of the magnetic flux density distribution of ICT has been significantly improved.

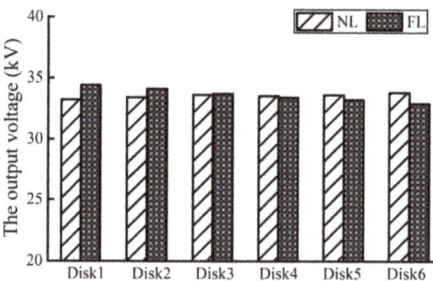

Figure 10. The DICT output voltage distribution of disks under no-load and a full load by FEM simulation after PSO. NL, no-load; FL, full load.

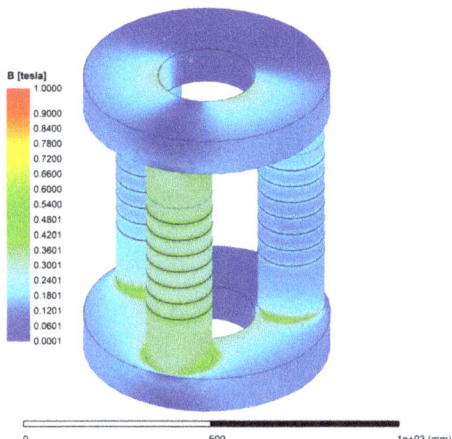

Figure 11. Distribution of the magnetic flux density in the 3D FEM model of the DICT.

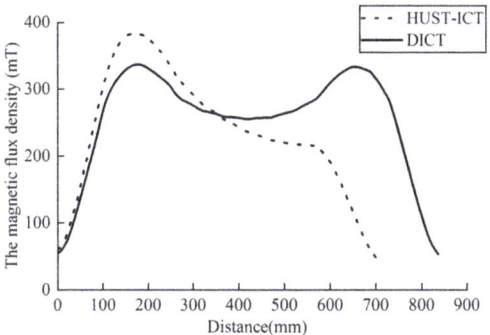

Figure 12. A comparison of the distribution of the magnetic flux density in the central axis of the A-phase core column between the HUST-ICT and the DICT.

The results based on PSO show that both σ_0 and σ_1 were less than 1.5%. However, σ tended to be larger in the FEM model, especially σ_1. The difference between the two simulation methods can be attributed to a minor current phase shift in the dummy primary windings. Compared with the circuit simulation model, the FEM model is more reliable. Therefore, the final results based on the FEM simulation are presented in Table 3. In comparison with the HUST-ICT under 200 kV/20 mA, the DICT has obvious advantages over ICT. The non-uniformity of the disks' output voltage decreases, from 3.5% to 1.9% under no-load and from 11.1% to 4.4% under a full load. Moreover, the load regulation is greatly reduced to 9.6%.

Table 3. Comparison of optimization results with 200 kV/20 mA.

Type	Non-Uniformity		Load Regulation
	No-Load	Full Load	
HUST-ICT	3.5%	11.1%	14.3%
DICT by PSO	1.9%	4.4%	9.6%

In addition, the PSO method takes only a few hours, whereas the manual optimization method takes several days or even weeks. In summary, the PSO method proved to be far superior to the manual optimization method.

The number of secondary winding turns was greatly reduced, especially for secondary windings in the upper disks. Moreover, the number of winding turns had a roughly symmetrical distribution, which reduced the number of winding specifications. As a result, this suggested higher feasibility for the project's implementation.

6. Conclusions

In this paper, the accuracy of the FEM model was verified by comparing test data of the HUST-ICT prototype with the simulation results, and consistent results were also verified in MATLAB/Simulink. The PSO algorithm was proposed for optimizing the design parameters of ICT. The structure of the DICT made the electric field evenly distributed, ensured the uniformity of the disks' output voltage, and greatly reduced the load regulation.

The PSO-based optimization method turned out to be highly effective for achieving better disk output voltage uniformity and load regulation for the DICT. In summary, it significantly saves the design time needed to improve an ICT's performance. The optimized design codes developed here can be used for all ICT-type high-voltage power supply systems. Future work is planned to develop a new prototype based on this method.

Author Contributions: Conceptualization, C.J. and J.Y.; methodology, C.J.; software, C.J.; validation, C.J. and J.Y.; investigation, C.J. and J.Y.; resources, J.Y.; data curation, C.J.; writing—original draft preparation, C.J.; writing—review and editing, J.Y.; project administration, J.Y. and M.F.; funding acquisition, M.F. All authors have read and agreed to the published version of the manuscript.

Funding: This research was funded by the Technological Innovation Program of Hubei Province, China (grant number 2017AEA107).

Data Availability Statement: The data that support the findings of this study are available from the corresponding author upon reasonable request.

Acknowledgments: We acknowledge the financial support provided by the Department of Science and Technology of Hubei Province.

Conflicts of Interest: The authors declare no conflict of interest.

References

1. Knyazeva, A.G.; Kushch, V.I.; Remnev, G.E.; Ezhov, V.V.; Smolyanskiy, E.A. Tin coating effect on the elastoplastic behaviour of ti film for electron beam exit window. *Vacuum* **2017**, *143*, 356–362. [CrossRef]
2. Chmielewski, A.G.; Al-Sheikhly, M.; Berejka, A.J.; Cleland, M.R.; Antoniak, M. Recent developments in the application of electron accelerators for polymer processing. *Radiat. Phys. Chem.* **2014**, *94*, 147–150. [CrossRef]
3. Parejo Calvo, W.A.; Duarte, C.L.; Machado, L.D.B.; Manzoli, J.E.; Geraldo, A.B.C.; Kodama, Y.; Silva, L.G.A.; Pino, E.S.; Somessari, E.S.R.; Silveira, C.G.; et al. Electron beam accelerators—Trends in radiation processing technology for industrial and environmental applications in latin america and the caribbean. *Radiat. Phys. Chem.* **2012**, *81*, 1276–1281. [CrossRef]
4. Uhmeyer, U. Ksi's cross insulated core transformer technology. *AIP Conf. Proc.* **2009**, *1149*, 1099–1103.
5. Cheng, K.; Yonghao, L.; Deming, L.I. Analysis of output voltage on a planar insulating core transformer. *Nuclear Sci. Tech.* **2012**, *22*, 15–18.
6. Yang, L.; Yang, J.; Liu, K.F.; Qin, B.; Chen, D.Z. A combined compensation method for the output voltage of an insulated core transformer power supply. *Rev. Sci. Instrum.* **2014**, *85*, 063302. [CrossRef] [PubMed]
7. Jiang, C.; Yang, J.; Tang, K.; Liu, T.; Xi, C.; Ye, J.; Yu, T.; Fan, M. A hybrid compensation method for ict high voltage power supply. *IEEE Trans. Appl. Supercond.* **2020**, *30*, 0600105. [CrossRef]
8. Cao, L.; Yang, J. Linear circuit model of the three-phase insulated core transformer power supply. *IEEE Trans. Nucl. Sci.* **2016**, *63*, 288–296. [CrossRef]
9. Hu, J.; Cao, L.; Yang, B.; Yang, J. Leakage inductance calculation of the insulated core transformer. *J. Huazhong Univ. Sci. Technol.* **2016**, *44*, 47–50.
10. Yang, B.; Cao, L.; Yang, J.; Yan, S.-C.; Tao, Y.-B. Equivalent circuit model for the insulated core transformer. *Nucl. Sci. Tech.* **2016**, *27*, 68. [CrossRef]
11. Graaff, R.V.D.J. High Voltage Electromagnetic Apparatus Having an Insulating Magnetic Core. U.S. Patent 3187208, 6 January 1965.
12. Luo, M.; Dujic, D.; Allmeling, J. Leakage flux modeling of medium-voltage phase-shift transformers for system-level simulations. *IEEE Trans. Power Electron.* **2019**, *34*, 2635–2654. [CrossRef]

13. Frost, R.E.P.; Pilgrim, J.A.; Lewin, P.L.; Spong, M. An investigation into the next generation of high density, ultra high voltage, power supplies. In Proceedings of the 2018 IEEE International Power Modulator and High Voltage Conference, Jackson, WY, USA, 3–7 June 2018; pp. 156–161.
14. Eberhart, R.C.; Kennedy, J. A new optimizer using particle swarm theory. In Proceedings of the Sixth International Symposium on Micro Machine and Human Science, Nagoya, Japan, 4–6 October 1995.
15. Sibalija, T.V. Particle swarm optimisation in designing parameters of manufacturing processes: A review (2008–2018). *Appl. Soft Comput. 84* **2019**, *84*, 105743. [CrossRef]
16. Zhou, P.; Ma, X.; Zhang, S.; Liu, Z.; Meng, Z.; Xiang, Z.; Wang, X.; Sun, T.; Lin, X.; Li, Y. Application of particle swarm optimization in the design of a mono-capillary x-ray lens. *Nucl. Instrum. Methods Phys. Res.* **2020**, *953*, 163077. [CrossRef]
17. Liu, Z.H.; Wei, H.L.; Li, X.H.; Liu, K.; Zhong, Q.C. Global identification of electrical and mechanical parameters in pmsm drive based on dynamic self-learning pso. *IEEE Trans. Power Electron.* **2018**, *33*, 10858–10871. [CrossRef]
18. Godio, A.; Santilano, A. On the optimization of electromagnetic geophysical data: Application of the pso algorithm. *J. Appl. Geophys.* **2018**, *148*, 163–174. [CrossRef]
19. Yan, R.Q.; Wang, T.; Jiang, X.; Zhong, Q.; Yue, X.Z. Design of high-performance plasmonic nanosensors by particle swarm optimization algorithm combined with machine learning. *Nanotechnology* **2020**, *31*, 375202. [CrossRef] [PubMed]
20. Akbari, M.; Rezaei-Zare, A.; Cheema, M.A.M.; Kalicki, T. Air gap inductance calculation for transformer transient model. *IEEE Trans. Power Deliv.* **2021**, *36*, 492–494. [CrossRef]
21. Li, D.; Chen, Q.; Jia, Z.; Ke, J. A novel active power filter with fundamental magnetic flux compensation. *IEEE Trans. Power Deliv.* **2004**, *19*, 799–805. [CrossRef]
22. Sarkar, S.; Roy, A.; Purkayastha, B.S.; Sarkar, S.; Roy, A.; Purkayastha, B.S. Application of particle swarm optimization in data clustering: A survey. *Int. J. Comput. Appl.* **2013**, *65*, 38–46.

MDPI
St. Alban-Anlage 66
4052 Basel
Switzerland
Tel. +41 61 683 77 34
Fax +41 61 302 89 18
www.mdpi.com

Electronics Editorial Office
E-mail: electronics@mdpi.com
www.mdpi.com/journal/electronics

www.ingramcontent.com/pod-product-compliance
Lightning Source LLC
LaVergne TN
LVHW070413100526
838202LV00014B/1448